Ethical Leadership and Pedagogical Transformation in AI-Driven Education

Vasileios Paliktzoglou
https://orcid.org/0009-0001-0326-1156
Bahrain Polytechnic, Bahrain

Mohamed Lahby
University Hassan II of Casabalanca, Morocco

Pushan Dutta
https://orcid.org/0000-0002-4765-3864
Amity University, Kolkata, India

Muthmainnah Muthmainnah
https://orcid.org/0000-0003-3170-2374
Universitas Al Asyariah Mandar, Indonesia

IGI Global Scientific Publishing
Publishing Tomorrow's Research Today

Vice President of Editorial	Melissa Wagner
Director of Acquisitions	Mikaela Felty
Director of Book Development	Jocelynn Hessler
Production Manager	Mike Brehm
Cover Design	Jose Rosado

Published in the United States of America by
IGI Global Scientific Publishing
701 East Chocolate Avenue
Hershey, PA, 17033, USA
Tel: 717-533-8845 | Fax: 717-533-7115
Website: https://www.igi-global.com E-mail: cust@igi-global.com

Library of Congress Cataloging-in-Publication Data

LCCN: (CIP Data Pending)
ISBN13: 9798260018408
Isbn13Softcover: 9798260018415
EISBN13: 9798260018422
British Cataloguing in Publication Data
A Cataloguing in Publication record for this book is available from the British Library.

Table of Contents

Detailed Table of Contents

This study explores the integration of Artificial Intelligence (AI) in education, emphasizing the interplay between governance, innovation, and ethics. Using secondary data from peer-reviewed articles, policy documents, and case studies, the research develops a comprehensive framework to guide responsible AI adoption. Key findings highlight that effective AI governance, grounded in transparency, accountability, fairness, and inclusivity, fosters innovation while ensuring ethical compliance. Ethical education and digital literacy are crucial for preparing students and educators to engage responsibly with AI technologies. The study underscores the importance of scalable, accessible, and context-sensitive AI solutions, alongside continuous evaluation using measurable metrics for learning outcomes, stakeholder engagement, and sustainability. This framework provides actionable guidance for institutions, policymakers, and researchers to implement AI in ways that enhance educational outcomes, promote equity, and uphold societal values

The concept of Artificial Intelligence (AI) is becoming an inseparable part of the educational sphere, influencing the process of teaching, learning, evaluation, and decision making of the institutions. Even though AI-powered applications and technologies, including learning analytics and automated assessment, provide efficiency and customization, they pose severe ethical issues, especially when it comes to algorithmic discrimination and data privacy. Algorithms that are biased would perpetuate educational disparities and the use of large amounts of data can jeopardize the privacy and autonomy of learners. The available studies tend to treat these concerns in technical or disjointed manner. The chapter takes the responsible AI approach and discusses how bias and privacy risks are created throughout the AI lifecycle when used in education. It suggests a humanistic approach to ethics

creative agency. Ethical concerns such as bias, data governance, and accountability are treated as integral to everyday pedagogical practice.

Artificial intelligence (AI) has appeared as a promising tool to support and develop assessments with efficiency, consistency, and scalability in grading (Hooda et al., 2022). Nevertheless, AI tools have been increasingly used in tertiary education, specifically in assessments, which necessitates an evaluation of their reliability and alignment with teacher evaluative standards (Vittorini, Menini & Tonelli, 2021). CoGrader is an AI-based grading platform that facilitates using rubrics to provide fast and accurate grading. However, the complexity of dealing with languages in terms of contexts, genres and writing objectives may present some challenges when using CoGrader. 128 student submissions were compared through a mixed-methods approach by three faculty members and CoGrader. The study aims to provide empirical insights into how effective CoGrader is as a trustworthy alternative to teacher grading and show how practical, accurate and validated it is in Foundation and Degree-level English courses to contribute to the ongoing discourse on AI in language learning and teaching.

The rapid integration of artificial intelligence (AI) into higher education has fundamentally reshaped teaching, learning, and assessment practices, raising critical questions about its viability in supporting meaningful learning outcomes. This study examines how AI is being utilised in assessment within higher education, with particular attention to its pedagogical implications and ethical challenges. Guided by the Technological Pedagogical Content Knowledge (TPACK) framework, the study analyses the perspectives of three Social Sciences lecturers on students' engagement with AI across disciplinary, pedagogical, and technological domains. Drawing on qualitative participant accounts, the findings reveal that while AI can enhance

Preface

INTRODUCTION

The rapid advancement of Artificial Intelligence (AI) is reshaping education in ways that were once confined to speculation. From adaptive learning platforms and intelligent tutoring systems to automated assessment and predictive analytics, AI is transforming not only how education is delivered, but also how it is governed, experienced, and understood. In this evolving landscape, questions of ethics and leadership have become inseparable from questions of innovation. It is within this context that *Ethical Leadership and Pedagogical Transformation in AI-Driven Education* has been developed.

As editors, we were motivated by a shared recognition that the integration of AI into education is not merely a technical or pedagogical challenge—it is fundamentally an ethical one. The deployment of AI systems introduces complex concerns related to data privacy, algorithmic bias, equity of access, autonomy, and surveillance. These issues demand more than reactive solutions; they require proactive, principled leadership and a commitment to embedding ethical considerations into every stage of technological adoption and educational transformation.

This volume brings together a diverse range of scholarly voices to explore these challenges and opportunities. Drawing on interdisciplinary expertise from education, computer science, philosophy, and public policy, the chapters collectively offer theoretical insights, empirical findings, case-based analyses, and actionable recommendations. Together, they form a comprehensive examination of how ethical leadership can guide the responsible integration of AI in education while fostering meaningful pedagogical transformation.

Central to this book is the idea that ethical AI in education must be both principled and practical. The contributions move beyond abstract discussions to propose concrete frameworks for ethical design, data governance, regulatory compliance, and inclusive implementation. They also foreground the evolving role of educators—not as passive adopters of technology, but as critical agents who shape, interpret, and mediate AI-driven learning environments. In doing so, the volume emphasizes that pedagogical transformation must remain grounded in human values, professional judgment, and social responsibility.

This publication seeks to advance the global discourse on ethical AI in education in several important ways. It addresses a critical gap at the intersection of AI ethics, digital pedagogy, and education policy, offering integrative perspectives that are often treated in isolation. It provides evidence-based insights and cross-disciplinary frameworks that can inform ongoing research and scholarly debate. It also contributes to shaping future research agendas, particularly in areas such as algorithmic accountability, student data ethics, and responsible educational technology innovation. Finally, it supports the development of ethical guidelines and governance models that can be adopted by institutions, policymakers, and technology developers alike.

The intended audience for this volume reflects the breadth of its concerns. Academic researchers will find a foundation for further inquiry into the ethical dimensions of AI in education. Educators and instructional designers will gain guidance on adopting and evaluating AI tools responsibly. Developers and engineers will encounter perspectives that challenge them to integrate ethical considerations into system design. Policymakers and educational leaders will find frameworks to support strategic decision-making and regulatory development. Graduate students and emerging scholars will discover a rich resource for understanding one of the most pressing issues in contemporary education.

By fostering dialogue across disciplines and sectors, this volume aims to contribute to the responsible evolution of AI-enhanced learning systems. It underscores that innovation must be guided not only by what is possible, but by what is just, equitable, and sustainable. Ethical leadership, in this regard, is not an abstract ideal but a practical necessity—one that shapes how technologies are designed, implemented, and ultimately experienced by learners.

We extend our sincere gratitude to the contributors whose work has made this volume possible. Their insights reflect both the urgency of the challenges we face and the possibilities for thoughtful, ethical progress. It is our hope that this book will serve as a catalyst for continued reflection, collaboration, and action in advancing AI-driven education that is both innovative and principled.

ORGANIZATION OF THE BOOK

In Chapter 1, the editors foreground the critical role of ethical leadership and governance in shaping responsible AI adoption within higher education. This chapter presents a comprehensive framework that brings together innovation and accountability, emphasizing that effective governance must be rooted in transparency, fairness, inclusivity, and continuous evaluation. It highlights the importance of digital literacy and ethical education as foundational elements in preparing both educators and learners to engage meaningfully with AI. By advocating for context-sensitive and scalable solutions, the chapter positions governance not as a constraint on innovation, but as its essential enabler.

Chapter 2 deepens the ethical discussion by examining the intertwined challenges of algorithmic bias and data privacy across the AI lifecycle. The editors emphasize that these risks are not isolated technical issues but systemic concerns that emerge at multiple stages of design and deployment. Through a human-centered and integrative approach, the chapter calls for ethical frameworks that move beyond fragmented solutions, promoting transparency, accountability, and respect for learner autonomy. It offers a timely reminder that responsible AI integration must address both fairness in outcomes and the protection of individual rights.

In Chapter 3, attention shifts to academic libraries as dynamic sites of AI-driven transformation. The editors explore how leadership—particularly visionary and ethical leadership—plays a pivotal role in reimagining library services, collection management, and institutional innovation. Drawing on global case studies, the chapter outlines how AI can enhance user experiences while also introducing new complexities that demand organizational readiness and ethical foresight. It underscores the need for cultivating AI-responsive cultures, professional competencies, and policy frameworks that ensure sustainable and responsible innovation in library systems.

Chapter 4 centers on the professional development of educators, arguing that effective AI integration depends fundamentally on teacher preparedness. The editors highlight the growing necessity for educators to develop both technical proficiency and ethical awareness in navigating AI tools. By proposing a comprehensive training model that integrates digital pedagogy, data literacy, and ethical reasoning, the chapter reinforces the idea that educators are not passive users of technology but active agents in shaping equitable and responsible learning environments.

Extending this perspective, Chapter 5 positions educators as central ethical actors in AI-enhanced education. The editors emphasize that ethical awareness cannot be reduced to compliance or technical knowledge alone; it must be embedded in the judgment, agency, and everyday practices of educators. The chapter explores how issues such as bias, transparency, and power asymmetries manifest in classroom contexts, arguing for a holistic approach that aligns ethical principles with institutional governance and educator capacity. In doing so, it advances a vision of AI integration that is both human-centered and socially responsive.

Chapter 6 introduces a distinctive perspective by examining AI integration within creative disciplines, specifically film and media education. The editors present AI as a mediating presence that reshapes notions of authorship, originality, and pedagogical responsibility. Rather than focusing solely on technical proficiency, the chapter emphasizes the importance of reflexivity, critical inquiry, and ethical awareness in designing learning experiences. It highlights how educators can foster creative agency while navigating the uncertainties introduced by AI, framing pedagogy as an inherently ethical and relational practice.

In Chapter 7, the editors turn to the domain of assessment, offering an empirical investigation into AI-assisted writing evaluation. This chapter critically examines the reliability and effectiveness of automated grading systems in comparison to human evaluators. While AI tools demonstrate potential in enhancing efficiency and consistency, the findings reveal important limitations related to linguistic complexity and contextual interpretation. The chapter contributes to ongoing debates about trust, validity, and the role of human judgment in assessment, underscoring the need for balanced and critically informed adoption of AI technologies.

Chapter 8 further explores assessment practices by examining educators' perspectives on AI's impact on student performance and learning integrity. The editors highlight a nuanced reality: while AI can support efficiency and engagement, its uncritical use may undermine deep learning and disciplinary understanding. Guided by pedagogical frameworks, the chapter underscores the importance of aligning technological use with educational goals, emphasizing that meaningful learning requires intentional oversight and ethical consideration.

Chapter 9 provides a comprehensive exploration of AI-driven learning environments and adaptive technologies. The editors outline the theoretical and technical foundations of these systems, emphasizing their capacity to deliver personalized, data-informed learning experiences. At the same time, the chapter raises important questions about the implications of continuous data collection and algorithmic decision-making. By examining intelligent tutoring systems, adaptive feedback mechanisms, and predictive analytics, it offers a balanced view of both the transformative potential and the ethical complexities of AI-enhanced learning environments.

Chapter 10 builds on this discussion by critically examining adaptive learning systems through an ethical lens. The editors highlight how personalization, while beneficial, introduces concerns related to bias, privacy, surveillance, and transparency. The chapter advocates for the integration of explainable AI and ethical risk mitigation strategies, emphasizing the need for frameworks that balance technological advancement with responsible governance. It reinforces the idea that innovation must be accompanied by accountability at every stage of the AI lifecycle.

Finally, Chapter 11 looks toward the future of AI in education, offering a forward-looking analysis of emerging trends and trajectories. The editors trace the evolution of AI from rule-based systems to more sophisticated, human-centered and generative models, highlighting their implications for teaching, learning, and institutional practices. The chapter underscores the importance of ethical governance, policy development, and interdisciplinary collaboration in shaping this future. It concludes by calling for sustainable and inclusive approaches that ensure AI contributes meaningfully to educational advancement.

Collectively, these chapters provide a rich and multidimensional exploration of ethical leadership and pedagogical transformation in AI-driven education, offering both critical insights and practical pathways for responsible innovation.

CONCLUSION

As this volume makes clear, the integration of Artificial Intelligence into education is not simply a matter of technological advancement—it is a question of leadership, responsibility, and the values that underpin educational practice. Across the chapters, a unifying insight emerges: ethical leadership is the cornerstone of meaningful and sustainable pedagogical transformation in AI-driven environments.

The contributions in this collection collectively illustrate that while AI holds immense potential to enhance learning, personalize instruction, and improve institutional effectiveness, these benefits are neither automatic nor evenly distributed. Without careful design, critical oversight, and principled governance, the same technologies risk reinforcing inequities, compromising privacy, and narrowing the scope of human agency. Ethical challenges such as algorithmic bias, data governance, transparency, and accountability are not peripheral concerns; they define the conditions under which AI can be trusted and legitimately integrated into education.

A central theme throughout this volume is the indispensable role of human actors—educators, leaders, developers, and policymakers—in shaping how AI is understood and applied. Educators, in particular, emerge not merely as users of AI systems but as ethical decision-makers whose judgment, awareness, and professional agency mediate the impact of these technologies on learners. Similarly, institutional leaders are called upon to cultivate cultures of responsibility, ensuring that innovation is aligned with equity, inclusivity, and long-term societal benefit.

The chapters also emphasize that ethical AI in education requires more than compliance with regulations or adherence to abstract principles. It demands the development of robust frameworks, continuous evaluation, and an openness to revision as technologies and contexts evolve. Whether through governance models, training initiatives, adaptive learning systems, or emerging policy directions, the work presented here underscores the importance of embedding ethics into every stage of the AI lifecycle.

Looking forward, the future of AI in education will be shaped by the choices made today—choices about what to prioritize, whom to include, and how to balance efficiency with integrity. The path ahead calls for collaboration across disciplines and sectors, as well as sustained critical inquiry into the broader implications of AI for knowledge, creativity, and human development.

This volume does not claim to offer definitive answers. Rather, it seeks to provide a foundation for ongoing dialogue and action. By bringing together diverse perspectives and practical insights, it invites readers to engage thoughtfully with the challenges and opportunities of AI in education.

Ultimately, the promise of AI in education lies not in the technology itself, but in our collective capacity to guide its use with wisdom, fairness, and ethical clarity. It is our hope that this book contributes to that endeavor, supporting a future in which innovation and integrity advance hand in hand.

Chapter 1

Ethical Leadership and Governance Frameworks for Responsible AI Adoption in Higher Education

Raed Atef
http://orcid.org/0009-0004-0012-4940
Independent Researcher, Palestine

ABSTRACT

This study explores the integration of Artificial Intelligence (AI) in education, emphasizing the interplay between governance, innovation, and ethics. Using secondary data from peer-reviewed articles, policy documents, and case studies, the research develops a comprehensive framework to guide responsible AI adoption. Key findings highlight that effective AI governance, grounded in transparency, accountability, fairness, and inclusivity, fosters innovation while ensuring ethical compliance. Ethical education and digital literacy are crucial for preparing students and educators to engage responsibly with AI technologies. The study underscores the importance of scalable, accessible, and context-sensitive AI solutions, alongside continuous evaluation using measurable metrics for learning outcomes, stakeholder engagement, and sustainability. This framework provides actionable guidance for institutions, policymakers, and researchers to implement AI in ways that enhance educational outcomes, promote equity, and uphold societal values

DOI: 10.4018/979-8-2600-1840-8.ch001

INTRODUCTION

The rapid evolution of Artificial Intelligence (AI) is transforming multiple sectors, most notably education, where its integration offers opportunities to enhance learning, streamline administration, and personalized instruction. Yet, this transformation also introduces complex ethical, social, and governance challenges that require deliberate leadership and responsible oversight (Awashreh & Mohamed, 2024). As institutions adopt AI tools for assessment, admissions, and pedagogy, questions surrounding bias, transparency, accountability, and privacy have intensified (Awashreh, 2025a). Consequently, the intersection of ethical leadership, AI governance, and innovation in education has become a central concern for policymakers and educators seeking to ensure that AI-driven reforms serve both human and institutional values (Rashid & Kausik, 2024).

AI's potential to revolutionize education is undeniable. Adaptive learning systems, predictive analytics, and automated administrative tools can improve efficiency, expand access, and foster individualized learning experiences (Awashreh, 2024 a). However, these same technologies also present risks—such as algorithmic bias, data misuse, and erosion of critical human agency—that may exacerbate educational inequities if left unregulated. Without ethical oversight and structured governance frameworks, AI implementation could reproduce systemic disparities and undermine trust in academic institutions (Wang et al., 2024). Therefore, achieving a balance between innovation and ethical responsibility is not optional; it is a governance imperative.

AI governance encompasses the ethical principles, institutional policies, and operational mechanisms that guide AI design, deployment, and evaluation. In higher education, such governance frameworks must promote both innovation and accountability through a multi-stakeholder approach that includes educators, policymakers, technologists, and community representatives. Effective governance ensures that AI systems are transparent, inclusive, and aligned with institutional missions to advance learning rather than commodify it (Cancela-Outeda, 2024). Within this framework, ethical leadership plays a crucial role in shaping institutional culture, defining ethical norms, and embedding human-centered values into technological decision-making.

Ethical education is equally central to this process. By integrating ethical reasoning, digital citizenship, and critical thinking into curricula, educational institutions can cultivate a generation of learners and professionals capable of evaluating the moral and societal implications of AI technologies (Abulibdeh, Zaidan & Abulibdeh, 2024). Ethical education also extends to AI developers, urging them to design systems that respect human dignity and equity. This dual emphasis—on governance structures and ethical literacy—creates a sustainable foundation for responsible AI innovation.

As societies increasingly rely on AI to shape educational policy and practice, the demand for cohesive, value-driven governance frameworks becomes urgent (Alonso-Rodríguez, 2024). This study explores how ethical leadership and AI governance frameworks can jointly foster innovation while safeguarding fundamental rights and fairness. It argues that aligning technological development with ethical imperatives enables AI to strengthen—not replace—the human dimensions of education. The study also identifies the mechanisms through which leadership can bridge the gap between ethical theory and institutional practice, contributing to an equitable and transparent model of AI adoption in higher education (Li, 2023).

While AI offers powerful opportunities for personalization, automation, and predictive analytics, it also poses dilemmas related to privacy, accountability, and social equity (Awashreh, 2024b). The absence of coherent governance frameworks magnifies these risks, creating uncertainty for educators and policymakers (Al-Zahrani & Alasmari, 2024). Addressing this gap requires not only technical regulation but also leadership capable of guiding AI transformation with moral clarity and institutional foresight.

Accordingly, this research is guided by the following central question:

How can ethical leadership and AI governance frameworks be designed to foster innovation while ensuring the responsible and equitable use of AI in higher education?

The objectives of the study are:

1. To examine the role of AI governance in promoting innovation and ethical responsibility within educational systems.
2. To develop ethical frameworks and leadership strategies that ensure fairness, accountability, and inclusivity in AI deployment.
3. To propose actionable policy and pedagogical recommendations that support responsible AI integration through collaborative governance.

The significance of this study lies in its dual contribution. Theoretically, it advances discourse at the intersection of AI ethics, governance, and educational leadership, offering a comprehensive understanding of challenges and opportunities. Practically, it provides policymakers and institutional leaders with frameworks to design governance models that align AI innovation with social and ethical integrity (Goosen & Mugumo, 2024). The study thus contributes to global efforts to guide AI's transformative potential toward equitable, transparent, and human-centered educational futures.

LITERATURE REVIEW

The integration of artificial intelligence (AI) in education has emerged as one of the most transformative developments in contemporary learning environments. Scholars increasingly emphasize its potential to reshape pedagogical approaches, enhance administrative efficiency, and enable more personalized, adaptive, and data-driven educational experiences (Leelavathi & Surendhranatha, 2024). Adaptive learning systems, for instance, tailor content delivery to individual learners' performance, preferences, and learning trajectories, creating dynamic and responsive educational experiences (Awashreh, 2026). Similarly, AI-powered tools—such as chatbots, virtual tutors, and predictive analytics—have redefined administrative processes, enabling educators to allocate more attention to instructional quality and student engagement. Collectively, these innovations signify a paradigm shift in the operational and pedagogical frameworks of educational institutions, highlighting AI's promise to foster inclusivity, innovation, and institutional efficiency (Awashreh & Hassiba, 2025a).

However, despite these promising advancements, the integration of AI in education presents complex ethical and governance challenges that warrant critical attention. Scholars caution that the rapid, and at times unregulated, deployment of AI systems may reproduce or exacerbate existing structural inequalities within educational contexts (Kamalov et al., 2023). Central ethical concerns include algorithmic bias, privacy violations, and the potential erosion of human judgment (Zhai et al., 2024). Algorithmic bias, for instance, can emerge from flawed or unrepresentative datasets, resulting in discriminatory educational outcomes where marginalized learners receive less favorable recommendations or assessments. Similarly, extensive data collection practices expose students and educators to significant privacy risks, raising critical questions about consent, transparency, and institutional accountability. Beyond technical and procedural issues, overreliance on AI also risks undermining essential human capabilities such as empathy, creativity, and critical thinking, potentially reshaping the human dimension of education in ways that could diminish holistic learning outcomes.

These challenges underscore the imperative for robust AI governance frameworks that ensure ethical, equitable, and transparent implementation. AI governance encompasses the rules, standards, and guiding principles that oversee the design, deployment, and monitoring of AI technologies. Effective governance, as highlighted by Mogavi et al. (2024), must strike a careful balance between promoting technological innovation and safeguarding ethical and social values, including fairness, accountability, and inclusivity. In the educational context, governance frameworks should employ a multi-stakeholder approach, engaging policymakers, educators, technologists, and civil society representatives to co-create policies that are both locally relevant and globally informed. Transparency is a fundamental principle, not only in algorithmic design but also in communicating AI-driven decisions to stakeholders in a manner that is understandable and accountable. Furthermore, fairness and inclusivity require deliberate efforts to mitigate digital divides and ensure equitable access to AI-enhanced learning opportunities (Cheong, 2024). Without such governance structures, AI integration risks reinforcing pre-existing inequalities, thereby undermining its transformative potential (Awashreh & Almi, 2026).

Complementing governance is the critical role of ethical education, which involves embedding moral reasoning, digital ethics, and critical awareness within curricula and institutional practices. Ethical education equips students, educators, and policymakers with the analytical tools needed to evaluate and navigate the societal implications of AI technologies (Awashreh & Al Ghunaimi, 2025). By fostering ethical literacy, institutions can cultivate responsible digital citizens capable of engaging with AI technologies conscientiously, ensuring that the benefits of innovation are realized without compromising human-centered values. Furthermore, ethical education extends to AI developers themselves, who are increasingly expected to embed principles such as non-maleficence, transparency, explainability, and accountability into the design and deployment of AI systems. As such, ethical awareness becomes not merely an academic or professional exercise but a societal necessity, critical to ensuring that AI advances human well-being, equity, and social justice.

At the policy and regulatory level, literature emphasizes the need for cohesive, adaptive, and context-sensitive AI governance frameworks that align global ethical standards with local realities. Fragmented or inconsistent governance models can inadvertently exacerbate existing disparities while stifling innovation (Mogavi et al., 2024). Consequently, scholars advocate for international collaboration to establish shared principles for AI in education while simultaneously remaining sensitive to cultural, economic, and institutional variations. This dual focus—on global alignment and local adaptability—ensures that governance mechanisms maintain legitimacy, responsiveness, and relevance across diverse educational systems. Such approaches also allow for iterative refinement, enabling policymakers and institutions to adapt AI frameworks to emerging technologies and evolving pedagogical needs.

Synthesizing these insights, literature consistently highlights the dual character of AI in education: its transformative potential and its ethical fragility. The convergence of research underscores that sustainable innovation depends on governance frameworks grounded in ethical principles, transparency, and inclusivity (Farahani, 2024). Moreover, integrating ethical education into governance strategies strengthens the capacity of institutions and societies to manage AI responsibly, cultivating a culture of accountability and awareness. As emphasized by Akinrinola et al. (2024), the future of AI-enhanced education hinges on a delicate balance between technological progress and ethical stewardship (Awashreh & Hassiba, 2025b). Ensuring that AI functions as a tool for empowerment rather than exclusion requires an ongoing commitment to aligning innovation with human-centered values, fostering equity, and embedding ethical reflection into all dimensions of educational practice. Ultimately, this body of literature affirms that the successful integration of AI in education relies on an interconnected approach, combining technological innovation, ethical literacy, and robust governance to create equitable, effective, and socially responsible learning environments.

METHODS

Research Approach

This study employs a secondary data analysis methodology to critically examine the intersection of AI governance, ethical education, and responsible innovation within higher education. The approach draws on existing literature, reports, and datasets to synthesize theoretical and empirical insights related to the ethical integration of AI in educational contexts. Data sources include peer-reviewed journal articles, international policy documents, regulatory frameworks, and case studies that explore governance mechanisms and ethical principles guiding AI in education (Cheong et al., 2023). This approach allows for a comprehensive and multi-perspective understanding of how AI technologies can be ethically implemented in higher education while maintaining accountability, transparency, and inclusivity (Ofosu-Ampong, 2024).

Research Procedures

The research process involved systematically identifying, selecting, and analyzing secondary sources that address key dimensions of AI governance and ethical education. Keywords such as AI governance, ethical leadership, responsible innovation, and higher education ethics were used in academic databases and Google Scholar to locate relevant studies. The collected materials were then evaluated, summarized, and thematically synthesized to identify recurring principles, frameworks, and gaps in existing scholarships. This structured process supports the development of an integrated conceptual framework that aligns with global efforts toward responsible and equitable AI adoption in education.

Data Collection

Peer-reviewed publications, policy reports, and institutional guidelines serve as the primary data sources for this research. These materials provide theoretical foundations and practical insights into how ethical governance can shape AI-driven educational transformation. Reports and international standards—particularly those related to data protection, algorithmic accountability, and digital ethics—inform the contextual understanding of governance in education. Case studies were also reviewed to illustrate the practical implications of AI governance across diverse educational systems. This triangulation of sources enables a holistic exploration of how institutions can adopt AI responsibly while safeguarding societal and ethical values.

Framework Development: Ethical Governance and Innovation in AI Education

Building on this synthesis, the study constructs a comprehensive ethical governance framework integrating three interdependent components—AI governance, innovation in education, and ethical education—as proposed by Roshanaei, Olivares & Lopez (2023). Each component represents a pillar of responsible AI adoption and reflects the balance between technological progress and moral accountability.

- AI Governance establishes the ethical foundations and regulatory structures for AI development and deployment. Core principles such as transparency, accountability, fairness, and inclusivity are emphasized to ensure that AI systems are aligned with human-centered values. Governance mechanisms must remain adaptive and participatory, enabling multi-stakeholder collaboration among policymakers, educators, technologists, and community actors to ensure that implementation reflects diverse social perspectives (Singhal et al., 2024).
- Innovation in Education focuses on harnessing AI's transformative potential to improve learning environments and institutional processes (Tan, 2023). Through personalized learning, adaptive pedagogy, and data-driven insights, AI can enhance both teaching quality and administrative efficiency. However, ethical innovation demands that such benefits be scalable, transparent, and accessible, particularly for underserved or marginalized learners. Ensuring equitable access is central to sustaining socially responsible AI adoption.
- Ethical Education forms the humanistic dimension of the framework, preparing stakeholders to critically engage with AI technologies. Ethical literacy—rooted in critical thinking and reflective judgment—enables students, educators, and developers to navigate complex moral and societal implications

(Awashreh & Al Ghunaimi, 2025). Integrating ethical education into curricula and professional training ensures that AI tools and policies are shaped by values of justice, empathy, and inclusion. Responsible AI design further promotes technologies that safeguard human dignity and prioritize social wellbeing (Fu & Weng, 2024).

Together, these three dimensions form a cohesive ethical leadership model that balances innovation with governance and ethics. By fostering collaboration, accountability, and inclusivity, the framework advances the responsible integration of AI in higher education and aligns with institutional missions to uphold transparency, fairness, and equity.

Table 1. Components of the ethical AI governance framework

Component	Key Focus Areas
AI Governance	- Ethical Principles: Transparency, accountability, fairness, inclusivity. - Regulatory Frameworks: Standards and adaptable policies for AI integration. - Stakeholder Collaboration: Engagement of policymakers, educators, technologists, and communities.
Innovation in Education	- Technological Advancements: AI for personalized learning, adaptive teaching, and efficiency. - Data-Driven Insights: AI analytics to improve institutional decision-making. - Scalability and Accessibility: Ensuring innovations benefit diverse learner populations.
Ethical Education	- Ethical Literacy: Developing critical thinking and ethical decision-making skills. - Responsible AI Design: Aligning technology with human-centered and societal values. - Equity and Inclusion: Promoting equal access to AI-enhanced learning opportunities.

Sources: Developed by researchers, 2024)

Framework Interactions and Ethical Leadership Nexus

The interactions within this framework illustrate the ethical leadership nexus, where governance, innovation, and education operate synergistically to promote responsible AI adoption.

- The Governance–Innovation Nexus highlights the necessity of creating flexible regulatory structures that encourage creativity while ensuring compliance with ethical and social standards (Goosen et al., 2024).

- The Governance–Ethics Nexus embeds ethical reflection into institutional governance, fostering cultures of accountability, transparency, and moral responsibility.
- The Innovation–Ethics Nexus ensures that technological advancements prioritize inclusivity, privacy, and fairness, preventing the reinforcement of existing inequalities (Alvarez et al., 2024).

Table 2. Interactions within the ethical governance framework

Interaction	Description
Governance–Innovation Nexus	Governance frameworks promote innovation while maintaining adherence to ethical and societal principles.
Governance–Ethics Nexus	Governance integrates moral reasoning into AI policy, promoting institutional responsibility and public trust.
Innovation–Ethics Nexus	AI innovations are guided by inclusivity, privacy, and fairness, ensuring equitable and human-centered outcomes.

(Sources: Developed by researcher, 2025)

Overall, the framework provides a holistic model for aligning ethical governance, educational innovation, and moral leadership in higher education. By integrating these dimensions, institutions can ensure that AI adoption enhances learning environments while upholding principles of justice, transparency, and societal well-being.

RESULTS

The findings of this study underscore the critical importance of ethical AI governance in driving innovation within educational systems. Effective governance frameworks not only facilitate technological progress but also ensure that innovation is guided by the principles of fairness, transparency, inclusivity, and accountability. Such frameworks enable institutions to harness the benefits of AI responsibly, ensuring that students, educators, and policymakers all benefit from equitable and trustworthy AI integration. Figure (2) presents a summary of the study's main findings in a simplified format.

Figure 1. Summary of key findings

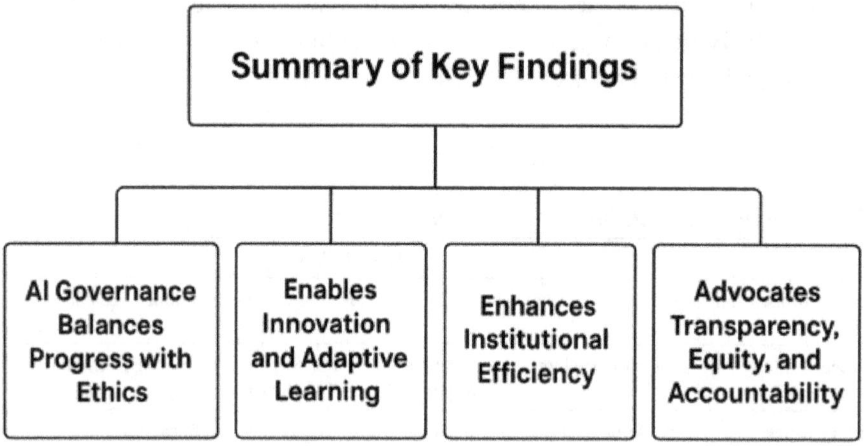

Role of AI Governance in Promoting Innovation in Education

AI governance serves as a cornerstone for balancing technological advancement with ethical responsibility in educational systems, providing structured oversight and policy guidance that cultivates environments conducive to adaptive learning, administrative efficiency, and data-informed decision-making (David et al., 2024). The analysis of existing frameworks and institutional practices reveals that effective governance not only encourages innovation but also ensures alignment with societal values and moral imperatives, highlighting its transformative potential across diverse educational contexts.

A central area where AI governance demonstrates its impact is in adaptive learning, where frameworks emphasizing transparency, fairness, and accountability support the development of systems that personalize education according to individual learner needs. These adaptive systems enhance learning outcomes by fostering differentiated instruction and promoting inclusivity, while collaboration among educators, technologists, and policymakers under a strong governance model maximizes AI's potential to revolutionize educational practices (Abdelkader et al., 2024).

In parallel, AI governance enhances institutional efficiency by guiding the responsible automation of administrative processes. This enables educators to devote more time to teaching and student engagement while ensuring safeguards for accuracy, transparency, and ethical accountability. Consequently, operational efficiency improves, institutional resources are allocated more effectively, and the broader educational ecosystem is strengthened (Igbokwe, 2023). Additionally, governance frameworks support data-driven decision-making by ensuring that institutional data are handled ethically, with integrity and confidentiality, and in compliance with privacy laws. Through these measures, institutions can make informed decisions to improve learning outcomes, identify curricular gaps, and enhance overall educational quality, demonstrating that AI can be both transformative and ethically grounded (Papagiannidis, Mikalef & Conboy, 2025).

Equally critical to governance is the establishment of ethical principles and frameworks that guide the responsible use of AI in education, mitigating risks such as algorithmic bias, discrimination, and privacy breaches. Ethical frameworks balance innovation with accountability, fairness, and human-centered values, fostering trust, equity, and transparency within educational ecosystems (Tahir, Amanat & Awan, 2024). Transparency and accountability ensure that AI systems and algorithms remain open to evaluation and public scrutiny, allowing stakeholders—students, educators, and policymakers—to understand AI-driven decision-making processes. Clear accountability mechanisms assign responsibility to developers and institutions, preventing misuse and reinforcing ethical integrity (Cheong, 2024).

Furthermore, fairness and inclusivity are central to responsible AI adoption, requiring routine auditing of algorithms to detect and correct biases, thereby preventing the reinforcement of existing social or educational disparities. Inclusive governance ensures that marginalized communities are not overlooked and that AI benefits are equitably distributed, positioning AI as a tool for empowerment rather than exclusion (Schwartz et al., 2024). Privacy and data protection remain essential, particularly given the sensitivity of student information. AI governance frameworks must comply with international regulations, such as the GDPR, and implement clear protocols for data collection, storage, and analysis. By safeguarding privacy and autonomy, these measures maintain trust and ensure that AI serves as a force for educational integrity and social justice (Huang, 2023).

In summary, AI governance and ethical frameworks are deeply interconnected, providing a foundation for educational innovation that is both effective and morally responsible. Grounded in transparency, accountability, fairness, inclusivity, and data protection, these frameworks ensure that AI enhances educational quality while upholding human dignity and equity, ultimately fostering sustainable and responsible progress across educational systems.

Key Insights on Balancing Innovation with Ethical Standards

The analysis reveals several critical insights on harmonizing technological innovation with ethical governance in higher education. First, responsible innovation emerges as a guiding principle. While AI-driven tools such as personalized learning platforms and intelligent administrative systems offer transformative potential, their deployment must be governed by ethical standards that prioritize equity, privacy, and transparency. Responsible innovation ensures that technological progress enhances education without deepening existing inequalities (Lim et al., 2023).

Second, collaborative governance models are essential for sustainable AI integration. The involvement of multiple stakeholders—educators, technologists, policymakers, students, and communities—creates a participatory environment that reflects diverse perspectives and mitigates ethical risks. Such inclusive governance fosters social legitimacy and ensures that AI applications address local educational contexts effectively (OECD, 2023).

Third, ethical literacy and education are foundational for ensuring that both educators and learners can critically engage with AI. Integrating ethics into AI-related curricula equips stakeholders with the ability to assess and question the implications of emerging technologies. This proactive approach cultivates a culture of responsibility, preparing future generations to navigate AI systems ethically and effectively (Isiaku et al., 2024).

Overall, the study highlights that ethical AI governance is both a strategic and moral necessity. Building adaptive, transparent, and inclusive governance frameworks allows institutions to achieve a balance between innovation and accountability. Such frameworks not only enhance learning outcomes and operational efficiency but also reinforce the ethical foundations of higher education.

In the evolving landscape of AI adoption, the challenge lies in maintaining a flexible yet principled governance model—one that promotes innovation while safeguarding human dignity, equity, and social responsibility. This study contributes to the broader dialogue on ethical leadership and AI governance, emphasizing that the future of education depends not only on technological advancement but on the moral vision that guides it (Awashreh, 2025c).

DISCUSSION

The integration of Artificial Intelligence (AI) into education represents a transformative opportunity to enhance learning outcomes, improve administrative efficiency, and bridge persistent educational disparities. In contexts such as the United States, the focus has increasingly shifted toward ensuring equitable access to AI tools, particularly for underserved communities, through government grants and private sector initiatives (Lin et al., 2023). However, despite these efforts, disparities in funding and access remain substantial, underscoring the urgent need for targeted policy interventions that guarantee AI's benefits reach all students equitably (Jindal et al., 2023). To achieve this, AI governance frameworks must be carefully aligned with both ethical and educational goals, embedding principles of transparency, accountability, fairness, and inclusivity as core components of trustworthy AI systems (Cheong, 2024).

Implementing AI governance across diverse educational systems presents complex challenges. Variations in infrastructure, policy environments, and institutional readiness necessitate adaptable governance frameworks capable of addressing issues such as data privacy, algorithmic bias, and digital literacy. Meaningful collaboration between policymakers, educators, and technologists is essential to tailor AI integration to the unique needs of different learner populations (OECD, 2023). Moreover, achieving an effective balance between governance and innovation remains crucial: governance must not stifle creativity, but rather guide innovation in alignment with societal and ethical values (Abulibdeh, Zaidan & Abulibdeh, 2024). Embedding ethical principles at the heart of AI governance ensures that AI contributes to improved educational outcomes while safeguarding fairness and social responsibility (Awashreh, 2025c).

Another critical dimension is ethical education, which prepares both students and educators to engage with AI technologies responsibly. Ethical literacy fosters a culture of reflection and accountability, enabling stakeholders to navigate the opportunities and risks of emerging technologies with informed judgment (Isiaku et al., 2024). Although AI offers substantial potential to advance personalized learning and optimize administrative systems, persistent challenges—such as scalability, accessibility, and uneven levels of digital literacy—must be addressed. Investments in technological infrastructure and digital skill development are therefore vital to enable widespread, equitable AI adoption (Kamalov et al., 2023).

Localized and flexible AI governance frameworks are particularly essential for addressing the needs of underserved and resource-constrained communities. Contextual governance ensures that ethical standards remain relevant to local realities while encouraging innovation through public–private partnerships that align technological advancement with moral responsibility (United Arab Emirates, 2024). Additionally, longitudinal and comparative studies are needed to assess the enduring impact of AI policies on learning outcomes and social equity, helping refine governance mechanisms over time (Ou, 2024). Ultimately, effective AI integration requires maintaining a careful balance between governance, innovation, and ethics to overcome resource constraints and regional disparities. Future research should thus emphasize long-term empirical assessments that measure AI's transformative potential in real-world educational contexts (Dwivedi et al., 2023).

The proposed framework—linking AI governance, innovation, and ethical education—holds profound implications for society, academia, and educational institutions, shaping the evolving landscape of responsible AI in higher education. For society, the governance–innovation nexus ensures that AI advances benefit all individuals equitably, particularly marginalized groups. By embedding ethical guidelines into AI policies and technologies, society gains from innovations that promote economic progress and social inclusion simultaneously. This approach prevents the reinforcement of inequalities and minimizes the creation of new forms of digital exclusion. Consequently, a governance system rooted in inclusivity, fairness, and transparency can help build a more just and empowered society, where technology serves as a catalyst for opportunity rather than marginalization (Sargiotis, 2024).

In the academic sphere, the governance–ethics nexus carries significant implications for how institutions design curricula and conduct research related to AI. By integrating ethical considerations into AI education policies, universities can cultivate a culture of responsibility, reflexivity, and accountability in technological innovation. Embedding AI ethics within educational programs equips future generations with the knowledge and sensitivity required to make responsible decisions about AI's design, deployment, and social impact. Academia thus plays a pivotal role in setting ethical standards, fostering interdisciplinary research, and advancing a collective understanding of AI's social, cultural, and economic dimensions (Camilleri, 2023).

For institutions, the innovation–ethics nexus demands a balance between technological advancement and moral responsibility. Universities and schools must not only embrace AI-driven innovation but also ensure that its adoption is guided by ethical principles that protect privacy, inclusivity, and fairness (Al-Zahrani & Alasmari, 2024). Institutional policies must therefore regulate AI deployment in ways that are both technically effective and ethically sound. Furthermore, fostering multi-stakeholder collaboration among policymakers, educators, technologists, and communities enhances institutional capacity to navigate the complex ethical landscape of AI. Such collaboration ensures that AI technologies reflect the values of the wider society and contribute to the common good (Herane, 2024).

Overall, the framework's emphasis on the interconnectedness of governance, innovation, and ethics offers a strategic roadmap for institutions, academia, and society to jointly navigate AI's challenges and opportunities. By ensuring that AI is guided by strong ethical principles, stakeholders can collectively advance toward a more inclusive, accountable, and sustainable educational future.

RECOMMNDATIONS

To effectively operationalize the AI governance framework in education, practical steps must be taken to address scalability, accessibility, and digital literacy while ensuring successful implementation across diverse educational contexts. Ensuring scalability requires the development of modular AI solutions that can expand in line with institutional needs, enabling schools and universities to accommodate growing user bases without compromising performance. Complementing this, fostering public–private partnerships can help deliver affordable AI tools, while strategic investment in essential AI infrastructure, including broadband connectivity and cloud-based systems, ensures that technological resources are robust and reliable. Conducting comprehensive needs assessments further identifies potential scalability challenges, allowing for the design of adaptive training programs that equip educators to leverage AI effectively as their institutions expand.

Equally critical is enhancing accessibility to AI technologies, particularly for underserved communities and low-resource environments. This involves providing government subsidies and incentives to reduce the financial barriers to adopting AI solutions and designing mobile-friendly systems that function efficiently in areas with limited infrastructure. Moreover, AI tools must be culturally and linguistically tailored to the local context, ensuring relevance and inclusivity. Targeted outreach and training initiatives in regions with constrained digital resources can further bridge equity gaps, enabling all learners and educators to benefit from AI-enhanced educational experiences.

Strengthening digital literacy represents another essential pillar for successful framework implementation. Integrating digital literacy and AI ethics into both student and educator curricula equips stakeholders with the knowledge and critical awareness necessary to navigate AI responsibly. Continuous professional development programs for educators enhance their proficiency in utilizing AI tools, while literacy initiatives aimed at marginalized communities ensure that technological empowerment is widespread and inclusive. By cultivating these capabilities, educational institutions can maximize the impact of AI technologies while minimizing risks associated with misuse or inequitable deployment.

Finally, the framework must be implemented with sensitivity to local contexts. Tailoring AI governance strategies to reflect cultural, infrastructure, and institutional realities ensures that policies are both relevant and effective. Pilot programs provide an opportunity to refine AI solutions based on empirical feedback and contextual data, while advisory boards composed of key stakeholders guarantee inclusive oversight and decision-making. By integrating these measures, educational institutions can achieve sustainable, equitable, and ethically aligned AI adoption, positioning innovation as a tool for empowerment rather than a source of exclusion.

Assessing the effectiveness and sustainability of AI governance in education requires a comprehensive set of measurable indicators that capture both technical and ethical dimensions. To begin with, scalability metrics are essential for understanding how widely AI tools are adopted and how their usage grows over time. Key indicators include adoption rate, user growth, infrastructure expansion, and cost efficiency, which together ensure that AI solutions can be scaled to meet the needs of diverse educational settings without compromising quality or accessibility (Awashreh, 2025b).

Closely linked to scalability, accessibility metrics evaluate whether AI tools are available to students and educators in low-resource environments. These metrics focus on access to AI-powered technologies, affordability, device compatibility, and the cultural and linguistic adaptability of AI solutions. By monitoring accessibility, institutions can ensure that AI integration does not exacerbate existing disparities, but rather promotes equitable access to educational resources, complementing scalability efforts.

In tandem, digital literacy metrics examine the preparedness of students and educators to engage effectively with AI technologies. Measures such as improvements in AI-related digital literacy scores, participation in educator training programs, user confidence in technology use, and community engagement initiatives provide critical insights into the capacity of educational stakeholders to leverage AI responsibly. These measures are intrinsically linked to both scalability and accessibility, as effective use depends on the ability to access and adopt AI tools meaningfully.

Equally important is evaluating the impact of AI on learning outcomes, which tracks changes in student performance, engagement, retention, and success in personalized learning pathways. By connecting adoption and literacy metrics to tangible educational results, institutions can determine whether AI technologies are truly enhancing learning experiences and addressing individual student needs. This naturally extends to stakeholder satisfaction and engagement, which assesses levels of satisfaction among students, educators, and administrators, as well as the quality of collaborations and feedback mechanisms during AI deployment. High engagement ensures that AI initiatives align with the expectations and needs of all stakeholders, reinforcing positive learning outcomes.

Governance and ethical standards metrics further strengthen this evaluation framework by focusing on compliance with ethical guidelines, transparency in AI decision-making processes, and the monitoring and resolution of reported ethical violations. These metrics ensure that innovation occurs within a responsible framework prioritizing fairness, accountability, and inclusivity, directly supporting both learning outcomes and stakeholder satisfaction. Finally, long-term sustainability metrics examine the continuity of funding, adaptability of governance frameworks, and integration of AI tools into core institutional practices, ensuring that AI adoption remains effective, resilient, and adaptable to future technological and educational developments.

Together, these interconnected metrics provide a holistic approach for continuous evaluation, linking technical performance, accessibility, digital literacy, educational impact, stakeholder engagement, ethical governance, and sustainability. Consequently, regular monitoring using these indicators enables policymakers, educators, and researchers to refine AI strategies, proactively address challenges, and sustain responsible innovation that benefits all learners within the educational system.

CONCLUSION

This study underscores the pivotal role of ethical leadership and AI governance in fostering innovation while maintaining the highest ethical standards within educational systems. By strategically aligning AI technologies with comprehensive governance frameworks, institutions can unlock AI's transformative potential while ensuring that equity, transparency, accountability, and inclusiveness remain central to educational advancement. The findings highlight the urgent need for dynamic, context-sensitive regulatory models capable of addressing pressing challenges such as algorithmic bias, data privacy, and the widening digital divide. Moreover, fostering ethical literacy and responsible AI design practices ensures that technological progress remains firmly rooted in human-centered values and social responsibility. The study further emphasizes the importance of localized and culturally responsive approaches, which account for the economic, institutional, and technological realities of different educational contexts to promote equitable AI integration worldwide.

The interconnectedness of governance, innovation, and ethics provides the foundation for a sustainable and ethically coherent vision of AI in education. The proposed framework integrates these three dimensions, ensuring that AI-driven transformation is guided by ethical leadership and transparent governance while advancing pedagogical innovation and institutional integrity. This holistic governance model envisions a responsible AI ecosystem where technology not only enhances learning outcomes but also reinforces the moral and social mission of education. The synergistic relationships among the governance–innovation, governance–ethics, and innovation–ethics nexuses are thus essential to ensuring that AI deployment enhances educational quality while minimizing ethical, cultural, and societal risks.

However, several avenues for future research can further deepen understanding of AI's ethical integration into education and its broader implications for governance and equity. First, empirical investigations are needed to examine how the proposed framework operates in real-world institutional contexts, including case-based and longitudinal studies that assess the impact of governance models on both innovation and ethical performance outcomes. Second, research should explore the influence of cultural, political, and regional variations on AI governance standards, highlighting how local norms shape responsible innovation across different educational systems. Understanding these contextual nuances can help develop adaptive, locally grounded AI policies that uphold ethical consistency while respecting diversity. Furthermore, examining the, long-term societal impacts of AI adoption, particularly on access, inclusion, and social mobility, remains crucial. Determining whether AI is contributing to reducing or reproducing structural inequities will provide vital insights for policymakers and educators alike. Finally, as AI technologies evolve, there is a pressing need to develop forward-looking ethical frameworks that address the complexities of advanced systems such as deep learning, neural networks, and generative AI, ensuring their responsible and human-centric implementation in educational environments.

In conclusion, this study presents a strategic and ethically grounded framework for the responsible adoption of AI in education. Yet, the continuing evolution of AI necessitates ongoing research, cross-sector collaboration, and ethical reflexivity to refine governance mechanisms and maintain trust in AI systems. By advancing such scholarship and practice, educators and leaders can ensure that AI's transformative potential is realized in ways that empower learners, strengthen institutional ethics, and promote societal well-being. Ultimately, ethical leadership and robust governance will determine whether AI serves merely as a technological innovation—or as a catalyst for a more equitable, accountable, and human-centered educational future.

ACKNOWLEDGMENT

The author acknowledges the use of ChatGPT, the free version, to assist in revising and editing the language throughout this chapter.

REFERENCES

Abdelkader, A. A. M., Hassan, H., & Abdelkader, M. (2024). The role of artificial intelligence in designing higher education courses: Benefits and challenges. In Lytras, M. D., Alkhaldi, A., Malik, S., Serban, A. C., & Aldosemani, T. (Eds.), *The evolution of artificial intelligence in higher education* (pp. 83–97). Emerald Publishing Limited., DOI: 10.1108/978-1-83549-486-820241005

Abulibdeh, A., Zaidan, E., & Abulibdeh, R. (2024). Navigating the confluence of artificial intelligence and education for sustainable development in the era of industry 4.0: Challenges, opportunities, and ethical dimensions. *Journal of Cleaner Production, 437*, 140527. DOI: 10.1016/j.jclepro.2023.140527

Akinrinola, O., Okoye, C. C., Ofodile, O. C., & Ugochukwu, C. E. (2024). Navigating and reviewing ethical dilemmas in AI development: Strategies for transparency, fairness, and accountability. *GSC Advanced Research and Reviews*, 18(3), 050-058. DOI: 10.30574/gscarr.2024.18.3.0088

Al-Zahrani, A. M., & Alasmari, T. M. (2024). Exploring the impact of artificial intelligence on higher education: The dynamics of ethical, social, and educational implications. *Humanities & Social Sciences Communications, 11*(1), 912. DOI: 10.1057/s41599-024-03432-4

Alonso-Rodríguez, A. M. (2024). Towards an ethical framework for artificial intelligence in education. *Teoría de la Educación. Revista Interuniversitaria, 36*(1), 31821. Advance online publication. DOI: 10.14201/teri.31821

Alvarez, J. M., Colmenarejo, A. B., Elobaid, A., Fabbrizzi, S., Fahimi, M., Ferrara, A., Ghodsi, S., Mougan, C., Papageorgiou, I., Reyero, P., Russo, M., Scott, K. M., State, L., Zhao, X., & Ruggieri, S. (2024). Policy advice and best practices on bias and fairness in AI. *Ethics and Information Technology, 26*(2), 31. DOI: 10.1007/s10676-024-09746-w

Awashreh, R. (2024a). Omani private universities: Debates between progress in human development but weak education quality. *The International Journal of Educational Organization and Leadership, 32*(1), 1–15. DOI: 10.18848/2329-1656/CGP/v32i01/1-15

Awashreh, R. (2024b). Be aware: Navigating challenges in AI-driven higher education. *The International Journal of Interdisciplinary Educational Studies, 20*(1), 203–218. DOI: 10.18848/2327-011X/CGP/v20i01/203-218

Awashreh, R. (2025a). Leadership strategies for managing change and fostering innovation over private higher education: Academic institutions in Oman. In R. Awashreh, *Evolving strategies for organizational management and performance evaluation* (pp. 399–422). IGI Global. DOI: 10.4018/979-8-3373-0149-5.ch018

Awashreh, R. (2025b). Managing business continuity and resilience in higher education institutions without compromising the quality of education. In R. Awashreh, *Enhancing resilience in business continuity management* (pp. 295–326). IGI Global. DOI: 10.4018/979-8-3693-8809-9.ch010

Awashreh, R. (2025c). Navigating leadership dynamics: Insights and strategies across domains. In *Optimizing leadership and governance in higher education* (pp. 203–232). IGI Global., DOI: 10.4018/979-8-3693-3534-5.ch010

Awashreh, R. (2026). Advancing innovative entrepreneurship in higher education: Suggested framework. In R. Awashreh, *Sustainable innovation in the Middle East and North Africa (MENA) region* (pp. 121–154). IGI Global. DOI: 10.4018/979-8-3373-0908-8.ch005

Awashreh, R., & Al Ghunaimi, H. (2025). Rethinking the PhD: Aligning higher education with market needs and practical skills. *Forum for Linguistic Studies, 7*(2), 254–264. DOI: 10.30564/fls.v7i2.7942

Awashreh, R., & Almi, H. (2026). Do universities need rankings?: Rethinking biases, transparency, and alternative models. In R. Awashreh & H. Almi, *Influence of university rankings on institutions: Ethics, controversies, and competition* (pp. 1–32). IGI Global. DOI: 10.4018/979-8-3373-7518-2.ch001

Awashreh, R., & Hassiba, A. (2025a). Revolutionizing education with AI: Personalized learning, predictive analytics, and gamification. In *Insights into digital business, human resource management, and competitiveness* (pp. 149–170). IGI Global., DOI: 10.4018/979-8-3693-9440-3.ch006

Awashreh, R., & Hassiba, A. (2025b). Democratizing personalized learning through mentorship reform in private higher education. In R. Awashreh, *Democratizing education with AI and the future of personalized learning* (pp. 207–236). IGI Global. DOI: 10.4018/979-8-3373-2302-2.ch007

Awashreh, R., & Mohamed, Y. (2024). Comparative study of leadership perceptions in government and education sectors: Insights from the UAE and Oman. *The International Journal of Organizational Diversity, 24*(2), 109–123. DOI: 10.18848/2328-6261/CGP/v24i02/109-123

Camilleri, M. A. (2023). Artificial intelligence governance: Ethical considerations and implications for social responsibility. *Expert Systems: International Journal of Knowledge Engineering and Neural Networks*. Advance online publication. DOI: 10.1111/exsy.13406

Cancela-Outeda, C. (2024). The EU's AI act: A framework for collaborative governance. *Internet of Things : Engineering Cyber Physical Human Systems, 27*, 101291. DOI: 10.1016/j.iot.2024.101291

Cheong, B. C. (2024). Transparency and accountability in AI systems: Safeguarding wellbeing in the age of algorithmic decision-making. *Frontiers in Human Dynamics, 6*, 1421273. DOI: 10.3389/fhumd.2024.1421273

Cheong, H.-I., Lyons, A., Houghton, R. W., & Majumdar, A. (2023). Secondary qualitative research methodology using online data within the context of social sciences. *International Journal of Qualitative Methods, 22*(2), 16094069231180160. DOI: 10.1177/16094069231180160

David, A., Yigitcanlar, T., Desouza, K., Li, R. Y. M., Cheong, P. H., Mehmood, R., & Corchado, J. (2024). Understanding local government responsible AI strategy: An international municipal policy document analysis. *Cities (London, England), 155*, 105502. DOI: 10.1016/j.cities.2024.105502

Dwivedi, Y. K., Kshetri, N., Hughes, L., Slade, E. L., Jeyaraj, A., Kar, A. K., Baabdullah, A. M., Koohang, A., Raghavan, V., Ahuja, M., Albanna, H., Albashrawi, M. A., Al-Busaidi, A. S., Balakrishnan, J., Barlette, Y., Basu, S., Bose, I., Brooks, L., Buhalis, D., & Wright, R. (2023). Opinion paper: "So what if ChatGPT wrote it?" Multidisciplinary perspectives on opportunities, challenges and implications of generative conversational AI for research, practice and policy. *International Journal of Information Management, 71*, 102642. DOI: 10.1016/j.ijinfomgt.2023.102642

Farahani, M. Sh. (2024). *Artificial intelligence and inequality: Challenges and opportunities*. Qeios., DOI: 10.32388/7HWUZ2

Fu, Y., & Weng, Z. (2024). Navigating the ethical terrain of AI in education: A systematic review on framing responsible human-centered AI practices. *Computers and Education: Artificial Intelligence, 7*, 100306. DOI: 10.1016/j.caeai.2024.100306

Goosen, W., & Mugumo, V. P. (2024). A framework for the application of AI in higher education in association with APPETD and Swiss Institute for Management and Innovation. In *Proceedings of the International Conference on Medical Imaging, Electronic Imaging, Information Technologies, and Sensors (MIEITS 2024)*. SPIE. DOI: 10.1117/12.3030740

Herane, M. (2024, January 16). AI in education, balancing innovation with ethics. *Higher Education Digest*. Retrieved from https://www.highereducationdigest.com/ai-in-education-balancing-innovation-with-ethics/

Huang, L. (2023). Ethics of artificial intelligence in education: Student privacy and data protection. *Science Insights Education Frontiers*, *16*(2), 2577–2587. DOI: 10.15354/sief.23.re202

Igbokwe, I. C. (2023). Application of artificial intelligence (AI) in educational management. *International Journal of Scientific and Research Publications*, *13*(3), 300. DOI: 10.29322/IJSRP.13.03.2023.p13536

Isiaku, L., Muhammad, A. S., Kefas, H. I., & Ukaegbu, F. C. (2024). Enhancing technological sustainability in academia: Leveraging ChatGPT for teaching, learning, and evaluation. *Quality Education for All*, *1*(1), 385–416. DOI: 10.1108/QEA-07-2024-0055

Jindal, M., Chaiyachati, K. H., Fung, V., Manson, S. M., & Mortensen, K. (2023). Eliminating health care inequities through strengthening access to care. *Health Services Research*, *58*(S3, Suppl 3), 300–310. DOI: 10.1111/1475-6773.14202 PMID: 38015865

Kamalov, F., Santandreu Calonge, D., & Gurrib, I. (2023). New era of artificial intelligence in education: Towards a sustainable multifaceted revolution. *Sustainability (Basel)*, *15*(16), 12451. DOI: 10.3390/su151612451

Leelavathi, R., & Surendhranatha, R. C. (2024). ChatGPT in the classroom: Navigating the generative AI wave in management education. *Journal of Research in Innovative Teaching & Learning*. Advance online publication. DOI: 10.1108/JRIT-01-2024-0017

Li, N. (2023). Ethical considerations in artificial intelligence: A comprehensive discussion from the perspective of computer vision. *SHS Web of Conferences*, 179(1), 04024. DOI: 10.1051/shsconf/202317904024

Lim, T., Gottipati, S., & Cheong, M. L. F. (2023). Ethical considerations for artificial intelligence in educational assessments. In *Creative AI tools and ethical implications in teaching and learning* (pp. 32–79). IGI Global., DOI: 10.4018/979-8-3693-0205-7.ch003

Lin, C. C., Huang, A. Y. Q., & Lu, O. H. T. (2023). Artificial intelligence in intelligent tutoring systems toward sustainable education: A systematic review. *Smart Learning Environments*, *10*(1), 41. DOI: 10.1186/s40561-023-00260-y

Mogavi, R. H., Deng, C., Kim, J. J., Zhou, P., Kwon, Y. D., Metwally, A. H. S., Tlili, A., Bassanelli, S., Bucchiarone, A., Gujar, S., Nacke, L. E., & Hui, P. (2024). ChatGPT in education: A blessing or a curse? A qualitative study exploring early adopters' utilization and perceptions. *Computers in Human Behavior: Artificial Humans*, *2*(1), 100027. DOI: 10.1016/j.chbah.2023.100027

OECD. (2023). *OECD digital education outlook 2023: Towards an effective digital education ecosystem*. OECD Publishing., DOI: 10.1787/9872e201-

Ofosu-Ampong, K. (2024). Artificial intelligence research: A review on dominant themes, methods, frameworks, and future research directions. *Telematics and Informatics Reports*, *14*, 100127. DOI: 10.1016/j.teler.2024.100127

Ou, S. (2024). Transforming education: The evolving role of artificial intelligence in students' academic performance. *International Journal of Education and Humanities*, *13*(2), 163–173. DOI: 10.54097/cc1x7r95

Pant, A., Hoda, R., Tantithamthavorn, C., & Turhan, B. (2024). Ethics in AI through the practitioner's view: A grounded theory literature review. *Empirical Software Engineering*, *29*(67), 67. Advance online publication. DOI: 10.1007/s10664-024-10465-5

Papagiannidis, E., Mikalef, P., & Conboy, K. (2025). Responsible artificial intelligence governance: A review and research framework. *The Journal of Strategic Information Systems*, *34*(2), 101885. DOI: 10.1016/j.jsis.2024.101885

Radu, R. (2021). Steering the governance of artificial intelligence: National strategies in perspective. *Policy and Society*, *40*(2), 178–193. DOI: 10.1080/14494035.2021.1929728

Rashid, A. B., & Kausik, M. A. K. (2024). AI revolutionizing industries worldwide: A comprehensive overview of its diverse applications. *Hybrid Advances*, *7*, 100277. DOI: 10.1016/j.hybadv.2024.100277

Roshanaei, M., Olivares, H., & Lopez, R. (2023). Harnessing AI to foster equity in education: Opportunities, challenges, and emerging strategies. *Journal of Intelligent Learning Systems and Applications*, *15*(4), 123–143. DOI: 10.4236/jilsa.2023.154009

Sargiotis, D. (2024). Fostering ethical and inclusive AI: A human-centric paradigm for social impact. SSRN *Electronic Journal.* DOI: 10.2139/ssrn.4879372

Schwartz, R., Vassilev, A., Greene, K., Perine, L., Burt, A., & Hall, P. (2024). *Towards a standard for identifying and managing bias in artificial intelligence* (NIST Special Publication 1270). National Institute of Standards and Technology. https://nvlpubs.nist.gov/nistpubs/SpecialPublications/NIST.SP.1270.pdf

Singhal, A., Neveditsin, N., Tanveer, H., & Mago, V. (2024). Toward fairness, accountability, transparency, and ethics in AI for social media and health care: Scoping review. *JMIR Medical Informatics*, *12*, e50048. DOI: 10.2196/50048 PMID: 38568737

Tahir, M., Amanat, I., & Awan, S. M. (2024). Ethical considerations and challenges in the integration of artificial intelligence in education: A systematic review. *Journal of Education and Management Studies*, *3*(4), 35–50. Advance online publication. DOI: 10.69565/jems.v3i4.314

Tallberg, J., Erman, E., Furendal, M., Geith, J., Klamberg, M., & Lundgren, M. (2023). The global governance of artificial intelligence: Next steps for empirical and normative research. *International Studies Review*, *25*(3), viad040. Advance online publication. DOI: 10.1093/isr/viad040

Tan, S. (2023). Harnessing artificial intelligence for innovation in education. In *Learning intelligence: Innovative and digital transformative learning strategies* (pp. 335–363). Springer., DOI: 10.1007/978-981-19-9201-8_8

United Arab Emirates. (2024). *UAE guiding principles on AI policy*. UAE Government. Retrieved from https://ai.gov.ae/wp-content/uploads/2024/10/UAE-Guiding-on-ai-policy-EN-V3.pdf

Wang, S., Wang, F., Zhu, Z., Wang, J., Tran, T., & Du, Z. (2024). Artificial intelligence in education: A systematic literature review. *Expert Systems with Applications*, *252*(Part A), 124167. DOI: 10.1016/j.eswa.2024.124167

Wu, C., Zhang, H., & Carroll, J. M. (2024). AI governance in higher education: Case studies of guidance at Big Ten universities. *Future Internet*, *16*(10), 354. DOI: 10.3390/fi16100354

Xue, L., & Pang, Z. (2022). Ethical governance of artificial intelligence: An integrated analytical framework. *Journal of Digital Economy*, *1*(1), 44–52. DOI: 10.1016/j.jdec.2022.08.003

Zawacki-Richter, O., Marín, V. I., Bond, M., & Gouverneur, F. (2019). Systematic review of research on artificial intelligence applications in higher education – where are the educators? *International Journal of Educational Technology in Higher Education, 16*(39), 39. Advance online publication. DOI: 10.1186/s41239-019-0171-0

Zhai, C., Wibowo, S., & Li, L. D. (2024). The effects of over-reliance on AI dialogue systems on students' cognitive abilities: A systematic review. *Smart Learning Environments, 11*(28), 28. Advance online publication. DOI: 10.1186/s40561-024-00316-7

Zhai, X., Chu, X., Chai, C. S., Jong, M. S. Y., Istenic, A., Spector, M., Liu, J. B., Yuan, J., & Li, Y. (2021). A review of artificial intelligence (AI) in education from 2010 to 2020. *Complexity, 2021*(1), 8812542. Advance online publication. DOI: 10.1155/2021/8812542

Chapter 2
Algorithmic Bias and Data Privacy in Education: Building Ethical Frameworks for Responsible AI Integration

Kartavya Sharma
http://orcid.org/0009-0008-0270-5369
Christ (Deemed to be) University, Delhi NCR, India

Neerja Nigam
http://orcid.org/0009-0009-2636-4500
Christ (Deemed to be) University, Delhi NCR, India

ABSTRACT

The concept of Artificial Intelligence (AI) is becoming an inseparable part of the educational sphere, influencing the process of teaching, learning, evaluation, and decision making of the institutions. Even though AI-powered applications and technologies, including learning analytics and automated assessment, provide efficiency and customization, they pose severe ethical issues, especially when it comes to algorithmic discrimination and data privacy. Algorithms that are biased would perpetuate educational disparities and the use of large amounts of data can jeopardize the privacy and autonomy of learners. The available studies tend to treat these concerns in technical or disjointed manner. The chapter takes the responsible AI approach and discusses how bias and privacy risks are created throughout the AI lifecycle when used in education. It suggests a humanistic approach to ethics by qualitatively synthesizing literature (2016-2025) to steer towards the seamless, transparent, and responsible introduction of AI in education.

DOI: 10.4018/979-8-2600-1840-8.ch002

1. INTRODUCTION

The quickly developing digital technologies revolutionized the educational systems of different countries around the world, as it changed the way teaching, learning, and managing the institutions were performed. In the last ten years, school systems are introducing their own digital learning platforms, online learning environments, and information-driven technologies to improve their instructional practice and operation. Artificial Intelligence (AI) is one of the most significant technological advances that have contributed to the modern-day education. One of the ways AI technologies are finding implementation into the educational ecosystem is to support personalized learning and automated administrative functions and influence decision-making based on data (Holmes et al., 2019; Zawacki-Richter et al., 2019).

At present, educational institutions use a broad spectrum of AI-based solutions, such as intelligent tutoring systems, automated grading sites, predictive analytics solutions, chatbots, and generative AI applications. The technologies enable institutions to process massive amounts of education information and generate insights that will benefit students and educators. In the case of intelligent tutoring systems, which are adaptive algorithms, customized learning processes are provided based on learning patterns and performance by the student. In the same measure, learning analytics systems process digital records of student engagement in learning management systems and determine patterns that can possibly point to academic difficulty or inactivity (Luckin et al., 2016).

The growing use of AI technologies is tightly related to the process of digital transformation in general education. The term digital transformation concerns a systematic adoption of highly developed technologies into the sphere of teaching, the organization of institutions, as well as academic infrastructure. Universities and schools are turning towards more integrated digital platforms, cloud-based infrastructures, and AI-enabled analytics systems to facilitate the processes of teaching, learning, and managing the institutions (Williamson, 2017). Consequently, numerous universities are turning themselves into so-called smart campuses, meaning that digital technologies are used to constantly gather and analyse data in helping academic and administrative faculties to make decisions.

In these digital learning ecosystems, AI technologies allow institutions to track the student learning patterns, test student engagement habits, and detect possible academic problems at an initial stage. One example of such measures is predictive analytics models, which examine past academic records to approximate the chance that the student is at risk of academic challenges or loss of interest in his or her education. The insights can help the institutions introduce specific interventions, which will help to enhance the success and retention rates of the students (Siemens and Baker, 2012). AI-based decision support systems are therefore becoming a more common tool to support academic advising, curriculum development and institutional planning.

Among the most common advantages of AI technologies in education, one can single out the opportunity to facilitate personalized learning. Conventional classroom set ups have the weakness of being unable to support various learning requirements even in terms of time, materials and educational groupings. Learning systems based on AI can counter this issue by breaking down individual learning behavior and adjusting teaching content to meet the needs of that learning behavior. Adaptive learning applications involve machine learning algorithms to assess the student performance and suggest personal learning paths according to the performance patterns and the learning preferences (Holmes et al., 2019). Through these systems students are able to study at their own speed and get in-depth feedback to aid them in gaining more knowledge and academic growth.

AI technologies improve the efficiency of institutions as well as the learning experiences. Academic institutions handle elaborate administrative tasks and processes such as enrollment of students, course time-tables, grading of students, and performance control and assessment. The extensive variety of the numerous routine tasks that can be automated using AI-based administrative tools, enables educators to prioritize their teaching and mentoring functions. The automated grading system, such as, can be utilized to assess assignments and give instant feedback to students, whereas predictive analytics system can assist administrators in detecting trends in academic performance and institutional results (Holmes et al., 2019).

Although there are such advantages, there are also serious ethical issues associated with the high pace of adoption of AI technologies in the education field. AI systems are extremely dependent on vast amounts of data to discover patterns and make predictions concerning the behavior of students or their academic achievements. The consistency and validity of such forecasts are, however, tied to the quality and extent to which the information applied in training algorithmic models is representative. In cases where training materials are biased or historically represent differences which are unjustly promoted through educational structures, AI technologies can replicate or even increase them unintentionally (Barocas and Selbst, 2016; Mehrabi et al., 2021).

Algorithms bias is connected to the biased results of an algorithm system as a result of biased data received when algorithms are deployed, or if the algorithm was designed with various assumptions and the context in which the algorithm will be applied. In an educational system, an algorithmic bias may affect the choices regarding the assessment of students, academic tracking, admissions, and distribution of learning resources. Since most models of the AI are typically based on past data, they might also be taking into consideration the trends that mirror the existing social inequalities. As an illustration, academic literature in the past might note the differences in the educational opportunities of the students who pertain to various socioeconomic backgrounds. Training predictive models with these datasets can cause them to learn a relationship with some demographic factors that falsely attributes poor academic performance to such factors (Baker and Hawn, 2021).

The fact that educational technologies have an algorithmic bias is especially alarming due to the rise in high-stakes decisions that are taken by AI systems and that impact the academic trajectory and future opportunities of students. Institutional decisions of the type of academic support programs, courses placements or student retention strategies might be informed by algorithmic predictions. When such projections are systematically disfavoring some population of students, then the resultant consequences can be seen to enhance disparities in the educational systems. As a consequence, researchers note that it is necessary to work on governance frameworks that create fairness, transparency, and accountability in AI -enabled educational technologies (Floridi et al., 2018; Dignum, 2019).

On the one hand, the issue of algorithmic bias is present; on the other hand, there is the problem of data privacy that has become one of the most important ethical problems with the introduction of AI into education. AI technologies are based on the accumulation and study of big data regarding academic success of students, their learning, and relations with online learning tools. Schools and colleges frequently gather the statistics including grades, attendance data, the number of assignments submitted, and engagement rates created in the digital learning platforms (Slade and Prinsloo, 2013).

Although this type of data has valuable insights to take into consideration in order to enhance the teaching and learning process, it also creates vital concerns about how personal data is gathered, stored, and processed in the educational system based on AI application. Students are usually weak in controlling the compilation and processing of their data especially when digital learning platforms become mandatory to participate in the coursework. Moreover, numerous institutions use the services of third-party technology developers that create and operate AI-powered learning platforms. Third-party providers can access personal information on students, and bringing up the issue of who owns the data, expresses consent, and their responsiveness towards students and their institutions (Williamson, 2017).

Surveillance in the learning context has also been an issue of concern with the emerging technology of learning analytics. Based on AIs, it is possible to track interactions of students with online learning platforms on a continuous basis, such as how often students log in, how much time they spend working with learning activities, and whether they engage in online discussion. Although this type of monitoring can assist teachers to be able to monitor specific learning issues and offer specific assistance to them, it can also establish conditions, in which a student feels constantly followed. Researchers have thus noted that data-driven innovation should be accompanied by a balance of privacy and autonomy of the individual (Prinsloo and Slade, 2017).

The other significant ethical issue is that there is no transparency when it comes to making decisions about algorithms. Most artificial intelligence systems are hard to understand complex machine learning models whose workings are hard to decipher. It is sometimes said that such systems are so opaque that their decision-making processes are perceived as black box algorithms in that users can easily understand them. When institutions of learning base decisions made on them to influence students, then learners and teachers might be unable to comprehend how particular forecasts or suggestions were arrived at. A lack of transparency may restore the lack of trust in AI technologies and complicate the process of detecting and redressing algorithmic errors/bias (Rudin, 2019).

To resolve these moral issues, it is more reasonable to expand the scope of the AI technologies regulation in education. Instead of defining algorithmic bias and data privacy as distant matters in technical space to be addressed, it is required to consider the two as interrelated problems that are embedded into AI-based educational environments. It is impossible to implement AI responsibly without involving educators, technologists, policymakers, and institutional leaders since it is only in collaboration with these stakeholders that the technologic innovation can be brought into accordance with the ethical principles and educational values (Floridi et al., 2018).

Although there has been a growing interest of AI ethics as an educational concept, the current literature tends to study algorithmic bias and data privacy individually. Technical research is often related to more efficient machine learning models or bias in datasets, whereas policy-related studies are concerned with legal regulations to safeguard personal information. Both sides of the argument have meaningful contributions; however, they cannot be used to assess the interplay of bias and privacy issues at the various stages of the AI system implementation in education (Williamson and Eynon, 2020).

This gap is filled in this chapter as it describes ethical implications of AI systems algorithmic bias and data privacy in lifecycle of AI systems in learning settings. Comprising an interdisciplinary review of literature and examining the ethical dangers of artificial intelligence technologies, the chapter will contribute to the creation of governance models that promote the responsible use of AI in learning. Finally, the ethical responsibility of adopting AI technologies is to create a balance between technological innovation and ethical responsibility in order to make AI-driven educational systems rule out unfairness, transparency, and biased opportunities to learn.

2. LITERATURE REVIEW

The implementation of Artificial Intelligence (AI) in the educational setup has garnered the growing academic interest as learning institutions embrace intelligent technologies to facilitate their educational, teaching, and management. Recent developments in machine learning, learning analytics and news decision systems have allowed educational institutions to gather and process vast quantities of student data which has presented new possibilities of enhancing learning outcomes and institutional performance. The personalized learning, adaptive learning, and data-driven governance of educational institutions have been discussed by researchers of different fields, including education, computer science, data ethics, and governance (Holmes et al., 2019; Zawacki-Richter et al., 2019).

Meanwhile, the quick implementation of AI systems has also attracted critical ethical issues. Researchers are starting to underline that AI technologies are not the neutral tools but the socio-technical systems in which the results of any data practice, algorithm design choices, and even the way institutions are governed (Floridi et al., 2018; Williamson and Eynon, 2020). With an increasing trend in the use of algorithmic systems in educational institutions to aid the decisionmaking process, the concerns regarding algorithmic bias, data privacy, transparency, and accountability have emerged as dominant themes in the Artificial Intelligence in Education (AIEd) literature. This part will be a review of current studies on these themes and determine the conceptual background of exploring ethical risks in AI-based learning settings.

Artificial intelligence stands out as a key area of transformation in educational systems; in this context, functions like message-scheduling, computer-generated reading tasks, collaborative learning exercises, and tutorial-focused computer-assisted education will be examined.

2.1 The Artificial Intelligence in Educational Systems The AI in Education

The use of AI technologies in the educational field has grown tremendously with the institutions trying to get up to date with the digital innovation in teaching and learning. Applications of AI systems in adaptive learning platforms, intelligent tutoring system, automated grade system, learning analytics dashboards, and generative AI applications are on the increase. The technologies are based on machine learning algorithms to evaluate patterns in the student behavior and come up with insights that are beneficial to both pupils and the teachers (Holmes et al., 2019).

Among the greatest AI technologies advances in the field of education, the creation of customized learning systems should be mentioned. Personalized learning can be defined as the instructional methods that provide diversification of the instructional matter over needs, skills and learning patterns of particular students. The adaptive learning systems of AI processes analyze the student performance data and dynamically change the learning content based on the learning progress and preference of students (Luckin et al., 2016). These systems enable the learners to study at their pace and have their own individualized feedback that helps in acquisition of knowledge and improvement of skills.

Learning analytics and predictive modelling are the other AI technologies that are used in institutional decision-making. Learning analytics refers to computerized systems that process the data obtained on the basis of digital learning systems to detect the patterns concerning the student interactions and academic performance. The insights can enable teachers and administrators to know the students who are likely to fail in academics and apply early interventions to help them enhance retention and churn out positive results in their learning (Siemens and Baker, 2012). As a result, AI technologies are being regarded as educational governance support mechanisms, which can be used in an evidence-based way.

The increasing use of AI technologies has also affected the changing role of a teacher in a digital learning setting. Instead of destroying the employment of human teachers, most researchers believe that AI systems serve as complimentary resources and help teachers by automating the process and offering analytical feedback (Holmes et al., 2019). As an example, automated grading systems have the potential to mark assignments and give instant feedback to educators so that they could put more effort into mentoring and assisting students in critical thinking and problem-solving.

Although such advantages exist, researchers have also expressed their concern that AI-powered educational systems could increase unwanted biases or strengthen the existing disparities in the educational institutions (Zawacki-Richter et al., 2019). These issues have inspired the growing amount of research on the ethical consequences of AI introduction in education.

2.2 Algorithms bias in educational artificial intelligence systems

Algorithms bias has become a topic of the most popular discussion of the ethical issues related to AI technologies. Algorithms bias means all outputs generated by algorithm systems are systematic and unfair and are caused by biased data, poor specifications of the model, or contextual conditions affecting the implementation of the system (Barocas and Selbst, 2016). Algorithms bias can affect institutional decisions that are related to student assessment, admissions, academic tracking, and resources access in educational settings.

Educational systems based on AI are usually trained on historic data sets to predict. These data sets can have patterns that indicate structural inequalities based on socioeconomic status, race, sex or geographic position. When such datasets are used to train machine learning models, these inequalities can be reproduced or amplified when such algorithms make predictions (Mehrabi et al., 2021). In its turn, predictive analytics systems intended to help predict students facing the risk of academic failure can label some demographic groups as high-risk based on the patterns that are present in the historical data. These classifications can affect some institutional choice on academic support programs and intervention strategies (Baker & Hawn, 2021).

The existing literature on algorithmic fairness suggests that bias in AI may appear at various cycles of the AI lifecycle. The bias can be created at the time of data collection when the training data used in the collection is insufficient to represent the various student groups. It can also happen when designing an algorithm when some variables have undue weight on model prediction. Moreover, bias can occur at the stage of the system implementation when it comes to interpreting algorithm outputs in the context of more general social and institutional circumstances.

A number of measures have been suggested against the alleviation of algorithmic bias in educational AI systems. One of them involves enhancing the representativeness of the training datasets so that algorithmic models can be representative of different student populations. The other strategy is to come up with fairness-conscious algorithms that use fairness indicators when training and interpreting models (Mehrabi et al., 2021). Along with that, researchers also highlight the significance of the algorithmic transparency and interpretability that allow the educators and administrators to see how the algorithmic predictions are made.

Nonetheless, the application of these solutions within the educational facilities is still a problem. Several of the AI technologies employed in learning are proprietary and not transparent in their algorithms due to the fact that most are developed by individual technology firms. It makes educational institutions tend to be very poor in assessing the fairness or reliability of such systems. This lack of transparency shows that there is a need to have more robust governance frameworks that would govern the adoption of AI in the educational setting.

2.3 Educational Technologies and Data Privacy/Surveillance

Besides the topic of the bias of the algorithms, data privacy has turned into a main theme in the discourse of AI implementation in the field of education. The use of AI systems is also dependent on big data sets with in-depth information regarding the academic achievements, behaviour tendencies, and their engagement with any online learning environment. The performance of schools and higher education regularly gathers information in the form of grades, attendance testing, submissions of assignments and metric measurement of engagements created by the learning centered systems (Slade and Prinsloo, 2013).

Although such data are useful to enhance the processes of teaching and learning, issues of personal information of students protection also emerge in terms of ethical concerns. Learning analytics technologies are used to constantly track student activity in digital learning space to generate comprehensive behavioral portraits that can be utilized in academic performance prediction or detect learning challenges (Drachsler and Greller, 2016). Even though this type of monitoring can assist in the implementation of early intervention strategies, it will also produce the environments where students become aware that they are always watched.

The growing application of surveillance technologies in the education sectors has thus raised issues regarding concerns of the equilibrium between information-based creativity and the rights of privacy. Researchers believe that when collecting data in large amounts, it could turn the educational setting into a monitored behavioral setting instead of an intellectual exploration (Williamson, 2017). Moreover, the intervention of third-party technology providers also makes the data ownership and accountability more complicated. The fact that many institutions have external vendors who operate the learning platforms and analytics systems, however, poses some concerns regarding how the student data is stored, disseminated, and utilized by third-party organizations.

The other significant question is the question of informed consent. In most learning institutions, learners are being required to utilize these digital learning tools in their coursework assignments and therefore, they have little room to choose when it comes to avoiding the practice of data collection. Researchers thus stress the importance of open data policy aimed at making clear how student data is gathered, processed and ensured in AI-enhanced educational systems.

2.4 AI-Driven Education Transparency and Accountability

In the context of education, responsible AI governance includes transparency and accountability as its mandatory elements. Artificial intelligence systems can resemble intricate computational frameworks and are unable to be easy to understand by the users the way that decisions are made. These black box systems can create predictions or suggestions without obvious ways of explaining how results were obtained.

In education, the unpredictability of the process in terms of algorithm systems can call in question the trust of students, teachers, and the administration of particular institutions. Scientists thus highlight the significance of explainable AI (XAI) aiming at creating models that can give interpretable result of algorithmic prediction (Rudin, 2019). Explainable AI methods provide users with the chance to learn how certain predictions are made and whether the results of algorithmic decision-making are appropriate to the courses and ethical standards.

Responsibility measures are also significant in responsible AI implementation. Governing systems in institutions should create a sense of accountability of decisions made by algorithmic systems. Teachers and managers ought to be in a position to challenge and analyze the outputs of algorithms or algorithms as opposed to blindly adhering to them. Through instituting accountability mechanisms, schools will be able to implement AI technologies in a way that will not substitute human decisions with machines.

2.5 Research Loophole and the Necessity of Ethical AI Frameworks

Despite the rapid growth in research on AI in education, there are a number of research gaps that are significant. To start with, most of the current literature discusses the areas of algorithmic bias and data privacy as two distinct ethical concerns, instead of exploring the interactions between the two problems in the larger lifecycle of AI systems. Technical research work has frequently been interested in making machine learning models better, whereas policy studies attach importance to legal regulations regarding data protection. These perspectives have not been combined in many studies to devise all-encompassing governance structures of AI-based educational systems.

Second, most of the researches study ethical issues when AI technologies are already at work in the academic setting. This nature of reactive approach restricts the capacity of institutions to be able to predict the onset of risk before it occurs. There is a need to have a proactive strategy that incorporates moral factors in the design, implementation, and oversight of AI systems.

Lastly, research on how schools can come up with a feasible governance model that would resolve the issues of algorithmic bias and data privacy coincidentally has not been conducted extensively. As AI technologies keep changing the educational frameworks, higher learning institutions need effective methods to put in place ethical AI practices that safeguard the rights of students as well as enhance technological advancement.

To resolve these gaps in research, educationists, technologists, policymakers, and ethicists must work together on an interdisciplinary basis. The chapter can be useful in designing the guidelines on governance that enable the responsible and equitable use of AI in education by analyzing the moral implications of algorithmic prejudice and privacy concerns to the context of AI-enabled learning systems.

3. RESEARCH GAP

The recent years have seen a significant body of academic interest towards the increasing use of Artificial Intelligence (AI) technologies in the education setting. The recent studies have reviewed a lot of AI use in education, such as intelligent tutoring systems, adaptive learning platforms, predictive analytics applications, automated grading systems, and learning analytics dashboards. These technologies have shown a great possibility of advancing the concept of personalized learning, increasing student engagement, and assisting the data-oriented institutional decision-making (Holmes et al., 2019; Zawacki-Richter et al., 2019).

The available literature mentions the potential of AI technologies to facilitate data-driven education as the methods allow institutions to process masses of data on students. Learning analytics systems enable teachers and administrators to keep track of the student responsiveness and performance trends, enhancing teaching approaches and institutional performance (Siemens and Baker, 2012). Predictive analytics models can also reveal students who are in danger of failure or dropping out of school so that early intervention plans to enhance retention and study success can be implemented (Baker and Hawn, 2021). On the same note, adaptive learning tools apply machine learning algorithms to customize learning material based on personal learning requirements and advanced (Luckin et al., 2016). This has resulted in the development of intelligent learning environments where the algorithmic systems are becoming more and more relevant in the decision making process in education.

Even with such technological advancements, researchers have become more concerned about the ethical issues of AI integration in education. Some of the most widely debated issues include algorithm bias, threats to data privacy, the absence of transparency, algorithm action, and the problem of responsibility with the introduction of AI-powered systems (Floridi et al., 2018; Williamson and Eynon, 2020). When AI systems produce unfair or discriminative results because of biased training data, erroneous design assumptions, or other external factors related to the system implementation, this is known as algorithmic bias (Barocas and Selbst, 2016; Mehrabi et al., 2021). Such biases can be applied in the context of education with the effects of such choices in the evaluation of students, the process of their admission to the organization, their division into academic tracks, as well as their share of institutional resources.

This has been accompanied by the problem of algorithmic bias and the issue of data privacy has become another worrisome ethical issue. AI systems are also dependent on colossal volumes of information that include personal and behavioral data on students. Schools and colleges buy and compile data regarding academic achievement, online learning experience, on-line communication and engagement with digital learning environments (Slade and Prinsloo, 2013). Although these data are invaluable toward bettering the learning outcomes, there are also pertinent issues of concern with how personal information is stored, handled and disseminated. There is also a limited control that students have on the way their data can be used, especially when the use of digital learning platforms is compulsory to take part in the academic process (Drachsler and Greller, 2016).

Despite the fact that the available literature contains valuable information about these ethical issues, there are still several significant drawbacks. First, there is a great number of studies that consider algorithmic bias, and data privacy individually, even though AI systems need personal data to make predictions and recommendations. Therefore, prejudice and privacy problems are intrinsically linked to each other and are to be reviewed collectively in AI-based academic systems.

Second, a significant portion of the available literature does not consider such ethical issues related to AI systems in terms of lifecycle. Ethical risks have the potential to appear throughout various points of constructing AI and its applications, such as data gathering, algorithm development, system implementation, and interpreting the outputs of algorithms by institutions. Nevertheless, most studies are concentrated on single steps of the AI implementation as opposed to studying the dynamics of ethical issues throughout the AI lifecycle.

Lastly, little research has offered viable governance practices that the learning institutions can implement to guarantee accountable AI adoption. Although such ethical standards like fairness, transparency, accountability, and protection of privacy are frequently mentioned by scholars, they are commonly regarded at a conceptual level without institutional strategies of their implementation.

In order to overcome those constraints, this chapter investigates the origin of the ethical risks, which arise in terms of algorithmic bias and data privacy throughout the lifecycle of AI technologies in education. The chapter lacks any original research and instead proposes a Responsible AI Governance Framework in Education based on the combination of insights in education, computer science, and digital ethics, to promote fairness, transparency, accountability, and responsible innovation in AI-driven educational systems.

4. METHODOLOGY

This chapter also follows a conceptual research design of qualitative methodology to explore the ethical issues linked with both algorithmic bias and data privacy in Artificial Intelligence (AI)-powered education systems. Conceptual research has been found to be most appropriate when researching on new phenomena in technology, empirical evidence might still be small or incomplete. Conceptual research, as opposed to primary data collection in form of a survey or an experiment, synthesizes the previous scholarly understanding and, in that way, outlines the conceptual patterns, conceptual relationships, and new problems in a field.

Algorithms favoring any group, privacy concerns, transparency and responsibility issues are all ethical considerations that are undergoing development in the scholarly community in regard to the integration of AI into educational programs. Thus, a conceptual research method allows performing the systematic study of the available literature and allows formulating a systematized perception of ethical risks of AI-based educational systems.

The interdisciplinarity of AI in the educational context is another need behind the use of the conceptual approach to research. The problem of ethics regarding the integration of AI cannot be limited to the technical operations of machine learning algorithms and involves interaction with various academic fields, such as, but not restricted to, educational technology, computer science, digital ethics, data governance, and public policy. Conceptual approach will allow merging the findings of all these different areas and help the study provide the presentation of the holistic framework of appearance of ethical issues in AI-driven educational setting.

4.1 Research Approach

The methodology applied in this chapter is qualitative and conceptual and made on the basis of systematic analysis and synthesis of existing academic literature. Conceptual studies are seen that have been extensively used in research fields that were new in conceptualizing research to the extent that little empirical evidence has been established.

Ethical issues about using algorithms to make decisions on the educational field become multidimensional and intricate in the context of AI-enabled education. Bias in an algorithmic context and privacy issues emerge in a form of interaction between the technological design, institutional practices, and governance. A qualitative conceptual approach allows the research to analyze these interactions and find trends in the current body of research on the issue of incorporation of ethical AI in education.

4.2 Research Design

The method used in the research is a systematic conceptual review and synthesis of academic literature published within the period of 2016 to 2025. This era marks one of the most important stages of the evolution of Ville franc Raichi Education: AIed. where learning analytics, predictive analytics tools, intelligent tutoring technologies and generative AI application boomed quickly.

The research plan will be based on three main steps:

Literature Identification

During the first step, the academic databases and research repositories were searched to find relevant scholarly publications. The search of the literature was done according to peer-reviewed articles that explore the intersection of Artificial Intelligence, education, algorithmic bias, and data privacy. Key search terms included:

- Artificial Intelligence in Education (AIEd)
- Artificial intelligence bias.
- Personal information in learning technology.
- Learning analytics ethics
- AI governance in education
- Responsible AI frameworks

The purpose of this step was to find the literature that was devoted to both technological uses of AI in education and ethical implications of technologies.

Thematic Categorization

The second stage involved the analysis of the research that was selected in order to determine the common themes in the literature in terms of ethical issues. The thematic categorization allowed splitting the research into numerous dimensions that were associated with ethical integration of AI to education. Key topics were algorithmic bias, data governance, privacy protection, transparency in making algorithmic decisions, institutional accountability, and AI regulatory scheme.

Conceptual Synthesis

During the last phase, the knowledge gained on the reviewed literature was synthesised into a conceptual framework of why ethical risks arise in the education system run by AI-driven learning systems. The synthesis is extended than a descriptive literature review since it defines conceptual connections among algorithmic bias, issues of data privacy, and generative practices of institutional governance.

4.3 Data Sources

The discussion which is made in this chapter is completely playing on secondary sources which is based upon peer-reviewed academic literature and scholarly publications. Conceptual research is commonly applied as secondary data analysis and is aimed at synthesizing the existing information and delivering the new theoretical implications in a domain.

The sources used in the literature review of the current study included several academic sources such as:

- scholarly peer-reviewed journal articles.
- academic book chapters and book edits.
- systematic literature reviews.
- AI Governance and digital ethics policy reports.
- educational technology and AI research papers in conferences.

Major academic databases that included Scopus, Web of Science, Google scholar, ERIC and IEEE Xplore were investigated to find relevant literature on AI technologies and educational innovation.

There were about 50 scholarly researches that were reviewed in order to generate an all-embracing view of ethical issues involved with integrating AI in education.

4.4 Selection Criteria

In order to achieve the required academic quality and relevancy of the literature that was utilized in this study, certain inclusion criteria were used when conducting the review. The following conditions were necessary to select the studies:

1. It explores how the technologies based on Artificial Intelligence are used in the education sphere including K-12 education, higher education facilities, or online learning systems.
2. The research focuses on such ethical concerns regarding AI technologies as the bias of algorithms, data privacy, or the control of AI systems.
3. The article has been reported in peer-reviewed journals, books or other credible academic publications.
4. The journal is in the timeframes of 2016-2025, as it reveals the latest trends in AI technologies and modern discourses on AI ethics.

4.5 Analytical Procedure

The thematic analysis was used in the literature analysis as it is a qualitative research method employed to determine patterns and conceptual relationships in the text information. The analysis entailed three steps.

Stage 1: Initial Coding

The ethical issues raised in the literature were identified and coded in the first stage. Some of the main terms were algorithmic bias, transparency, fairness, data governance, surveillance, accountability, and explainability.

The subject becomes familiar with objects within a specific category.<|human|>Stage 2: Thematic Organization

Primary familiarity with objects in a given category.

Stage 2: Thematic Organization

Other similar codes were clustered into larger thematic groups that represented the mammoth ethical aspects in regards to the use of AI in education. These included:

- binary features of other sources of resistance to algorithms in education data.
- privacy threats of learning analytics systems.
- surveillance use in AIs based learning environments.
- governance issues associated with the implementation of AI in schools.

Stage 3: Conceptual Integration

During the last phase, the determined themes were incorporated into a conceptual framework that explains the beginnings of ethical risks at any point of the AI systems lifecycle in the education area.

4.6 Research Limitations

Despite the fact that conceptual research offers good information on the new technological and ethical issues, it has its limitations. The research applies only secondary data sources that are based on the existing literature and fails to present primary empirical information about institutions involved in education and AI developers. Therefore, the essay does not pay a lot of attention to real observations but rather theoretical understandings regarding AI application.

Also, although interdisciplinary studies across various academic fields were included in attempt to ensure that such studies were not missed in the review process, some of the relevant studies might not have been incorporated in the review process. Further studies could expand the scope of the current research through empirical research involving the investigation on how the problems of algorithmic bias and data privacy are manifested within the context of individual educational institutions.

Irrespective of these restrictions, the research conceptual approach achieved in this chapter offers a powerful theoretical framework of grasping the ethical issues regarding AI-based education and is able to create the frameworks of governance that allow responsible AI-integration.

5. ETHICAL RISK THROUGHOUT AI LIFECYCLE IN EDUCATION

The implementation of Artificial Intelligence (AI) technologies in education settings has developed immense potentials of customized learning, predictive analytics, and data-driven institutional decision-making. Intelligent tutoring systems, adaptive learning platforms, and learning analytics tools are part of artificial intelligence used in education to enable education institutions to examine student progress and establish specific learning interventions. Nevertheless, in addition to the above, there are also ethical issues associated with the use of AI in education, such as algorithmic bias, privacy of data, transparency, and institutional responsibility. There is consensus among scholars that these ethical concerns must be considered throughout the lifecycle of AI systems, from the collection of data, development of algorithms, the deployment of the system itself, and the interpretation of the algorithmic results by the institution (Floridi et al., 2018; Holmes et al., 2019).

The life cycle perspective of ethical risks is of special significance since AI systems are developing in interdependent development and implementation phases. Relying on big datasets, sophisticated machine learning algorithms, and institutional governance practices determine the interpretation and application of algorithmic predictions by educational AI technologies. Ethical risk can arise in various forms at every stage this lifecycle. As an example, biased sample sets might result in discriminatory forecasts, opaque algorithms might encompass transparency in decision-making, and automated analytics systems might impact on high-stakes academic selections that determine the course of education of students. A review of ethical risks at each stage of an AI lifecycle hence gives a holistic perspective on the interplay between algorithmic bias and data privacy issues in the educational systems (Williamson and Eynon, 2020; Zawacki-Richter et al., 2019).

5.1 Data Collection and Data Set Bias

The collection, processing and preparation of datasets that are to be used to train machine learning models represents the first phase of AI lifecycle. AI systems in the educational setting are dependent on vast amounts of student data that are obtained through the online learning platforms. Such data sets usually involve academic performance records, course attendance records, attendance, interaction in online learning, and behavior measurement per data gathered by learning management systems and education platforms. Learning analytics technologies keep on collecting such data to determine patterns of student engagement, performance, and predict academic performance, as well as to help implement personalized learning interventions (Siemens and Baker, 2012; Ferguson, 2019).

Although the predictive power of the large-scale educational data is high because of the availability of large datasets, such information quality and representativeness are essential determinants of the trustworthiness and impartiality of AI systems. The algorithms of machine learning are susceptible to the data that is employed in the training. In case these datasets are biased historically or reflect structural disparities in educational systems, then the resulting models can reproduce such disparities or create new ones. It has been demonstrated by scholars that biases in algorithms, presented by means of biased or incomplete datasets, often result in discriminatory consequences despite the apparent technical accuracy of the algorithms (Barocas and Selbst, 2016; Mehrabi et al., 2021).

In education, dataset bias can be an outcome of the training data being an inappropriate representation of a particular group of students relative to a particular education group. As an example, a dataset that is based on institutions that cover a particular socioeconomic or geographic community might not give a true picture of the diversity of learners at large education systems. The application of predictive models built using such data can result in inaccurate predictions or disadvantage specific groups of students once applied to other educational environments.

There might also be bias on datasets due to lack of equality in availability of digital learning materials. Learners with poor socioeconomic status might have low access to a good and reliable internet connection, access to digital devices, or good study conditions. As a result, they might not interact in the same way as more technology-accessible students do in the platform of online education. The machine learning platforms that use lowered online interactions as an indicator of educational danger can therefore label the students as non-engaged or less productive, notwithstanding the reality that there is high student capability (Williamson and Eynon, 2020).

On top of the problem of representation, there are other concerns of privacy and informed consent about the data collection stage. Learning centers and institutions are gathering more and more comprehensive behavioral information via digital learning platforms in many cases without the full disclosure of how it will be processed or how it will be shared. Though students can officially agree to data collection by mandated institutional policies, such agreement is often clogged in elaborate terms of service, which are hard to comprehend. In addition, students usually have no choice regarding these data practices as it would imply that they have to participate in the academic activities at the cost of doing so. These circumstances bring up moral concerns regarding the possibility of students sensibly controlling their own information in AI-powered educational systems (Slade and Prinsloo, 2013; Williamson, 2017).

5.2 Model Bias and Algorithm Design

The second phase of AI lifecycle entails the training and design of machine learning algorithms. In this phase, the developers choose the input variables, program model structures and train models with past datasets. These choices also play a major role in the ways AI systems can process educational data and make predictions about performance among students.

Machine learning algorithms detect statistical correlation in sets of data to estimate future results. Such correlations are, however, not always causal because they can equally be due to underlying social inequalities inherent in the data. Indicatively, predictive analytics systems aimed at forecasting students who are likely to underperform in academics are usually based on the attendance logs, course attendance statistics, and internet usage tendencies. These indicators might be constant signals of student engagement, but they can be also related to the socioeconomic conditions which influence access to an educational opportunity (Holmes et al., 2019).

Under the circumstances where algorithm models are overly dependent on such variables and are not synchronized with contextual factors they can produce biased forecasts to particular groups of students. To illustrate, part-time students with a need to work to sustain their education might lessen their time life with the online learning platforms than students who have sufficient financial support. Algorithms resulting in reading less engagement as a predictor of low academic performance can thus classify such students as high-risk learners.

The other major ethical issue that can be seen in relation to the design of algorithms is the problem of transparency and explainability. Most developed machine learning algorithms often tend to work as black box or rather deep learning algorithms, the inner workings of which are often hard to comprehend. Although these models can be highly predictive, they are not transparent, which makes the educators and administrators hard to comprehend the way in which the predictions are produced. Such a lack of transparency may undermine the confidence in AI technologies and the possibility of detecting and rectifying any mistakes or bias in the algorithms (Rudin, 2019).

Since the outcomes of the algorithmic forecasts can affect significant educational choices, the researchers point at the necessity of explainable algorithms that can provide intelligible information about how predictive models will operate in the educational system (Floridi et al., 2018).

5.3 Implementation of AI Systems in Academic Centres

The third phase of the AI lifecycle is the implementation of AI technologies in the sphere of education. At this level, artificial intelligence systems will be implemented in organizational systems like learning management systems, student information systems, and online learning systems. These technologies once implemented start impacting daily academic activities with teachers and administrators acting based on algorithm intelligence.

A significant ethical issue in the deployment process is that there can be a high-stakes educational decision affected by an algorithmic prediction. Predictive analytics systems are present in cases where they attempt to detect students who might need further academic attention. Although these systems can assist institutions to direct their resources, it can also be dangerous when people use the outcomes of the algorithmic prediction as the objective results of student ability.

The study of decision-making in automated settings identifies the phenomenon of automation bias, according to which people trust automated systems too much despite the fact that automated systems can deliver an inefficient forecast or even a corrupt forecast (Cummings, 2017). Automation bias can also be used in school settings to encourage teachers to be overly dependent on algorithmic suggestions in terms of assessing student performance in a way that they interfere with any interventions. This kind of dependence can diminish the importance of the professional judgment and miss contextual aspects that determine the learning results.

The other issue related to the use of AI is the increase in surveillance before the digital learning field. Learning analytics systems constantly monitor the student activity, such as frequency of their log-in, the time that they are on course materials, and their involvement in online discussions. Though these streams of data can be very helpful in the understanding of the work with students, they can also generate conditions when students are exposed to constant surveillance. It is also criticized that even such surveillance practices can disturb student autonomy and produce a behavioral focus in studying spaces instead of intellectual experimentation (Williamson, 2017).

5.4 Institutional Governance and Ethics Accountability

The last AI lifecycle stage is institutional governance and ethics to control AI systems. Governance should be effective, which is crucial to make sure that AI technologies will be applied in a responsible manner, and in accordance with the values of education. The structures that govern the industry should be used to control data gathering procedures, judgment of the algorithm, and the responsibility tools of AI-informed decision-making.

The increased dependency on external technology vendors is one of the problems of governance of AI. Most learning institutions utilize AI-based services created by non-governmental corporations without having much insight into the algorithms used or the ways the data is processed. Such a dependence may curb institutional transparency and decrease the capacity of educators to assess the ethical relevance of AI systems adopted by their institutions (Williamson and Eynon, 2020).

To eliminate these threats, researchers focus on the necessity to implement ethical AI governance that includes the principles of fairness, transparency, accountability, and privacy protection (Floridi et al., 2018). Such frameworks are supposed to set the standards of assessing the algorithmic systems and tracking the potential biases and that the student data can be used and not abused or accessed by unauthorized parties.

Interdisciplinary partnership between educators, data scientists, policymakers, and experts in ethics is also necessary to practice good governance. Educational institutions can achieve this objective by involving moral issues in the forms of institutional decision-making in order to make sure that AI technologies are concerned not only with advancing technological innovations but also with enhancing educational equity.

5.5 Consequences on responsible AI integration

One of the issues that can be analyzed when looking at ethical risks throughout the AI lifecycle is the significance of a proactive approach to AI governance within education. Instead of trying to address ethical issues once they arise, the institutions must consider the ethical considerations at all the steps to developing and implementing AI systems.

The implementation of AI should be carefully incorporated with paying attention to the diversity of the datasets, the clarity of the algorithm and administrative controls that would guarantee student privacy and autonomy. Educational institutions need to make sure that datasets to be used to train machine learning models have diverse student populations andAL predictions need to be plotted within corresponding contextual frameworks.

Monitoring and appraisal should also be undertaken in order to establish the unintended effects of AI use in learning institutions. With the development of AI technologies, the institutions need to evaluate its effects on student outcomes, institutional practices, and education equity on a regular basis. During continuous assessment, the education systems can come up with adaptive ways of governing that would address emerging ethical issues.

Finally, the ethical incorporation of AI into education is based on the willingness to prioritize technological change and safeguard unaltered educational principles in institutions. A lifecycle view on ethics in AI can guide educational institutions to be more aware of how ethical hazards arise, and work out ways to enhance justice, openness, and responsibility.

6. BUILDING A RESPONSIBLE AI GOVERNANCE FRAMEWORK TO EDUCATION

The growth of the use of Artificial Intelligence (AI) in education has led to significant ethical issues in connection with algorithmic bias, data privacy, and transparency. With the common use of AI technologies in the learning analytics, adaptive learning platforms, and institutional decision-making systems, the educational institutions should formulate governance frameworks that will promote equity, accountability, and responsible application of the AI technologies (Floridi et al., 2018; Holmes et al., 2019).

The multi-layered AIG policy is necessary to ensure responsible AI governance, and the proposed approach involves technical controls, institutional policies, and ethical regulations. According to the literature, this chapter suggests a Responsible AI Governance Framework in Education that consists of five major elements that include ethical data governance, bias-conscious algorithm design, transparent system deployment, institutional oversight, and ongoing monitoring (Williamson and Eynon, 2020). All these factors combined will enable institutions to plan and establish AI systems that safeguard student data, minimize bias in algorithms, and achieve ethical digital learning systems.

6.1 Ethical Data Governance

Responsible AI systems in education rely on the aspect of ethical data governance. To facilitate the predictive analytics and personalized learning, AI technologies use student data on their academic performance, engagement patterns, and learning behaviors (Siemens and Baker, 2012; Ferguson, 2019).

Institutions should make sure that data on students should be gathered, stored and utilized in a manner that upholds privacy and autonomy. Being open and very clear regarding the methods of gathering and utilizing data is the key to establishing trust between students and educators (Slade and Prinsloo, 2013).

Strong data protection policies should also be implemented by institutions such as secure systems of storage, and limited access to sensitive information. Contracts with third-party providers of technology should specify ownership of the data and guard against student data misuse (Williamson, 2017).

Data minimization is yet another crucial tenet as it ensures that AI systems will gather only such data as needed by the intended purposes. This minimizes the threat to privacy and restricts unnecessary monitoring in online classrooms (Floridi et al., 2018).

6.2 Bias-Aware Algorithm Design

The second element aims at creating bias-conscious algorithms. AI systems are based on learning historical data that can be full of social or institutional inequalities. Consequently, such biases can be reproduced or multiplied by algorithmic models unwillingly (Barocas and Selbst, 2016; Mehrabi et al., 2021).

In order to solve this problem, the developers are advised to use fairness metrics and bias-detection algorithms when creating AI models. These approaches are useful in determining the discrepancies in algorithm predictions between various demographic groups.

The role of educational institutions must also be considered in the context of the assessment of AI technologies prior to their use. Educators, data scientists and policymakers can collaborate to make sure that AI systems promote equity and inclusiveness in education (Baker and Hawn, 2021).

6.3 Open AI Systems Implementation

A crucial part of the responsible AI governance is transparency. Most AI systems are complex black boxed systems; that is, they cannot easily allow an educator and students to understand the way the algorithmic decisions are made.

Transparency can be enhanced with explainable AI methods that should help understand the way of how predictions are made and what may cause bias or errors (Rudin, 2019).

Academic institutions are also expected to communicate with the learners freely concerning the application of AI technologies in learning platforms. Being transparent about the use of AI systems to analyse their information or make suggestions foster trust and accountability (Holmes et al., 2019).

6.4 Institutional Oversight and Accountability

Implementation of AI responsibility needs well-built institutional governance structures. The universities ought to put in place regulatory tools like ethics committees or AI governance boards to test AI technologies prior to implementation.

Such committees are able to determine the correspondence of AI systems to the institutional values of fairness, transparency, and data protection (Floridi et al., 2018).

The institutions ought to also establish feedback systems through which students and educators can present their concerns regarding the use of algorithmic decisions. These systems can be used to detect possible ethical concerns and make AI technologies regularly assessed.

6.5 Continuous Monitoring and Ethical auditing

The last element of the governance structure is constant monitoring. Development of AI systems can pose new ethical threats as the system continues to interact with new information and learning conditions.

Institutions can monitor bias or unintended consequences of the AI systems by regularly auditing their algorithms and assessing their performance. Such audits can be based on demographic dissimilarity of AI outputs and the policy of institutional data governance (Williamson & Eynon, 2020).

The external audits can also enhance transparency and increase the trust of the population in the AI-driven educational technologies.

7. CONCLUSIONS TO SMART CAMPUS GOVERNANCE

The increased application of the Artificial Intelligence is also making smart campuses ecosystems. Smart campuses are the one that implement technologies that can include but not limited to the IoT devices, cloud platforms, and learning analytics systems to enhance the efficiencies of institutions and the learning experience.

AI systems enable the universities to process extensive data regarding the student engagement, academic performance, and campus services. Such technologies assist in decision-making that is data-based and at the same time allow the institutions to tailor learning experiences (Holmes et al., 2019).

Nevertheless, there are also concerns regarding the data privacy and surveillance, as well as the accountability of the algorithms used in the integration of smart campus technologies. Data collection on digital platforms can lead to more risks of misuse or unethical surveillance in case such governance mechanisms are not put in place (Williamson & Eynon, 2020).

Hence, there is a need to make AI governable to make sure that technological innovation does not undermine student rights and institutional transparency.

8. FUTURE RESEARCH DIRECTIONS

Despite the fact that this chapter offers a conceptual framework through which the responsible AI governance in the education sector works, the research needs to be further developed to explore how the principles of governance work in the real-life educational settings.

Future researches may include empirical case studies of the implementation of AI technologies at universities like predictive analytics systems or smart tutoring platforms as well as the effect of governance structures on decision-making (Holmes et al., 2019).

The other direction in research is the investigation of the stakeholder views. Several problems may be perceived differently by students, educators, and administrators: data privacy, transparency of algorithms, and fairness are some of them. By learning about these views, it will be possible to develop more reliable AI systems (Williamson and Eynon, 2020).

Education, computer science, ethics, and policy studies interdisciplinary research will also be crucial in coming up with holistic AI governance models.

9. CONCLUSION

Artificial Intelligence is altering the education system since it allows customized learning, data-driven decision-making, and better management of institutions. Adaptive learning platform, intelligent tutoring systems, and learning analytics tools are the technologies that are becoming more and more part of digital learning environments.

Although these advantages exist, there are also major ethical issues brought about by the use of AI in terms of algorithmic bias, data privacy and transparency. This chapter was able to discuss these challenges by focusing on ethical risks in the various phases of AI lifecycle such as data collection, algorithm design, system deployment and institution governance.

The chapter is relevant to the literature because it suggests a Responsible AI Governance Framework of Education comprising five major components, such as ethical data governance, bias-conscious algorithm design, transparent deployment of the system, institutional oversight, and ongoing monitoring.

REFERENCES

Baker, R. S., & Hawn, A. (2021). Algorithmic bias in education. *International Journal of Artificial Intelligence in Education, 31*(4), 1052–1092. DOI: 10.1007/s40593-021-00285-9

Barocas, S., & Selbst, A. D. (2016). Big data's disparate impact. *California Law Review, 104*(3), 671–732.

Cummings, M. L. (2017). Automation bias in intelligent time critical decision support systems. In *AIAA Infotech at Aerospace Conference*. DOI: 10.4324/9781315095080-17

Dignum, V. (2019). *Responsible artificial intelligence: How to develop and use AI in a responsible way*. Springer. DOI: 10.1007/978-3-030-30371-6

Drachsler, H., & Greller, W. (2016). Privacy and analytics: It's a delicate issue a checklist for trusted learning analytics. *Journal of Educational Technology & Society, 19*(1), 89–99.

Ferguson, R. (2019). Ethical challenges for learning analytics. *Journal of Learning Analytics, 6*(3), 25–30. DOI: 10.18608/jla.2019.63.5

Floridi, L., Cowls, J., Beltrametti, M., Chatila, R., Chazerand, P., Dignum, V., Luetge, C., Madelin, R., Pagallo, U., Rossi, F., Schafer, B., Valcke, P., & Vayena, E. (2018). AI4People—An ethical framework for a good AI society. *Minds and Machines, 28*(4), 689–707. DOI: 10.1007/s11023-018-9482-5 PMID: 30930541

Holmes, W., Bialik, M., & Fadel, C. (2019). *Artificial intelligence in education: Promises and implications for teaching and learning*. Center for Curriculum Redesign.

Luckin, R., Holmes, W., Griffiths, M., & Forcier, L. (2016). *Intelligence unleashed: An argument for AI in education.* Pearson.

Mehrabi, N., Morstatter, F., Saxena, N., Lerman, K., & Galstyan, A. (2021). A survey on bias and fairness in machine learning. *ACM Computing Surveys, 54*(6), 1–35. DOI: 10.1145/3457607

Prinsloo, P., & Slade, S. (2017). Ethics and learning analytics. *British Journal of Educational Technology, 48*(2), 387–392.

Rudin, C. (2019). Stop explaining black box machine learning models for high stakes decisions and use interpretable models instead. *Nature Machine Intelligence, 1*(5), 206–215. DOI: 10.1038/s42256-019-0048-x PMID: 35603010

Siemens, G., & Baker, R. (2012). Learning analytics and educational data mining: Towards communication and collaboration. In *Proceedings of the 2nd International Conference on Learning Analytics and Knowledge* (pp. 252–254). DOI: 10.1145/2330601.2330661

Slade, S., & Prinsloo, P. (2013). Learning analytics: Ethical issues and dilemmas. *The American Behavioral Scientist*, *57*(10), 1510–1529. DOI: 10.1177/0002764213479366

Williamson, B. (2017). Big data in education: The digital future of learning, policy and practice.

Williamson, B., & Eynon, R. (2020). Historical threads, missing links, and future directions in AI in education. *Learning, Media and Technology*, *45*(3), 223–235. DOI: 10.1080/17439884.2020.1798995

Zawacki-Richter, O., Marín, V. I., Bond, M., & Gouverneur, F. (2019). Systematic review of research on artificial intelligence applications in higher education–where are the educators? *International Journal of Educational Technology in Higher Education*, *16*(1), 39. DOI: 10.1186/s41239-019-0171-0 [illegible] (2012). Learning analytics and educational data mining: [illegible] communication and collaboration. In [illegible] [illegible]

[illegible] (2011). [illegible]

[illegible] 2. [illegible]

[illegible] 2021 [illegible]

[illegible]

Chapter 3
Leadership in Artificial Intelligence in Academic Libraries:
Strategies to Transform User Services, Collection Management, and Institutional Innovation

Jogen Sharma
http://orcid.org/0000-0001-7151-0137
KIIT (Deemed to be) University, India

ABSTRACT

Use of Artificial Intelligence technologies poses a fundamental shift in the academic library, fundamentally altering the delivery model of services, the working process and the leadership paradigm. This study discussing the role of visionary leadership, ethical leadership and organizational preparedness in the implementation of AI in the library through sustainablity. This study related to transformational leadership, distributed leadership and reflect the AI use in library operations. By examining world case studies, AI-based interactive experiences, the paper comes up with best practices, challenges and strategic directions to be undertaken by leaders of libraries. The study highlights the effectiveness of implementing AI and it's technological complexity on the development of AI-receptive organisational cultures, the establishment of professional skills, the development of solid ethical policies and the preservation. This study makes essential contributions to the discussion of leadership in library and information science.

DOI: 10.4018/979-8-2600-1840-8.ch003

1. INTRODUCTION

AI and the Significant Revolution of Academic Libraries

The introduction of artificial intelligence in academic libraries is one of the core reconfigurations of library services, operations and leadership roles within higher education ecosystems. Academic libraries can play a central role in the ongoing development of critical discourses surrounding AI by adapting to AI literacy, demystifying technology and fostering interdisciplinary partnerships to develop and understand how AI may impact research and learning. Recent data indicate that the number of libraries exploring or implementing AI tools has steadily increased over time, with most (67%) of libraries actively exploring or implementing AI tools as of 2025, compared to 63% in 2024. Nevertheless, 7 percent of academic libraries have already reached the level of a complete implementation of AI systems up to September 2024, which shows that the growth prospects are significant and the lack of good leadership guidance is crucial.

This change is not only technological but also includes a basic change in leadership paradigms of libraries. The job of library heads has shifted from the old ways of collection management and circulation control to strategic innovation, evidence-based decision-making and organisational change management. Contemporary library executives are visionary strategists who coordinate tricky technological implementations, navigate ethical challenges inherent in data-driven systems, develop organizational capability to pursue unceasing innovation and view technological innovation as a way to promote instead of disenfranchising the key values of libraries.

The greater digital transformation agenda of higher education further supports this change. Universities are placing greater demands on libraries to utilise emerging technologies to help students achieve greater success, assist faculty in their research, demonstrate their value to an institution in terms of data analytics and support the institution in achieving its objectives, such as accreditation, research impact assessment and learning analytics. This institutionalised position makes library leaders organisational change agents, many of whose choices and actions have far-reaching effects throughout institutions.

Figure 1. Digital and AI adoption in academic libraries (1960-2025) timeline

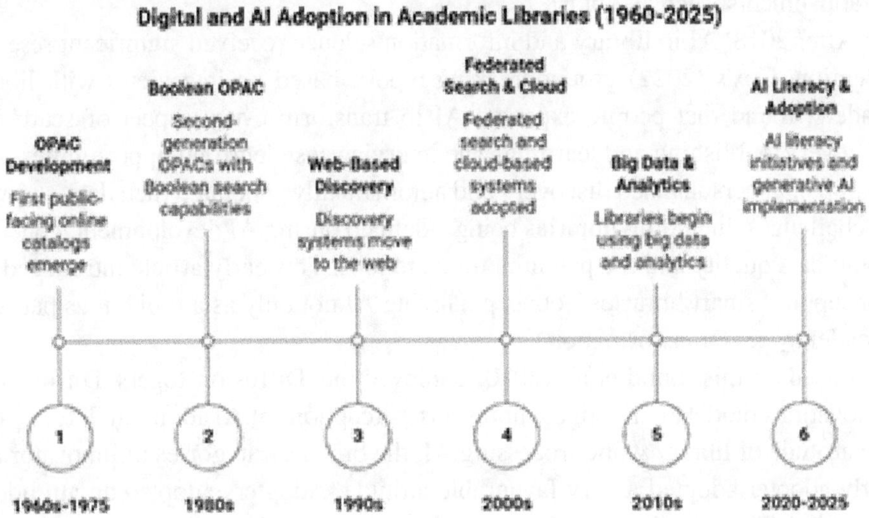

2. LITERATURE REVIEW

Artificial intelligence (AI) has been profoundly transforming scientific disciplines and higher education in recent years, particularly in the academic libraries of all sizes. Early scholarly discussions about AI proposed computationally precise rule-based algorithms. For example, Nakai and Kanehisa (1992) presented one of the first expert system approaches, discussing how to predict protein localization sites. By developing an AI-powered rule system capable of processing massive amounts of biological data, they demonstrated that what had previously seemed impossible was now feasible. Although grounded in genomics, their work laid a foundation for subsequent AI applications across the various information environments.

The expansion of machine learning (ML) across various sectors has been well-documented. For instance, Yassin et al. (2017) conducted a systematic literature review on ML-based diagnostic systems for breast cancer, highlighting both the maturity of image-led ML and the need for standardized practices in this critical care setting as pressing matters. Similarly, Tufail et al. (2023) systematically categorised modern ML models across multiple areas. They summarised the supervised, unsupervised and reinforcement learning techniques, as well as the current challenges of implementation for them. These articles illustrate the much broader development in AI and set the scene for its increased importance within information establishments, such as libraries.

After 2018, AI in library and information science received significant research attention. Cox's (2022) groundbreaking report, based on interviews with library leaders, found that people expected AI to transform every aspect of searching, discovery, publishing and learning. The interviewees identified opportunities—for example, in personalised discovery and automatically generated metadata—as well as challenges, including libraries being sidelined during AI development, concerns about data quality and the potential threat to jobs. This early article introduced the concept of "smart libraries," conceptualizing AI not only as a tool but as part of a broader system transformation.

Based on this, Lund et al. (2020) deployed the' DiffusionRogers' Diffusion of Innovations model to investigate librarians' perceptions of AI adoption. It found that the attitude of library work processing AI, the broader categories of innovator and early adopter adopted a very favourable attitude. Adopters adopted an attitude of suspicion. Their findings emphasised the importance of training and digital skills, as well as organisational readiness.

Several studies have looked at the AI adoption framework. Zhoksitir et al. (2022) were anchored in the Artificial Intelligence Library Services Innovative Conceptual Framework (AI-LSICF), which lateralizes AI with university libraries' digital transformation strategies. In this research, it was argued that AI requires strategic planning and librarian training and that its implementation should conform to the principles of service innovation.

Similarly, Cao et al. (2018) articulated a "smart library" from three aspects of technology, service and human resources, finding that the technological core of an intelligent library system is formed by combining AI cloud computing and data mining.

From the perspective of environmental scanning, Wheatley and Hervieux (2022) stated that, despite some research libraries in the North American region having begun to establish artificial intelligence hubs or incorporate AI into their strategies, overall engagement with AI remains limited in strategic terms. Interpreting these findings, a gap exists between the potential of technology and its actual implementation.

Recent studies have tended to focus on generative AI and its applications in librarianship. In Johnston et al. (2024), 2,500 university students were surveyed about their attitudes and use of generative AI tools (utilising Generative AI technology, such as the keyboard in Romeo's Restaurant, Roce Afd sentings). Students were familiar with tools like Grammarly, primarily for language aid purposes, but had reservations about academic writing entirely produced by generative AI. As they observed, their results stress the necessity of institutional polices and allowing all-comers fair treatment.

Adetayo (2023) further explored AI chatbots, focusing on potential applications in academic libraries for ChatGPT, including reference services, cataloguing and user guidance. However, dangers were noted such as inaccuracy, bias and picking up automatic systems and the study recommended "hybrid man–AI "service modes.

Cox (2022) investigated how AI might impact the professional skills of academic libraries, identifying eleven potential directions for AI knowledge discovery in libraries. Publications on the studies suggested that librarians might move toward "hybrid" professional identities increasingly. They will combine technical prowess with the ability to handle traditional content expertly, thus striking a balance as well as they can.

3. TECHNOLOGICAL WAVE IN ADOPTION IN ACADEMIC LIBRARIES

3.1. Transformational Leadership and AI Adoption

To interpret the present state of AI implementation, it is necessary to take into account the historical context of the adoption of the past waves of technological use by academic libraries. This evolutionist outlook brings about adoption, resistance trends, evolution and eventual integration trends that guide contemporary AI leadership approaches.

Academic libraries developed out of manuscript collections to printed collections maintained using card catalogs- physical collections that needed a lot of manual work to organize bibliographically, to track circulation and to provide patrons with services. This period, beginning with the founding of libraries up to the 1960s, entrenched some of the fundamental library principles such as intellectual freedom, equitable access, preservation and service to users that continue to be foundational beliefs today.

3.2. The OPAC Revolution (1960s-2000s)

Online Public Access Catalogs (OPACs) began in the early 1960s, a technology that was the first significant technological break in library operations. The library materials at the Ohio State University were under development in 1967 by Frederick Kilgour who was working on creating an online searchable database which saw the first publicly accessible OPAC system launched in 1975. This innovation allowed users of libraries to search collections either by title, or author, or by call number on their own without the intermediation of the librarian.

3.3. Opac and Advance Serach

The usability issues of the first-generation OPACs (1975-1980s) were that the new system was highly specific in terms of the exact wording and spelling, as only the correct spelling and wording would achieve successful search. But with the second generation of the OPAC systems in the 1980s, Boolean logic operations (AND, OR, NOT), help screens and circulation integration, searchability and user experience dramatically improved. The third generation OPAC came with the introduction of World Wide Web in 1991, which allowed online access, multimedia resources that were hyperlinked, electronic journal integration, cloud computing and finally national and global connections among consortia.

This OPAC development illustrates the way in which libraries adopted technological change whilst encountering the problem of implementation resistance to change by the users, requirement of staff training, continual enhancement of the system and adjustment of the organization. The process of gradually replacing the card catalogs with the use of digital systems took decades and involved long-term organizational commitment, vision of the leadership and staff development, which can be directly applied to AI implementation nowadays.

3.4. Resources and the Age of Big Data (1990s-2010s)

The advent of internet and commercial database systems in the 1970s transformed the collection and services in libraries radically. In 1972, Dialog with six bibliographic databases was the first commercial database, but systems continued to be costly and not user-friendly and were utilized by information experts, not end-users. The 1980s were the years of the spread of various databases and commercial services and the use of CD-ROMs became possible by the end of the decade.

The internet revolution of the 1990s changed the library services by being able to discover web-based and distributed access as well as integration of electronic resources with the traditional holdings. Libraries gradually turned to electronic formats in place of print, necessitating new cataloging processes, licensing deals, access control systems and technologies. Such a shift required flexibility of the organization, retraining of the staff and management that could negotiate swift technological transformation - setting precedents in modern AI application.

Big data culture, predictive analytics and data-driven decision-making models became a reality in the 2010s and the early 2020s. Libraries started to deploy integrated library systems (ILS), discovery systems, usage analytics and institutional repositories - systems that are data intensive and demand new skills, as well as create novel privacy and ethics issues. The next-generation integrated library systems offer single discovery and delivery platforms across format and consortial borders, including support of metadata enhancement, user experience customisation and integration with institutional systems.

Figure 2. Library technology innovation and leadership requirement milestones

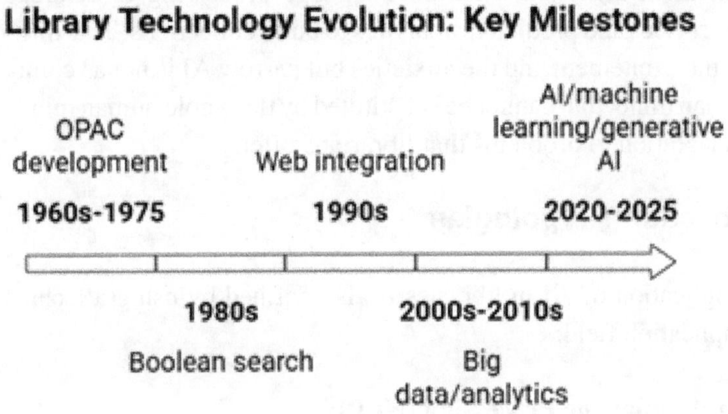

4. THE NEW ACADEMIC LIBRARY ECOSYSTEM ROLE OF AI

4.1. Typologies and Definitions of AI

In order to speak about the implementation of AI in libraries, it is necessary to have clear definitional frameworks. Several typologies of artificial intelligence have different features, functions and consequences on library services.

Narrow AI (Weak AI): The only form of AI that currently exists is the Narrow AI (Weak AI), which is meant to be executed to accomplish specific tasks within fixed criteria and it cannot generalise outside the designated areas. Voice assistants (Siri, Alexa), recommendation systems (Netflix, Amazon), chatbots and even ChatGPT created by OpenAI can be listed as contemporary examples that are referred to as narrow AI, even though their performance in particular areas is impressive. Narrow AI is a perfect system in its field of expertise and fails to transfer knowledge to new issues and to learn in general across fields.

General AI (Strong AI): Artificial General Intelligence or general artificial intelligence (also known as general artificial intelligence, or general AI, AI) is a hypothetical state of artificial intelligence that can interpret, learn and accomplish any intellectual task that humans can. General AI is hypothetical there is no available such system and general AI is still a matter of speculation when it comes to the application of general AI in libraries.

In the case of academic libraries, this is a critical distinction all existing and predictable AI applications are small AI systems that are task-oriented, such as recommendation algorithms, natural language processing to catalogue, chatbot reference services and predictive analytics to build collections. This difference must moderate the excitement and the anxieties but narrow AI is not as competent in the global human mind, that cannot be substituted by the whole human mind, contextual skill, or adaptation to problems that librarians offer.

4.2. Application Typologies

The application of AI in libraries is also defined by using a technical method and an application field:

a) **Natural Language Processing (NLP):**

AI can process, comprehend and create human language, which drives chatbots, robotic cataloging, text classification, topic modeling, sentiment analysis and text summarization.

b) Machine Learning:

Algorithms that discover the patterns in the data without specific programming allow recommendation systems, predictive analytics, the ability to forecast the behaviour of users and customise it.

c) Deep Learning:

Advanced neural network designs that allow more complex pattern recognition and are especially useful in image recognition, content analysis and advanced language understanding, which form the basis of modern chatbots.

d) Generative AI:

Generators of novel content (text, images, audio) by training on training data, such as large language models (LLMs) such as ChatGPT, DALL-E and domain-specific models, run in libraries.

4.3. Mapping AI Tools That are Already Implemented in Academic Libraries

There are various AI tools used in academic libraries around the world in various areas of operation:

[a] Discovery and Recommendation Systems:

Ex Libris Primo Research Assistant uses retrieval-augmented generation (RAG) technology, which is a combination of central discovery indexes and a large language model (LLM), or any combination thereof, to deliver intelligent search results. This system overcomes the conventional constraints of discovery by reasoning about user intent, which involves natural language query interpretation and more contextual summaries of results as opposed to traditional results lists.

[b] Automated Cataloguing and Metadata:

The Library of Congress is adopting human-in-the-loop processes by which machine learning proposes subject headings and lists of authors in authority files, which are then reviewed and chosen by catalogers. Finland-created Annif is an example of an artificial intelligence-based system of automated subject indexing with encouraging accuracy levels in text classification. In the University of Oulu, AI systems are used to process parts of cataloging processes that used to demand a lot of manual work.

[c] Virtual Reference and Chatbots:

ChatBook prototypes are the first generative AI-based models that provide multi-modal interaction experience that integrates oral histories, speeches, photographs, biographies and cultural narratives offered by the National Library of Singapore. Such systems enable users to communicate with historical figures and fictional characters, developing critical AI literacy and uncovering new uses of generative AI in cultural interactions.

[d] Predictive Analytics and Decision Support:

Libraries have adopted predictive analytics models to manage collection demand, forecast resources demand, detect patterns of use, optimize budgetary allocation, facilitate evidence-based weeding and retention decisions.

[e] Information integration:

Academic libraries are beginning to support institutional learning analytics projects, including data about circulation, resource access and citation analysis to student success prediction systems.

Figure 3. Academic libraries and primary technologies AI-enabled around the world

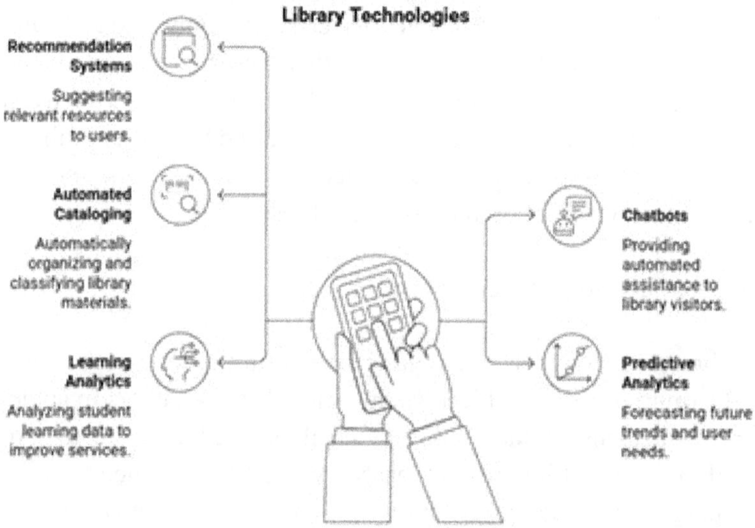

4.4. Theoretical Background

Leadership Paradigms in an Age of AI

A practical implementation of AI in academic libraries must be based on solid leadership theories that describe how organizations embrace innovations, how they handle change, how they develop a culture of excellence and how they maintain the change. Three theoretical models are particularly useful when library leaders engage in the process of implementing AI.

The Transformational Leadership Theory is the Fourth Concept That Will be Explored

The transformational theory of leadership as developed by James MacGregor Burns (1978) in his study of political leaders and elaborated by Bernard Bass (1985) in the organizational setting, offers the necessary frameworks of understanding how leaders facilitate technological change.

Burns theorised transformational leadership as taking place when an individual or individuals interact with others in a manner that leaders and followers elevate each other to new levels of motivation and morality. This is very opposite to the transactional leadership that emphasizes on exchange relationships and obedience by reward or punishment.

Bass added to the theory of Bass and Burns by establishing that transformational leaders encourage their followers to achieve more than was initially envisioned through creating awareness of the relevance of outcomes, stimulating critical thinking and generating intellectual stimulation. Bass defined transformational leadership to have four essential elements:

Idealized Influence

Leaders show model behaviors, gain the trust and respect and paint pictures of what people desire, which makes the followers want to follow the leaders.

Inspirational leaders motivate by inspiring high expectations, appealing to symbols and emotional appeals and fostering a group spirit with a shared goal.

Intellectual Stimulation

Leaders stimulate the followers to think, question assumptions, innovate in problem-solving and look at a problem in a new light.

Individual Consideration

Leaders offer mentoring, coaching, professional development and individualised attention to the needs and level of development of followers.

In the case of AI implementation in libraries, transformational leadership is observed with library leaders who communicate powerful visions of how AI can enhance library values question conventional ways of service provision motivate employees to explore new technologies, offer long-term support of learning and skill development and demonstrate belief that AI can be used to augment rather than subvert the fundamental library missions.

Studies prove that transformational leaders who are librarians regard AI not as something to be simply used but as truly useful to organisational innovation, which has a direct impact on the readiness to adopt and the success of the implementation. Transformational leaders of libraries create cultures in which employees see AI as enhancing their professional skills and not as a substitute to their jobs- an important psychological conditioning factor between successful and unsuccessful implementations or defiant ones.

4.5. The Distributed Leadership Theory

Distributed leadership theory is another theory that opposes traditional hierarchical theories, which suggest that leadership roles and duties are limited to a few individuals in organisations, but instead extend to a number of people. Distributed leadership recognises that expertise, innovation and leadership competence are spread across the organisation at all levels.

Distributed leadership is characterised by the fact that leadership functions are not limited to formal managers but spread to various people in an organisation, which has been beneficial to libraries in terms of innovation, better coordination, learning and organisational resilience. This strategy is especially useful with AI implementation, whereby expertise could be held by IT specialists, subject librarians, systems administrators, staff of Public services and other people, but not necessarily by a formal leader of the library per se.

Distributed leadership within the context of AI implies establishing task forces with subject matter experts as leaders of AI pilots, empowering representatives of departments to be change agents, learning networks, and various manifestations of leadership through formal roles, technical expertise, as change agents and peer influence. This strategy is decentralizing the role of AI and the accountability of its success, avoiding reliance on individual visionary figures and establishing a capacity within organizations to be continuously innovative.

4.6. Theory of Innovation Diffusion and Adoption Process

The theory of Diffusion of Innovations by Rogers provides a complementary framework for understanding AI adoption within academic library populations.

Rogers finds 5 stages of the innovation adoption process:

- **Knowledge/Awareness**: People get to know there are innovations.
- **Persuasion**: The people have positive or negative attitudes towards the innovations.
- **Rational Choice**: people make decisions to either accept or reject innovations.
- **Application**: Practical people put innovations into practice.
- **Confirmation**: Adoptee people want support in adoption.

Rogers also recognizes 5 categories of adopters depending on the adoption timing:

Being aware of these categories can enable library executives to understand that not every single employee will be able to embrace AI at once or be enthusiastic about it. Successful strategies attract innovators and early adopters as advocates, offer compelling evidence to make decisions early on the majority, counteract the doubt of the late majority and acknowledge that some laggards may never adopt AI- need varying change management strategies.

Five factors affect the innovation-diffusion process perceived advantage, compatibility with existing practices, perceived complexity, trialability (room to experiment) and observability (visibility of results). To expedite the adoption of AI, a library leader may show visible benefits to professional practice and service to patrons make sure it can work with the library's values and workflows reduce perceived complexity by providing training and support not commit to it before trying it and show visible outcomes of initial work.

Figure 4. Comparative leadership models to implement AI in academic libraries

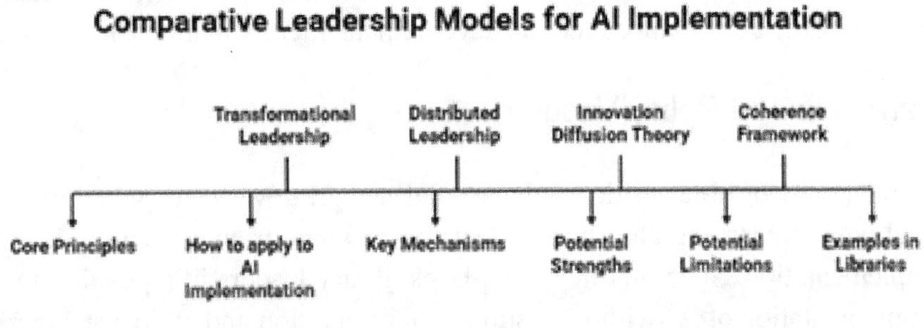

5. ORGANISATIONAL CHANGE MANAGEMENT AND CULTURE

The successful AI implementation goes beyond the technology implementation to the actual change in the organization culture. The literature regarding organisational change presents repetitive obstacles and facilitators that leaders of the library should strategically overcome.

5.1. AI Implementation Barriers in Libraries

Resistance to Change: The most common causes of traditional resistance are the fear of losing a job, a perceived challenge to professional identity, comfort with existing work processes, doubt in the efficacy of technologies and the belief that AI is devaluing the ideals of the library. Certain library workers doubt that AI is actually enhancing their service to patrons or is only doing it in response to cost-saving requirements.

Poor AI Literacy

The majority of the library staff have an idea of conceptualisation about AI and little practical knowledge about AI tools and a significant lack of understanding about the ethical implications. Such knowledge gap is a source of understandable opposition individuals are reluctant to back up initiatives that they do not know or feel that they are unprepared to do it.

Resource Limitation

Due to tight budgetary constraints, many academic libraries are not able to invest in either technological infrastructure, personnel training, or vendor solutions. The scarcity of resources will create prioritisation decisions, in which AI investments will compete with the traditional collection development, facility maintenance and staff.

Governance and Policy Vacuum

The majority of libraries do not have a defined AI governance structure, institutional policy regarding algorithmic decision-making, or an ethical guideline on AI implementation. Such a policy gap places library leaders in a position to face the implementation of AI without institutional orientation and ethical standards.

Vendor and Ecosystem Complexity

Academic libraries rely on the integrated library system, discovery platforms and external vendors to supply several AI-based services. The use of AI by vendors is incredibly different some are equipped with advanced and complex AI features, others are significantly out of pace with developing standards.

5.2. Organisational Readiness Enabling Factors

Leadership Vision and Commitment

Organizations with articulated leadership vision that provide how AI will be integrated into the institutional missions, values and strategic goals achieve greater success in implementation. Leaders who present convincing arguments, offer visible action and resource allocation show the seriousness of organizations with respect to AI transformation.

Change Agent Networks

The identification and empowerment of change agents-enthusiastic employees at each level of the organisation, ready to become champions of AI projects, communicate with non-believers, practice new behaviours and support their peers is one of the strategies that significantly increases the speed of adoption. Legitimacy Change agents manage to conquer resistance using relationships and credibility more than authority.

Capacity Building and Professional Development

When organizations allocate resources to formal AI literacy training and offer learning opportunities, assist with conference attendance and encourage professional growth, it encourages staff confidence and competence. Employees that feel empowered to deal with AI tools show increased adoption rates.

Participatory Implementation Approaches

Organizations with participative approaches, in which employees are involved in the implementation decision-making of AI, in the design of the system and in policymaking are more satisfied and adopted compared to top-down mandates. Engagement fosters ownership and reveals valuable local knowledge that informs effective implementation.

Open Communication

Honest and frank communication on issues of concern, successes, implementation difficulties and decision rationale fosters trust and resistance can be better handled when the rationale is clear. Constant communication demonstrates that leadership is serious about AI and is attentive to legitimate concerns.

Figure 5. Academic library AI change management process flowchart

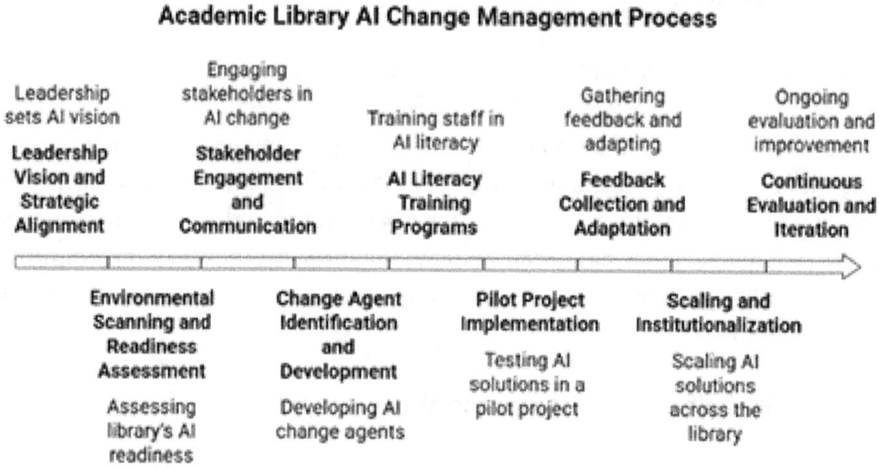

6. AI APPLICATIONS IN ACADEMIC LIBRARIES SURVEY

6.1. Cataloging and Metadata Enhancement Intelligence

Smart cataloguing is one of the oldest and most developed uses of AI in libraries and it suits a long-standing operating problem the manual construction and upkeep of bibliographic records and metadata of high quality are resource-consuming.

Technical Overview and Workflows

Conventional cataloguing processes entail librarian inspection of tangible or digital objects, intellectual topic research, establishment of original cataloguing documents by adherence to MARC standards, authority file validation and incorporation into discovery systems. These have proven to be processes that require the expert judgment, specialized understanding of the classification systems and a lot of time investment- a normal time of 30-45 minutes per item is anticipated to be spent in doing original cataloging.

Artificial intelligence (AI) is used to automate parts of this workflow using natural language processing (NLP). Machine learning models that are trained on existing cataloging records are learned to identify trends between document content and the correct metadata elements, subject classification and terms in authority files. Upon encountering new objects, these systems will harvest content, emit likely metadata values, anticipate subject classifications and provide authority file assignments — metadata suggestions for human consideration instead of automation.

The Human-in-the-Loop Model

Human-in-the-loop (HITL) workflows are used in the Library of Congress and even larger academic libraries as it is acknowledged that AI systems can work best under human supervision. In HITL cataloguing processes, automated systems will do the first round metadata extraction and production librarians will verify system suggestions as valid catalogers will accept, amend or reject system suggestions validated metadata will be added to the system. This is the most effective way to embrace AI efficiency and still have the quality of human expertise.

Case Studies and Outcomes

University of Oulu Library in Finland implemented AI-based cataloging systems that addressed some of the metadata processing tasks in their libraries and saved many hours in processing time, without any change in the quality of the metadata. The Library of Congress's human-in-the-loop style of cataloguing has been found to have 90 per cent accuracy in several categories of cataloguing, with machine propositions providing substantial grounds upon which the cataloger can perform their work efficiently. Annif is an open-source software framework developed by the National Library of Finland specifically to index the subject of manuscripts automatically and with promising results in a wide range of different languages and document types.

Practical Implications and Issues

Although intelligent cataloging promises to achieve good results, there are obstacles to it, which need a close consideration:

Training Data Quality

AI models trained with incomplete, inconsistent or biased historical cataloging recreates and even exacerbates any underlying bias.

Specialized Collections

AI systems are most effective on standard materials in training data domains, non-traditional, rare, or specialized materials offer more challenges.

Complexity of Authority Control

Correct subject classification and allocation of authority files is more difficult to automate than bibliographic description.

Change Management

Cataloging personnel will need to move away the task execution and embrace quality examination and exception processing-they will need other skills and they would be a threat to the staff confidence.

Figure 6. Main AI cataloging systems - features, vendors, implementation scope and reported results

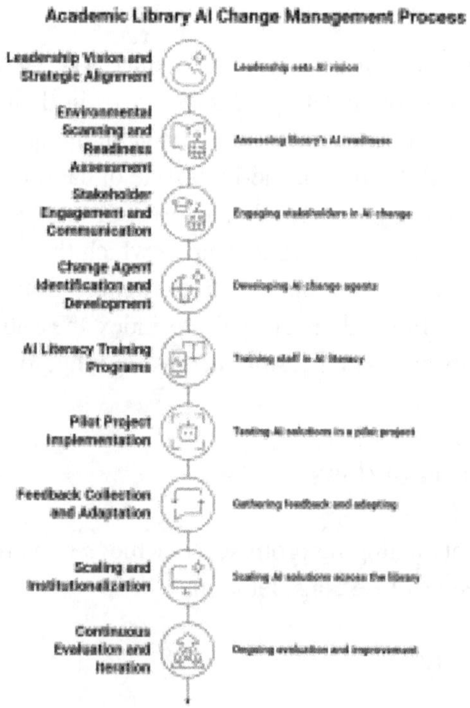

6.2. Discovery Systems and Recommendation Systems

Recommendation systems are advanced AI applications that tailor user experiences by providing them with resources that best fit their interests, learning abilities and information requirements.

Technical Architecture and Algorithms Approaches

The current recommendation systems use a variety of algorithm families with diverse goals:

Collaborative Filtering

Makes recommendations based on the identification of a similarity with an user based on their behavior/preferences with the assumption that similarity in past likes will translate into similar likes in the future.

Content-Based Filtering

This algorithm proposes items based on the feature of the items and the similarities between items and those that the user has already consumed.

Hybrid Approaches

Use a mixture of collaborative and content based approach in which the user behavior, item attributes and context are combined.

Knowledge-Based Systems

Recommend on the basis of explicit knowledge on objects and user preferences and is effective in complex domains when preferences of the users become hard to infer based on behavior.

The AI recommendation systems at the University of Oulu are used to recommend reading materials, depending on the academic program and past search history of users which enhances the system to a much greater extent, increasing user engagement and decreasing the time required to get relevant reading materials. These systems can work out the pattern of interaction between the user, the focus of academic discipline, taking courses and previous utilization of resources to create individualized suggestions.

User Experience and Engagement Effects

Studies show that individualized recommendations enhance user interaction, satisfaction in library discovery services, less friction in locating resources and the perception of library value. Users find it useful when they can find relevant resources otherwise they would not have found the same by using the traditional browsing and searching.

Privacy Issues and Ethical Implications

Nonetheless, the suggestions bring immense privacy-personalization conflicts. To make personalized recommendations, user data, such as search history, access patterns, reading time, materials that can be downloaded and demographics, must be collected and analyzed. Customers are increasingly resistant to disclosing personal data unless they clearly comprehend the data collection, storage and usage and retention techniques.

The privacy-personalisation trade-off is convoluted in terms of libraries keeping the principles of intellectual freedom, user privacy and equal access. Commercial web sites feel free to use information about users to make the best use of profit margins libraries are forced to find a balance in how to give the advantages of personalization and at the same time offer high privacy protection beyond the expectation of commercial websites.

Privacy-Respecting Personlization Strategies

Privacy approaches based on the users acknowledge this to be neither banning of personalizing the users nor unregulated data gathering.

Instead, libraries can:

Adopt Privacy-by-Design

Collect the least amount of data to the services intended.

Enable User Control

It is the ability of users to access, process and destroy personal data.

Apply Anonymization and Encryption, Secure data with technical means.

Use Privacy-Saving Methods

Federated learning and differential privacy make analytics without sensitive data centralization.

Ensure Tracking Management and HTTPS

Use HTTPS encryption audit and control 3rd party tracking scripts enable users to see company data practices.

Be Transparent: Express Clearly Data Practices, Policies and User Rights

Figure 7. Recommendation system architecture in academic libraries

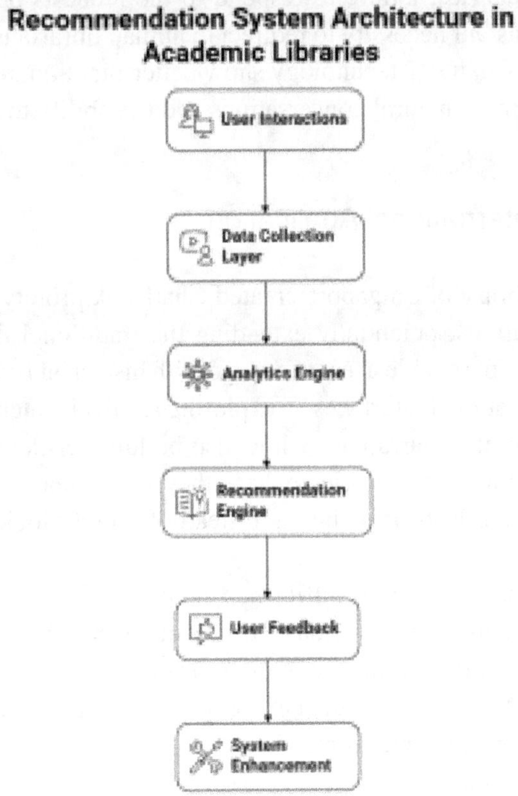

6.3. Virtual Reference, Chatbots and Conversational AI

AI chatbots are fast emerging library applications to the classic issues of reference service limitations on availability, asynchronous service provision desired by customers and availability limits of human reference librarians.

Library Chatbots Evolution and Capabilities

First generation library chatbots used simple rule-based systems that had limited conversation and were scripted and had a limited range of domain knowledge. Modern systems take advantage of large language models (LLMs) and natural language processing that allows more advanced dialogues, contextual consideration and other responsive details.

The classical constraints of chatbots were the final topic coverage, inability to serve complicated queries, failure to respond to the requests not listed in preset domains and the constant necessity to redirect to human librarians. Recent systems such as those using ChatGPT technology show better functionality on a variety of types of questions, more natural conversations and the ability to deal with nuance and complexity.

Case Studies: International Application

The National Library of Singapore created ChatBook prototypes as generative AI-powered applications, potentially extending the traditional reference service. The multimodal systems enable users to engage with historical figures and fictional characters in conversational interfaces by exploring archival materials, biographies, oral histories and cultural narratives, while also building critical AI literacy. The users interact with Singapore Stories, where they get to learn historical context by conversing with the historical figures instead of merely looking up historical information.

Reference chatbots are used to fulfill the first point of contact with the patron at the University of Toronto and various North American universities they answer frequent questions regarding hours, policies, access to resources and basic research advice. Complex questions are directed to the human librarians through systems to handle high-volume routine questions.

Limitations in functionality and Human-Librarian Integration

Although it has improved, studies have shown that chatbots fail to offer reference services solely. AI systems do not have the human experience, empathy, contextual assessment and problem resolution that is typical of expert librarianship. Multifaceted consultations of research, subtle questions of discipline and dealing with ethical issues and situations with patrons that demand emotional intelligence still are best left to human librarians.

Best implementations use hybrid designs chatbots will address simple questions, answer quick queries with frequent questions and refer users to the right resources or to librarians. Librarians are concerned with complicated consultations, research, individual training and challenges in which human judgment is necessary.

Ethical Concerns and Accuracy Concerns

Large language model chatbots pose new challenges. The responses produced by LLM can be hallucinating (confident false information), or outdated, due to the constraints of the training corpus, or biased due to the training corpus being composed of biased views. These constraints are particularly worrying for libraries, where accuracy and reliability are central.

Figure 8. Chatbot deployments in global libraries- technologies, capabilities and reported outcomes

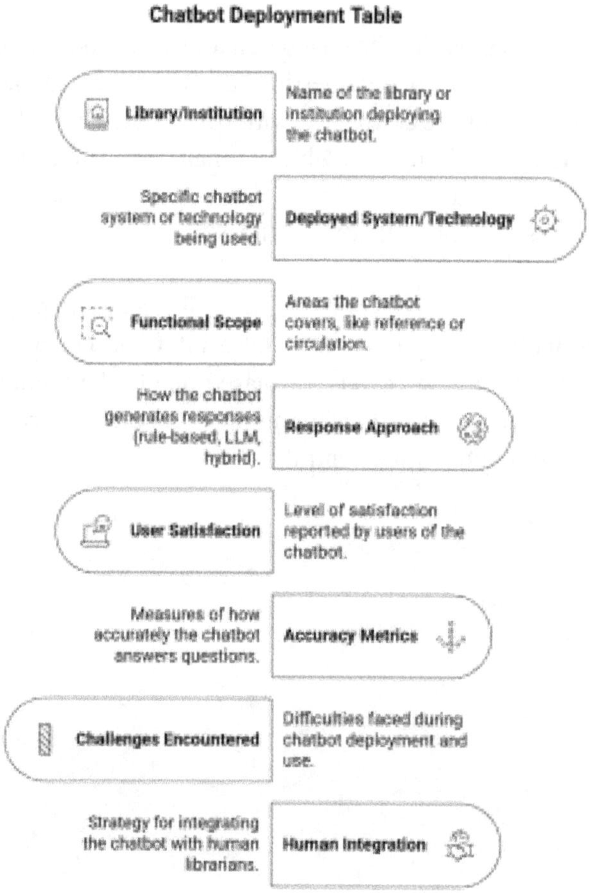

Predictive Analytics of Collection Development and User Behaviour

The use of predictive analytics is one of the most powerful AI applications to library operations that allow developing collections using data, distributing resources and succeeding with users.

Collection Development Applications

The common collection development approach is based on the judgment of the librarian, patron requests, subject knowledge and market awareness. Although useful, these methods only give partial insight into new demand trends, usage trends, or give predictive signs of what lies ahead.

Predictive analytics systems apply machine learning algorithms to historical use data, user demographics, institutional trends and externalization to predict future collection needs. Predictive systems are used by studying that circulation patterns, e-resource usage, citation trends, research publication patterns and course enrollments in order to determine which type of resource is in growth, which areas of research are emerging and which is anticipated to be in demand.

To manage their materials, libraries use clustering algorithms (K-Means, DB-SCAN) and NLP to classify the materials, determine the collections not used by users, predict the needs of the users and aid data-driven weeding policies. Not only can collections that used to accumulate dust be discovered and promoted, digitized, or removed, but also save on the shelf space and budgetary allocation.

Impact of Research and Institutional Analytics

Academic libraries are becoming more involved in research analytics efforts at the institutional level based on predictive student success analytics systems. Such systems combine library resource use records with institutional student information systems and determine the patterns of use that are associated with academic performance. Libraries that can prove that students accessing the library resources perform better in retention, better grades and improved graduation rates reinforce institutional positioning and prove worth to the administrators.

Predictive analytics can also be used to assist research impact, that is, predictive analytics with citation patterns to evaluate research impact, publication patterns to evaluate research impact and research collaboration networks to evaluate research impact, but these are metrics used to justify institutional accreditation and research funding.

User Success and Engagement Prediction

Libraries also implement predictive models to identify at-risk students at the beginning of an academic term so that they can be proactively intervened with. Through information search habits, library utilization, course attendance and demographic indicators, students who are at risk of course failure or dropping out are predicted in the model. Academic support services collaborate with libraries to offer specific interventions.

Implementation Issue and Concerns

Implementation of predictive analytics involves a number of practical and ethical challenges that have to be addressed:

Data Quality and Integration: Needs clean data incorporation of disparate library frameworks, institutional frameworks and external sources of data.

Algorithmic Bias: Predictive algorithmic models used on historical data replicate past biases, which can benefit the majority at the disadvantage of the minority.

Explainability: Black boxes are complex machine learning models that do not make predictions explaining underlying factors, thus making it more difficult to validate and build trust.

Implications of Privacy: Predictive analytics involves a need to collect vast volumes of data, which generates privacy vulnerabilities and discriminatory effects when used.

Ethical Decision-Making: Predictions in resource allocation or interventions pose an ethical dilemma in terms of fairness, autonomy and harm.

7. ARTIFICIAL INTELLIGENCE AND ETHICS IN LIBRARIES: LEADERSHIP PROBLEMS

Although the potential of AI in improving library services is immense, there are severe challenges that emerge during implementation that demand careful leadership, ethical considerations and effective governance systems.

7.1. Algorithms Bias and Information Justice

Algorithms bias has a substantial impact on information search and discovery systems and has far-reaching consequences on accessing information and intellectual freedom.

Biases are caused by various sources and appear in the stages of implementation.

Sources of Algorithmic Bias:

- **One-Sided Training Data:**

AI models trained on historical data replicate and amplify existing biases. AI models acquire the historical biases in the event that the cataloging records indicate past discriminations or the collection development of the library included discriminatory policies.

- **Labeling Bias:**

Bias in modeling is a human labeling of training data which adds subjective judgments to the models.

- **Sample Bias:**

The model trained on data that do not represent the entire population (e.g., a collection of mostly Western academic materials to represent international collections) results in a model biased towards specific regions, cultures, or viewpoints.

- **Algorithmic Bias:**

Some algorithms are biased towards specific qualities or groups.

- **Deployment Bias:**

Implementation options such as threshold settings or ranking algorithms cause bias in the prediction-to-user-facing translation.

- **Symptoms in Library Systems:**

Algorithms bias in library discovery systems are realized as indexical bias (biased selection of material in collections) and content bias (biased views in the selected materials). As an example, when the circulation patterns trained in the recommendation systems are driven by the interests and views of mostly white, wealthy and English-speaking user groups, then the suggestions made to different users will be systematically biased toward Western, English-language, mainstream content at the expense of the minority, international and different views.

This is an inherent contradiction of the library principle of equal access and intellectual freedom. In cases where AI systems are ready to discriminate against certain perspectives or authors and favor others systematically, it equates to limiting users to different access to varied information even though some of the collections may seem exhaustive.

- **Mitigation Strategies:**

LIS practitioners contribute significantly to the reduction of algorithmic bias by use of several tactics:

- **Ethical Data Curation:** Training data should be structured in a complete manner to describe different views, geographical locations, authors and opinions.
- **Algorithmic Audits:** Frequent bias testing of the systems by demographic groups, geographical regions and interests.
- **Transparency and Explainability:** The use of explainable AI (XAI) strategies that allow learning about the decision-making mechanisms used by systems to identify bias.
- **Diverse Teams:** Making certain that there is diversity in the AI development, implementation and oversight teams with the aim of uncovering blind spots.
- **Inclusive Governance:** Developing feedback systems that would detect any bias experienced in systems by communities.

7.2. Data Privacy and User Trust

The privacy of data is one of the underlying issues to libraries where part of the ethical obligation is to safeguard the confidentiality of patrons, as well as safeguard intellectual freedom. The use of AI normally demands a lot of data gathering- establishing vulnerabilities and introducing new privacy concerns.

What are the Privacy Problems of Using AI?

Massive Data Gathering: Personalization, recommendation and predictive analytics demand elaborate user data such as search history, resource access profile, demographics and behavioral inferences.

Data Retention and Security: Stored information must be highly secured, which poses a threat of data leakage and unauthorized access.

Secondary-use data that has been provided in support of one goal (e.g., a recommendation) can also be accessed to support other goals (e.g., user profiling, compliance monitoring), which can pose unexpected privacy threats.

- **De-Anonymization:** The data obtained even after de-anonymization can be identified again with the help of other data sources or subtle patterns.
- **Regulatory Compliance:** Data Minimisation, Consent Management and User Rights. Global privacy laws (GDPR, CCPA) require data minimisation, consent management and user rights.
- **Privacy-Sensitive Artificial Intelligence Methods:**

The ethical AI development based on privacy-by-design principles is minimizing privacy risks:

- **Differential Privacy:** It is a mathematical method that introduces noise to data, allowing statistical analysis and computations without revealing any particular individual's identity.
- **Federated Learning:** Methods in computational learning that allow model training with heterogeneous data distribution without sensitive data centralisation.
- **Encryption and Anonymization:** Technical security controls data stored/in transit.
- **Minimization of Data:** Gathering of information that is required.
- **User Control:** It allows the user to see, manipulate, edit and delete personal information.
- **Transparency:** Openness of information practices, policies and user privileges.

Establishing and Retaining Client Trust

Reliability is crucial in encouraging customers to utilise library systems, particularly AI-driven systems that raise concerns about privacy.

The way libraries can establish trust is:

- **Honest Policies:** Easy-to-understand and transparent privacy policies in plain language describing how they work with data.
- **Explicit Consent**: Seeking informed consent to collecting or using personal data and such consent has simple opt-out provisions.
- **Obvious Secrecy:** It shows that the organisation takes the notion of data security seriously, both in terms of technology (https) and personnel (Chief Privacy Officers).
- **Responsive Governance:** Resolving privacy issues in time and admitting errors and taking corrective actions.
- **Frequent Audits:** Conducting privacy compliance and data practices assessment on a regular basis.

7.3. Change Resistance and Staff Concerns

Although AI has potential positive outcomes, library employees are usually subject to anxiety about the implementation demanded sensitive leadership:

- **Job Displacement Fears:** Employees will be interested in the fear that they will lose their jobs due to cataloging, reference services, or other services being automated, leaving them with fewer hours or less expertise. Although

AI does not often replace librarians, the leadership has to communicate the issues in a refined manner and offer the believable justification.

- **Professional Identity Threats:** In the case of librarians whose identity is based on expertise (cataloging, reference), the automation of AI poses a threat to the very identity of the profession. The leadership should assist personnel in imagining more expanded and strategic roles that embrace their skillsets and AI potentials.
- **AI Literacy Gaps:** The team that does not have the knowledge of AI and does not have any experience with AI tools, of course, is reluctant to support the adoption. This will need long term education and training.
- **Value Conflicts:** There are professional library workers who doubt the idea of AI really promoting library missions or exerting cost-reduction and managerial efficiency. Libraries will need to demonstrate that AI benefits the interests of patrons and corporate objectives, which extend beyond operational cost savings.
- **Equity and Access Concerns:** Some employees are concerned that AI solutions may create bias against vulnerable groups or that a move to adopt AI by libraries can be perceived as a departure from human values of service.
- These issues can be addressed by continuing the dialogue, being transparent, participating in the implementation decision, identifying the valid concerns and demonstrating the dedication to ethical AI practices that address the values of the library.

8. ETHICS AND GOVERNANCE ETHICS PRINCIPLES IN LIBRARIES

8.1. Guiding Principles of Ethical AI

The implementation of AI raises issues that must be tackled through extensive ethical principles and mechanisms that would guarantee that that AI application is beneficial to the libraries without causing harm.

There are several AI ethics statements expressed by various organizations libraries can use it to their advantage to collect these in their own, discipline-specific wikis and frameworks.

Transparency and Explainability: The libraries are to use the explainable AI (XAI) techniques that disclose how systems arrive at their decisions, allowing the staff and users to reason, analyze and challenge the AI-assisted suggestions or decisions. Users should be able to know why systems suggest specific resources or mark them as at-risk.

Accountability: explicit delegation of responsibility on the performance of the AI system, accuracy, bias, privacy protection and ethical adherence is accountable instead of spreading responsibility among vendors, IT workers and administrators. The libraries must create positions that are specifically to handle AI governance and oversight.

- **Fairness and Non-Discrimination:** AI systems must not in some way routinely discriminate against specific groups of people because of some protected characteristic or exacerbate past discriminations. Fairness is provided by way of regular bias audit, having diverse development teams and inclusive governance.
- **Privacy and Data Protection:** Libraries are expected to reduce the amount of data collected, protect the collected data, gain informed consent and allow its users to control personal information, as well as to adhere to the regulations of privacy. System design should not consider privacy as an after-thought.
- **Benefit and Non-Maleficence:** The use of AI should be proven beneficial to library users, employees, or institutions and not harmful. Libraries must evaluate the implications of AI investments on how well it services customers, augment the capacity of the staff, or help in advancing the institutions missions- not just save money.
- **Human Autonomy and Agency:** AI needs to complement and not substitute human judgment where it can be found that human autonomy is critical. The libraries are supposed to have rational human control over AI systems, especially on consequential decisions that involve people.
- **Consistency with Library Values**: AI application must support fundamental libraries values of access, intellectual freedom, privacy and inclusivity instead of making technology ability subordinate to these values. AI must be used to fulfill the mission of libraries as trusted community institutions not turn libraries into surveillance machinery or data collection instruments of the corporation.

8.2. Governance Frameworks and Policies of the Institutions

The ethical principles must be translated into practice through tangible governance systems to provide policies, decision-making procedures and control systems.

- **AI Governance Committee:** Institution should form cross-functional committees that are represented by library administration, IT, public services, technical services, human resources and (preferably) community representatives. These committees manage the adoption of AI, scrutinize the ethical concerns, develop policies, audit systems and solve issues.

- **Policy to use AI:** It must include clear institutional policies on authorized use of AI (as opposed to prohibited use), authorized vendors and tools of AI, data collection and retention standards, data privacy, mitigation of bias, transparency and explainability expectations and community complaints mechanisms.
- **Algorithmic Impact Assessment:** Institutions ought to run impact assessment of the potential benefits, risks, bias potential and privacy implications, stakeholder concerns and mitigation strategies of any significant AI systems, before they are deployed.
- **Frequent Audits and Review:** AI systems must be periodically reviewed and evaluated based on metrics of performance (accuracy, precision, recall), indicators of bias, user satisfaction, compliance with privacy and consistency with institutional values.
- **Transparency Reports:** The institution must release transparency reports that detail AI systems in use, their uses, evaluation findings including bias and accuracy rates, privacy and incidents or concerns.
- **Mechanism of Complaints and Appeal:** The libraries are to put in place a mechanism by which staff, users and other members of the community can bring their concerns regarding the use of AI systems, seek audits, appeal decisions and seek redress in case they are harmed.

The diagram of the organizational chart/ framework must show Senior Leadership (approves AI strategy), AI Governance Committee (monitors implementation, policy), Technical Review Team (assesses systems), Community Advisory Panel (reflects interests of users) and individual tracks Policy Development, Impact Assessment, Bias Auditing, Privacy Compliance, Stakeholder Communication and Evaluation/ Continuous Improvement.

9. BUILDING AND AI LITERACY IN LIBRARY PROFESSIONALS

The key element to successfully deploying the AI systems is the capacity to develop organizational capacity- making sure that the library professionals have the knowledge, skills and confidence to operate the AI technologies.

9.1. AI Literacy: Definitions and Components

AI literacy is a critical competency in a modern librarian and its definitions are still developing and facing challenges.

The AI literacy has several components:

- **Conceptual Knowledge:** Understanding of the basic concepts of AI, types, capabilities, limitations and general conceptual knowledge of the various AI strategies.
- **Technical Awareness:** Technical knowledge of technical components, data needs, types of algorithms and system architectures to the extent of assessing AI systems and determining constraints.
- **Practical Skills:** The skills to work with AIs, to analyze the results, to troubleshoot the simplest problems and to implement AI functionalities into the working routine.
- **Ethical Discipline:** The awareness of moral considerations, privacy issues, the possibility of bias and responsible AI ethics.
- **Critical Thinking:** The Capacity to be sceptical of AI systems, critical of claims, knowing what to do and what is inappropriate and make this decision.
- Importantly, AI literacy is not about understanding how to program or possessing profound technical skills it is about having informed awareness, which is sufficient to make informed decisions as a professional and use AI responsibly.

9.2. Relevant Hulls AI Literacy Research

The survey study reports high levels of AI illiteracies among library employees:

- **Conceptual Awareness:** Librarians are mostly familiar with AI and understand its application few (7-15) are well conceptually informed.
- **Practical Experience:** A very small part (usually 5-20%) has dealt with AI tools in practice the majority are theory only conscious.
- **Ethical Framework:** Fewer librarians have delved into ethical issues or even conducted biases audits, privacy analysis, or governance arguments.
- **Application in Disciplines:** The librarians often have no ideas on how AI can be applied in their particular duties (cataloguing, reference, collection development).
- **Confidence and Agency:** Most people in the library profession have low levels of confidence in their understanding of AI and feel like they are not involved in the decisions related to AI in the workplace.

These loopholes have a comprehensible opposition to the use of AI and restrict the functionality of the libraries in terms of installing, maintaining and constantly advancing AI systems.

9.3. AI Literacy Around the World

Workforce AI literacy has been identified as an issue of importance and several organizations have created training and resources:

- **ACRL AI Literacy Framework**

The Association of College & Research Libraries created an AI literacy framework, which bases AI education specific to libraries on funding principles, use of tools and ethical concerns. This model is used in designing training programs and curriculum.

- **Clarivate AI Literacy Essentials**

It is a self-paced eight-week micro-course jointly created by Clarivate (a vendor of library services) and LibTechInsights that offers flexible learning based on the ACRL model. The program equips library teams to be knowledgeable stakeholders in institutional AI pathways by offering hands-on and library-related training.

- **ProQuest Professional Development**

ProQuest (key library supplier) has webinars, workshops and online material related to AI literacy, training on the tool and advice on implementation.

- **Government Initiatives**

Other international organizations such as UNESCO formulate AI ethics and literacy guidelines that apply to libraries and cultural establishments.

- **Institutional Programs:** Other individual libraries create their own tailored AI training to meet their systems, priorities and staff needs.

9.4. AI Capacity Building Strategies

Libraries can use a complex strategy to establish organizational AI literacy and capacity:

- **Formal Training:** Institute general AI literacy education of the entire workforce and position-specific training of jobs interacting with AI systems. Training should be based on formal curricula such as ACRL framework instead of haphazard training.
- **Communities of Practice:** Introduce community of practice among staff, where employees share knowledge, talk about applications, find solutions to problems and gain practical knowledge together in groups.
- **Leadership Development:** Make sure that the leaders of the library have adequate AI literacy to make strategic decisions, formulate governance and spearhead implementation.
- **Vendor Partnerships:** Capitalize on vendor expertise by means of training, consultation and demonstrations. Make vendors sufficiently documented, trained and supportable.
- **Conference and Continuing Education**: Support staff will be invited to attend library conferences, AI-centered workshops and continuing education where they will learn among their peers and receive expert training.
- **Testing and Pilot Projects:** Provide employees with a chance to test AI tools in the low-risk setting to acquire some experience and become more confident in their use before it is implemented on a large scale.
- **Mentoring and Coaching**: Call on technology-experienced personnel to mentor colleagues with AI skills, particularly with one-on-one support and advice.
- **Recognition and incentives:** Recognize AI learning and implementation initiatives by staff by promoting, providing leadership opportunities and professional recognition.

10. CASE STUDIES: GLOBAL LEADING BEST PRACTICE IN AI

The analysis of institutions that have done it successfully offers tangible examples of how to approach leadership, the implementation process and insights.

10.1. North America: AI-Based Learning Analytics and Decision Support

North American academic libraries are forming more partnerships with institutional leaders to use AI as the basis of student success analytics and learning analytics programs.

This paper examines four contexts of Learning Analytics:

North American educational bodies utilize predictive analytics that detect at risk students early within academic terms such that interventions are made early enough before the students become disadvantaged academically. Libraries provide the circulation data, access information at a resource and research participation indicators to such predictive models.

It has been shown that students who are able to use library services perform better (greater GPA, higher retention, raise in graduation rates) than those with little library use. Being in a position to identify students who are at risk whilst at the same time monitoring their use of library resources, then institutions can be able to recommend specific library interventions.

- **Leadership Strategies:** Effective implementations in North America show that a number of leadership strategies are effective.
- **Strategic Alignment:** Library leaders actively participated in institutional leadership when it came to defining how libraries support student success analytics and learning initiatives.
- **Staff Development:** Institutions made substantial investment in developing the training of library personnel to be familiar with learning analytics situations, data interpretation and positive communication of library value.
- **Vendor Partnerships:** Libraries chose those vendors who had learning analytics systems that were compatible with library data and values.
- **Privacy Leadership:** Libraries were at the forefront in institutional discourses of privacy, data storage and ethical analytics practices.
- **Visible Value Demonstration:** Libraries, in a very obvious way, explained the direct effect of their resources and services on the success of the students and this is why they should be invested in, even in the settings of tight budgets.
- **Challenges and Lessons:**

Privacy contradictions between the institutional wish to know using predictive analytics.

Seeing to it that diverse populations of students use analytics as an advantage and not a disadvantage that biased models have imposed.

Handling personnel issues regarding big data cuts on individual service.

Holding intellectual freedom and customer privacy amid institutional appetite of information.

10.2. Europe: Machine Learning in Library Science and Publication Management

European institutions have been the first to make use of machine learning in bibliometric analysis, research evaluation and scholarly communication infrastructure.

- **The Acquisition of LIBRA.I. Project (EU-Funded Initiative):**

European Union funded LIBRARI. project seeks to introduce AI into media and learning literacy training inside public libraries making libraries places of AI education. This multi-national project acknowledges the fact that libraries are playing vital roles in building AI literacy within different communities and librarians are engaging in workshops and helping to build structures. The project includes the releases in various languages, which is a sign of adherence to linguistic and cultural accessibility.

- **Knowledge Communication Applications:**

Machine learning is being used in European libraries to:

- **Bibliometric Analysis:** A review of publication pattern, citation patterns, network of research collaboration and the metrics of impact.
- **Repository Management:** Institutional repositories In automated metadata enhancement, subject classification and content recommender systems in institutional repositories.
- **Research Assessment:** Accreditation, funding and strategic planning Supporting research evaluation.
- **Leadership Approaches:**
- **Collaborative Infrastructure:** European libraries collaborated on a regional basis in consortia and networks in order to create common infrastructure that lessened personal load.
- **Ethical Governance:** GDPR regulatory framework was an advantage to European institutions, which caused institutions to go privacy-by-design.
- **Community Engagement:** European efforts focused on integrating the community in AI creation, which is a democratic principle.

10.3. Asia: Shrewd Digital Reference Systems and Cultural Applications:

The Asian institutions have been the first ones to implement new applications of the AI in the digital reference and cultural heritage practices.

- **University of Oulu (Finland - Europe): Suggestion systems:**

The University of Oulu Library implemented AI-based recommendation systems that recommend reading materials according to the academic program and search history of the users. Such an undertaking reveals:

- **The Program-Based Personalization**: Program based recommendations were personalized based on institutional knowledge of academic programs and curricula.
- **Integration of Search Behavior**: Systems examined previous searches and discovered research interests and suggested related materials.
- **Significant Impact:** The recommendation system had a great influence on the level of involvement and time is spent on finding the sources of interest.
- **National Library of Singapore: ChatBook and Multi-Modal AI.**
- ChatBook prototypes, which are generative AI-based applications of AI to new service offerings, were the first of its kind to be developed by the National Library of Singapore.

ChatBook Technical Features:

- **Multi-Modal Interaction:** Systems merge oral history interviews, speeches, photographs, archival documents, biographies and cultural narratives available by using conversational interfaces.
- **Conversational Learning:** This is a mode of interaction with historical figures or fictional characters, where the user gets to know about the past of Singapore by conversational means instead of conventional information search.
- **Critical AI Literacy Development:** As people have a pleasant experience with AI, they also acquire knowledge about the performance and limitations of AI during direct interaction.
- Cultural Heritage Preservation ChatBook is an example of AI preserving and offering new opportunities to access cultural heritage and enhancing national identity and the interest of people in cultural institutions.

Leadership Implications:

- **Innovation Leadership:** ChatBook leadership needed leadership that would allow them to experiment with the new technologies of generative AI and be comfortable with taking risks that may not yield results.
- **Public Mission Focus:** It was implemented with more emphasis on the involvement of the people and cultural conservation as opposed to focused operational efficiency.
- **Technology Adaptation:** Leadership responded to the quickly changing generative AI features and adjusted the strategies as technology developed.

11. AI-BASED TRANSFORMATION LEADERSHIP FRAMEWORK

Combining theoretical bases, international case studies and pragmatic analysis to make a complete synthesis is a framework that will help library leaders navigate the process of AI transformation.

11.1. The Five-Component Leadership Framework

This model combines the features of transformational leadership (Bass), coherence and change management (Fullan and Quinn), diffusion of innovations (Rogers) and ethical decision-making:

Component 1:
Strategic Visioning and Alignment:

- A clear expression of how AI would contribute to the development of library missions, values and institutional objectives.
- Make it clear how AI is of interest to patrons, employee growth, institutional relationships.
- Secure apparent executive dedication and allocation of resources in favor of vision.
- Never stop to strengthen vision by communicating, making decisions and allocating resources.

Component 2:
Organizational Preparedness and Capacity Building.

- Complete AI preparedness analysis that reveals the lack of infrastructure, skills, governance, culture.

- Establish elaborate AI literacy initiatives to equip library employees to the right depths.
- Invest in technological infrastructure, which will be required to implement AI.
- Create change agent networks that enable distributed leadership.
- Promote innovation and learning cultures.

Component 3:
Ethical Governance and Accountability.

- Develop the governance systems that have a proper sense of responsibility on the performance and ethics of AI systems.
- Establish policies concerning comprehensive AI by covering approved uses, data management, privacy, bias mitigation.
- Carry out algorithmic impact testing prior to the implementation of major systems.
- Adopt routine audit strategies measuring prejudice, accuracy, data confidentiality.
- Establish transparency, complaint and appeal systems, which allow stakeholders to input.

Component 4:
Stakeholder Engagement and Communication:

- Participate in the implementation decision process of AI, involving library employees and integrating their experience and responding to concerns.
- Develop open and continuous consultation regarding AI activities, reasons, advancements, issues.
- Create local advisory boards on behalf of users in the governance of AI.
- Overcoming resistance should be achieved through dialog, engaging the skeptics into pilot projects and proving value.
- Communicate achievements and experience with failures publicly.

Component 5:
Ongoing Review and Recurrent Enhancement:

- Determine evidence-based evaluation strategies to measure the performance of AI systems as per the desired results.
- Develop feedback loop that allows stakeholder feedback on how to make improvements on the iterations.

- Look out at unwanted effects such as bias, intrusion on privacy, effects on service quality.
- Encourages experimentation and rational risk-taking and holds oneself accountable.
- Disclose the review of shares publicly, making them a field contribution.

11.2. Strategy and Strategic Planning

Prior to the introduction of AI, libraries are to carry out thorough preparedness evaluation, which involves the determination of organizational capacity and strategic priorities.

Assessment Dimensions:

- **Infrastructure / Technology:** IT infrastructure, data management level, cloud computing maturity, cybersecurity level.
- **Staff Skills & Training:** Leading AI skills, tech adoption history, change management history, training physicality.
- **Governance & Policy:** Current governance systems, policy making procedures, privacy guidelines, codes of ethics.
- **Data Management:** Data quality, integration, retention, privacy.
- **Strategic Alignment:** Mission clarity in the institution, stakeholder involvement and resource dedication.
- **Ethical Framework:** Current ethical interaction, diversity and inclusion, accessibility guarantee.
- **Maturity Model:**

  Evaluation findings usually show that there are different levels of organization maturity in the following dimensions:
- **First**: Flexible, improvised, reactive strategies scanty infrastructure informal governance.
- **Developing**: new practices primitive infrastructure new policies and governance.
- **Advanced**: Structured methods well-developed infrastructure full-fledged governance.
- **Optimized:** Vision culture of continuous improvement forward-looking adaptation combined ethical practices.

  Libraries evaluate maturity on a spectrum and the priority developments are determined ahead of the entire AI adoption.

12. AI IN LINE WITH INSTITUTIONAL OBJECTIVES: INSTITUTIONAL ACCREDITATION, STUDENT SUCCESS, RESEARCH IMPACT

The application of AI must be provable in terms of institutional objectives and promotion of quantifiable results and not a demonstration of technology as a phenomenon.

12.1. Facilitating Accreditation and Quality Assurance

There is a growing trend in which accreditation agencies require institutions to use the power of data analytics to provide quality assurance and learning outcomes assessment and continuous improvement. The libraries can place AI in the context of institutional accreditation by:

- **Student Learning Outcomes**: Add to the pool of learning analytics with library resource utilization data, identify a correlation between library use and student achievement.
- **Institutional Effectiveness:** Predicting resources, collections and service directions with predictive analytics and aligning library services with the needs of the institution.
- **Research Impact Assessment:** Accompanying metrics of research evaluation, bibliometric analysis and tracking of research output needed to meet accreditation requirements.
- **Accessibility and Inclusivity:** Use of artificial intelligence to determine and overcome obstacles to equal access, so that more diverse cohorts of students have access to services.

12.2. Developing Research Support and Impact

Libraries are also starting to embrace the institutional research goal in AI-enhanced research support services:

Research Analytics: This offers research impact evaluation and publication tracking and as well as collaboration network analysis to facilitate researcher productivity and institutional branding.

Easy Discovery: Intelligent Discovery systems and improved discovery systems that assist in researchers to locate pertinent literature effectively.

Emerging Research Discovery: Predictive analytics to reveal new areas of research and interdisciplinary cooperation.

12.3. Enabling Student Success Initiatives

Student achievement is the ultimate institutional objective and the libraries are placed at the forefront:

- **Predictive Intervention:** This is identifying the at-risk students at an early stage so that specific library interventions can be administered before they start to get into academic trouble.
- **Learning Analytics Incorporation:** Donating library information to institutional learning analytics, showing library contribution to retention, GPA, graduation rates.
- **Individualized Orchestration**: Personalized research support on the recommendation systems and AI based reference services were shown to achieve individualized guidance based on student learning requirements.
- **Accessibility Support:** Multilingual, AI-based accessibility assistance and student-centered learning support by various student groups.

13. EVALUATION CONTINUOUS IMPROVEMENT FEEDBACK LOOPS

The transformation of AI in a sustainable way should be done with systematically evaluated methods of evaluating the performance of the system, defining the problems and advising on the gradual enhancement.

13.1. AI Driven Library Key Performance Indicators

The libraries are advised to implement extensive KPI to evaluate the performance of AI system in various aspects:
Service Quality Metrics:

- The satisfaction of the users with the use of AI (surveys, feedback)
- Success rates (finding needed resources) Discovery
- Rates of reference questions resolution (the chatbots answering questions)
- Mean time-to-resource (speed of users finding material)

Operational Efficiency:

- Cost per record, time per record efficiency in cataloging.
- Scalability (queries served per hour) of reference service.

- Efficiency of management of collections (acquisitions per budget dollar)

Equity and Access:

- Demographic group utilization (providing equal access to services)
- Audit results (discrimination testing on algorithms)
- Measures of accessibility compliance.

User Engagement:

- Use and engagement rates of discovery system.
- Recommendation acceptance rates (users on recommendations)
- Chatbot interaction and customer satisfaction.

Institutional Impact:

- Correlation of student success with library use.
- The use of research support influences publication/citation measures.
- Reputation contribution- institutional positioning.

Ethical Compliance:

- Cases of privacy breach and their response.
- Audit findings/bias audit findings and remediation.
- Preparation and accuracy of transparency reports.
- Frequency and effectiveness of Governance meetings.

13.2. Agile Feedback and Continuous Improvement

Libraries must use rapid iteration and improvement agile methods:

- **Quick Cycles of Feedback:** Seek staff and user feedback on a regular basis, make a quick improvement.
- **A/B testing:** Compare alternative methods (e.g. recommendation algorithms) by controlled testing.
- **Participatory Improvement:** Involve the stakeholders in determining the areas of improvement.
- **Learning Culture:** Failures in learning frame learning as an informing experience on how to improve.

- **Open Discussion:** Summarize feedback on evaluations, progress undertaken and current issues.

14. FUTURE PROJECTIONS AND SUGGESTIONS

14.1. Research Frontiers and Emerging Technologies

Generative AI and Large Language Models: Although ChatGPT and similar systems are in the focus at the moment, the library implementation is still in its infancy. Further progress can probably involve more advanced research support, natural language query interfaces and knowledge synthesis.

- **Federated Learning and Privacy-Preserving AI:** With an increase in privacy concerns, federated methods that allow joint AI development without centralized pain data are bound to increase. The use of consortial AI can be seen as a future innovation in libraries.
- **Explainable AI and Interpretability:** Technical developments in XAI will allow more interpretable AI systems to be created to deal with the existing issues of black boxes. This openness is critical to library applications in which reasonableness of systems is important considerations of fairness and trust.
- **Human-AI Collaboration:** Future library AI is unlikely to be focused on automation, but human-AI collaboration, where AI will act as an auxiliary, but not substitute, to librarian expertise. This shared paradigm is consistent with the values of the library that focus on human judgment and service.
- **Voice Interfaces and Multimodal Access:** Library services will be more accessible and interactive, especially when voice-based library interfaces, chat-based searching interfaces and multimodal interactions are implemented to make library services more accessible to consumers with accessibility requirements.

14.2. Artificial Intelligence Maturity and Strategic Growth (2025-2030) Roadmap

2025-2026: Foundation Building:

- Undertake organizational preparedness tests.
- Create AI literacy policies and regulations.
- Carry out pilot projects.
- Build change agent networks

2027-2028: Expansion and Integration:

- Scale pilot successful library services.
- Increase AI intelligence on all levels of staff.
- Combine AI programs and institutional policies.
- Formulate initial generation ethics and audit system.

2029-2030: Leadership Optimization:

- Make AI an important component of operation and strategy.
- Produce superior applications to meet new requirements.
- In the publication, presentation at conferences, mentoring of other institutions.
- Decades of practices and new guidance should be constantly improved.

14.3. Library Leadership Recommendations

In the case of Individual Library Leaders:

Taking time to become personally AI literate, working with new technologies and research.

Express convincing institutional vision of relating AI to library values and missions.

Develop multi-skilled teams of leadership comprising technologists, service professionals, ethicists and community representatives.

Externalize participatory governance that guarantees authentic stakeholder voice.

Do not compromise on this ethical values do not yield to technology potentiality at core values expense.

14.4. Institute Professional Code of Ethical AI in Libraries

Establish peer learning networks so that institutions can share the experiences and lessons.

Campaign on AI governance to allow the value of libraries (intellectual freedom, privacy) to be safeguarded by policy.

Advance worldwide discourse on AI ethics and accountable practices.

- **For Library Consortia:**
- Learn team AI development strategies that would offload individuals and develop collective capacity.
- Formulate common governance systems and codes of ethics.
- Establish the federated learning possibilities that would ensure collaborative analytics without data centralization.

- The integration of AI literacy, ethics and leadership across the curriculi should be ensured instead of a non-elective discipline.
- Equip future leaders (AI-enabled library world).
- Promote continuing education to practicing librarians with ease.

In the case of Researchers and Scholars:

- Keep exploring the use of AI applications in libraries and record both successes and failures.
- Provide to knowledge on ethical AI in services.
- See the impact of AI on the different categories of users and equity commitments of libraries.
- Learn about human-AI collaborative model development that develops library missions.

CONCLUSION

Academic libraries are at a deep junction in the history of its institution. The potential of artificial intelligence is real, as it can contribute to improving the user services, simplifying the operations, facilitating institutional objectives and allowing the librarian to concentrate on high-value professional work. Nonetheless, this possible can only be converted into institutional value in the event that AI implementation is beneficial to the library, is given careful strategic management and is subjected to strict ethical standards.

The pieces of evidence provided in this chapter allow concluding that the effective use of AI will not be based on the technological advancedness as much as it will be premised on the ability of the company to see the vision, prepare the organization and be committed to ethical standards. The recommendation systems of the University of Oulu, the ChatBook innovations of the National Library of Singapore and the student success analytics of North American institutions are all examples of how AI can serve to benefit the library missions when the decisions related to the implementation are thoughtful in terms of what it should use, moral values and strategic alignment.

The transformational leadership theory helps in illuminating the way in which leaders of libraries motivate their employees to consider change, improve aspirations and advance common values. Distributed leadership principles embrace the fact that agents of change are found within organizations and that genuine involvement enhances the effect of change. According to Rogers, the innovation diffusion model elucidates the adoption patterns, which can help the leader tailor the engagement approach to different employees. The model of coherence proposed by Fullan and Quinn focuses on collaborative cultures, coherent strategies and moral purpose.

Such theoretical grounds are invaluable not because they are always the source of success but because they help us see the way out of the maze of organizational politics, make strategic decisions and relate immediate implementation decisions to institutional change. Together with the applied frameworks, international case studies and individual recommendations introduced in this paper, these grounds give library administrators the required conceptual and practical instruments.

The ethical issues that AI brings algorithmic bias, privacy and displacement concerns, value clashes are not something that can be brushed off or decidedly diminished. These issues are worthwhile consideration, open recognition and long term governance dedication. Libraries that make themselves unique not as the ones that blindly follow the emerging technologies but as those who carefully apply AI to the service of well-considered values will eventually become the most trusted and appreciated by their communities.

A way ahead needs library leaders who both drive change and protect values who are open-minded to technological potential and remain steadfast in their devotion to access, privacy and intellectual freedom who enable employees by being participatory leaders as well as by creating an organizational capacity and who in their actions and resource disbursements profess that AI is human and organizational rather than the other way around.

This time is unprecedented in the case of academic libraries that have been placed as strategic entities in institutional change. Libraries that learn to embrace AI change yet remain morally purposeful, create communities that are inclusive and develop further accountability will become reliable leaders in guiding higher education in an AI-transformed world without losing the values that universities are meant to stand. The future of AI in higher education will significantly be dependent on the quality of the leadership of libraries in this transformation.

REFERENCES

Adetayo, A. J. (2023). Artificial intelligence chatbots in academic libraries: The rise of ChatGPT. *Library Hi Tech News*, *40*(3), 18–21. DOI: 10.1108/LHTN-01-2023-0007

Cao, G., Liang, M., & Li, X. (2018). How to make the library smart? The conceptualization of the smart library. *The Electronic Library*, *36*(5), 811–825. DOI: 10.1108/EL-11-2017-0248

Cox, A. (2022). How artificial intelligence might change academic library work: Applying the competencies literature and the theory of the professions. *Journal of the Association for Information Science and Technology*, *74*(3), 367–380. DOI: 10.1002/asi.24635

Johnston, H., Wells, R. F., Shanks, E. M., Boey, T., & Parsons, B. N. (2024). Student perspectives on the use of generative artificial intelligence technologies in higher education. *International Journal for Educational Integrity*, *20*(1), 2. Advance online publication. DOI: 10.1007/s40979-024-00149-4

Lund, B., Omame, I., Tijani, S., & Agbaji, D. (2020). Perceptions toward Artificial Intelligence among Academic Library Employees and Alignment with the Diffusion of Innovations' Adopter Categories. *College & Research Libraries*, *865*, 865. Advance online publication. DOI: 10.5860/crl.81.5.865

Nakai, K., & Kanehisa, M. (1992). A knowledge base for predicting protein localization sites in eukaryotic cells. *Genomics*, *14*(4), 897–911. DOI: 10.1016/S0888-7543(05)80111-9 PMID: 1478671

Ravyse, W. S., Blignaut, A. S., Leendertz, V., & Woolner, A. (2016). Success factors for serious games to enhance learning: A systematic review. *Virtual Reality (Waltham Cross)*, *21*(1), 31–58. DOI: 10.1007/s10055-016-0298-4

Tufail, S., Riggs, H., Tariq, M., & Sarwat, A. I. (2023). Advancements and Challenges in Machine Learning: A comprehensive review of models, libraries, applications and algorithms. *Electronics (Basel)*, *12*(8), 1789. DOI: 10.3390/electronics12081789

Wheatley, A., & Hervieux, S. (2019). Artificial intelligence in academic libraries: An environmental scan. *Information Services & Use*, *39*(4), 347–356. DOI: 10.3233/ISU-190065

Yassin, N. I., Omran, S., Houby, E. M. E., & Allam, H. (2017). Machine learning techniques for breast cancer computer aided diagnosis using different image modalities: A systematic review. *Computer Methods and Programs in Biomedicine*, *156*, 25–45. DOI: 10.1016/j.cmpb.2017.12.012 PMID: 29428074

Chapter 4
AI Training for Educators: Building Ethical, Inclusive, and Competent Teaching Practices in the Age of Artificial Intelligence

Raffi Akbar Saputra
http://orcid.org/0009-0001-6286-9209
Universitas Esa Unggul, Indonesia

Binastya Anggara Sekti
http://orcid.org/0000-0001-5489-4888
Universitas Esa Unggul, Indonesia

ABSTRACT

Artificial intelligence is increasingly embedded in education, requiring educators to develop both technical understanding and ethical judgment. This chapter examines how AI-focused professional development can strengthen pedagogy while promoting fairness, privacy, and responsible use. It explores the growing influence of AI tools such as adaptive learning systems, automated assessment, and personalized tutoring, and highlights the need for teachers to understand algorithmic bias, data protection, and transparent decision-making. Drawing on case studies and established frameworks, the chapter proposes a comprehensive model for AI educator training that integrates ethical principles, digital pedagogy, and data literacy. It argues that equipping teachers with strong AI literacy is essential for ensuring equitable implementation and preparing learners to engage critically with AI technologies.

DOI: 10.4018/979-8-2600-1840-8.ch004

1. INTRODUCTION

The integration of artificial intelligence in educational environments has transformed traditional teaching paradigms, creating unprecedented opportunities and challenges for educators worldwide. Educational institutions are increasingly adopting AI-powered tools ranging from intelligent tutoring systems to automated assessment platforms, fundamentally reshaping how knowledge is transmitted and evaluated. This technological shift demands that educators develop new competencies that extend beyond traditional pedagogical skills to encompass technical literacy, ethical awareness, and critical understanding of algorithmic systems. Artificial intelligence is the driving force of change, focusing on the needs and demands of the student (Tapalova & Zhiyenbayeva, 2022).

The use of artificial intelligence in education is not entirely new. Early experiments in AI-assisted instruction can be traced back to the 1980s with the development of intelligent tutoring systems such as SCHOLAR and GUIDON. These early systems aimed to simulate human tutoring through rule-based reasoning and adaptive feedback. Although their capabilities were limited by computational constraints, they laid the conceptual foundation for contemporary AI-enhanced learning environments. The emergence of machine learning and generative AI has significantly expanded these possibilities, transforming AI from experimental tools into widely accessible educational technologies.

The rapid proliferation of AI technologies in classrooms has outpaced the preparation of teachers to effectively utilize these tools. Many educators find themselves navigating complex AI systems without adequate training or support, leading to suboptimal implementation and potential ethical violations (Daher, 2025). The absence of comprehensive professional development programs creates a critical gap between technological capabilities and pedagogical readiness, ultimately affecting student learning outcomes and data privacy.

Furthermore, the ethical dimensions of AI deployment in education require educators to act as gatekeepers who can identify and mitigate potential harms. Issues such as algorithmic bias, data surveillance, and automated decision-making present new challenges that traditional teacher education programs have not addressed (Omidvar & Meihami, 2025). Educators must develop the capacity to critically evaluate AI systems, understand their limitations, and advocate for student welfare in increasingly automated learning environments. AI has become an influential force shaping modern society, raising urgent ethical questions about responsibility, fairness, transparency, and human dignity (Sekti, 2025a).

Figure 1. The teacher role evolution

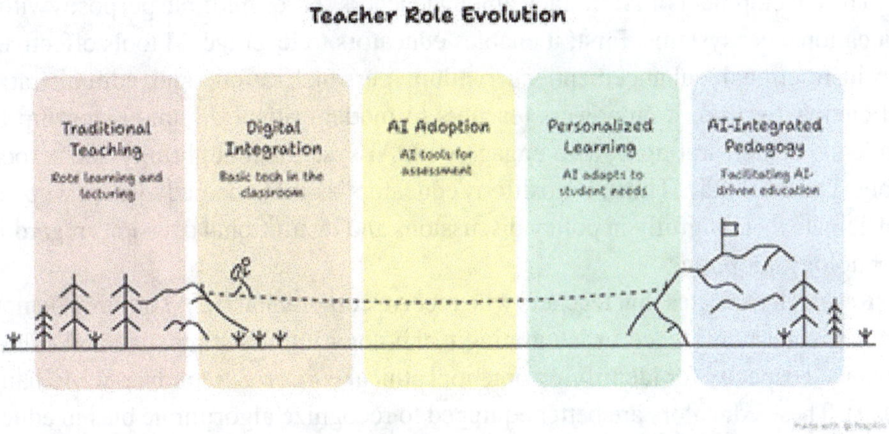

Figure 1 illustrates the shift in teacher responsibilities from traditional content delivery toward hybrid roles involving technological mediation, ethical evaluation, and learning design. In AI-enhanced environments, teachers act not only as instructors but also as critical evaluators of algorithmic outputs and facilitators of student engagement with AI systems.

Recent international surveys indicate that more than 60% of teachers report insufficient preparation to critically evaluate AI tools, while a majority anticipate significant AI influence on their instructional practice within the next five years (Krumsvik, 2020).

This chapter addresses these challenges by proposing a comprehensive framework for AI training that equips educators with the knowledge, skills, and ethical foundations necessary for responsible technology integration. The discussion encompasses technical competencies, pedagogical adaptations, ethical considerations, and policy implications, providing a holistic approach to professional development in the age of artificial intelligence.

1.1 The Imperative for AI Literacy in Education

AI literacy has emerged as a fundamental competency for contemporary educators, comparable in importance to traditional literacies such as reading, writing, and digital fluency. The concept extends beyond mere technical proficiency to encompass critical understanding of how AI systems function, their societal implications, and their potential impact on student learning and development (Lee et al., 2026). Educators with robust AI literacy can make informed decisions about technology selection, implementation strategies, and appropriate use cases within their instructional contexts.

The development of AI literacy among teachers serves multiple purposes within educational ecosystems. First, it enables educators to leverage AI tools effectively for instructional enhancement, curriculum personalization, and administrative efficiency. Second, it empowers teachers to model critical digital citizenship for students, demonstrating how to engage with AI systems thoughtfully and responsibly (Daher, 2025). Third, it positions educators as informed advocates who can participate meaningfully in policy discussions and institutional decisions regarding technology adoption.

Research indicates that teachers who receive comprehensive AI training demonstrate greater confidence in integrating technology into their practice and exhibit enhanced capacity for identifying potential ethical concerns (Omidvar & Meihami, 2025). These educators are better equipped to recognize algorithmic bias in educational applications, understand data privacy implications, and implement safeguards that protect student welfare. Moreover, they can facilitate student learning about AI in age-appropriate ways, preparing learners for a future where artificial intelligence permeates professional and personal spheres.

1.2 Educator and Student Perspectives in AI Integration

Interviews conducted in multiple national contexts reveal that practicing teachers often experience AI adoption as both empowering and destabilizing. While some report increased efficiency in grading and lesson preparation, others express anxiety regarding surveillance, loss of professional autonomy, and uncertainty about ethical boundaries. For example, teachers in Singapore's AI literacy pilot program noted that although automated feedback tools reduced marking time by up to 30%, they required additional oversight to ensure fairness and contextual sensitivity.

From the student perspective, generative AI tools are often perceived as accessible learning companions rather than assessment threats. However, students also report confusion regarding appropriate usage boundaries and fear of punitive responses when policies are unclear. These perspectives highlight the necessity of training that addresses not only technical implementation but also relational trust, transparency, and shared understanding.

Student experiences with AI tools often differ from educator perceptions. Many students view generative AI systems as learning companions that support exploration and idea generation. However, ambiguity in institutional policies can create uncertainty regarding appropriate use. Educator training programs should therefore include strategies for co-developing AI usage guidelines with students to foster transparency and trust.

1.3 Objectives and Structure of the Chapter

This chapter pursues four primary objectives that address the multifaceted nature of AI training for educators. The first objective examines the theoretical foundations of AI literacy within educational contexts, exploring how concepts from computer science, pedagogy, and ethics converge to create a comprehensive framework for teacher competency. This analysis establishes the intellectual groundwork for understanding why certain knowledge domains and skill sets are essential for effective AI integration in teaching practice. As a transformative technology reshaping educational systems, artificial intelligence refers to computational systems that simulate aspects of human intelligence, including reasoning, pattern recognition, language processing, and adaptive decision-making, to support teaching, learning, assessment, and institutional operations (Sekti, 2025b).

The second objective focuses on practical implementation by presenting detailed frameworks, curriculum models, and training methodologies that institutions can adopt or adapt for their specific contexts. This includes examination of successful case studies from various geographic and institutional settings, highlighting both effective practices and common pitfalls (Pham, 2025). The discussion emphasizes scalable approaches that can be implemented across diverse educational environments, from well-resourced institutions to settings with limited technological infrastructure.

The third objective addresses the ethical and legal dimensions of AI in education, providing educators with conceptual tools and practical strategies for navigating complex moral terrain. This includes detailed exploration of algorithmic bias, data privacy regulations, surveillance concerns, and equity considerations (Kooli & Chakraoui, 2025). The chapter presents frameworks for ethical decision-making that educators can apply when evaluating AI systems or developing policies for technology use in their classrooms and institutions.

The final objective examines policy implications and governance structures necessary for sustaining effective AI training programs. This analysis considers institutional policies, national frameworks, and international standards that shape the landscape of AI in education (Pham, 2025). The discussion provides recommendations for policymakers, administrators, and educational leaders seeking to create supportive environments for teacher professional development in AI literacy and ethical practice.

While existing studies have examined AI literacy, ethics, or digital pedagogy in isolation, this chapter advances an integrated perspective that connects ethical governance, classroom practice, institutional policy, and lived educator experience within a single training architecture. Rather than treating AI competence as a technical add-on, the chapter conceptualizes it as a professional transformation process that reshapes teacher identity, agency, and responsibility in AI-mediated learning environments. This integrative framing constitutes the chapter's primary contribution to the literature.

2. THEORETICAL FOUNDATIONS OF AI LITERACY FOR EDUCATORS

Understanding the theoretical underpinnings of AI literacy requires examination of multiple disciplinary perspectives that converge in educational practice. The conceptualization of AI literacy for educators draws from computer science education, critical pedagogy, information ethics, and professional development theory to create an integrated framework that addresses technical, pedagogical, and ethical dimensions simultaneously.

2.1 Defining AI Literacy in Educational Contexts

AI literacy in educational settings encompasses more than basic understanding of artificial intelligence technologies. It represents a multidimensional competency framework that includes technical knowledge about how AI systems function, critical awareness of their societal implications, and practical skills for effective and ethical implementation in teaching and learning contexts (Lee et al., 2026). This comprehensive definition recognizes that educators need different types of knowledge and capabilities depending on their roles, subject areas, and institutional contexts.

Figure 2. The synergy of AI literacy for educators

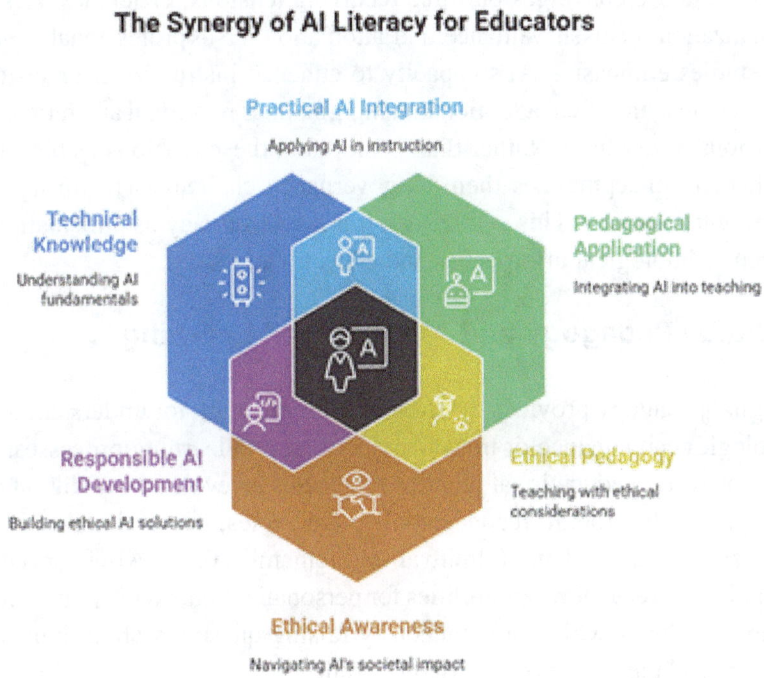

The technical dimension of AI literacy includes understanding fundamental concepts such as machine learning algorithms, neural networks, natural language processing, and computer vision. Educators do not need to become computer scientists, but they should develop conceptual understanding sufficient to make informed decisions about AI tool selection and implementation (Baxmann et al., 2025). This includes recognizing the difference between various types of AI systems, understanding their capabilities and limitations, and identifying appropriate use cases for different educational objectives.

Beyond technical knowledge, AI literacy encompasses critical and ethical dimensions that enable educators to evaluate AI systems through multiple lenses. This includes understanding how training data influences algorithmic outputs, recognizing potential sources of bias, and assessing the transparency and accountability of AI systems used in educational setting (Daher, 2025). Educators with strong critical AI literacy can ask probing questions about the systems they use, advocate for student welfare, and participate meaningfully in institutional decisions about technology adoption and policy development.

The literature converges on three recurring tensions: efficiency versus equity, personalization versus surveillance, and automation versus professional agency. While some studies emphasize AI's capacity to enhance instructional precision, others caution against uncritical adoption that marginalizes relational and human-centered dimensions of teaching. Rather than positioning these tensions as binary choices, this chapter conceptualizes them as governance challenges requiring structured training interventions. This synthesis reframes AI literacy as a mediation practice between technological affordances and educational values.

2.2 Digital Pedagogy and AI-Enhanced Learning

Digital pedagogy provides the theoretical framework for understanding how AI technologies can enhance or transform teaching and learning processes. The integration of AI into educational practice represents an evolution of digital pedagogy that requires educators to reconceptualize their roles, instructional strategies, and relationships with students (Omidvar & Meihami, 2025). AI-enhanced learning environments create new possibilities for personalization, adaptive instruction, and real-time feedback while simultaneously raising questions about human agency, creativity, and the nature of knowledge itself.

The concept of adaptive learning exemplifies how AI technologies can support pedagogical innovation. Adaptive learning systems use algorithms to analyze student performance data and adjust content delivery, pacing, and difficulty levels based on individual needs and progress patterns (Lin et al., 2025). These systems promise to address long-standing challenges in education by providing personalized learning experiences at scale. However, they also require educators to develop new competencies in data interpretation, system oversight, and pedagogical decision-making within technologically mediated environments.

AI technologies also enable new forms of formative assessment that provide more frequent and detailed feedback to both students and teachers. Automated essay scoring, intelligent tutoring systems, and learning analytics dashboards offer insights into student understanding that were previously impossible or prohibitively time-consuming to generate (de Putter-Smits et al., 2025). Educators must learn to interpret these data streams, integrate algorithmic assessments with human judgment, and maintain holistic understanding of student learning that encompasses dimensions not easily measured by AI systems.

The pedagogical integration of AI also raises fundamental questions about the goals and methods of education. When AI systems can provide instant answers, facilitate skill practice, and generate personalized content, educators must reconsider what knowledge and capabilities students need to develop. This shift emphasizes higher-order thinking skills such as critical analysis, creative problem-solving, ethical reasoning, and collaborative communication that complement rather than compete with AI capabilities (Hanshaw & Sullivan, 2025).

2.3 Ethical Frameworks for AI in Education

Ethical frameworks provide essential conceptual tools for navigating the complex moral landscape of AI deployment in educational settings. Multiple ethical traditions and principles inform how educators should approach AI integration, including consequentialist considerations of benefits and harms, deontological principles of rights and duties, virtue ethics emphasizing character and professional integrity, and care ethics focusing on relationships and responsibility (Kooli & Chakraoui, 2025).

The principle of beneficence requires that AI applications in education should actively promote student welfare and learning outcomes. This means carefully evaluating whether specific AI tools genuinely enhance educational experiences or merely provide technological novelty without substantive benefit. Educators must consider questions such as: Does this AI system improve learning outcomes? Does it support student agency and engagement? Does it free teacher time for higher-value interactions? The answers to these questions should guide implementation decisions and ongoing evaluation of AI tools in educational practic (Pham, 2025).

Equally important is the principle of non-maleficence, which obligates educators to avoid or minimize potential harms associated with AI deployment. These harms can take multiple forms, including privacy violations through excessive data collection, psychological impacts from constant monitoring, reinforcement of biases through flawed algorithms, and erosion of student autonomy through over-reliance on automated systems (Daher, 2025). Educators need frameworks for identifying potential harms, assessing their likelihood and severity, and implementing safeguards that protect students from negative consequences of AI integration.

Justice and equity considerations form another critical dimension of ethical AI use in education. AI systems can perpetuate or amplify existing inequalities if they are trained on biased data, designed without consideration of diverse user needs, or deployed in ways that advantage already privileged population (Kooli & Chakraoui, 2025). Educators must develop sensitivity to these equity concerns and advocate for fair, inclusive AI implementation that serves all students regardless of background, ability, or identity. This includes attention to the digital divide, linguistic diversity, accessibility for students with disabilities, and cultural responsiveness in AI system design and deployment.

2.4 AI Inclusion and Accessibility

Inclusive AI in education requires deliberate design choices that account for linguistic diversity, disability access, and cultural representation. AI systems trained primarily on English-language datasets may produce biased educational content for multilingual learners, while adaptive systems that rely on standardized behavioral patterns may disadvantage neurodiverse students. Educator training must therefore incorporate accessibility awareness and encourage critical evaluation of AI systems across diverse learner populations.

Although scholars generally agree that AI literacy is becoming a core competency for educators, their conceptualizations differ in emphasis. Daher (2025) focuses primarily on critical perspectives and ethical awareness in AI-mediated learning environments, while Lee et al. (2026). frame AI literacy through measurable competency frameworks linked to technological proficiency. Meanwhile, Kooli & Chakraoui (2025) extend the discussion to policy and governance dimensions. Taken together, these perspectives suggest that AI literacy should not be understood solely as a technical skill but as an integrated competency encompassing ethics, pedagogy, and institutional awareness.

3. DESIGNING COMPREHENSIVE AI TRAINING PROGRAMS FOR EDUCATORS

Effective AI training programs for educators require careful design that addresses multiple dimensions of competency development while remaining responsive to diverse institutional contexts and teacher needs. The following sections outline core components, pedagogical approaches, and implementation strategies for comprehensive professional development in AI literacy and ethical practice.

3.1 Core Competency Framework

A robust competency framework for AI training identifies the specific knowledge, skills, and dispositions that educators need to integrate AI effectively and ethically into their practice. Research suggests that comprehensive AI literacy for teachers encompasses at least five interconnected competency domains: technical understanding, pedagogical application, ethical reasoning, data literacy, and advocacy and leadership (Lee et al., 2026).

Technical understanding forms the foundation of AI literacy, providing educators with conceptual knowledge about how artificial intelligence systems function. This includes familiarity with basic AI concepts such as machine learning, algorithms, training data, and model evaluation. Educators should understand the difference between narrow AI and general AI, recognize various AI applications in educational contexts, and grasp fundamental principles of how algorithms learn from data and generate predictions or recommendations (Mannuru et al., 2025). While educators need not become programmers, this conceptual foundation enables informed decision-making about AI tool selection and implementation.

Pedagogical application competencies enable educators to leverage AI tools strategically to enhance teaching and learning. This domain includes skills such as:

1) Evaluating AI educational tools for alignment with learning objectives and pedagogical approaches
2) Designing learning activities that appropriately integrate AI systems
3) Facilitating student interaction with AI tools in ways that promote learning and critical thinking
4) Assessing the impact of AI integration on student engagement, understanding, and outcomes
5) Adapting instructional strategies based on insights from AI-generated analytics

These competencies require educators to think critically about when and how AI can genuinely improve educational experiences versus when human interaction and traditional methods remain superior (Omidvar & Meihami, 2025).

Ethical reasoning represents a crucial competency domain that distinguishes mere technical proficiency from responsible professional practice. Educators must develop capacity to identify ethical issues arising from AI use, analyze them through multiple ethical frameworks, and make principled decisions that prioritize student welfare and rights. This includes recognizing algorithmic bias, understanding privacy implications of data collection, evaluating fairness in automated assessment, and considering the long-term social impacts of AI integration in education (Daher, 2025).

Data literacy has emerged as an essential competency in the age of AI-enhanced education. Educators need to understand how educational data is collected, stored, analyzed, and used by AI systems. This includes interpreting learning analytics dashboards, recognizing limitations and potential biases in data-driven insights, and protecting student privacy in data-intensive environments (Pham, 2025). Data literacy also encompasses understanding data governance policies, informed consent procedures, and legal frameworks such as GDPR and FERPA that regulate educational data use.

Finally, advocacy and leadership competencies position educators as active agents in shaping how AI is deployed in their institutions and profession. This includes participating in policy discussions, advocating for ethical AI implementation, collaborating with colleagues to develop best practices, and contributing to broader conversations about the future of education in an AI-enhanced world (Kooli & Chakraoui, 2025). Educators with strong advocacy competencies can influence institutional decisions, support colleagues in developing AI literacy, and ensure that student interests remain central in technology adoption processes.

3.2 Curriculum Models and Training Approaches

Effective AI training curricula balance theoretical knowledge with practical application, providing educators with both conceptual understanding and hands-on experience using AI tools in educational contexts. Several curriculum models have emerged from successful training programs worldwide, each with distinct advantages for different institutional settings and teacher populations.

The modular competency-based model organizes training content into discrete units focused on specific competency areas. Each module addresses a particular aspect of AI literacy, such as understanding machine learning, evaluating algorithmic bias, implementing adaptive learning systems, or protecting student data privacy. Educators can complete modules sequentially or select those most relevant to their immediate needs and interests (de Putter-Smits et al., 2025). This approach offers flexibility for teachers with varying levels of prior knowledge and different time availability, making it particularly suitable for in-service professional development where educators must balance training with ongoing teaching responsibilities.

The project-based learning model engages educators in authentic tasks that require them to apply AI concepts and tools to real educational challenges. Rather than studying AI in abstract terms, teachers work on projects such as evaluating AI tools for their specific subject area, designing an AI-enhanced unit plan, analyzing student data from learning analytics systems, or developing ethical guidelines for AI use in their schools (Hanshaw & Sullivan, 2025). This approach promotes deep learning through active engagement and produces immediately applicable outcomes that teachers can implement in their practice.

The community of practice model emphasizes collaborative learning and ongoing professional dialogue among educators exploring AI integration. This approach recognizes that AI literacy develops not only through formal instruction but also through sustained conversation, shared problem-solving, and collective reflection on practice. Communities of practice may meet regularly to discuss readings, share experiences with AI tools, troubleshoot implementation challenges, and develop institutional guidelines for ethical AI use (Lin et al., 2025). This model is particularly effective for building institutional capacity and creating supportive cultures around AI innovation in education.

Figure 3. AI training curriculum models

AI Training Curriculum Models

Characteristic	Flexibility	Time Investment	Collaborative Element	Practical Application	Theory Depth
Modular	High	Low	Low	Medium	Low
Project-Based	Medium	Medium	High	High	Medium
Community of Practice	Low	High	High	Medium	High
Hybrid	Variable	Variable	Medium	High	High

As shown in Figure 3, the hybrid model provides the most balanced approach by combining the scalability of modular learning, the contextual relevance of project-based activities, and the collaborative strength of communities of practice.

Hybrid models combine elements from multiple approaches to create comprehensive training experiences that leverage the strengths of each model while mitigating their limitations. For example, a hybrid program might begin with modular content delivery to build foundational knowledge, progress to project-based application where educators implement AI tools in their teaching, and culminate in ongoing participation in a community of practice for sustained professional learning and support (Patias, Miteva, & Peltekova, 2026). These hybrid approaches often prove most effective for developing robust, durable AI literacy that translates into changed practice and improved student outcomes.

3.3 International Case Studies in AI Teacher Training

In Finland, AI training integrated into preservice teacher education has been piloted across multiple universities. Evaluations indicate that over 70% of participating student teachers reported increased confidence in identifying algorithmic bias, and nearly 60% demonstrated improved ability to design AI-supported lesson plans assessed through performance rubrics. The Finnish model's emphasis on ethical reflection workshops alongside technical experimentation illustrates how integrated training can produce measurable professional growth (Mannuru et al., 2025).

In India, several state-level digital education initiatives have begun incorporating AI awareness modules for rural teachers. These programs emphasize low-bandwidth AI tools and focus on data ethics, recognizing infrastructural constraints. Early program evaluations show increased teacher awareness of privacy risks even in environments with limited AI deployment, demonstrating that ethical literacy does not require high technological penetration.

In Singapore, the Ministry of Education has implemented a comprehensive professional development program focused on AI literacy for in-service teachers. The program combines online learning modules with face-to-face workshops and ongoing mentorship support. A distinctive feature is its emphasis on subject-specific AI applications, recognizing that mathematics teachers, language teachers, and science teachers need somewhat different competencies and face distinct challenges in integrating AI into their disciplines (Lee et al., 2026). This differentiated approach has enhanced program relevance and teacher engagement, leading to higher implementation rates of AI-enhanced pedagogies across Singapore's education system.

The United States has seen multiple initiatives at state and district levels, with varying approaches and outcomes. The AI4K12 initiative, developed by the Association for the Advancement of Artificial Intelligence and the Computer Science Teachers Association, provides resources and guidelines for teaching AI across grade levels. While primarily focused on student learning, the initiative has spawned professional development programs that prepare teachers to facilitate AI education (Omidvar & Meihami, 2025). These programs emphasize the integration of AI concepts across curriculum areas rather than treating AI as a separate subject, promoting interdisciplinary thinking and broad-based AI literacy among educators.

In developing regions, AI training initiatives often address unique challenges related to infrastructure limitations, resource constraints, and digital divides. The African School on Internet Governance has included AI literacy components in its teacher training programs, recognizing that African educators need competencies not only for using AI tools but also for critically evaluating their appropriateness in local contexts and advocating for equitable technology policies (Kooli & Chakraoui, 2025). These programs often emphasize low-tech and offline approaches to AI education, developing teacher capacity to teach AI concepts even without extensive computational resources.

4. ETHICAL AND LEGAL DIMENSIONS OF AI IN EDUCATIONAL PRACTICE

The integration of AI into educational settings raises complex ethical and legal questions that educators must navigate as part of their professional responsibility. This section examines key ethical challenges including algorithmic bias, data privacy, surveillance concerns, and equity considerations, while also exploring the legal frameworks that govern AI use in education.

4.1 Understanding and Addressing Algorithmic Bias

Algorithmic bias represents one of the most significant ethical challenges in AI-enhanced education. Bias can enter AI systems through multiple pathways including biased training data, flawed algorithm design, or inappropriate application of systems to contexts different from those for which they were developed. When biased AI systems are used for high-stakes decisions such as student assessment, academic tracking, or resource allocation, they can perpetuate or amplify educational inequalities (Daher, 2025).

Training data bias occurs when the datasets used to develop AI systems do not adequately represent the diversity of student populations. For example, an automated essay scoring system trained primarily on essays written by native English speakers from middle-class backgrounds may systematically undervalue the work of multilingual students or those from different socioeconomic contexts. Similarly, facial recognition systems used for attendance tracking or proctoring have demonstrated significantly higher error rates for individuals with darker skin tones, raising serious concerns about racial bias and equity (Kooli & Chakraoui, 2025).

Algorithm design bias can manifest when the objectives, assumptions, or optimization criteria embedded in AI systems reflect narrow or inappropriate definitions of educational success. An AI tutoring system designed to optimize for test scores might neglect other important learning outcomes such as creativity, critical thinking, or social-emotional development. Educators need competencies to evaluate AI systems not only for their technical performance but also for the values and priorities encoded in their design (Omidvar & Meihami, 2025).

Addressing algorithmic bias requires multiple strategies that educators can implement at institutional and classroom levels:

1) Conducting equity audits of AI systems before implementation to identify potential bias in their operation across different student populations
2) Maintaining human oversight of AI-generated decisions, particularly for high-stakes outcomes that significantly affect student opportunities
3) Advocating for transparency from AI vendors regarding training data, algorithm design, and bias mitigation strategies
4) Implementing diverse teams for AI evaluation and selection to bring multiple perspectives to technology adoption decisions
5) Regularly monitoring AI system outcomes disaggregated by student demographics to detect emergent bias patterns

These strategies position educators as active agents in ensuring fairness rather than passive consumers of potentially biased technology.

4.2 Data Privacy and Protection in AI-Enhanced Learning Environments

The operation of AI systems in education typically requires extensive collection, processing, and analysis of student data. This data-intensive nature of AI raises significant privacy concerns that educators must understand and address to fulfill their ethical and legal obligations to protect students. Privacy challenges in AI-enhanced education extend beyond traditional concerns about data security to encompass issues of surveillance, consent, data ownership, and secondary uses of information collected for educational purposes (Anwar et al., 2025).

Educational AI systems collect diverse types of data including academic performance metrics, behavioral information, engagement patterns, learning preferences, social interactions, and sometimes biometric data such as facial recognition or keystroke patterns. The aggregation and analysis of these data streams can reveal intimate details about students' cognitive abilities, emotional states, personal interests, and family circumstances. While such insights may enhance personalization and instructional effectiveness, they also create risks of privacy violation, unauthorized disclosure, and potential misuse of sensitive information (Zhai, Wibowo, & Li, 2024).

Legal frameworks governing educational data privacy vary across jurisdictions but generally impose obligations on educational institutions and technology providers to protect student information. In the United States, the Family Educational Rights and Privacy Act (FERPA) regulates access to educational records, while the Children's Online Privacy Protection Act (COPPA) provides additional protections for children under 13. The European Union's General Data Protection Regulation (GDPR) establishes comprehensive data protection requirements including principles of data minimization, purpose limitation, and individual rights to access and deletion (Sun, 2023).

Educators need practical understanding of these legal frameworks and their implications for AI implementation. Key privacy principles that should guide educational practice include:

1) Data minimization: Collect only the data necessary for legitimate educational purposes, avoiding excessive surveillance or collection of information unrelated to learning objectives. Educators should critically evaluate whether proposed AI systems require appropriate levels of data access or demand unnecessary intrusion into student privacy.
2) Informed consent: Ensure that students and parents understand what data is being collected, how it will be used, who will have access, and what choices they have regarding participation. This requires clear, accessible communication rather than lengthy legal documents that few people read or understand.

3) Purpose limitation: Use educational data only for the purposes for which it was collected, resisting pressures to repurpose student information for commercial, administrative, or research uses without explicit additional consent. Educators should be particularly vigilant about AI systems that might share or sell student data to third parties.
4) Security safeguards: Implement appropriate technical and organizational measures to protect student data from unauthorized access, breaches, or misuse. This includes understanding how AI vendors protect data and ensuring that institutional policies establish clear security standards for educational technology.
5) Student rights: Respect student rights to access their data, correct inaccuracies, and in some cases request deletion. Educators should facilitate these rights rather than viewing them as obstacles to system operation.

4.3 Navigating Surveillance and Autonomy Concerns

The extensive monitoring capabilities of AI systems in education raise concerns about surveillance that extends beyond privacy to encompass issues of autonomy, trust, and the nature of the educational relationship. When students know they are constantly monitored by AI systems that track their attention, engagement, emotional states, and academic performance, this awareness may alter their behavior, inhibit authentic expression, and create psychological stress (Hanshaw & Sullivan, 2025).

Figure 4. How to ethically implement AI surveillance in education

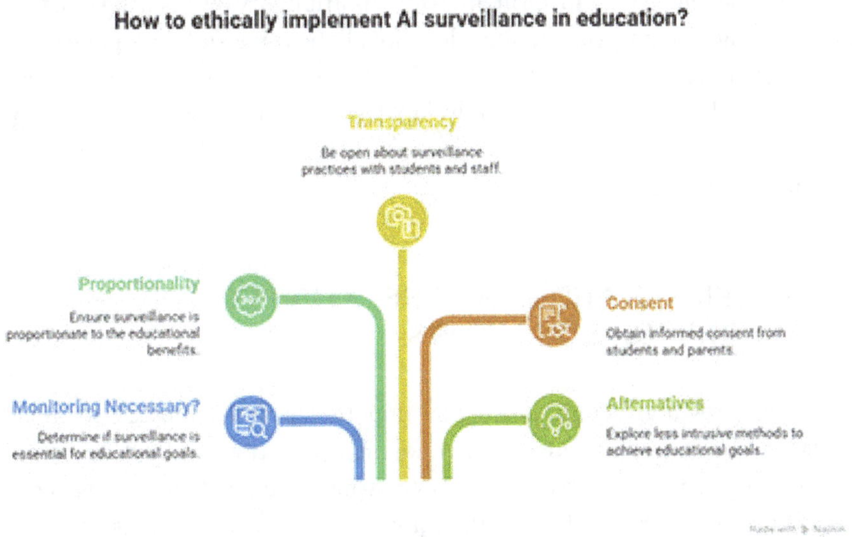

Figure 4 outlines a decision pathway educators can use when evaluating surveillance-based AI tools, emphasizing transparency, proportionality, and student participation in decision-making.

Educational surveillance through AI takes multiple forms. Learning management systems track when students access materials, how long they engage with content, and which resources they find most helpful. Proctoring systems use webcams and algorithms to monitor test-takers for suspicious behavior, eye movements, and background activities. Classroom management systems analyze student attention and engagement, sometimes providing real-time feedback to teachers about who appears focused or distracted. While these surveillance capabilities promise to enhance learning and maintain academic integrity, they also create environments of constant observation that may undermine student autonomy and trust (Omidvar & Meihami, 2025).

The ethical challenge for educators lies in balancing legitimate uses of AI-enabled monitoring with respect for student autonomy and dignity. Not all forms of data collection constitute problematic surveillance. Tracking student progress through learning activities serves clear educational purposes and enables personalized support. However, continuous monitoring of student behavior, emotions, and attention crosses into surveillance territory that raises ethical concerns, particularly when implemented without meaningful student input or consent (Daher, 2025).

Educators can adopt several principles to navigate surveillance concerns responsibly. First, implement the principle of transparency by clearly communicating to students what is being monitored, why, and how the information will be used. Students should not discover monitoring systems after the fact or through inadvertent disclosure. Second, apply the principle of proportionality by ensuring that the extent of monitoring is appropriate to the educational objective and does not exceed what is necessary to achieve legitimate goals. Third, create opportunities for student voice and choice in how monitoring systems are designed and implemented, recognizing that students are stakeholders whose perspectives should inform decisions about surveillance practices.

5. CHALLENGES AND BARRIERS TO EFFECTIVE AI TRAINING FOR EDUCATORS

Despite growing recognition of the importance of AI literacy for educators, numerous challenges impede the development and implementation of effective training programs. These barriers operate at multiple levels including individual, institutional, systemic, and societal, requiring coordinated responses that address root causes rather than merely treating symptoms.

5.1 Resource Constraints and the Digital Divide

Resource limitations represent a fundamental barrier to widespread AI training for educators, particularly in under-resourced schools and regions. Effective professional development requires investment in training programs, expert facilitators, technological infrastructure, and release time for teachers to participate in learning activities. Many educational systems struggle to fund these investments, especially when faced with competing priorities such as reducing class sizes, updating facilities, or providing basic educational materials (Kooli & Chakraoui, 2025).

The digital divide exacerbates resource challenges by creating stark disparities in access to the technologies that enable both AI training and subsequent classroom implementation. Schools serving low-income communities often lack reliable internet connectivity, modern computing devices, and technical support infrastructure necessary for meaningful engagement with AI tools. Teachers in these settings may receive training on AI systems they cannot actually implement due to technological constraints, leading to frustration and wasted professional development resources.

Geographic inequalities compound these challenges, with rural and remote areas frequently experiencing more limited access to both training opportunities and technological infrastructure. Teachers in isolated locations may lack access to in-person professional development and face bandwidth limitations that prevent participation in online training. International disparities are even more pronounced, with educators in many developing countries having minimal exposure to AI technologies and virtually no access to specialized training programs. Teaching, learning, and assessment activities can be implemented across diverse physical and virtual environments, including remote and underserved areas, to improve educational access and outcomes (Susanto et al., 2023).

Addressing resource barriers requires multi-level interventions including:

1) Increased public and private investment in educational technology infrastructure, prioritizing equity in distribution to ensure under-resourced communities receive adequate support
2) Development of low-cost and open-source AI training resources that reduce financial barriers to professional development access
3) Creation of training models that accommodate limited technology access, including offline components and low-bandwidth alternatives
4) Implementation of regional training centers that pool resources and provide shared access to professional development opportunities for educators from multiple schools or districts

5) Advocacy for policy changes that recognize AI literacy as an essential component of teacher preparation and mandate adequate funding for professional development

These strategies acknowledge that addressing resource constraints requires both immediate practical solutions and longer-term systemic change.

5.2 Institutional Resistance and Governance Gaps

Institutional resistance to AI integration and AI training initiatives stems from multiple sources including organizational inertia, competing priorities, skepticism about technology benefits, and concerns about risks. Educational institutions are inherently conservative organizations that change slowly, and the rapid pace of AI development creates tensions between institutional stability and technological innovation. Administrators may hesitate to invest resources in AI training when they perceive the technology as experimental, potentially problematic, or likely to be superseded by newer innovations.

Governance gaps create additional barriers by leaving unclear who is responsible for decisions about AI adoption, training requirements, ethical standards, and quality assurance. In many educational institutions, technology decisions are made by IT departments with limited input from educators or pedagogy experts, leading to misalignment between available tools and instructional needs. Conversely, educators may select AI tools without adequate consideration of privacy implications, security requirements, or institutional policies, creating risks and compliance problems.

The absence of clear governance structures for AI in education means that critical questions often remain unresolved. Who decides which AI systems are acceptable for classroom use? What standards should guide vendor selection? Who evaluates whether AI tools are effective and ethical? How should student data be protected? What training is required before teachers can use AI systems? Without institutional frameworks that address these questions, AI integration proceeds haphazardly with inconsistent practices and inadequate safeguards.

Teacher unions and professional associations play complex roles in navigating institutional resistance and governance challenges. While these organizations advocate for professional development resources and teacher welfare, they may also resist changes perceived as threatening to teacher autonomy, increasing workload, or enabling surveillance of educator performance through AI-enabled monitoring. Productive engagement with these stakeholders requires acknowledging legitimate concerns while building shared understanding of how AI training can empower rather than undermine educators.

Overcoming institutional resistance and governance gaps requires deliberate organizational change strategies. Successful approaches include establishing cross-functional committees that bring together educators, administrators, IT professionals, and other stakeholders to develop shared governance frameworks. Creating pilot programs that demonstrate benefits while addressing risks can build institutional confidence in AI integration. Developing clear policies that establish roles, responsibilities, standards, and accountability mechanisms provides necessary structure for responsible AI adoption.

5.3 Ethical Dilemmas in AI-Powered Assessment and Decision-Making

The use of AI systems for student assessment and educational decision-making presents particularly challenging ethical dilemmas that many educators feel ill-equipped to navigate. These dilemmas arise from tensions between efficiency and fairness, standardization and individualization, human judgment and algorithmic objectivity, creating situations where there are no clearly right answers but only more or less ethically defensible choices.

Automated assessment systems exemplify these dilemmas. AI-powered essay grading promises consistent scoring, rapid feedback, and freed teacher time for higher-value instructional activities. However, these systems may fail to recognize creative or unconventional responses, privileging formulaic writing that matches algorithmic expectations. They may also introduce or perpetuate biases based on language use patterns, writing styles, or cultural references that differ from those in training data (Daher, 2025). Educators must decide whether the benefits of automated grading justify these limitations and risks, recognizing that their choices affect students' academic outcomes and opportunities.

Predictive analytics for student success present another ethically complex application of AI in education. These systems analyze multiple data points to identify students at risk of academic failure, course dropout, or other negative outcomes. Early identification enables targeted interventions that may prevent problems before they become severe. However, prediction is not destiny, and labeling students as at-risk based on algorithmic assessments may create self-fulfilling prophecies where reduced expectations lead to diminished performance. Furthermore, such systems may perpetuate historical inequalities by identifying as at-risk students from demographic groups that have historically faced educational barriers, thereby reinforcing rather than disrupting patterns of disadvantage.

AI-driven placement and tracking decisions raise similar concerns. When algorithms recommend students for advanced, standard, or remedial academic tracks based on prior performance data and demographic characteristics, they make determinations with profound impacts on educational trajectories and life opportunities. While proponents argue that data-driven placement is more objective than human judgment, critics note that algorithms may encode and automate historical biases while stripping away the contextual understanding and holistic assessment that educators bring to such decisions.

Educators face ethical responsibility to interrogate these systems, understand their limitations, and advocate for appropriate human oversight of high-stakes decisions. This requires not only technical knowledge about how AI systems function but also ethical frameworks for evaluating when algorithmic decision-making is appropriate, what safeguards are necessary, and how to ensure that efficiency gains do not come at the cost of fairness and student welfare. Training programs must equip teachers with both the analytical tools and the moral courage to question systems, challenge problematic practices, and prioritize student interests over technological convenience.

6. POLICY AND GOVERNANCE FRAMEWORKS FOR AI IN EDUCATION

Effective integration of AI into educational practice requires comprehensive policy and governance frameworks that establish standards, allocate responsibilities, ensure accountability, and protect stakeholder interests. This section examines policy considerations at institutional, national, and international levels, providing recommendations for governance structures that support responsible AI adoption while enabling innovation and continuous improvement.

6.1 Institutional Policies for Responsible AI Implementation

Figure 5. The institutional AI governance cycle, illustrating how policy development, system selection, implementation, professional development, and evaluation form an integrated, iterative process for responsible AI adoption in educational settings

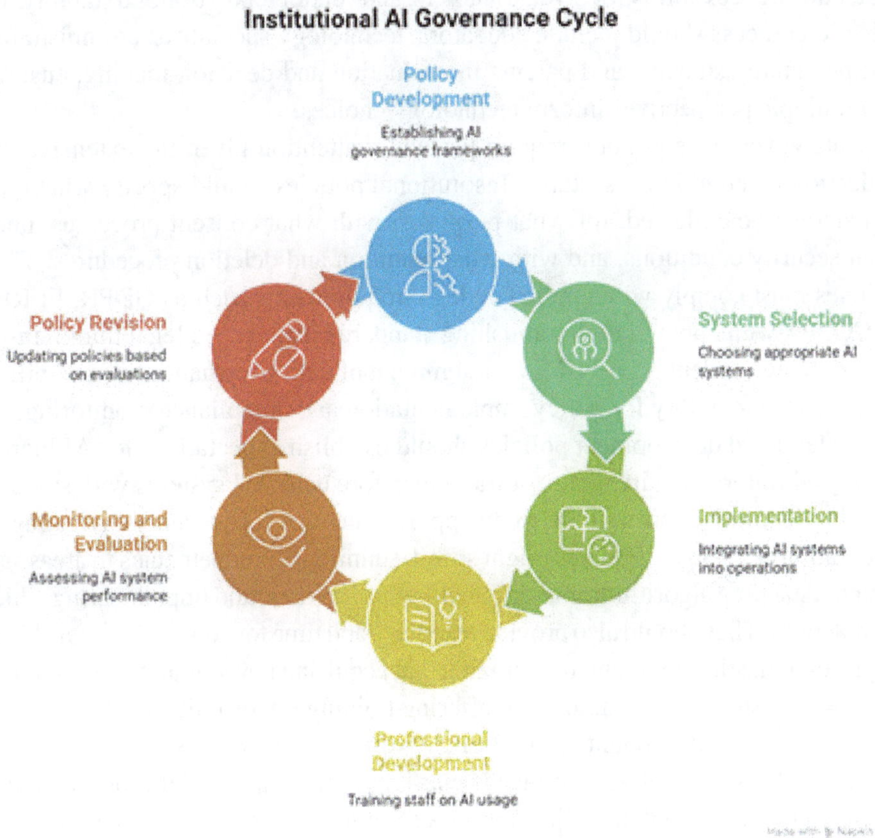

Educational institutions need clear policies that govern AI system selection, implementation, evaluation, and ongoing oversight. These policies should address multiple dimensions including pedagogical appropriateness, ethical standards, data protection, vendor management, and professional development requirements. Well-designed institutional policies provide clarity for educators about what is expected and permitted, protect students from potential harms, and establish accountability mechanisms for ensuring compliance with standards.

Policies for AI system selection should establish criteria and processes for evaluating potential tools before adoption. These criteria might include alignment with institutional educational philosophy, evidence of effectiveness for intended purposes, transparency about algorithm design and training data, data privacy and security protections, accessibility for diverse learners, and vendor reputation and stability. The selection process should include educators, technology specialists, administrators, and potentially students and parents in evaluation and decision-making, ensuring that multiple perspectives inform technology choices.

Data governance policies require particular attention given the extensive data collection inherent in AI systems. Institutional policies should specify what types of data can be collected, for what purposes, with what consent processes, under what security conditions, and with what retention and deletion procedures. These policies must comply with applicable legal requirements such as GDPR, FERPA, or COPPA while potentially establishing standards that exceed legal minimums to better protect student privacy. Clear assignment of data governance responsibilities ensures accountability for policy implementation and compliance monitoring.

Professional development policies should establish expectations for AI literacy among educators, requirements for training before using AI systems with students, ongoing learning opportunities, and support structures for teachers navigating AI integration challenges. Policies might specify minimum competencies in areas such as understanding algorithmic bias, protecting student data, and implementing ethical AI practices. They should also provide resources and time for educators to participate in professional development, recognizing that acquiring new competencies requires institutional support beyond merely offering training opportunities.

Evaluation and accountability policies establish mechanisms for assessing whether AI systems deliver promised benefits, identifying problems or unintended consequences, and making adjustments based on evidence. These policies should specify what data will be collected to evaluate AI effectiveness and impact, how this evaluation data will be analyzed and reported, who is responsible for conducting evaluations, and what decision processes follow from evaluation findings. Regular evaluation enables evidence-based improvement and prevents continued use of ineffective or harmful systems simply because they have been adopted.

6.2 National Frameworks and Educational Technology Standards

National educational authorities play crucial roles in establishing frameworks that guide AI integration across school systems, teacher preparation programs, and educational research. These frameworks can provide coherence and quality assurance while allowing flexibility for local adaptation and innovation. Countries that have developed comprehensive national AI in education strategies offer valuable models for others seeking to support responsible technology integration.

National frameworks typically address several key areas including curriculum standards for AI literacy, teacher certification requirements, data protection regulations, research and development priorities, and funding mechanisms for infrastructure and professional development. Effective frameworks balance multiple objectives such as promoting innovation, ensuring equity, protecting rights, and maintaining quality. They also establish coordination mechanisms across different government agencies, recognizing that AI in education intersects with technology policy, data protection law, education standards, and other policy domains.

Teacher preparation and certification standards represent an important policy lever for ensuring educator AI literacy. National frameworks can establish competencies that preservice teachers must demonstrate before certification, require teacher education programs to incorporate AI literacy content, and mandate continuing education in AI for practicing teachers. These requirements signal the importance of AI competencies while creating incentives for teacher education institutions to develop and deliver relevant training. However, standards must be carefully designed to be achievable given available resources and to allow flexibility for different subject areas and educational contexts.

Data protection and privacy frameworks at the national level establish legal requirements and enforcement mechanisms that provide stronger protections than institutional policies alone can offer. Comprehensive data protection laws specify rights and responsibilities, establish oversight bodies with investigative and enforcement powers, and create accountability for violations. Educational data often receives special protection in recognition of the vulnerability of student populations and the sensitivity of information collected in school settings. National frameworks should address consent requirements, data minimization principles, security standards, cross-border data flows, and individual rights regarding personal information.

Research and evidence-generation policies can accelerate understanding of effective AI integration practices and identify potential problems early. National frameworks might fund research on AI effectiveness in education, establish pilot programs that test innovative approaches under controlled conditions, require evaluation of large-scale AI implementations, or create repositories of evidence and best practices that educators and policymakers can access. Investment in research and evaluation infrastructure ensures that policy development and practice improvement rest on solid evidence rather than speculation or vendor marketing claims.

6.3 International Standards and Cross-Border Considerations

International organizations and agreements play increasingly important roles in shaping AI in education, particularly as educational technology companies operate globally and AI systems trained in one country are deployed in others. International standards can promote interoperability, establish baseline ethical principles, facilitate cross-border learning, and address challenges that transcend national boundaries. However, they must also respect cultural diversity, varied educational traditions, and different developmental contexts.

UNESCO's Recommendation on the Ethics of Artificial Intelligence, adopted in 2021, provides a comprehensive framework that addresses AI across all sectors including education. The recommendation establishes principles such as respect for human rights and dignity, environmental sustainability, transparency and explainability, and accountability. It specifically addresses AI in education, emphasizing the importance of human agency and oversight, quality and equity in education, and protection of vulnerable populations. While not legally binding, the UNESCO recommendation influences national policy development and provides a common reference point for international discussions.

The OECD has also contributed to international AI governance through principles and recommendations that emphasize human-centered values, transparency, robustness and safety, accountability, and inclusive growth. The OECD's work on digital education and skills development provides frameworks for thinking about how education systems can prepare learners for an AI-influenced future. These international frameworks help establish shared language and concepts that facilitate cross-border dialogue and cooperation on AI in education challenges.

Cross-border data flows present particular challenges for educational AI systems. Many AI tools used in education are provided by multinational companies that may store and process student data in multiple jurisdictions. When data protection laws differ across countries, questions arise about which standards apply and how rights can be enforced. International agreements on data protection and transfer can provide clarity, though significant variations persist in how different regions balance innovation, privacy, and security concerns. Educational institutions using international AI systems must understand where student data is stored and processed and what protections apply in those jurisdictions.

International professional organizations for educators play important roles in developing and disseminating best practices for AI integration. Organizations such as the International Society for Technology in Education (ISTE) create standards and resources that inform professional development globally. These organizations facilitate knowledge exchange across borders, enabling educators to learn from international experiences and adapt successful approaches to their own contexts.

They also provide platforms for collective advocacy on issues such as ethical AI use, educator professional development needs, and equity concerns.

7. FUTURE DIRECTIONS IN AI TRAINING FOR EDUCATORS

The landscape of AI in education continues to evolve rapidly, requiring that professional development approaches remain dynamic and forward-looking. This section explores emerging trends, anticipated challenges, and opportunities that will shape the future of AI training for educators over the coming decade.

Practical examples of generative AI in education include tools such as ChatGPT for lesson planning assistance, Bard for multilingual content generation, and AI-supported learning analytics dashboards that provide real-time insights into student engagement patterns.

7.1 Emerging Technologies and Pedagogical Innovation

Emerging AI technologies are expected to significantly reshape educational practices, creating both opportunities and challenges for educators. Generative AI systems capable of producing text, images, and multimedia content require teachers to reconsider traditional approaches to assessment, academic integrity, and the authenticity of student work. At the same time, multimodal AI systems that process diverse forms of data—such as text, diagrams, and visual media—can provide richer feedback and enable personalized instructional materials tailored to individual learning preferences. To effectively integrate these technologies, educators must develop competencies that allow them to evaluate AI tools critically and apply them in ways that enhance rather than replace human-centered teaching.

At the same time, emerging technologies such as emotional AI and AI-enhanced virtual or augmented reality introduce new ethical and pedagogical considerations. Emotional AI systems that attempt to detect student engagement or affective states may offer timely support for struggling learners but also raise concerns related to privacy, accuracy, and potential misuse. Similarly, AI-driven immersive learning environments can simulate complex scenarios and enable collaborative experiences beyond traditional classrooms, yet they require careful instructional design to ensure meaningful learning outcomes. Consequently, future training programs for educators must address both the technical understanding of these technologies and the ethical frameworks needed to guide their responsible use in educational settings.

7.2 Lifelong Learning and Continuous Professional Development

The rapid advancement of artificial intelligence means that one-time training is insufficient to maintain educators' competencies throughout their careers. Instead, AI professional development must evolve toward continuous learning models that support ongoing adaptation and skill refinement. This shift requires moving beyond occasional training workshops toward sustained learning ecosystems that offer multiple pathways for competency development. Approaches such as microlearning modules allow educators to engage with concise, targeted content during flexible timeframes, ensuring that training remains responsive to emerging technologies, research developments, and evolving pedagogical practices.

Collaborative learning structures also play an important role in sustaining professional growth. Communities of practice and professional learning networks enable educators to share experiences, exchange strategies, and collectively develop knowledge about effective AI integration. Complementary support mechanisms such as just-in-time learning resources, mentoring systems, and AI-assisted help platforms can provide timely guidance when educators encounter challenges in implementing AI tools. Additionally, credentialing systems such as micro-credentials and digital badges can recognize the progressive development of AI-related competencies, motivating continuous professional learning while providing institutions with evidence of educators' evolving expertise..

7.3 Cultivating Critical AI Literacy as a Core Educational Value

Perhaps the most important future direction for AI training involves elevating critical AI literacy from a technical skill to a fundamental educational value comparable to critical thinking, ethical reasoning, or scientific literacy. This vision positions AI literacy not as mastery of particular tools or techniques but as a disposition of thoughtful, questioning engagement with technological systems and their social implications. Achieving this vision requires cultural change within education that recognizes AI literacy as essential to contemporary teaching practice and student preparation for civic participation (Walter, 2024).

Critical AI literacy refers to a set of interconnected competencies that go beyond technical understanding of artificial intelligence. It includes the ability to recognize when AI systems are used, critically evaluate their appropriateness, and understand how these systems may reflect or amplify the values and biases of their designers. Developing this literacy among educators requires professional development that not only teaches tools and ethical principles but also encourages reflection on broader questions about the purpose of education, the relationship between humans and technology, and the societal implications of AI. Equally important is fostering educator agency, enabling teachers to actively shape how AI is implemented in their classrooms and institutions rather than simply adapting to technological change..

7.4 Evaluating the Impact of AI Training Programs

Effective AI training initiatives require systematic evaluation beyond participant satisfaction surveys. Impact assessment should include pre- and post-training competency measurement, classroom implementation tracking, student outcome analysis, and longitudinal follow-up to assess sustained behavioral change. Mixed-method approaches combining self-efficacy scales, lesson plan analysis, and institutional policy shifts offer more robust insight into program effectiveness (Santomartino & Yi, 2022).

Emerging studies suggest that teachers who complete structured AI literacy programs demonstrate increased confidence in ethical decision-making and reduced reliance on unverified AI outputs. However, long-term evidence remains limited, underscoring the need for continued empirical research on training impact.

Beyond teacher self-efficacy, impact evaluation should also examine downstream student outcomes, including changes in assessment design, critical AI awareness among learners, and shifts in classroom dialogue around ethical technology use. Institutional indicators such as policy revisions, procurement standards, and data governance reforms can further signal systemic transformation. Longitudinal tracking is particularly important, as short-term confidence gains may not translate into sustained behavioral change without organizational reinforcement.

A structured evaluation framework for AI training should include four key indicators:

(1) educator AI competency development measured through pre- and post-training assessments,
(2) classroom implementation rates of AI-supported pedagogy,
(3) student outcomes including critical AI awareness and engagement, and
(4) institutional policy development related to ethical AI governance.

8. CONCLUSION

This chapter has moved from conceptual foundations to governance implications, illustrating how ethical AI training must operate simultaneously at classroom, institutional, and policy levels.

The integration of artificial intelligence into educational systems represents one of the most significant transformations in the history of formal education. This transformation creates both tremendous opportunities for enhancing teaching and learning and serious risks to student welfare, privacy, and equity. Whether AI ultimately serves to democratize education and improve outcomes for all learners or exacerbates existing inequalities depends significantly on the preparation and competency of educators who implement these technologies in classrooms and schools.

This chapter has argued that comprehensive AI training for educators is essential to realizing the positive potential of AI while mitigating its risks. Such training must address multiple dimensions including technical understanding of how AI systems function, pedagogical knowledge for effective integration of AI tools, ethical frameworks for navigating complex moral terrain, data literacy for protecting student privacy, and advocacy competencies for shaping institutional policies and practices. The frameworks, case studies, and recommendations presented here provide foundations for developing effective programs adapted to specific circumstances.

The challenges to implementing effective AI training for educators are substantial, including resource constraints, institutional resistance, governance gaps, and the rapid pace of technological change. Addressing these challenges requires coordinated action at multiple levels from individual educators developing their own competencies, to institutions creating supportive policies and professional development opportunities, to national governments establishing frameworks and standards, to international organizations facilitating cross-border cooperation and knowledge exchange.

Several key principles should guide ongoing efforts to build educator AI literacy and competency. Human agency and oversight must remain central in educational AI systems, where technology should augment and support human teaching rather than replace educator judgment and professional discretion. Equity and inclusion must be prioritized in both the design of training programs and the implementation of AI systems, ensuring accessibility for educators in diverse contexts including under-resourced schools and developing regions. Privacy and dignity must be protected through thoughtful data governance, meaningful consent processes, and appropriate limits on surveillance. Critical thinking and ethical reasoning are as important as technical skills in preparing educators for AI-enhanced teaching, and professional development must be ongoing rather than episodic, recognizing that AI technology and best practices evolve continuously.

Looking forward, the most pressing need is for cultural change within education that recognizes AI literacy as a core professional competency rather than an optional specialization. When understanding AI becomes as fundamental to teaching as knowledge of child development, assessment principles, or instructional design, the profession will be positioned to engage with these technologies thoughtfully and effectively. Achieving this vision requires commitment from all stakeholders in education including teachers, administrators, policymakers, teacher educators, technology developers, and researchers.

The stakes in this endeavor extend beyond improving educational outcomes or maintaining institutional competitiveness. At its core, the question of AI training for educators concerns what kind of educational system and what kind of society we wish to create. Educators are uniquely positioned to influence these outcomes through their daily choices about technology use, their advocacy for policies that protect student interests, their modeling of critical engagement with technology for students, and their collective voice in shaping the future of their profession. However, they can fulfill these responsibilities only if provided with the training, resources, support, and institutional structures necessary for informed, ethical practice.

Ultimately, AI training for educators is not merely a technological adaptation project but a democratic and ethical endeavor. It determines who benefits from AI, who bears its risks, and how educational values are preserved in algorithmically mediated environments.

The work of training educators for AI-enhanced teaching is ongoing and will never be complete given the continuous evolution of technology and society. By attending to technical, pedagogical, ethical, and policy dimensions simultaneously, and by centering human welfare and educational values in all decisions about technology integration, educators and educational systems can navigate the AI revolution in ways that honor their fundamental commitments to student learning, growth, and flourishing. The future of education in the age of artificial intelligence will be shaped by the wisdom, skill, and ethical commitment that educators bring to this technological transformation.

REFERENCES

Anwar, N., Rahaman, R., Widodo, A. M., Sekti, B. A., Erzed, N., Santiago Tangkudung, R. R., . . . Budhisantosa, N. (2025). Sustainable cybersecurity in the AI era: Innovations in green computing and security. In *Sustainable Information Security in the Age of AI and Green Computing* (pp. 603–620). DOI: 10.4018/979-8-3693-8034-5.ch030

Daher, R. (2025). Integrating AI literacy into teacher education: A critical perspective paper. *Discover Artificial Intelligence*, *5*(1), 217. Advance online publication. DOI: 10.1007/s44163-025-00475-7

de Putter-Smits, L. G. A., Pols, C. F. J., Dekkers, P. J. J. M., Runhaar, P. R., Timmer, M., & Van der Veen, J. T. (2025). Exploring the role of generative AI in science teacher education programs: A qualitative study. *International Journal of Educational Research Open*, *9*, 100492. Advance online publication. DOI: 10.1016/j.ijedro.2025.100492

Hanshaw, G., & Sullivan, C. (2025). Exploring barriers to AI course assistant adoption: A mixed-methods study on student non-utilization. *Discover Artificial Intelligence*, *5*(1), 178. Advance online publication. DOI: 10.1007/s44163-025-00312-x

Kooli, C., & Chakraoui, R. (2025). AI-driven assistive technologies in inclusive education: Benefits, challenges, and policy recommendations. *Sustainable Futures : An Applied Journal of Technology, Environment and Society*, *10*, 101042. Advance online publication. DOI: 10.1016/j.sftr.2025.101042

Krumsvik, R. J. (2020). Home schooling, remote teaching and digital Bildung in societal crisis. *Nordic Journal of Digital Literacy*, *15*(2), 71–85. DOI: 10.18261/issn.1891-943x-2020-02-01

Lee, S. C., Baby, T., Vongvit, R., Lee, J., Kim, Y. W., Cha, M. C., & Yoon, S. H. (2026). Development and validation of Generative AI Competence Scale (GenAIComp) among university students. *Technology in Society*, *84*, 103059. Advance online publication. DOI: 10.1016/j.techsoc.2025.103059

Lin, J., Liao, Z., Dai, J., Wang, M., Yu, R., Yang, H., & Liu, C. (2025). Digital and artificial intelligence-assisted cephalometric training effectively enhanced students' landmarking accuracy in preclinical orthodontic education. *BMC Oral Health*, *25*(1), 623. Advance online publication. DOI: 10.1186/s12903-025-05978-4 PMID: 40275285

Mannuru, N. R., Shahriar, S., Teel, Z. A., Wang, T., Lund, B. D., Tijani, S., … Vaidya, P. (2025). Artificial intelligence in developing countries: The impact of generative artificial intelligence (AI) technologies for development. *Information Development, 41*(3 Special Issue: "Artificial Intelligence initiatives"), 1036–1054. DOI: 10.1177/02666669231200628

Omidvar, S., & Meihami, H. (2025). Exploring the "what" and "how" of opportunities and challenges of AI in EFL teacher education. *Computers and Education: Artificial Intelligence*, *9*, 100443. Advance online publication. DOI: 10.1016/j.caeai.2025.100443

Patias, I., Miteva, D., & Peltekova, E. (2026). Using Old Lessons for New AI – A Trainer for Project Risk Management. In *Lecture Notes in Computer Science* (Vol. 16119 LNAI, pp. 155–167). DOI: 10.1007/978-3-032-05607-8_16

Pham, S. T. H. (2025). An empirical investigation of the experience of educators and politicians with the emergence of artificial intelligence in education. *Technology in Society*, *83*, 102965. Advance online publication. DOI: 10.1016/j.techsoc.2025.102965

Santomartino, S. M., & Yi, P. H. (2022). Systematic Review of Radiologist and Medical Student Attitudes on the Role and Impact of AI in Radiology. *Academic Radiology*, *29*(11), 1748–1756. DOI: 10.1016/j.acra.2021.12.032 PMID: 35105524

Sekti, B. A. (2025a). Foundations of Artificial Intelligence Ethics. In *Navigating Social Trust in the AI Era* (pp. 23–47). DOI: 10.4018/979-8-3373-7011-8.ch002

Sekti, B. A. (2025b). Machine Learning vs. AI: Key Concepts. In *Implementing Enterprise Cybersecurity With AI* (pp. 1–27). DOI: 10.4018/979-8-3373-2252-0.ch001

Sun, J. C. (2023). Gaps, guesswork, and ghosts lurking in technology integration: Laws and policies applicable to student privacy. *British Journal of Educational Technology*, *54*(6), 1604–1618. DOI: 10.1111/bjet.13379

Susanto, G. W. A., Maulana, H., Putri, P. H., Purwaningrahayu, R. D., Wijaya, A. A., Sekti, B. A., & Karuniawan, A. (2023). Stability Analysis to Select the Stable and High Yielding of Black Soybean (Glycine max (L) Merril) in Indonesia. *International Journal of Agronomy*, *2023*, 1–14. Advance online publication. DOI: 10.1155/2023/7255444

Tapalova, O., & Zhiyenbayeva, N. (2022). Artificial Intelligence in Education: AIEd for Personalised Learning Pathways. *Electronic Journal of e-Learning*, *20*(5), 639–653. DOI: 10.34190/ejel.20.5.2597

Walter, Y. (2024). Embracing the future of Artificial Intelligence in the classroom: The relevance of AI literacy, prompt engineering, and critical thinking in modern education. *International Journal of Educational Technology in Higher Education, 21*(1), 15. Advance online publication. DOI: 10.1186/s41239-024-00448-3

Zhai, C., Wibowo, S., & Li, L. D. (2024). The effects of over-reliance on AI dialogue systems on students' cognitive abilities: A systematic review. *Smart Learning Environments, 11*(1), 28. Advance online publication. DOI: 10.1186/s40561-024-00316-7

Chapter 5
Building Ethical Awareness in AI-Enhanced Educator Training for Responsible and Inclusive Learning Environments

Rampelli Manojkumar
http://orcid.org/0000-0002-8141-0321
BVRIT HYDERABAD College of Engineering for Women, India

Padmavati E. Gundgurti
BVRIT HYDERABAD College of Engineering for Women, India

T. Aditya Sai Srinivas
http://orcid.org/0009-0006-6164-7029
Ravindra College of Engineering for Women, India

Ramesh Babu Pittala
http://orcid.org/0000-0003-2420-8183
Anurag University, India

Aravinda Swamy Konda
Malla Reddy College of Engineering and Technology, India

Bansilal Bairwa
REVA University, India

ABSTRACT

Artificial intelligence is increasingly embedded in educational practices, reshaping teaching, learning, assessment, and institutional decision-making. While AI-enabled systems promise efficiency, personalization, and data-informed insights, they also introduce significant ethical challenges related to algorithmic bias, data privacy, transparency, accountability, and power asymmetries. This chapter examines these

DOI: 10.4018/979-8-2600-1840-8.ch005

ethical challenges and argues that responsible AI adoption in education requires more than technical solutions or regulatory compliance. It positions educators as central ethical actors whose awareness, judgment, and agency are critical in mediating AI use in classrooms. By aligning ethical principles with educator capacity and governance structures, the chapter contributes to advancing fair, inclusive, and human-centered AI-enhanced learning environments.

INTRODUCTION

Artificial intelligence (AI) has rapidly transitioned from a peripheral innovation to a foundational component of contemporary educational ecosystems, influencing teaching practices, learning design, assessment mechanisms, and institutional decision-making. AI-driven tools now support adaptive learning systems, automated grading, predictive analytics, and personalized feedback, offering the promise of enhanced efficiency, scalability, and learner-centered education. However, as AI becomes embedded within everyday educational practices, it simultaneously introduces a range of ethical challenges that fundamentally reshape the professional responsibilities of educators. These challenges are no longer speculative or distant; rather, they are immediate, practical, and deeply consequential for issues of fairness, trust, inclusion, and human agency in education (Akgun & Greenhow, 2022; Holmes et al., 2022). Educators increasingly find themselves positioned as intermediaries between complex AI systems and learners, expected to use these technologies effectively while remaining accountable for their pedagogical and ethical implications, often without adequate preparation or institutional support.

A growing body of scholarship emphasizes that ethical concerns in AI-enhanced education extend well beyond technical accuracy or system performance. Algorithmic bias, opacity in automated decision-making, and extensive data collection practices pose significant risks to equity and student rights, particularly when AI systems are deployed without sufficient transparency or contextual understanding. Studies have shown that biases embedded in training data or system design can disadvantage already marginalized learners, reinforcing structural inequalities under the guise of objectivity (Holmes et al., 2022; Yu & Yu, 2023). At the same time, the widespread use of learning analytics and AI-powered monitoring tools raises concerns related to surveillance, consent, data ownership, and long-term data governance, issues that educators are often ill-equipped to address due to limited awareness of how such systems function (Chen, 2024). The opacity of many AI systems further complicates ethical practice, as educators may struggle to explain or justify AI-generated outcomes to students, thereby undermining transparency, trust, and pedagogical accountability.

Despite increasing recognition of these challenges, ethical engagement with AI in education has largely remained fragmented across policy discourse, technical research, and isolated curriculum initiatives. Yu and Yu (2023) demonstrate that while research on AI ethics in education has expanded significantly, it often lacks coherence and practical integration into teacher education and professional development. National AI strategies similarly reveal a disconnect between ethical aspirations and educational practice. Schiff (2022) argues that many policy frameworks emphasize AI for economic growth and workforce readiness while neglecting the role of education in cultivating ethical understanding and critical engagement with AI. As a result, educators are frequently treated as passive implementers of AI systems rather than as ethical agents capable of questioning, shaping, and contextualizing AI use. This gap is particularly concerning given the rapid proliferation of generative AI tools, such as large language models, which introduce new ethical dilemmas related to academic integrity, authorship, dependency, and misinformation across disciplines (Jeyaraman et al., 2023).

Recent scholarship increasingly converges on the view that responsible AI in education cannot be achieved through technological design or regulatory frameworks alone, but must be grounded in human judgment, ethical reflection, and educator agency. Porayska-Pomsta (2024) argues for a proactively responsible approach to AI in education, emphasizing shared accountability among educators, institutions, and developers. Similarly, Domínguez Figaredo and Stoyanovich (2023) highlight the importance of responsible AI literacy that foregrounds stakeholder perspectives and ethical reasoning rather than tool-centric competence. Efforts to embed ethics into higher education curricula and professional training further reinforce this shift, advocating interdisciplinary, context-sensitive approaches that address fairness, privacy, and cultural values alongside technical understanding (Alam, 2023; Aler Tubella et al., 2024). Importantly, ethical frameworks must also be attentive to global and cultural diversity, as ethical priorities and educational realities vary significantly across regions, particularly in the Global South (Kiemde & Kora, 2022). Within this broader context, educators emerge as central ethical actors whose awareness, judgment, and reflective practice are critical to ensuring that AI supports inclusive, equitable, and human-centered learning environments rather than undermining them.

While artificial intelligence is often framed as a universal catalyst for educational innovation, emerging scholarship highlights that its ethical implications are profoundly context-dependent, particularly across Global North and Global South settings. In many regions of the Global South, AI adoption in education unfolds within constraints related to infrastructure, regulatory capacity, and asymmetric data economies, raising distinct ethical concerns around inclusion, equity, and shared benefit (Mutambara, 2025; Henadirage & Gunarathne, 2025). Rather than merely replicating Western models of AI-enabled education, these contexts expose how AI systems can reinforce structural inequalities through uneven access, opaque platform governance, and data extractivist practices that prioritize institutional or commercial value over learner rights (Poyares, 2025). Ethical AI in education must therefore be understood not as a uniform technical standard, but as a situated practice shaped by geopolitical, economic, and institutional conditions.

Within these uneven AI ecosystems, educators increasingly perform what can be understood as ethical labor—the ongoing cognitive, emotional, and professional work of interpreting algorithmic outputs, mediating student concerns, and compensating for the opacity of AI systems in everyday pedagogical practice. Recent studies show that while professional development can strengthen teacher agency in addressing ethical challenges of AI-enhanced education, educators' capacity to act ethically is often constrained by institutional policies, procurement decisions, and governance structures that lie beyond their control (Mouta et al., 2025; Jin et al., 2025). This highlights a critical limitation of approaches that position educators as sole ethical intermediaries. Ethical responsibility for AI in education cannot rest on individual agency alone but must be supported by institutional protections, transparent adoption policies, and shared accountability mechanisms. Foregrounding ethical labor at the outset underscores that responsible AI adoption is not only a matter of educator competence, but also of institutional commitment to fairness, transparency, and sustainable professional practice.

This chapter positions ethical awareness as a core professional competence for educators operating in AI-enhanced learning environments. Rather than treating ethics as an ancillary concern or post hoc compliance requirement, it argues that ethical reflection must be systematically embedded within educator training and professional development. Ethical awareness, as conceptualized here, involves understanding the social and pedagogical implications of AI systems, recognizing ethical risks, engaging critically with algorithmic outputs, and advocating for transparency and accountability within institutional structures. By focusing on educator-centered ethics training, the chapter responds to persistent gaps identified in the literature between ethical discourse and practical implementation (Farooqi et al., 2024). It advances the argument that educators, when equipped with ethical literacy and supported by institutional frameworks, can serve as ethical leaders in AI adoption, fostering learning environments that respect human agency, protect student data, and promote fairness and inclusion. The sections that follow build on this foundation by examining specific ethical challenges of AI in education, proposing structured models for integrating ethics into educator training, and exploring institutional and policy frameworks that support responsible and sustainable AI use in educational contexts.

AI AND ETHICAL CHALLENGES IN MODERN EDUCATION

The growing adoption of artificial intelligence in education has transformed pedagogical practices, assessment systems, and institutional decision-making processes. AI-driven technologies are now routinely used for personalized learning, automated grading, learning analytics, early warning systems, and generative content creation. While these systems promise efficiency, scalability, and data-informed insights, they also introduce profound ethical challenges that directly affect educational equity, learner autonomy, and institutional accountability. Unlike traditional educational technologies, AI systems do not merely support instruction; they actively participate in decision-making, shaping how learners are evaluated, categorized, and supported. As a result, ethical concerns related to bias, privacy, transparency, and accountability are no longer peripheral considerations but central issues that influence the legitimacy and trustworthiness of AI-enhanced education (Memarian & Doleck, 2023). As shown in Figure 1, concerns related to bias, privacy, transparency, and accountability form the core ethical dimensions of AI-enhanced education.

Figure 1. AI and ethical challenges in modern education

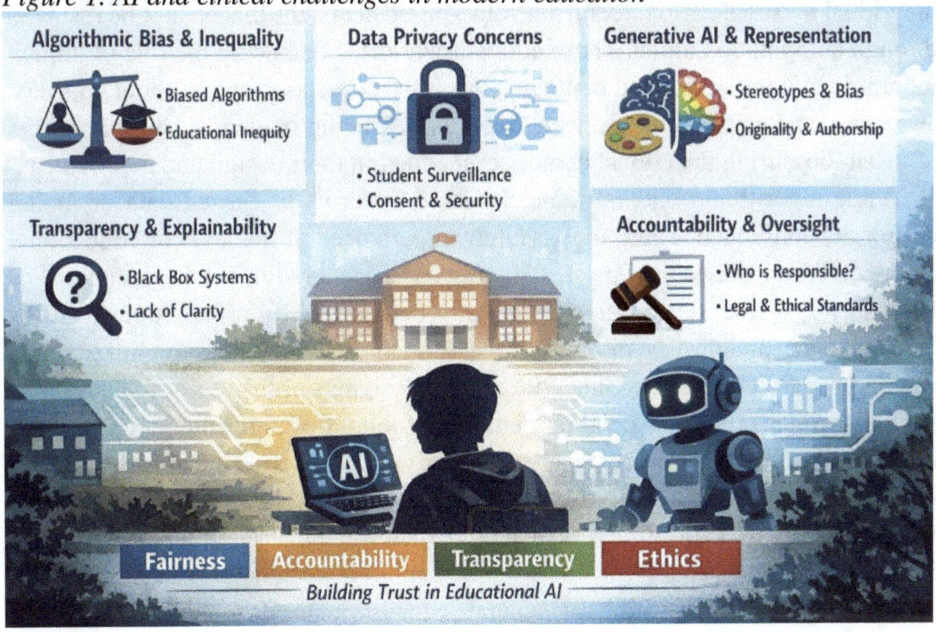

Algorithmic Bias and Educational Inequality

Algorithmic bias is one of the most extensively examined ethical challenges in educational AI. Bias occurs when AI systems produce systematically unfair outcomes for certain groups of learners due to skewed data, inappropriate proxies for learning, or design assumptions that fail to account for contextual diversity. Baker and Hawn (2022) demonstrate that educational datasets often reflect historical inequities related to socioeconomic status, race, language background, and access to learning resources. When such datasets are used to train predictive models or automated assessment systems, these inequities can become embedded in algorithmic outputs, reinforcing disadvantage under the appearance of objectivity. In high-stakes contexts such as grading, placement, and academic risk prediction, biased algorithms can significantly influence students' educational trajectories, often without their awareness or ability to contest outcomes.

Importantly, algorithmic bias in education cannot be understood solely as a technical malfunction. Kizilcec and Lee (2022) argue that fairness in educational AI is inherently normative, as different definitions of fairness prioritize different ethical values. For example, optimizing for equal outcomes may conflict with optimizing for individual personalization, requiring value-based decisions that cannot be resolved through computation alone. These ethical trade-offs underscore the role of human judgment in interpreting and deploying AI systems responsibly. Without educator awareness and critical engagement, AI tools risk being treated as neutral arbiters of merit, obscuring the ethical choices embedded in their design and deployment.

While algorithmic bias is often discussed in terms of flawed data or model design, its consequences are most acutely experienced at the level of educational practice. When biased or opaque AI outputs shape grading, risk prediction, or learner categorization, educators frequently become the frontline ethical buffers who must interpret, justify, or mitigate these outcomes in interactions with students and parents. Rather than residing with system designers or institutions, the responsibility for managing the social and emotional fallout of algorithmic decisions is often informally transferred to teachers. This dynamic places educators in ethically precarious positions, particularly when they are expected to reconcile algorithmic recommendations with professional judgment in the absence of transparency or institutional guidance.

This responsibility-shifting can generate what has been conceptualized as ethical labor—the ongoing, largely unrecognized work of correcting, compensating for, or explaining algorithmic bias within everyday teaching practice. Ali et al. (2025) emphasize that bias remediation in AI systems is rarely complete or context-sensitive, requiring human intervention to prevent harm. When such intervention becomes routine, educators may experience cumulative ethical strain and emotional exhaustion. Oberg (2025) links these systemic ethical conflicts to *moral injury* in teaching, where professionals are constrained by institutional systems that compel them to act in ways that conflict with their ethical commitments. Framing bias remediation as ethical labor highlights that the ethical costs of AI adoption are not evenly distributed, but often absorbed by educators without formal recognition, workload adjustment, or organizational support.

Interrogating Bias Beyond Technical Fixes

Recent scholarship emphasizes the need to move beyond purely technical approaches to bias mitigation toward more critical and reflective perspectives. Gaskins (2023) highlights the limitations of speculative or surface-level bias interventions, arguing instead for liberatory design approaches that center marginalized voices and challenge dominant power structures in technology development. In educational settings, this perspective calls for educators to actively interrogate how AI systems define success, represent learners, and prioritize certain forms of knowledge over others. Bias is not only reflected in outcomes but also in what is measured, what is ignored, and whose experiences are considered valuable within AI-driven educational models.

This critical orientation is particularly important as AI systems increasingly influence curricular content, feedback mechanisms, and learner identities. When educators lack the conceptual tools to recognize bias, they may unintentionally legitimize inequitable practices by relying on algorithmic recommendations without question. Ethical challenges, therefore, arise not only from biased systems themselves but from uncritical patterns of use that transfer authority from human educators to opaque technological systems.

Representational Bias and Generative AI in Learning Contexts

The emergence of generative AI introduces new ethical dimensions related to representation, creativity, and knowledge construction. Text-to-image and language-based AI systems can reproduce and amplify stereotypes embedded in their training data, shaping how learners perceive social identities, professions, and cultural norms. Vartiainen et al. (2025) demonstrate that children interacting with generative AI systems may internalize biased representations unless guided by intentional pedagogical interventions. This raises concerns about how AI-generated content influences learners' understanding of diversity, inclusion, and social justice.

Generative AI also challenges traditional notions of authorship and originality, complicating ethical discussions around academic integrity and learning ownership. These challenges are not isolated incidents but part of broader systemic dynamics.

Dieterle et al. (2024) conceptualize the ethical implications of educational AI as cyclical, emphasizing how AI systems shape educational practices, generate new data, and subsequently evolve in ways that reinforce existing norms and biases. This cyclical effect highlights the need for ongoing ethical oversight rather than one-time ethical evaluations.

Data Privacy and Surveillance in AI-Driven Education

Data privacy represents another major ethical challenge associated with AI-enhanced education. AI systems rely heavily on extensive data collection, often capturing detailed information about learners' behaviors, performance patterns, and interactions. Learning analytics platforms, in particular, aggregate and analyze large volumes of student data to generate predictions and interventions. Liu and Khalil (2023), in their systematic review, identify persistent concerns related to informed consent, data minimization, purpose limitation, and transparency in learning analytics practices. Students are frequently unaware of what data are collected, how they are processed, and for what purposes they are used beyond immediate instructional goals.

These concerns are further complicated by institutional and regional contexts. Prinsloo and Kaliisa (2022) highlight that data protection frameworks vary significantly across regions, particularly in parts of the Global South, where regulatory infrastructures may be fragmented or underdeveloped. This uneven landscape increases the risk of data exploitation and misuse, especially when educational institutions adopt AI tools developed by global technology providers. Prinsloo et al. (2022) argue that student data privacy challenges cannot be solved through technological safeguards alone but require ethical deliberation, institutional commitment, and shared responsibility among stakeholders.

Rethinking Privacy Beyond Individual Protection

While privacy is often framed as an individual right, scholars caution against treating it as the sole or dominant ethical concern. Komljenovic (2022) argues that focusing narrowly on data privacy risks obscuring broader questions about value creation, power, and commodification in digitalized higher education. AI-driven education systems increasingly operate within data economies where learner data generate institutional and commercial value. Ethical challenges, therefore, extend beyond consent and compliance to include questions about who benefits from data extraction and how educational values are reshaped in the process. This perspective underscores the need for educators and institutions to engage critically with the political and economic dimensions of AI adoption.

Ethical Implications of Learning Analytics in Teacher Education

AI and learning analytics are not only used to monitor students but also increasingly applied within teacher education and professional development contexts. Salas-Pilco et al. (2022) note that AI-driven analytics in teacher education can support reflective practice and personalized training pathways, but they also raise ethical concerns related to surveillance, performance monitoring, and professional autonomy. When educators themselves become subjects of data-driven evaluation, ethical risks mirror those faced by students, including loss of agency and increased pressure to conform to algorithmically defined norms of effectiveness.

These dynamics highlight the importance of preparing educators not only as users of AI but also as critical subjects within AI-mediated systems. Ethical challenges in education are thus relational, affecting students, teachers, and institutions simultaneously.

Ethical Challenges Beyond the Western Context: Data Extractivism and Power Asymmetries

While much of the literature on AI ethics in education has been shaped by Western regulatory and institutional contexts, emerging scholarship highlights that ethical challenges manifest differently—and often more acutely—in Global South settings. One critical concern is data extractivism, where learner data are systematically collected from local educational contexts and processed, monetized, or governed by external actors with limited accountability to the communities from which the data originate. Martínez (2026) conceptualizes this phenomenon as *epistemic extractivism*, in which knowledge, experiences, and data generated by marginalized populations are appropriated without reciprocal benefit or meaningful local agency. In educational AI systems, this dynamic is reflected in learning analytics platforms and generative tools that draw on extensive behavioral and performance data from students and educators while offering limited transparency regarding data ownership, reuse, or long-term value creation.

These extractive dynamics are closely linked to asymmetric data flows, where local learners and institutions supply data to global technology providers who retain control over algorithms, infrastructures, and decision-making processes. In contexts with weaker regulatory frameworks, such asymmetries can intensify dependency on external platforms, reducing institutional capacity to audit systems, contest outcomes, or align AI deployment with local educational priorities. Maimela and Mbonde (2025), examining South African universities, demonstrate how AI-driven curriculum and platform adoption can conflict with decolonisation efforts when technological systems embed epistemic assumptions and governance models misaligned with local social and cultural values. Rather than serving as neutral tools for transformation, AI systems may inadvertently reproduce colonial patterns of knowledge extraction and authority, positioning Global South institutions as data providers rather than co-governors of educational innovation.

Learning analytics and AI-enabled monitoring further complicate these power relations by introducing surveillance practices that reshape teacher–student relationships. Calderwood (2025) shows that digitized surveillance in blended and AI-supported learning environments fosters performativity, compliance, and self-monitoring, often at the expense of trust and relational pedagogy. In Global South contexts, where institutional safeguards and collective bargaining mechanisms may be limited, such surveillance can disproportionately burden educators and students, normalizing intrusive data practices as conditions of participation. These dynamics reinforce platform dependency, as institutions rely on proprietary systems that define what counts as engagement, performance, and success, while constraining educators' ability to resist or reinterpret algorithmic judgments.

Taken together, these perspectives illustrate that ethical challenges in AI-enhanced education cannot be fully understood without attending to global power asymmetries, data extractivism, and regulatory unevenness. Ethical risks are not confined to biased outputs or privacy breaches, but extend to structural conditions that shape who controls educational data, whose knowledge is privileged, and who bears the consequences of AI-mediated decisions. Recognizing these dynamics is essential for developing ethical frameworks that move beyond Western-centric assumptions and address the political economy of educational AI. This global lens reinforces the need for institutional governance and educator training approaches that explicitly account for power, dependency, and contextual vulnerability—issues that are examined further in subsequent sections on educator preparation and institutional responsibility.

Transparency, Explainability, and Trust in Educational AI

Transparency and explainability are central to ethical AI deployment in education. Many AI systems operate as black boxes, offering predictions or recommendations without clear explanations of how decisions are made. Cheong (2024) argues that such opacity undermines wellbeing and trust, particularly in contexts where AI outputs influence high-stakes educational outcomes. Without explainability, educators and learners cannot meaningfully question or contest algorithmic decisions, weakening procedural fairness.

Efforts to promote explainable AI emphasize the need for systems that provide understandable rationales for their outputs. Akhtar et al. (2024) outline best practices for transparency and accountability in explainable AI, stressing that explanations must be tailored to stakeholders' needs rather than technical audiences alone. In educational settings, explainability is essential for maintaining pedagogical integrity and ensuring that AI supports, rather than replaces, professional judgment.

Accountability and Legal Responsibility in AI-Mediated Decisions

Accountability remains a persistent ethical challenge in AI-enhanced education. When AI systems influence decisions, responsibility can become diffused across developers, institutions, and educators. Agrawal (2024) highlights the importance of public policy frameworks that clearly define accountability structures to sustain trust in AI systems. In educational contexts, ambiguity around responsibility can leave educators vulnerable to blame for decisions shaped by opaque algorithms, while institutions and vendors evade scrutiny.

Legal and procedural transparency is particularly important in assessment contexts. Al Fraidan (2025) demonstrates how procedural transparency and legal accountability are essential for sustaining trust in AI-mediated language assessment. These findings reinforce the need for institutions to establish clear governance frameworks that delineate roles, responsibilities, and mechanisms for redress.

Toward an Integrated FATE Perspective

In response to these interconnected challenges, scholars increasingly advocate for integrated ethical frameworks grounded in Fairness, Accountability, Transparency, and Ethics (FATE). Memarian and Doleck (2023), through their systematic review, demonstrate that fragmented ethical interventions are insufficient to address the complex risks posed by educational AI. Instead, ethical governance must be systemic, embedding ethical considerations across design, deployment, evaluation, and educator training.

Taken together, these ethical challenges illustrate that AI in education is not a neutral tool but a powerful sociotechnical system that reshapes educational values, practices, and relationships. Addressing these challenges requires more than technical fixes or policy statements; it demands sustained ethical awareness, critical engagement, and institutional commitment. This recognition sets the stage for the next section, which explores how AI ethics can be systematically integrated into educator training and professional development to support responsible and inclusive learning environments. The comparative literature review on ethical challenges in AI-enabled education is given in Table 1.

Table 1. Comparative literature review on ethical challenges in AI-enabled education

Author(s) & Year	Context / Domain	Main Contribution
Baker & Hawn (2022)	Educational AI; learning analytics	Explains how algorithmic bias arises from educational data and modeling choices.
Gaskins (2023)	Educational technology; critical design	Frames algorithmic bias as a sociotechnical issue requiring liberatory design approaches.
Kizilcec & Lee (2022)	AI ethics in education	Argues that algorithmic fairness involves normative ethical trade-offs beyond technical solutions.
Dieterle et al. (2024)	AI in education systems	Introduces cyclical ethical effects of AI through feedback loops in educational practice.
Vartiainen et al. (2025)	Generative AI in education	Shows how generative AI influences children's understanding of algorithmic bias.
Liu & Khalil (2023)	Learning analytics; data protection	Synthesizes privacy and data protection challenges in learning analytics.
Prinsloo & Kaliisa (2022)	Learning analytics; Global South	Highlights contextual and regulatory challenges of data privacy in African education systems.
Prinsloo et al. (2022)	Student data governance	Positions student data privacy as an institutional rather than purely technical issue.
Komljenovic (2022)	Digitalised higher education	Reframes ethics from privacy toward data value extraction and commodification.
Salas-Pilco et al. (2022)	Teacher education; AI analytics	Reviews ethical risks of AI and analytics in teacher education contexts.
Al Fraidan (2025)	AI-based language assessment	Emphasizes procedural transparency and legal accountability in AI-mediated assessment.
Cheong (2024)	Algorithmic decision-making	Links transparency and accountability to trust and wellbeing in AI systems.
Akhtar et al. (2024)	Explainable AI (XAI)	Identifies best practices for transparency and accountability in explainable AI.
Agrawal (2024)	AI policy and governance	Advocates enforceable accountability frameworks for ethical AI governance.
Memarian & Doleck (2023)	Higher education AI governance	Consolidates FATE as a comprehensive framework for ethical AI in higher education.

INTEGRATING AI ETHICS INTO EDUCATOR TRAINING

As artificial intelligence becomes increasingly embedded in educational practice, the need to integrate ethical awareness into educator training has emerged as a critical priority. Educators are no longer passive users of educational technologies but active agents who shape how AI systems are interpreted, implemented, and legitimized within learning environments. However, research consistently shows that many teachers lack sufficient AI literacy, ethical preparedness, and confidence to critically engage with AI-driven tools (Brandão et al., 2024; Nazaretsky et al., 2022). This gap highlights the importance of designing professional development frameworks that go beyond technical skill acquisition to foster ethical reasoning, critical digital literacy, and informed decision-making. Integrating AI ethics into educator training requires a holistic approach that addresses knowledge, values, agency, and institutional context simultaneously. Figure 2 presents a holistic model for integrating AI ethics into educator training, linking AI literacy, agency, and critical digital literacy.

Figure 2. Integrating AI ethics into educator training

Building Teacher AI Literacy Through Professional Development

AI literacy is a foundational prerequisite for ethical engagement with AI in education. Without a basic understanding of how AI systems function, educators are unlikely to recognize ethical risks or question algorithmic outputs. Ding et al. (2024) demonstrate that case-based professional development approaches can significantly enhance teachers' AI literacy by exposing them to realistic classroom scenarios involving AI-supported decision-making. These cases enable educators to explore not only how AI tools operate but also how their design assumptions and limitations influence pedagogical outcomes. Such contextualized learning experiences are particularly effective in helping teachers connect abstract ethical principles with everyday instructional practices.

Integrative reviews further suggest that professional development for AI should be continuous, interdisciplinary, and practice-oriented. Brandão et al. (2024) emphasize that teacher training must evolve alongside advances in generative AI, addressing emerging ethical challenges related to authorship, assessment integrity, and student dependency. Rather than positioning AI literacy as a one-time competency, effective professional development frames it as an ongoing learning process that adapts to technological change. This perspective aligns with the broader understanding that ethical competence is dynamic, requiring educators to continuously update their knowledge and reflective practices.

Teacher Agency and Ethical Decision-Making in AI-Enhanced Contexts

Ethical integration of AI in education depends not only on knowledge but also on teacher agency. Mouta et al. (2025) argue that professional learning environments must empower teachers to exercise ethical judgment, challenge technological determinism, and adapt AI use to local pedagogical values. Their educational design research highlights that teachers are more likely to address ethical challenges effectively when they perceive themselves as decision-makers rather than mere implementers of AI systems. This sense of agency enables educators to negotiate ethical tensions, such as balancing personalization with fairness or efficiency with human oversight.

Agency is closely linked to trust in AI systems. Nazaretsky et al. (2022) show that teachers' trust in AI-powered educational technology is shaped by transparency, explainability, and opportunities for professional dialogue. Professional development programs that explicitly address ethical concerns—rather than focusing solely on functional benefits—can improve trust by helping teachers understand both the capabilities and limitations of AI. Importantly, trust does not imply unquestioning acceptance; rather, it reflects informed confidence grounded in ethical awareness and critical understanding.

Ethical Labor, Emotional Burden, and Professional Sustainability

As AI systems become embedded in teaching and assessment practices, educators increasingly engage in what can be described as ethical labor—the sustained human work required to responsibly manage, interpret, and compensate for AI-mediated decisions. Fassbender (2024) conceptualizes this role through the notion of *teacher–AI centaur labor*, where teachers continuously collaborate with AI systems while retaining ethical responsibility for pedagogical outcomes. This labor includes ongoing monitoring of AI outputs, explaining opaque or contested algorithmic decisions to students, and mediating disputes arising from AI-supported assessment, feedback, or content generation. Crucially, while AI systems may automate instructional tasks, they do not automate ethical accountability; instead, this responsibility is absorbed by educators in everyday practice.

The cumulative demands of ethical labor have significant implications for professional sustainability. Oberg (2025) demonstrates that when educators are repeatedly required to act against their professional judgment or ethical commitments due to systemic constraints, they may experience *moral injury*, manifested as emotional exhaustion, frustration, and burnout. In AI-enhanced environments, such moral distress can arise when teachers are expected to defend or remediate algorithmic outcomes without transparency, authority, or institutional backing. Ethical labor thus extends beyond individual competence, highlighting the risk of role overload when ethical oversight is treated as an informal expectation rather than a recognized and supported component of professional work. Integrating AI ethics into educator training must therefore address not only skills and knowledge, but also the emotional and organizational conditions under which ethical judgment is exercised.

Assessing Ethical Reasoning in Educator Training

If ethical awareness and judgment are to be recognized as core professional competencies, they must be made visible and assessable within educator training programs. However, existing professional development models often prioritize technical proficiency in AI use while overlooking educators' capacity for ethical reasoning. Reeves (2022) argues that ethical capability is best understood as a form of professional judgment that integrates awareness of risk, contextual interpretation, and reflective decision-making. From this perspective, assessing ethical competence does not require standardized testing, but structured opportunities for educators to demonstrate how they reason through complex, value-laden scenarios.

Building on this approach, case-based professional development offers a practical mechanism for assessing ethical reasoning in AI-enhanced education. Ding et al. (2024) show that instructional cases involving AI-supported classroom scenarios can support teachers' reflective engagement with ethical dilemmas, enabling them to question algorithmic recommendations, anticipate unintended consequences, and adapt decisions to local contexts. Drawing on these insights, ethical reasoning in educator training can be assessed using a conceptual rubric that foregrounds judgment rather than compliance. Key dimensions include: ethical awareness, reflected in the ability to identify risks and biases in AI outputs; critical judgment, demonstrated by questioning or overriding algorithmic recommendations when necessary; contextual reasoning, which accounts for cultural, institutional, and learner-specific factors; and advocacy capacity, involving the ability to escalate ethical concerns through appropriate governance channels. Such assessment frameworks translate abstract ethical principles into observable professional practices, responding directly to the need for actionable and sustainable ethics integration in educator training.

Critical Digital Literacy as a Foundation for Ethical Awareness

Critical digital literacy has emerged as a central component of ethical educator training in AI-enhanced environments. Unlike functional digital skills, critical digital literacy emphasizes the ability to analyze, evaluate, and question digital technologies within their social, cultural, and political contexts. Ilomäki et al. (2023), in their systematic review, identify critical digital literacy as essential for enabling educators to recognize power relations, bias, and ethical implications embedded in digital tools. This perspective is particularly relevant for AI systems, which often operate invisibly while exerting significant influence over learning processes.

Pedagogical frameworks for critical digital literacy encourage educators to move beyond tool-centric approaches toward reflective and dialogic practices. Knight et al. (2023) advocate for pedagogies that foreground questioning, interpretation, and ethical critique, enabling educators to unpack how AI systems shape meaning, representation, and authority in education. Empirical studies further demonstrate that teachers who engage with critical digital literacy concepts are more likely to integrate ethical discussions into their teaching practices. Gouseti et al. (2024) show that educators who perceive critical digital literacy as integral to teaching are better equipped to address ethical dilemmas related to data use, automation, and algorithmic decision-making.

Developing Ethical Sensitivity Through Contextual and Collaborative Learning

Ethical awareness in educator training is strengthened through collaborative and context-sensitive learning environments. Bilki et al. (2023) illustrate how virtual exchange and dialogic learning approaches can support the development of critical digital literacy and ethical sensitivity among pre-service and in-service teachers. By engaging educators in reflective discussions across cultural and institutional contexts, such approaches highlight the situated nature of ethical challenges and discourage one-size-fits-all solutions.

Case-based and design-based learning approaches further support ethical integration by enabling educators to experiment with AI tools while reflecting on ethical implications. Ding et al. (2024) demonstrate that different types of instructional cases—ranging from success stories to ethical dilemmas—can help teachers anticipate risks, evaluate trade-offs, and develop ethical reasoning skills. These approaches align with the view that ethical competence is best cultivated through practice-oriented reflection rather than abstract instruction alone.

Assessing Digital and Ethical Competence in Educator Training

Assessment plays a critical role in legitimizing ethical awareness within educator training programs. Nguyen and Habók (2024) review tools for assessing teacher digital literacy and highlight the need for assessment frameworks that capture not only technical proficiency but also ethical understanding and critical judgment. Traditional assessment models often prioritize measurable skills, overlooking reflective and ethical dimensions that are more difficult to quantify. This gap can undermine the perceived importance of ethics in professional development.

Integrating ethical assessment requires innovative approaches that value reflective writing, scenario analysis, and collaborative inquiry. Such assessments signal that ethical reasoning is a core professional competency rather than an optional add-on. Moreover, ethical assessment practices reinforce the idea that educators are accountable not only for what they teach but also for how they engage with technology in ethically responsible ways.

Data Ethics and Informal Professional Learning Environments

Educator training increasingly occurs in informal and digitally mediated environments, including online communities, learning platforms, and AI-supported professional learning tools. Pammer-Schindler and Rosé (2022) highlight that these environments raise distinct data-related ethical concerns, such as consent, transparency, and surveillance of professional learning activities. Educators may be unaware that their learning behaviors are being tracked, analyzed, and potentially used for purposes beyond professional development.

Integrating data ethics into educator training involves making these processes visible and fostering informed consent. Ethical awareness training must therefore address not only classroom applications of AI but also the ethical dimensions of professional learning technologies themselves. This reflexive approach reinforces educators' capacity to critically engage with AI systems across multiple roles—as teachers, learners, and institutional stakeholders.

Ethical Reasoning and Computational Perspectives

Emerging research explores how ethical reasoning can be supported through computational approaches and AI system design. Sholla and Reshi (2024) argue that ethical reasoning should be integrated into AI systems themselves, enabling technologies to support ethical decision-making rather than merely optimize performance. While such approaches are still evolving, they highlight the importance of aligning educator training with broader developments in trustworthy AI.

From a professional development perspective, these insights underscore the need to help educators understand how ethical values can be operationalized within AI systems. Akbar et al. (2024) propose a taxonomy of challenges related to trustworthy AI, including transparency, robustness, and accountability.

Toward Integrated Models of Ethical Educator Training

Taken together, the literature suggests that integrating AI ethics into educator training requires comprehensive and systemic models that address literacy, agency, critical reflection, and institutional context. Ethical awareness cannot be effectively cultivated through isolated workshops or technical tutorials. Instead, it must be embedded within sustained professional learning pathways that align pedagogical goals with ethical values.

By fostering AI literacy, critical digital literacy, and ethical reasoning, educator training programs can prepare teachers to navigate the complexities of AI-enhanced education responsibly. Such preparation enables educators to act as ethical leaders who advocate for fairness, transparency, and inclusion while leveraging AI to support meaningful learning. This integrated approach provides a foundation for institutional and policy-level frameworks, which are examined in the following section, to sustain responsible AI use across educational systems.

INSTITUTIONAL AND POLICY FRAMEWORKS FOR RESPONSIBLE AI USE

The ethical integration of artificial intelligence in education cannot be sustained through individual awareness or classroom-level practices alone. As AI systems increasingly shape teaching, learning, assessment, and institutional decision-making, responsibility must be distributed across institutional structures and policy frameworks that govern how these technologies are selected, deployed, evaluated, and contested. Educational institutions are no longer neutral sites of technology adoption; they function as regulatory environments where ethical values are translated into operational practices. In this context, institutional and policy frameworks serve as the backbone of responsible AI use, determining whether ethical principles such as fairness, accountability, transparency, and human oversight remain aspirational ideals or become enforceable standards. Recent scholarship emphasizes that ethical AI in education requires coordinated governance mechanisms that align technological innovation with educational values, public trust, and social justice (Filgueiras, 2024; Memarian & Doleck, 2023). Figure 3 outlines the institutional and policy frameworks required to support responsible AI use in education.

Figure 3. Institutional and policy frameworks for responsible AI use in education

Institutional Governance as Ethical Stewardship

Institutions of education occupy a central position in the AI ecosystem, mediating between policy mandates, technological vendors, educators, and learners. Governance in this context extends beyond administrative compliance to include ethical stewardship of AI technologies. Filgueiras (2024) conceptualizes education governance as a normative process that shapes civic values, participation, and trust, arguing that AI governance in education must be understood as part of broader democratic accountability. Decisions about AI procurement, data governance, and algorithmic deployment implicitly define what counts as legitimate knowledge, fair assessment, and acceptable risk. When institutions adopt AI systems without transparent governance processes, ethical responsibility becomes fragmented, often leaving educators and learners exposed to harms without clear avenues for redress.

Institutional governance frameworks must therefore establish explicit ethical mandates that guide AI adoption across the educational lifecycle. Chan (2023) proposes a comprehensive AI policy education framework that embeds governance within the core missions of teaching and learning. This framework emphasizes the alignment of institutional AI policies with curricular goals, professional development, and assessment practices. Rather than treating AI governance as a purely technical or legal matter, Chan argues that policy education should be integrated into academic culture, enabling educators and administrators to share a common ethical language. Such integration helps bridge the gap between high-level policy statements and day-to-day pedagogical practice, ensuring that ethical principles are enacted consistently rather than selectively.

The Role of National and Supranational AI Policy in Education

Institutional AI governance does not occur in isolation but is shaped by national and supranational policy environments that define regulatory boundaries and ethical expectations. Schiff (2022) critically examines national AI strategies and highlights a persistent tension between economic priorities and educational ethics. Many national policies frame education primarily as a pipeline for AI talent development, emphasizing skills acquisition and workforce readiness while neglecting the ethical dimensions of AI use within educational systems themselves. This instrumental view risks subordinating educational values to technological agendas, positioning AI as an unquestioned driver of progress rather than a sociotechnical system requiring ethical scrutiny.

The emergence of regulatory instruments such as the European Union's AI Act represents a significant shift toward enforceable governance of AI systems. Kim et al. (2025) analyze the EU AI Act's risk-based approach, which categorizes AI systems according to their potential impact on fundamental rights and societal harm. Educational AI systems used for assessment, student profiling, or decision-making may be classified as high-risk, triggering obligations related to transparency, human oversight, and accountability. While such regulations strengthen protections, they also introduce complexity for educational institutions, which must interpret legal requirements within pedagogical contexts that are often fluid and culturally specific. This regulatory complexity underscores the need for institutional capacity-building to translate policy mandates into educationally meaningful practices.

Ethical Principles as Foundations for Governance Frameworks

Ethical principles play a foundational role in shaping AI governance frameworks, providing normative guidance for institutional decision-making. Nguyen et al. (2023) identify core ethical principles for AI in education, including fairness, inclusivity, transparency, accountability, and respect for learner autonomy. These principles resonate across international guidelines and scholarly discourse, yet their practical implementation remains uneven. One of the key challenges is translating abstract ethical values into operational criteria that can guide procurement, system design, and evaluation. Holmes et al. (2022) advance a community-wide ethical framework for AI in education that emphasizes shared responsibility among stakeholders, including educators, learners, developers, and policymakers. This framework challenges hierarchical governance models by advocating participatory approaches that incorporate diverse perspectives into ethical deliberation. In institutional settings, participatory governance can take the form of ethics committees, stakeholder consultations, and co-design processes that allow ethical concerns to be identified early and addressed collaboratively. Such approaches not only enhance ethical robustness but also foster trust by demonstrating institutional commitment to transparency and inclusion.

The Corporate "Black Box": Procurement, Vendor Power, and Institutional Accountability

As artificial intelligence systems are increasingly procured through commercial vendors, ethical governance in education is shaped not only by institutional values but by procurement practices that often operate as corporate "black boxes." Coglianese (2024) highlights that AI procurement frequently limits public and institutional visibility into algorithmic design, training data provenance, and system update cycles. In educational contexts, this opacity constrains institutions' ability to evaluate risks, enforce ethical standards, or adapt systems to pedagogical needs. Decision-making authority is effectively shifted upstream to vendors, while accountability for outcomes remains downstream with institutions and educators.

This procurement opacity intensifies power asymmetries within algorithmic education ecosystems. Cobo and Rivera-Vargas (2023) argue that educational institutions adopting AI technologies often lack the organizational and technical capacities required to interrogate vendor claims, audit system behavior, or negotiate governance conditions. As a result, educators' professional authority may be curtailed by systems they did not design and cannot fully explain. When algorithmic outputs influence assessment, personalization, or student monitoring, responsibility for ethical justification is frequently diffused—vendors control system logic, institutions approve deployment, and educators are left to manage consequences at the point of practice.

Accountability diffusion is further exacerbated by data governance constraints embedded in vendor contracts. Huang (2023) shows that student data protection and privacy risks are often intensified when institutions lack clear ownership or control over data generated through AI-enabled platforms. In such cases, ethical responsibility becomes fragmented, weakening institutional capacity to safeguard learner rights or respond effectively to harm. These dynamics demonstrate that ethical AI governance in education cannot be achieved without addressing procurement as a core site of ethical risk, rather than treating it as a purely administrative or technical process.

Institutional Ethical AI Procurement Checklist

To translate ethical principles into enforceable institutional practice, procurement processes must be guided by explicit governance criteria. Drawing on governance-oriented AI scholarship, an Institutional Ethical AI Procurement Checklist can support educational institutions in mitigating opacity and restoring accountability at the point of adoption (Coglianese, 2024; McKay, 2024). Key dimensions include:

1. Explainability guarantees: Contracts should require vendors to provide intelligible explanations of system logic and decision pathways to non-technical stakeholders.
2. Bias audit access: Institutions should retain the right to request or conduct independent audits to assess potential discriminatory impacts.
3. Data ownership and protection clauses: Clear provisions must define data ownership, retention, reuse, and deletion, ensuring alignment with student privacy obligations (Huang, 2023).
4. Educator override mechanisms: Systems should incorporate human-in-the-loop safeguards that preserve educators' authority to override or contextualize algorithmic outputs in pedagogical decision-making (McKay, 2024).

Embedding such criteria into procurement workflows shifts ethical governance from aspirational policy to operational control. It also redistributes ethical responsibility across institutional actors, reducing the burden placed on individual educators and reinforcing shared accountability for AI-mediated educational decisions.

Governing Emerging AI Paradigms in Education

AI governance frameworks must remain adaptive to emerging technological paradigms that introduce new ethical risks. Large language models and generative AI systems, for example, raise concerns related to epistemic authority, misinformation, authorship, and dependency. Yan and Liu (2025) propose an ethical framework for

AI education that explicitly addresses the unique challenges posed by large language models, including hallucinated outputs and overreliance on AI-generated knowledge. These challenges complicate traditional governance assumptions, as risks may not be immediately observable or easily measurable. Institutional policies must therefore incorporate mechanisms for continuous ethical review and horizon scanning to anticipate emerging risks. Static policy documents are insufficient in rapidly evolving AI landscapes. Adaptive governance requires feedback loops that integrate empirical evidence, educator experiences, and learner perspectives into policy revision processes. This dynamic approach aligns with the understanding that ethical AI governance is not a one-time intervention but an ongoing institutional practice.

FATE as an Integrative Institutional Governance Lens

The Fairness, Accountability, Transparency, and Ethics (FATE) framework has gained prominence as a comprehensive lens for AI governance in higher education. Memarian and Doleck (2023), through their systematic review, demonstrate that FATE principles provide a structured approach for addressing ethical risks across AI systems' lifecycles. In institutional contexts, FATE serves as a practical governance tool by linking ethical values to actionable domains such as data management, algorithmic evaluation, and stakeholder communication. Fairness requires institutions to assess whether AI systems disproportionately disadvantage specific groups of learners or educators. This assessment may involve bias audits, inclusive data practices, and monitoring of outcomes across demographic categories. Accountability demands clear assignment of responsibility for AI-mediated decisions, including documentation of decision processes and mechanisms for appeal. Transparency entails providing meaningful explanations of AI systems' functions, limitations, and impacts, tailored to non-technical audiences. Ethics integrates these elements by grounding governance practices in educational values rather than efficiency metrics alone. Together, FATE principles enable institutions to move from fragmented ethical interventions toward coherent governance strategies.

Accountability Beyond Transparency

Accountability remains one of the most challenging aspects of AI governance in education. Novelli et al. (2024) conceptualize accountability as a multifaceted construct involving answerability, enforceability, and institutional capacity. In educational settings, accountability requires not only that institutions can explain

AI-driven decisions but also that they can correct harms and prevent recurrence. This goes beyond transparency, which, while necessary, is insufficient on its own.

Williams et al. (2022) argue that transparency often functions as an aspirational goal rather than an operational mechanism. Educational institutions may disclose information about AI systems without providing meaningful opportunities for scrutiny or redress. Effective accountability requires governance structures that translate transparency into action, such as independent audits, ethics review boards, and formal complaint mechanisms. These structures signal institutional willingness to assume responsibility for AI-related outcomes rather than deflect blame onto technology providers or individual educators.

Institutional Responsibility and Risk Management

Responsible AI governance in education also involves proactive risk management. Institutions must anticipate potential harms associated with AI adoption and implement safeguards accordingly. This includes conducting impact assessments prior to deployment, monitoring system performance, and establishing contingency plans for system failures. Risk management frameworks should be informed by ethical principles rather than solely by legal compliance, recognizing that some harms may be ethically significant even if they fall outside regulatory thresholds.

In this regard, governance frameworks must balance innovation with precaution. Overly restrictive policies may stifle pedagogical experimentation, while permissive approaches risk exposing learners and educators to unmitigated harms. Ethical governance requires nuanced judgment that considers contextual factors, educational goals, and stakeholder perspectives.

Educating Stakeholders for Ethical Governance

Governance frameworks are only as effective as the people who implement and sustain them. Bogina et al. (2022) emphasize the importance of educating AI stakeholders about fairness, accountability, transparency, and ethics. In educational institutions, this includes administrators, educators, IT staff, and procurement officers. Ethical governance cannot be delegated exclusively to technical experts or compliance units; it must be embedded across institutional roles.

Stakeholder education supports participatory governance by enabling informed engagement with ethical issues. When educators and learners understand governance frameworks, they are better positioned to question AI use, report concerns, and contribute to ethical decision-making. This participatory dimension reinforces democratic values and strengthens institutional legitimacy.

Aligning Governance with Educational Values

A recurring concern in the literature is the risk that AI governance frameworks prioritize efficiency, performance metrics, or economic competitiveness at the expense of educational values. Filgueiras (2024) cautions that governance models driven primarily by managerial logics may undermine core educational commitments to equity, critical thinking, and human development. Institutional policies must therefore articulate explicit value commitments that guide AI adoption and evaluation. Chan's (2023) framework reinforces the importance of aligning AI policy education with institutional culture. When ethical principles are embedded in teaching, research, and governance practices, institutions create coherent ecosystems that reinforce responsible AI use. This alignment reduces the likelihood of ethical fragmentation, where policies exist on paper but fail to influence practice.

Global Diversity and Contextual Sensitivity in AI Governance

AI governance frameworks must also be sensitive to global diversity and contextual variation. Ethical priorities, regulatory capacities, and educational traditions vary across regions, making universal governance models inadequate. While supranational regulations such as the EU AI Act provide valuable benchmarks, institutions must adapt governance practices to local contexts. This includes considering cultural norms, resource constraints, and historical inequities that shape how AI is experienced by learners and educators.

Contextual sensitivity is particularly important in cross-border educational partnerships and technology procurement, where governance responsibilities may be shared across jurisdictions. Institutions must navigate overlapping regulatory regimes while maintaining ethical coherence.

From Aspirational Ethics to Institutional Practice

A central challenge in AI governance is moving from aspirational ethics to enforceable practice. Ethical guidelines and policy statements are necessary but insufficient without mechanisms for implementation and evaluation. Governance frameworks must specify roles, responsibilities, and procedures, ensuring that ethical principles are operationalized across institutional processes. This includes embedding ethics into procurement criteria, staff training, curriculum design, and evaluation metrics.

Regular review and adaptation of governance frameworks are also essential. As AI technologies evolve, new ethical risks emerge, requiring ongoing institutional learning and responsiveness. Governance should thus be viewed as a living process rather than a static set of rules.

Toward Sustainable and Trustworthy AI Governance in Education

Taken together, the literature underscores that responsible AI use in education depends on coherent institutional and policy frameworks that integrate ethical principles with operational mechanisms. Governance must be participatory, adaptive, and value-driven, capable of addressing both current and emerging challenges. By embedding fairness, accountability, transparency, and ethics into institutional structures, educational institutions can foster trust, protect learner rights, and support inclusive innovation.

This section highlights that ethical responsibility for AI adoption cannot rest solely on individual educators. Institutions and policymakers play a decisive role in shaping the conditions under which AI is used, determining whether it reinforces inequality or contributes to equitable and human-centered learning environments. The concluding section synthesizes these insights and offers strategic recommendations for embedding ethical awareness into educator training, institutional governance, and future AI policy development.

CONCLUSIONS AND RECOMMENDATIONS

This chapter shows that ethical awareness in AI-enhanced educator training is necessary but not sufficient on its own. Artificial intelligence in education is a sociotechnical shift that reshapes teaching practices, professional roles, and governance structures. Ethical challenges such as bias, privacy, surveillance, and accountability are embedded in everyday educational decisions and affect contexts unevenly, particularly in Global South systems. Educators play a key mediating role between AI tools and learners, but this role increasingly involves ethical labor that is often informal and unsupported. Without strong institutional and policy frameworks, placing ethical responsibility mainly on educators can lead to overload and moral distress. Responsible AI adoption therefore requires shared accountability and alignment between training, governance, and educational values.

AI ethics should be embedded as a core professional competence in educator training, with a focus on ethical reasoning, contextual judgment, and the ability to question algorithmic outputs. Institutions must strengthen governance through clear AI procurement and deployment policies, including transparency, bias checks, and educator override mechanisms. Participatory decision-making structures are needed to reduce the ethical burden on individuals. At the policy level, education-specific AI regulation and capacity building are essential, especially in contexts with limited regulatory resources, to ensure ethical and inclusive use of AI in education.

REFERENCES

Agrawal, G. (2024). Accountability, trust, and transparency in AI systems from the perspective of public policy: Elevating ethical standards. In *AI healthcare applications and security, ethical, and legal considerations* (pp. 148–162). IGI Global. DOI: 10.4018/979-8-3693-7452-8.ch009

Akbar, M. A., Khan, A. A., Mahmood, S., Rafi, S., & Demi, S. (2024). Trustworthy artificial intelligence: A decision-making taxonomy of potential challenges. *Software, Practice & Experience*, *54*(9), 1621–1650. DOI: 10.1002/spe.3216

Akgun, S., & Greenhow, C. (2022). Artificial intelligence in education: Addressing ethical challenges in K-12 settings. *AI and Ethics*, *2*(3), 431–440. DOI: 10.1007/s43681-021-00096-7 PMID: 34790956

Akhtar, M. A. K., Kumar, M., & Nayyar, A. (2024). Transparency and accountability in explainable AI: Best practices. In *Towards ethical and socially responsible explainable ai: Challenges and opportunities* (pp. 127–164). Springer Nature Switzerland. DOI: 10.1007/978-3-031-66489-2_5

Al Fraidan, A. (2025). Procedural Transparency and Legal Accountability to Sustain AI-Mediated Language Assessment in Saudi Arabia. *SAGE Open*, *15*(4), 21582440251396113. DOI: 10.1177/21582440251396113

Alam, A. (2023). Developing a curriculum for ethical and responsible AI: A university course on safety, fairness, privacy, and ethics to prepare next generation of AI professionals. In *Intelligent communication technologies and virtual mobile networks* (pp. 879–894). Springer Nature Singapore. DOI: 10.1007/978-981-99-1767-9_64

Aler Tubella, A., Mora-Cantallops, M., & Nieves, J. C. (2024). How to teach responsible AI in Higher Education: Challenges and opportunities. *Ethics and Information Technology*, *26*(1), 3. DOI: 10.1007/s10676-023-09733-7

Ali, S. I., Albadoo, S. F., & Al Mubarak, M. (2025). Ethical Ramifications and Remedial Approaches on Bias in Artificial Intelligence. In *Sustainable Digital Technology and Ethics in an Ever-Changing Environment* (Vol. 2, pp. 95–108). Springer Nature Switzerland. DOI: 10.1007/978-3-031-86708-8_8

Baker, R. S., & Hawn, A. (2022). Algorithmic bias in education. *International Journal of Artificial Intelligence in Education*, *32*(4), 1052–1092. DOI: 10.1007/s40593-021-00285-9

Bilki, Z., Satar, M., & Sak, M. (2023). Critical digital literacy in virtual exchange for ELT teacher education: An interpretivist methodology. *ReCALL, 35*(1), 58–73. DOI: 10.1017/S095834402200009X

Bogina, V., Hartman, A., Kuflik, T., & Shulner-Tal, A. (2022). Educating software and AI stakeholders about algorithmic fairness, accountability, transparency and ethics. *International Journal of Artificial Intelligence in Education, 32*(3), 808–833. DOI: 10.1007/s40593-021-00248-0

Brandão, A., Pedro, L., & Zagalo, N. (2024). Teacher Professional Development for a Future with Generative Artificial Intelligence—An Integrative Literature Review. *Digital Education Review, 45*(45), 151–157. DOI: 10.1344/der.2024.45.151-157

Calderwood, S. J. (2025). Surveillance Digitisation, Performativity, and Teacher-Student Relationships in a Blended Learning Setting. *Postdigital Science and Education*, 1–25.

Chan, C. K. Y. (2023). A comprehensive AI policy education framework for university teaching and learning. *International Journal of Educational Technology in Higher Education, 20*(1), 38. DOI: 10.1186/s41239-023-00408-3

Chen, H. (2024). The ethical challenges of educational artificial intelligence and coping measures: A discussion in the context of the 2024 World Digital Education Conference. Science Insights Education Frontiers, 20(2), 3263-3281.

Cheong, B. C. (2024). Transparency and accountability in AI systems: Safeguarding wellbeing in the age of algorithmic decision-making. *Frontiers in Human Dynamics, 6*, 1421273. DOI: 10.3389/fhumd.2024.1421273

Cobo, C., & Rivera-Vargas, P. (2023). What is 'algorithmic education' and why do education institutions need to consolidate new capacities? In *The new digital education policy landscape* (pp. 210–225). Routledge. DOI: 10.4324/9781003373018-14

Coglianese, C. (2024). Procurement and artificial intelligence. In *Handbook on Public Policy and Artificial Intelligence* (pp. 235–248). Edward Elgar Publishing. DOI: 10.4337/9781803922171.00026

Dieterle, E., Dede, C., & Walker, M. (2024). The cyclical ethical effects of using artificial intelligence in education. *AI & Society, 39*(2), 633–643. DOI: 10.1007/s00146-022-01497-w PMID: 36185064

Ding, A. C. E., Shi, L., Yang, H., & Choi, I. (2024). Enhancing teacher AI literacy and integration through different types of cases in teacher professional development. *Computers and Education Open, 6*, 100178. DOI: 10.1016/j.caeo.2024.100178

Domínguez Figaredo, D., & Stoyanovich, J. (2023). Responsible AI literacy: A stakeholder-first approach. *Big Data & Society*, *10*(2), 20539517231219958. DOI: 10.1177/20539517231219958

Farooqi, M. T. K., Amanat, I., & Awan, S. M. (2024). Ethical considerations and challenges in the integration of artificial intelligence in education: A systematic review. *Journal of Excellence in Management Sciences*, *3*(4), 35–50. DOI: 10.69565/jems.v3i4.314

Fassbender, W. J. (2024). "I can almost recognize its voice": AI and its impact on ethical teacher-centaur labor. *English Teaching*, *23*(1), 104–117. DOI: 10.1108/ETPC-08-2023-0101

Filgueiras, F. (2024). Artificial intelligence and education governance. *Education, Citizenship and Social Justice*, *19*(3), 349–361. DOI: 10.1177/17461979231160674

Gaskins, N. (2023). Interrogating algorithmic bias: From speculative fiction to liberatory design. *TechTrends*, *67*(3), 417–425. DOI: 10.1007/s11528-022-00783-0 PMID: 36160677

Gouseti, A., Lakkala, M., Raffaghelli, J., Ranieri, M., Roffi, A., & Ilomäki, L. (2024). Exploring teachers' perceptions of critical digital literacies and how these are manifested in their teaching practices. *Educational Review*, *76*(7), 1751–1785. DOI: 10.1080/00131911.2022.2159933

Henadirage, A., & Gunarathne, N. (2025). Barriers to and opportunities for the adoption of generative artificial intelligence in higher education in the global south: Insights from Sri Lanka. *International Journal of Artificial Intelligence in Education*, *35*(1), 245–281. DOI: 10.1007/s40593-024-00439-5

Holmes, W., Porayska-Pomsta, K., Holstein, K., Sutherland, E., Baker, T., Shum, S. B., Santos, O. C., Rodrigo, M. T., Cukurova, M., Bittencourt, I. I., & Koedinger, K. R. (2022). Ethics of AI in education: Towards a community-wide framework. *International Journal of Artificial Intelligence in Education*, *32*(3), 504–526. DOI: 10.1007/s40593-021-00239-1

Huang, L. (2023). Ethics of artificial intelligence in education: Student privacy and data protection. *Science Insights Education Frontiers*, *16*(2), 2577–2587. DOI: 10.15354/sief.23.re202

Ilomäki, L., Lakkala, M., Kallunki, V., Mundy, D., Romero, M., Romeu, T., & Gouseti, A. (2023). Critical digital literacies at school level: A systematic review. *Review of Education*, *11*(3), e3425. DOI: 10.1002/rev3.3425

Jeyaraman, M., Ramasubramanian, S., Balaji, S., Jeyaraman, N., Nallakumarasamy, A., & Sharma, S. (2023). ChatGPT in action: Harnessing artificial intelligence potential and addressing ethical challenges in medicine, education, and scientific research. *World Journal of Methodology*, *13*(4), 170–178. DOI: 10.5662/wjm.v13.i4.170 PMID: 37771867

Jin, Y., Yan, L., Echeverria, V., Gašević, D., & Martinez-Maldonado, R. (2025). Generative AI in higher education: A global perspective of institutional adoption policies and guidelines. *Computers and Education: Artificial Intelligence*, *8*, 100348. DOI: 10.1016/j.caeai.2024.100348

Kiemde, S. M. A., & Kora, A. D. (2022). Towards an ethics of AI in Africa: Rule of education. *AI and Ethics*, *2*(1), 35–40. DOI: 10.1007/s43681-021-00106-8

Kim, B. J., Jeong, S., Cho, B. K., & Chung, J. B. (2025). AI Governance in the Context of the EU AI Act. *IEEE Access : Practical Innovations, Open Solutions*, *13*, 144126–144142. DOI: 10.1109/ACCESS.2025.3598023

Kizilcec, R. F., & Lee, H. (2022). Algorithmic fairness in education. In *The ethics of artificial intelligence in education* (pp. 174–202). Routledge. DOI: 10.4324/9780429329067-10

Knight, J., Dooly, M., & Barberà, E. (2023). Getting smart: Towards critical digital literacy pedagogies. *Social Semiotics*, *33*(2), 326–349. DOI: 10.1080/10350330.2020.1836815

Komljenovic, J. (2022). The future of value in digitalised higher education: Why data privacy should not be our biggest concern. *Higher Education*, *83*(1), 119–135. DOI: 10.1007/s10734-020-00639-7 PMID: 33230347

Liu, Q., & Khalil, M. (2023). Understanding privacy and data protection issues in learning analytics using a systematic review. *British Journal of Educational Technology*, *54*(6), 1715–1747. DOI: 10.1111/bjet.13388

Maimela, C., & Mbonde, P. (2025). Artificial intelligence in South African universities: Curriculum transformation and decolonisation—aid or obstacle? *Frontiers in Sociology*, *10*, 1543471. DOI: 10.3389/fsoc.2025.1543471 PMID: 40697567

Martínez, M. A. (2026). Epistemic extractivism in engaged urban and housing research: Implications and counter-measures. *International Journal of Urban and Regional Research*, 1468-2427.70055. DOI: 10.1111/1468-2427.70055

McKay, M. H. (2024, June). Realizing the Promise of AI Governance Involving Humans-in-the-Loop. In *International Conference on Human-Computer Interaction* (pp. 107–123). Cham: Springer Nature Switzerland. DOI: 10.1007/978-3-031-76827-9_7

Memarian, B., & Doleck, T. (2023). Fairness, Accountability, Transparency, and Ethics (FATE) in Artificial Intelligence (AI) and higher education: A systematic review. *Computers and Education: Artificial Intelligence*, *5*, 100152. DOI: 10.1016/j.caeai.2023.100152

Mouta, A., Torrecilla-Sánchez, E. M., & Pinto-Llorente, A. M. (2025). Comprehensive professional learning for teacher agency in addressing ethical challenges of AIED: Insights from educational design research. *Education and Information Technologies*, *30*(3), 3343–3387. DOI: 10.1007/s10639-024-12946-y

Mutambara, A. G. (2025). *Artificial Intelligence: A driver of inclusive development and shared prosperity for the Global South*. CRC Press. DOI: 10.1201/9781003511014

Nazaretsky, T., Ariely, M., Cukurova, M., & Alexandron, G. (2022). Teachers' trust in AI-powered educational technology and a professional development program to improve it. *British Journal of Educational Technology*, *53*(4), 914–931. DOI: 10.1111/bjet.13232

Nguyen, A., Ngo, H. N., Hong, Y., Dang, B., & Nguyen, B. P. T. (2023). Ethical principles for artificial intelligence in education. *Education and Information Technologies*, *28*(4), 4221–4241. DOI: 10.1007/s10639-022-11316-w PMID: 36254344

Novelli, C., Taddeo, M., & Floridi, L. (2024). Accountability in artificial intelligence: What it is and how it works. *AI & Society*, *39*(4), 1871–1882. DOI: 10.1007/s00146-023-01635-y

Oberg, G. (2025). Moral injury in teaching: The systemic roots of ethical conflict and emotional burnout in education. *Educational Review*, •••, 1–24.

Pammer-Schindler, V., & Rosé, C. (2022). Data-related ethics issues in technologies for informal professional learning. *International Journal of Artificial Intelligence in Education*, *32*(3), 609–635. DOI: 10.1007/s40593-021-00259-x

Porayska-Pomsta, K. (2024). A manifesto for a pro-actively responsible AI in education. *International Journal of Artificial Intelligence in Education*, *34*(1), 73–83. DOI: 10.1007/s40593-023-00346-1

Poyares, M. (2025). Migrant Data Extractivism: Tech and Borders at the Limit of Rights. *International Migration (Geneva, Switzerland)*, *63*(4), e70065. DOI: 10.1111/imig.70065

Prinsloo, P., & Kaliisa, R. (2022). Data privacy on the African continent: Opportunities, challenges and implications for learning analytics. *British Journal of Educational Technology*, *53*(4), 894–913. DOI: 10.1111/bjet.13226

Prinsloo, P., Slade, S., & Khalil, M. (2022). The answer is (not only) technological: Considering student data privacy in learning analytics. *British Journal of Educational Technology*, *53*(4), 876–893. DOI: 10.1111/bjet.13216

Reeves, B. (2022). Assessing ethical capability: A framework for supporting teacher judgement of student proficiency. *Australian Educational Researcher*, *49*(4), 779–804. DOI: 10.1007/s13384-021-00442-y

Salas-Pilco, S. Z., Xiao, K., & Hu, X. (2022). Artificial intelligence and learning analytics in teacher education: A systematic review. *Education Sciences*, *12*(8), 569. DOI: 10.3390/educsci12080569

Schiff, D. (2022). Education for AI, not AI for education: The role of education and ethics in national AI policy strategies. *International Journal of Artificial Intelligence in Education*, *32*(3), 527–563. DOI: 10.1007/s40593-021-00270-2

Sholla, S., & Reshi, I. A. (2024). Ethical reasoning in technology: using computational approaches to integrate ethics into AI systems. Journal of Information, Communication and Ethics in Society.

Vartiainen, H., Kahila, J., Tedre, M., López-Pernas, S., & Pope, N. (2025). Enhancing children's understanding of algorithmic biases in and with text-to-image generative AI. *New Media & Society*, *27*(9), 5342–5368. DOI: 10.1177/14614448241252820

Williams, R., Cloete, R., Cobbe, J., Cottrill, C., Edwards, P., Markovic, M., Naja, I., Ryan, F., Singh, J., & Pang, W. (2022). From transparency to accountability of intelligent systems: Moving beyond aspirations. *Data & Policy*, *4*, e7. DOI: 10.1017/dap.2021.37

Yan, Y., & Liu, H. (2025). Ethical framework for AI education based on large language models. *Education and Information Technologies*, *30*(8), 10891–10909. DOI: 10.1007/s10639-024-13241-6

Yu, L., & Yu, Z. (2023). Qualitative and quantitative analyses of artificial intelligence ethics in education using VOSviewer and CitNetExplorer. *Frontiers in Psychology*, *14*, 1061778. DOI: 10.3389/fpsyg.2023.1061778 PMID: 36968737

Chapter 6
Teaching With Machines:
Ethical AI Integration and Creative Pedagogies in Film and Media Education

Azalia Primadita Muchransyah
http://orcid.org/0000-0002-3737-4837
Bina Nusantara University, Indonesia

ABSTRACT

This chapter examines the integration of artificial intelligence in film and media education as a pedagogical condition that reshapes relationships between educators, students, creative practice, and institutional expectations. Advancing the concept of teaching with machines, it approaches AI not as a neutral tool or automated authority, but as a mediating presence that structures learning through relational, interpretive, and ethically situated interaction. In creative and practice-based disciplines, AI unsettles established assumptions about authorship, assessment, originality, and responsibility. The chapter argues that meaningful engagement with AI in education depends less on technical mastery than on pedagogical intention. By foregrounding uncertainty, reflexivity, and care, it explores how educators can design process-oriented learning environments that sustain critical inquiry, human judgment, and creative agency. Ethical concerns such as bias, data governance, and accountability are treated as integral to everyday pedagogical practice.

INTRODUCTION

The increasing presence of artificial intelligence (AI) in educational settings has reshaped how teaching, learning, and creative practice are imagined and enacted. In

DOI: 10.4018/979-8-2600-1840-8.ch006

film and media education, AI tools are now routinely used for script development, image generation, editing, recommendation analysis, and audience forecasting. These technologies promise efficiency and expanded creative possibilities, yet they also unsettle long-standing pedagogical assumptions about authorship, expertise, and agency. Rather than appearing as a distant or future-oriented technology, AI is increasingly embedded in the everyday workflows of students and educators, shaping how creative decisions are made, justified, and evaluated. Teaching with machines is therefore not simply a matter of adopting new tools, but of rethinking how knowledge is produced, mediated, and assessed in environments where human and algorithmic intelligences intersect (UNESCO, 2023).

This chapter contributes to ongoing debates on AI in education by shifting the focus from AI as an instructional tool to AI as a pedagogical mediator; a system that actively participates in shaping creative processes, decision-making, and learning relationships. While existing discourse often frames AI either as an instrument to be mastered or as a risk to be governed, such perspectives tend to overlook the situated, everyday realities of classroom practice. Empirical studies suggest that educators and students encounter AI not as a stable or transparent system, but as a probabilistic and sometimes unreliable collaborator that requires interpretation and negotiation. For example, studies of higher education classrooms show that instructors are already redesigning assessments in response to generative AI, while simultaneously expressing uncertainty about how to integrate it effectively and ethically (Lee et al., 2024). Similarly, student-centered research indicates that learners use AI for ideation, drafting, and problem-solving, but remain concerned about accuracy, authorship, and overreliance (Zafar et al., 2024; Chan & Hu, 2023).

These findings point to a more complex pedagogical reality than dominant narratives of efficiency or disruption suggest. Rather than simply "using" AI, students engage in iterative processes of prompting, evaluating, and revising outputs; practices that foreground uncertainty, experimentation, and partial understanding as central conditions of learning. This aligns with critical perspectives that conceptualize AI not as a neutral tool, but as a system shaped by data histories, cultural assumptions, and embedded values (Khoo et al., 2022; Zylinska, 2020). From this perspective, learning with AI involves not only technical interaction but also epistemic negotiation: understanding how knowledge is produced, where it comes from, and how it should be interpreted.

In response, this chapter approaches AI as a mediating presence that reshapes relations between students, educators, and creative practice. This relational perspective foregrounds how meaning emerges through interaction: between human intention, algorithmic output, and institutional context. It also aligns with emerging pedagogical approaches that emphasize experimentation over mastery and process over product. Empirical classroom-based studies demonstrate that integrating AI into project-based learning environments can shift attention toward metacognitive skills, critical evaluation, and reflective practice, particularly when students are required to document their workflows and decision-making processes (Charles et al., 2025; Brand, 2024). Such approaches are especially relevant in film and media education, where creative processes are iterative, collaborative, and interpretive.

At the same time, the integration of AI into educational practice raises significant ethical and institutional challenges. Issues of consent, data provenance, bias, and authorship are not abstract concerns but lived realities in classrooms and creative projects (UNESCO, 2023). Students may rely on systems trained on opaque datasets, reproduce algorithmic biases, or struggle to define the boundaries between assistance and authorship. Empirical research further highlights tensions around trust and transparency, showing that undisclosed AI use can affect educator–student relationships and collaborative dynamics (Kloker et al., 2024). In addition, institutional factors, such as uneven access to tools, lack of training, and unclear policies, shape how AI is adopted and experienced in practice (Lee et al., 2024). Ethical engagement with AI, therefore, cannot be reduced to compliance with external guidelines; it must be understood as an ongoing pedagogical practice grounded in reflection, accountability, and contextual awareness (Association of Southeast Asian Nations, 2025).

By focusing on teaching with machines rather than teaching about machines, this chapter examines how AI reshapes pedagogical relationships in film and media education. It argues that meaningful AI integration depends less on technical proficiency than on cultivating critical, ethical, and reflective capacities: the ability to question algorithmic authority, evaluate outputs, and situate creative decisions within broader social and cultural contexts. In doing so, the chapter positions itself at the intersection of media studies, pedagogy, and AI ethics, offering a framework that connects theoretical reflection with classroom practice. Ultimately, it suggests that education is not merely adapting to AI but actively shaping how future creative practitioners understand, use, and critically engage with intelligent systems in an evolving media landscape.

BACKGROUND

Artificial intelligence has become embedded in educational environments not through a single technological breakthrough, but through a gradual normalization of automated systems across everyday academic practices. Writing assistants, image generators, transcription tools, recommendation systems, and analytics dashboards are now routinely encountered by students and educators alike. This incremental integration has made AI less visible as a discrete technology and more present as an infrastructural condition of contemporary education (UNESCO, 2023). In film and media education, this normalization is particularly pronounced, as creative workflows have long relied on digital tools that blur the boundaries between human intention and technical mediation. AI extends this trajectory by introducing systems that not only assist production but also actively generate, predict, and evaluate creative outputs (Zylinska, 2020).

Within higher education discourse, AI is frequently framed in terms of efficiency, scalability, and personalization. Such framings emphasize optimization (faster feedback, adaptive learning pathways, automated assessment), often positioning AI as a solution to structural constraints such as large class sizes or limited instructional resources (Organization for Economic Co-operation and Development, 2021). Policy documents and institutional strategies tend to privilege measurable outcomes, framing AI as a neutral instrument for improving performance and productivity (Association of Southeast Asian Nations, 2025). Empirical studies, however, suggest a more uneven reality. Educators report mixed levels of preparedness and uncertainty regarding how to integrate generative AI into teaching, often adapting assessments reactively rather than through established pedagogical frameworks (Lee et al., 2024). While these narratives highlight legitimate institutional concerns, they risk obscuring the pedagogical implications of delegating interpretive and evaluative functions to algorithmic systems. In creative disciplines, where learning outcomes are not easily standardized, this tension becomes particularly visible.

Critical scholarship on digital education has long emphasized that technologies do not simply support learning but actively shape what counts as knowledge, competence, and success (Bucholc et al., 2022). AI intensifies this dynamic by operating through probabilistic models trained on historical data, embedding assumptions about norms, values, and relevance into automated processes. Unlike earlier educational technologies that primarily mediated access or delivery, AI systems increasingly participate in judgment, selection, and interpretation (Khoo et al., 2022). When such systems are introduced into classrooms, they carry these assumptions, influencing how students understand creativity, originality, and expertise. The challenge for educators, therefore, is not only to manage AI use but to make its mediating role visible and discussable.

Recent debates around generative AI underscore a broader cultural shift toward process-oriented engagement with technology. Rather than treating AI outputs as authoritative or final, many practitioners approach them as provisional, iterative, and open to reinterpretation. This reframing positions AI-generated content as material for thinking rather than as an endpoint of production (Zylinska, 2020). Empirical research on student use of generative AI reflects similar dynamics: students often use AI for brainstorming, drafting, and iterative refinement, while simultaneously expressing concerns about accuracy, authorship, and overreliance (Zafar et al., 2024; Chan & Hu, 2023). Trust in generative systems, in this context, is not a matter of accuracy alone but of negotiated use, shaped through experimentation, critique, and contextual judgment (New Scientist, 2025). In educational settings, this orientation opens possibilities for pedagogies that foreground inquiry over mastery, positioning uncertainty as a productive condition of learning rather than a failure to be corrected.

Ethical concerns further complicate AI's role in education. Questions of data consent, bias, authorship, and accountability are often addressed through institutional guidelines or technical safeguards (UNESCO, 2023). However, such approaches can inadvertently distance ethics from everyday practice, treating it as an external constraint rather than an integral part of pedagogical engagement. Empirical studies indicate that students and educators alike experience ethical tensions in practice, particularly regarding academic integrity, transparency, and appropriate use of AI (Bùi & Tong, 2025; Kloker et al., 2024). Ethical issues are frequently framed as compliance matters, what students and educators should not do, rather than as reflective practices embedded in creative decision-making. In classrooms, ethical dilemmas emerge in situated ways: when students rely too heavily on generated content, when creative ownership becomes ambiguous, or when automated feedback reinforces normative aesthetic standards. These moments reveal ethics not as a checklist but as an ongoing negotiation embedded in teaching and learning processes (Zylinska, 2020).

The background for teaching with machines, then, is not defined by a lack of regulation or technical knowledge, but by a growing mismatch between how AI systems operate and how education has traditionally conceptualized learning. Pedagogical models premised on linear progression, individual authorship, and transparent evaluation struggle to accommodate systems characterized by opacity, collective data histories, and probabilistic reasoning (Khoo et al., 2022). This mismatch is also reflected in assessment practices, where traditional product-oriented evaluation often fails to capture AI-mediated processes of ideation, iteration, and collaboration (Zhao, 2025). Addressing this tension requires moving beyond instrumental approaches to AI adoption and toward pedagogical frameworks that recognize mediation, relationality, and responsibility as central to contemporary education.

Within film and media education, these concerns are amplified by the field's close relationship to cultural production and representation. Creative work does not occur in a vacuum; it circulates within social, political, and economic contexts that shape which stories are told and how they are valued (Zylinska, 2020). AI systems trained on existing media archives risk reinforcing dominant genres, aesthetic conventions, and cultural hierarchies unless their limitations are actively interrogated. At the same time, emerging classroom practices show that AI can function as a creative partner in processes such as story development, visual ideation, and editing experimentation, provided that students are guided to critically evaluate and contextualize its outputs (Kharrufa & Johnson, 2024). Teaching with machines, therefore, becomes a matter of cultivating awareness: helping students understand not only how AI tools function, but how they participate in broader cultural dynamics (UNESCO, 2023).

This background situates the chapter's intervention: to examine AI not as an external disruptor of education, but as a mediating actor that reshapes pedagogical relations, creative practice, and ethical responsibility (Zylinska, 2020). By foregrounding the lived experience of teaching and learning with AI, the chapter builds toward a framework that emphasizes critical engagement, reflexivity, and care in an increasingly automated educational landscape. Rather than resolving uncertainty, teaching with machines asks educators and students to learn how to dwell within it responsibly (UNESCO, 2023).

MAIN FOCUS OF THE CHAPTER

This chapter advances a pedagogical framework that reframes artificial intelligence not as an external instructional aid but as an active mediator within educational practice. Building on the background discussion of AI's infrastructural normalization and ethical implications, this section articulates how teaching with machines reshapes core dimensions of pedagogy, including agency, authorship, trust, creativity, and care. The following subsections examine these dynamics in detail, moving from relational understandings of human–machine interaction to the practical and ethical tensions that emerge in AI-mediated learning environments. Rather than isolating technical skills or policy compliance, the focus remains on how educators and students navigate uncertainty, responsibility, and meaning-making when creative work is produced in collaboration with algorithmic systems.

Teaching With Machines, Not Through Them

The central argument of this chapter is that artificial intelligence should be understood not as an instructional shortcut or an automated tutor, but as a mediating presence within pedagogical relationships (Zylinska, 2020; UNESCO, 2023). Teaching with machines foregrounds the relational dynamics between students, educators, creative tools, and institutional expectations. Rather than positioning AI as an authority that delivers answers, this approach treats AI systems as interlocutors, entities whose outputs are shaped by data histories, probabilistic reasoning, and embedded cultural assumptions (Bucholc et al., 2022). This framing shifts attention away from efficiency-driven adoption toward questions of interaction, interpretation, and responsibility.

In film and media education, this distinction is particularly consequential. Creative learning has long involved working with tools that shape form and meaning, from cameras and editing software to distribution platforms (Zylinska, 2020). AI extends this lineage while introducing a new degree of opacity and generativity. Outputs emerge not from linear instruction but from iterative prompting, revision, and negotiation (New Scientist, 2025). Teaching with machines, therefore, requires educators to shift emphasis from correct outcomes to interpretive processes: how ideas are formed, questioned, and reshaped through interaction with nonhuman systems. What students learn is not simply how to produce an acceptable artifact, but how to navigate a process in which agency is distributed across human intention and machine inference (UNESCO, 2023).

This shift toward process-oriented engagement is increasingly reflected in empirical studies of higher education. Research shows that educators are already modifying assessment formats in response to generative AI, often moving away from product-based evaluation toward process-oriented and reflective approaches (Lee et al., 2024). At the same time, these studies highlight persistent uncertainty among instructors about how to implement such changes effectively and consistently. Teaching with machines addresses this gap by offering a pedagogical framework that connects conceptual principles with classroom practice, emphasizing interpretive engagement, transparency, and critical reflection.

This pedagogical stance also positions itself in contrast to more instrumental or tool-oriented approaches to AI integration, which tend to prioritize efficiency, automation, or skill acquisition. Rather than treating AI as a productivity enhancer, teaching with machines aligns more closely with critical and relational pedagogies that emphasize situated knowledge, interpretive judgment, and ethical responsibility. Learning occurs not when students accept machine outputs, but when they interrogate how those outputs come into being and what values they reflect (Bucholc et al., 2022). In this sense, AI becomes less a tool to be mastered and more a condition through which critical thinking and creative judgment are exercised.

The distinction between instrumental uses of AI and a relational pedagogy of teaching with machines is summarized in Table 1, which contrasts how authority, agency, assessment, and ethics are configured across these two approaches.

Table 1. From teaching through machines to teaching with machines

Pedagogical Dimension	Teaching Through Machines	Teaching With Machines
Role of AI	Instructional aid or automated tutor	Mediating, generative interlocutor
Role of Educator	Overseer of tool use and outcomes	Pedagogical mediator and ethical guide
Student Agency	Compliance with AI-assisted efficiency	Reflexive engagement and interpretive judgment

continued on following page

Table 1. Continued

Pedagogical Dimension	Teaching Through Machines	Teaching With Machines
View of Knowledge	Stable, correct, and optimizable	Provisional, situated, and negotiated
Assessment Focus	Output quality and originality	Process, decision-making, and reflection
Treatment of Error	Mistakes to be minimized or corrected	Resource for inquiry and critique
Ethical Orientation	Compliance and detection	Transparency, accountability, and care

Source: Author's synthesis based on Zylinska (2020), UNESCO (2023), Organization for Economic Co-operation and Development (2021), and Bucholc et al. (2022)

Trust, Uncertainty, and the Generative Process

A recurring challenge in AI-enhanced education is trust. Students often oscillate between overreliance on generated content and skepticism toward its legitimacy (UNESCO, 2023). Teaching with machines reframes trust not as confidence in accuracy, but as awareness of limits. Trust becomes conditional, negotiated, and reflective rather than absolute. Students learn not to ask whether AI is "right," but under what conditions its outputs might be helpful, misleading, or ethically problematic (Zylinska, 2020).

Empirical studies of student experience reinforce this reframing. Survey-based research shows that students widely use generative AI for brainstorming, drafting, and problem-solving, while simultaneously expressing concerns about accuracy, bias, and overdependence (Chan & Hu, 2023; Zafar et al., 2024). This ambivalence suggests that trust is not a stable condition but an evolving negotiation shaped by context, task demands, and perceived reliability. Teaching with machines makes this negotiation explicit, positioning trust as something to examine rather than assume critically.

Generative systems operate through uncertainty. They produce plausible continuations rather than verified knowledge, offering suggestions that may inspire, mislead, or provoke critique (New Scientist, 2025). When educators invite students to examine how AI arrives at particular responses, uncertainty becomes a learning resource rather than a risk to be managed away. Moments of error, inconsistency, or bias can thus be treated as occasions for analysis and discussion rather than disruptions to be corrected (UNESCO, 2023).

This orientation aligns with broader understandings of generative technologies as processes rather than products. The emphasis shifts from what the machine produces to how students engage with the act of generation itself—through iteration, comparison, refusal, and reinterpretation (Zylinska, 2020). Teaching with machines cultivates epistemic humility, encouraging learners to recognize both the affordances and constraints of automated systems (Bucholc et al., 2022). Such humility is essential in creative education, where confidence must coexist with openness to revision and critique.

Creativity, Authorship, and Ethical Friction

AI complicates longstanding assumptions about creativity and authorship in education. In creative disciplines, originality has traditionally been associated with individual expression and intentional decision-making. Generative systems disrupt this framework by producing content that is neither fully authored nor entirely autonomous (UNESCO, 2023). Teaching with machines does not resolve this ambiguity; instead, it brings it into focus. Authorship becomes a shared, layered, and sometimes contested practice rather than a singular claim (Bucholc et al., 2022).

These tensions become especially visible in project-based and creative assessments. Empirical research shows that when students use generative AI in multimedia assignments, their understanding of authorship and originality shifts, often prompting reflection on how creative labor should be evaluated (Charles et al., 2025). Such findings reinforce the need to assess not only final outputs but also the processes through which AI is used, adapted, or resisted.

Ethical friction emerges when students submit AI-generated work without reflection, when stylistic homogeneity replaces experimentation, or when creative risk is avoided in favor of algorithmic predictability (Khoo et al., 2022). These moments are not failures of discipline but signals of deeper pedagogical questions: What counts as creative labor? Where does responsibility reside when outputs are co-produced with machines? How should educators respond when boundaries between assistance and substitution become blurred? Rather than treating such questions as violations, this chapter frames them as central learning opportunities.

Teaching with machines invites ethical reflection as part of creative practice rather than enforcing rigid prohibitions. Students are encouraged to articulate their decision-making processes, disclose their use of AI tools, and critically assess the implications of machine involvement (UNESCO, 2023). Ethics becomes situated and dialogic—embedded in practice rather than imposed externally (Zylinska, 2020). In this sense, ethical friction is not an obstacle to learning but a productive condition that reveals how creative, technical, and moral decisions intersect in AI-mediated environments.

Pedagogical Care in Automated Environments

Another key focus of this chapter is the role of care in AI-mediated education. Automated systems are often introduced under the promise of personalization. However, they can inadvertently standardize learning experiences by privileging dominant linguistic, aesthetic, or cultural patterns (Organization for Economic Co-operation and Development, 2021). Teaching with machines foregrounds the educator's role as a mediator who attends to difference, context, and vulnerability (Zylinska, 2020). Care, in this sense, is not opposed to technology but actively shapes how technology is integrated.

At the same time, institutional conditions shape how care can be enacted. Research on AI adoption in higher education highlights persistent challenges, including uneven access to tools, limited staff training, and gaps in institutional guidance (Lee et al., 2024). These constraints mean that care must extend beyond classroom interaction to encompass infrastructural realities that affect participation and equity.

Care manifests in how assignments are designed, how feedback is framed, and how students are supported as they navigate unfamiliar tools. It also involves recognizing that students experience AI technologies unevenly, shaped by prior exposure, linguistic background, access to resources, and cultural norms (Association of Southeast Asian Nations, 2024). A pedagogy of care resists one-size-fits-all adoption and adapts AI use to local conditions and student needs (UNESCO, 2023), helping prevent the amplification of existing inequalities.

Teaching with machines is therefore not about delegating responsibility to technology, but about reaffirming the educator's role in shaping ethical and inclusive learning environments. Machines may generate content, but educators remain responsible for framing its meaning and consequences.

From Technical Competence to Critical Fluency

Finally, the chapter argues for a shift from technical competence toward critical fluency. Knowing how to prompt an AI system or edit its outputs is insufficient on its own. Students must also develop the capacity to question how systems are trained, whose knowledge they reproduce, and which voices they marginalize (Bucholc et al., 2022). Critical fluency extends beyond operational skill to include cultural, ethical, and political awareness.

Emerging research underscores the importance of prompt literacy as part of this broader competence. Studies suggest that students who develop more deliberate and reflective prompting strategies achieve better learning outcomes, as prompt construction mediates their engagement with AI systems. In creative disciplines, this includes shaping narrative, visual, and conceptual outputs through iterative and critically informed interaction.

Teaching with machines, therefore, emphasizes interpretive skills: reading machine outputs critically, situating them within cultural and historical contexts, and recognizing their ethical and political dimensions (Zylinska, 2020). This approach prepares students not only to use AI tools but to participate responsibly in creative and educational ecosystems shaped by automation (UNESCO, 2023).

Rather than treating AI literacy as a discrete skill set, this chapter frames it as an ongoing practice; one that evolves alongside technologies and requires continuous reflection (New Scientist, 2025). Teaching with machines thus becomes less about mastering tools and more about cultivating ethical, creative, and critical agency in an uncertain technological landscape.

SOLUTIONS AND RECOMMENDATIONS

Translating the conceptual framework for teaching with machines into pedagogical practice requires principled yet adaptable approaches. Rather than offering prescriptive rules, this section proposes strategies to address the relational, ethical, and epistemic challenges outlined above. These strategies support learning environments in which AI functions as a site of inquiry rather than a shortcut. Table 2 summarizes these approaches.

Table 2. Pedagogical strategies for teaching with machines

Pedagogical Strategy	Learning Focus	Example Practice	Pedagogical Rationale
Process-oriented assignments	Critical thinking and agency	Students submit AI interaction logs and reflective commentaries	Shifts the evaluation from the product to the learning process
AI use documentation	Transparency and reflexivity	Prompt histories, rejected outputs, revision notes	Makes decision-making visible and assessable
Disclosure statements	Ethical accountability	Written explanation of how AI contributed to the work	Reframes integrity as explanation rather than concealment
Prompt comparison exercises	Bias and framing awareness	Students test multiple prompts and analyze differences	Reveals how human input shapes machine output
Ethical dilemma tasks	Situated ethical reasoning	Revising biased AI outputs or refusing AI use	Treats ethics as practice, not abstraction

Source: Adapted from Beetham & Sharpe (2019), Selwyn (2021), Zylinska (2020), and UNESCO (2023).

Designing Assignments Around Process, Not Output

One of the most effective ways to teach with machines is to redesign assignments so that learning outcomes emphasize process rather than final products (UNESCO, 2023). Empirical research supports this shift, showing that process-based assessment better captures higher-order thinking, metacognitive development, and iterative learning in AI-assisted contexts (Zhao, 2025).

Process-oriented assignments encourage students to document their interactions with AI systems: what they asked, what they received, what they rejected, and why (Zylinska, 2020). This documentation makes decision-making visible and assessable, allowing educators to evaluate critical thinking, reflexivity, and ethical awareness (Beetham & Sharpe, 2019).

In creative disciplines, this approach aligns with established studio pedagogies that value drafts, revisions, and reflective practice. AI interaction logs and annotated workflows extend rather than disrupt these traditions.

Embedding Disclosure and Reflexivity as Norms

Rather than treating AI use as something to be policed, this chapter recommends normalizing disclosure as a pedagogical practice (UNESCO, 2023). Reflexive statements help students articulate how AI contributed to their work, fostering a more nuanced understanding of authorship (Zylinska, 2020; Selwyn, 2021).

Transparency also supports trust. Research indicates that disclosure of AI use is positively associated with perceptions of fairness, collaboration, and academic integrity (Kloker et al., 2024). Framing disclosure as a learning tool encourages honesty and critical engagement rather than concealment.

Teaching Prompting as Critical Inquiry

Prompting functions not only as a technical skill but as a form of inquiry. Students can compare prompts, analyze variations in outputs, and reflect on embedded assumptions (Zylinska, 2020).

Empirical classroom studies show that structured prompting activities help students use AI both as a creative collaborator and as a reflective tool for understanding concepts (Kharrufa & Johnson, 2024). This reinforces prompting as a critical practice rather than mere optimization.

Integrating Ethical Friction Into Assessment

Teaching with machines incorporates ethical ambiguity into learning design. Assignments can require students to confront issues of bias, authorship, and responsibility.

Assessment can include criteria such as transparency of AI use, quality of reflection, and ability to critique outputs. These align with emerging frameworks for AI-integrated assessment that emphasize accountability and interpretive judgment (Zhao, 2025).

Supporting Educators Through Collective Pedagogy

AI pedagogy should not be a burden for individuals. Collaborative spaces allow educators to share practices and develop shared norms (Selwyn, 2021).

This is particularly important given that many educators report feeling underprepared to integrate AI and seek institutional support (Lee et al., 2024). Collective approaches enable more consistent and reflective implementation across programs.

Prioritizing Care and Context in Implementation

Finally, AI integration must remain context-sensitive (Zylinska, 2020). Students vary in access, familiarity, and comfort with AI, and equitable pedagogy requires flexibility.

Student research shows both enthusiasm and anxiety regarding AI use, including concerns about dependency and unclear expectations (Chan & Hu, 2023; Bùi & Tong, 2025). Recognizing these experiences allows educators to design more supportive environments.

Care-based implementation ensures that technological adoption does not override student well-being or equity (Eubanks, 2018). Teaching with machines ultimately sustains meaningful educational relationships within technologically mediated environments.

The recurring tensions that emerge across these dimensions, ranging from authorship ambiguity to institutional pressures, can be understood not as problems to be resolved through restriction, but as conditions that call for pedagogical response. These tensions and their corresponding teaching-with-machines strategies are summarized in Table 3.

Table 3. Pedagogical tensions and responsive teaching practices

Pedagogical Tension	Common Institutional Response	Teaching-with-Machines Response
Authorship ambiguity	Prohibition or plagiarism detection	Reflexive disclosure and relational authorship
Overreliance on AI	Surveillance and restriction	Guided critique and interpretive use
Assessment integrity	Tool bans or standardization	Process-based and reflective assessment
Student anxiety	Technical training emphasis	Dialogic support and pedagogical care
Pressure for efficiency	Automation of feedback and grading	Reaffirmation of educator judgment

Source: Author's synthesis drawing on UNESCO (2023), Association of Southeast Asian Nations (2024; 2025), Bucholc et al. (2022), and Zylinska (2020).

FUTURE RESEARCH DIRECTIONS

While this chapter has outlined a conceptual and pedagogical framework for teaching with machines, it does not claim to exhaust the questions raised by AI's integration into educational practice. On the contrary, the relational, ethical, and contextual issues identified here point toward a research agenda that must remain responsive to technological change, institutional diversity, and lived pedagogical experience. Future research is therefore necessary not only to evaluate the effects of AI adoption, but to deepen understanding of how teaching and learning are reconfigured over time in algorithmic environments.

Importantly, emerging empirical studies suggest that AI integration in higher education is uneven, context-dependent, and often marked by uncertainty among both educators and students (Lee et al., 2024; Zafar et al., 2024). These findings reinforce the need for research that moves beyond adoption metrics toward examining how pedagogical relationships, assessment practices, and forms of agency are reshaped in practice. The subsections that follow outline key areas where sustained empirical, theoretical, and methodological inquiry can extend the chapter's arguments and support more reflective, equitable, and context-sensitive approaches to AI in education.

Building on the pedagogical arguments developed in this chapter, Table 4 maps key areas for future research on teaching with machines, identifying central questions and methodological directions.

Table 4. Future research directions for teaching with machines

Research Area	Key Questions	Suggested Approaches
Longitudinal learning	How do student–AI relations evolve?	Longitudinal qualitative studies
Pedagogical labor	How does AI reshape educator workload and identity?	Interviews, institutional ethnography
Assessment and values	What forms of knowledge become legible or rewarded?	Policy analysis, assessment design studies
Cultural contexts	How does AI pedagogy vary across regions and languages?	Comparative and postcolonial studies
Creative education	How is authorship negotiated in hybrid creative work?	Studio ethnography, practice-based research
Ethics in practice	How do students learn ethical judgment with AI?	Reflective writing analysis, classroom observation

Source: Author.

Teaching, Learning, and Agency in Algorithmic Environments

Teaching with machines remains an emergent pedagogical condition rather than a stabilized field of practice. As generative systems become embedded in educational workflows, research must increasingly attend to how AI reshapes learning relations, institutional norms, and epistemic authority. Empirical studies indicate that educators often experience ambiguity about how to integrate AI into teaching meaningfully, even as adoption increases (Lee et al., 2024).

Rather than treating AI as a discrete intervention, future inquiry should conceptualize it as an evolving condition that reorganizes educational practice across classroom, institutional, and policy levels. This shift directs attention toward questions of agency: how students and educators negotiate responsibility, authority, and meaning in environments where machine-generated outputs are increasingly normalized.

Longitudinal Studies of Learning With AI

A significant gap in current scholarship is the lack of longitudinal research examining how sustained engagement with AI systems shapes learning over time. Existing empirical work tends to focus on short-term perceptions or immediate performance outcomes (Zafar et al., 2024; Chan & Hu, 2023), offering limited insight into how relationships with AI evolve.

Future research should trace how students' engagements with AI develop across semesters and programs. Do learners become more critical, more dependent, or more strategically selective in their use of AI tools? Studies suggest that student attitudes are already mixed: combining enthusiasm for efficiency and personalization with concerns about accuracy, trust, and skill development (Chan & Hu, 2023).

Longitudinal approaches would also allow researchers to examine whether pedagogical strategies such as process-based assessment, disclosure practices, and reflective engagement produce durable forms of critical agency. Such work is particularly important in creative disciplines, where iterative practice and identity formation unfold over extended periods.

Pedagogical Labor and the Role of the Educator

Another underexplored area concerns the changing labor of educators. Teaching with machines requires instructors to redesign assignments, negotiate ethical ambiguity, and support students navigating unfamiliar technological conditions. Empirical evidence suggests that many educators feel underprepared for these demands and seek clearer institutional guidance (Lee et al., 2024).

Future research should therefore make pedagogical labor more visible. This includes examining how educators balance authority and facilitation when AI systems generate content, as well as the emotional and ethical dimensions of supporting students dealing with uncertainty, overreliance, or distrust.

Comparative studies across institutional contexts can further illuminate how policy environments shape pedagogical autonomy, particularly in systems where AI adoption is encouraged without corresponding investment in training or support.

AI, Assessment, and Epistemic Values

Assessment remains a central site of tension in AI-mediated education. Empirical studies indicate that AI use is already prompting shifts in assessment design, particularly in project-based and creative work (Charles et al., 2025). These shifts highlight the inadequacy of traditional evaluation models focused solely on output and originality.

Future research should explore alternative assessment frameworks that foreground process, reflection, and decision-making. Evidence suggests that AI-supported feedback can enhance learning outcomes, particularly in iterative and formative contexts (Zhao, 2025), but also raises concerns about bias, trust, and overreliance.

More broadly, research should examine how AI reshapes epistemic values within education. What forms of knowledge become visible, measurable, and rewarded? How do algorithmic systems privilege certain forms of coherence, fluency, or normativity? Addressing these questions connects assessment design to deeper concerns about what counts as meaningful learning.

Student Perspectives, Trust, and Learning Experience

While theoretical frameworks often emphasize pedagogy and ethics, empirical studies highlight the importance of student experience in shaping AI integration. Students report both benefits, such as efficiency, ideation support, and personalized learning, and concerns related to trust, accuracy, and academic integrity (Zafar et al., 2024; Bùi & Tong, 2025).

Research should further examine how students navigate these tensions in practice. For example, studies suggest that transparency in AI use is closely tied to trust in collaborative and educational settings (Kloker et al., 2024). This has direct implications for pedagogical design, particularly in group-based creative work where authorship and contribution are negotiated.

Future work should also explore how students from different cultural, linguistic, and disciplinary backgrounds experience AI-mediated learning differently, contributing to more inclusive and context-sensitive pedagogies.

Cultural Contexts and Non-Western Pedagogies

Much of the existing literature on AI and education remains grounded in Western institutional contexts. Future research must more carefully attend to how teaching with machines unfolds in diverse cultural, linguistic, and economic settings.

Context-sensitive research can examine how local infrastructures, languages, and pedagogical traditions shape the use of AI. In Southeast Asian contexts, for example, the interaction between AI systems and multilingual, culturally diverse learning environments raises important questions about representation, bias, and accessibility.

Such work is essential for avoiding the reproduction of global inequalities through AI systems and for developing pedagogical models that are responsive to local conditions rather than universally imposed.

Creative Education and Experimental Pedagogies

Creative disciplines offer a particularly valuable site for future research. Empirical studies in adjacent fields demonstrate that integrating AI into project-based learning environments can shift both student perceptions and assessment expectations (Charles et al., 2025).

In film and media education, research can explore how students use AI tools in processes such as scripting, storyboarding, and editing, and how these practices reshape understandings of authorship and creative labor. Studies also suggest that teaching prompt design and critical evaluation of AI outputs can enhance learning outcomes (Kharrufa & Johnson, 2024).

Practice-based and ethnographic approaches are especially well suited to capturing these dynamics, as they foreground process, experimentation, and situated meaning-making.

Ethics as Pedagogical Practice

While ethical frameworks for AI are increasingly well developed, future research should focus on how ethics is practiced in classrooms. Empirical work indicates that students' ethical perceptions are shaped by discipline, context, and institutional guidance (Bùi & Tong, 2025).

Research should therefore examine how ethical reasoning develops through interaction, reflection, and dialogue rather than through abstract instruction alone. This includes exploring how students navigate issues such as authorship, attribution, and bias in everyday creative and academic practices.

Institutional Governance and Policy Alignment

Teaching with machines is shaped by institutional policies, many of which remain in flux. Empirical studies show that, in some contexts, instructors receive little guidance on integrating AI, leading to inconsistent practices and uncertainty (Lee et al., 2024).

Future research should examine how policies are interpreted and enacted in practice, as well as how they align with, or fail to align with, pedagogical realities. Comparative work can illuminate how different governance models support or constrain experimentation, reflexivity, and ethical engagement.

Methodological Innovation in Studying AI Pedagogy

Finally, future research must also evolve methodologically. Studying teaching with machines requires approaches that capture interaction, process, and reflexivity. Mixed methods, design-based research, and participatory approaches are particularly valuable in this regard.

Emerging studies that analyze interaction logs, reflections, and student workflows demonstrate the potential of such approaches for understanding how AI is used in practice (Kim et al., 2024). Involving educators and students as co-researchers can further ground research in lived experience.

Toward an Ongoing Pedagogical Conversation

Rather than offering definitive solutions, this chapter positions teaching with machines as an ongoing pedagogical conversation. Future research plays a crucial role in sustaining this conversation by grounding theoretical claims in empirical practice while remaining attentive to context and change.

By integrating empirical evidence with conceptual inquiry, future scholarship can ensure that AI in education is not reduced to efficiency or automation, but remains oriented toward critical engagement, creative practice, and ethical responsibility.

CONCLUSION

Teaching with machines is not simply a matter of adopting new tools or updating technical competencies. It entails a reconfiguration of pedagogical relations: between educators and students, between institutions and knowledge, and between human judgment and algorithmic mediation. Throughout this chapter, artificial intelligence has been approached not as an autonomous agent or neutral assistant, but as a sociotechnical presence that reshapes how authority, creativity, and responsibility are distributed within educational environments.

Rather than positioning AI as either a threat to education or a solution to its structural challenges, the chapter has advanced a relational understanding of pedagogy grounded in interaction, interpretation, and care. Empirical research reinforces this position, showing that both educators and students navigate AI with a mixture of opportunity, uncertainty, and ambivalence (Lee et al., 2024; Zafar et al., 2024). These findings underscore that AI integration is not a purely technical process but a deeply pedagogical one.

A central claim of this chapter is that pedagogy remains a fundamentally human practice, even in automated environments. Teaching involves judgment, attentiveness, and ethical deliberation; capacities that cannot be delegated to algorithmic systems without diminishing the educational encounter itself. While AI systems may generate outputs or simulate dialogue, responsibility for learning remains relational, grounded in the interactions between educators and students.

The chapter has also shown how teaching with machines destabilizes conventional understandings of authorship and assessment. Empirical studies of AI-assisted learning highlight the need to evaluate not only outputs but also processes, decisions, and forms of engagement (Charles et al., 2025; Zhao, 2025). In this context, academic integrity is reconfigured as transparency, reflexivity, and accountability rather than the absence of machine involvement.

Attention to context remains essential. AI systems are not experienced uniformly, and differences in access, language, and institutional support shape how teaching with machines is enacted. Without such attention, AI risks reinforcing existing inequalities even as it promises innovation.

Equally important is the role of care. Teaching with machines introduces uncertainty, anxiety, and ethical complexity into learning environments. Addressing these dimensions requires pedagogical approaches grounded in dialogue, trust, and responsiveness to student experience.

Ultimately, the future of education in algorithmic environments depends less on technological sophistication than on pedagogical intention. Teaching with machines can either reinforce efficiency-driven models of learning or open space for more reflective, inclusive, and humane educational practices.

In this sense, teaching with machines is not about learning from machines, but learning with and about them. It invites educators and students to reconsider what education is for, whose knowledge is valued, and how responsibility is shared in increasingly automated environments. By foregrounding relationality, care, and critical agency, this chapter offers a framework for engaging AI not as a replacement for pedagogy but as a condition that makes its ethical and human dimensions more visible than ever.

OPEN DATA STATEMENT

No new empirical data were generated for this study. All referenced materials are publicly available through institutional, governmental, and organizational sources as cited in the References section.

OPEN CONTRIBUTORSHIP STATEMENT

This chapter was conceptualized, researched, and written solely by the author. All analytical interpretations and conclusions are the author's own.

ACKNOWLEDGMENT

This research received no specific grant from any funding agency in the public, commercial, or not-for-profit sectors. The author acknowledges using ChatGPT (OpenAI, GPT-5) and Grammarly as digital writing and editing aids to refine language and maintain stylistic consistency. No generative tools were used to produce or analyze data; all interpretations and syntheses reflect the author's original scholarly work.

REFERENCES

Association of Southeast Asian Nations. (2024). *ASEAN guide on AI governance and ethics*. ASEAN Secretariat.

Association of Southeast Asian Nations. (2025). *Expanded ASEAN guide on generative AI governance and ethics*. ASEAN Secretariat.

Beetham, H., & Sharpe, R. (Eds.). (2019). *Rethinking pedagogy for a digital age: Principles and practices of design* (3rd ed.). Routledge., DOI: 10.4324/9781351252805

Bùi, T. T. D., & Tong, T. V. A. (2025). The impact of AI writing tools on academic integrity: Unveiling English-majored students' perceptions and practical solutions. *AsiaCALL Online Journal*, *16*(1), 83–110. Advance online publication. DOI: 10.54855/acoj.251615

Bucholc, M., Komornik, Ł., & Piasna, A. (2022). The world algorithmic order: Data, platforms, and the global condition. *Big Data & Society*, *9*(1), 1–12. DOI: 10.1177/20539517221078981

Chan, C., & Hu, W. (2023). *Students' voices on generative AI: Perceptions, benefits, and challenges in higher education*. arXiv. https://doi.org//arxiv.2305.00290DOI: 10.48550

Charles, K., Yousuf, A., Chow Chua, H., Matthews, S., Harnett, J., & Hinton, T. (2025). AI in action: Changes to student perceptions when using generative artificial intelligence for the creation of a multimedia project-based assessment. *European Journal of Pharmacology*, *998*, 177508. Advance online publication. DOI: 10.1016/j.ejphar.2025.177508 PMID: 40086582

Eubanks, V. (2018). *Automating inequality: How high-tech tools profile, police, and punish the poor*. St. Martin's Press.

Kharrufa, A., & Johnson, I. G. (2024). The potential and implications of generative AI on HCI education. DOI: 10.1145/3658619.3658627

Khoo, O., Sreberny, A., & Thiranagama, S. (Eds.). (2022). *Environment, media and popular culture in Southeast Asia*. Amsterdam University Press., DOI: 10.5117/9789463722642

Kim, N. W., Ko, H.-K., Myers, G., & Bach, B. (2024). ChatGPT in data visualization education: A student perspective (Preprint). /arXiv.2405.00748DOI: 10.1109/VL/HCC60511.2024.00022

Kloker, S., Bazanya, M., & Kateete, T. (2024). I don't trust you (anymore)! The effect of students' LLM use on lecturer-student trust in higher education. DOI: 10.58653/nche.v12i1.6

Lee, D., Arnold, M., Srivastava, A., Plastow, K., Strelan, P., Ploeckl, F., Lekkas, D., & Palmer, E. (2024). The impact of generative AI on higher education learning and teaching: A study of educators' perspectives. *Computers & Education. Artificial Intelligence*, *6*, 100221. Advance online publication. DOI: 10.1016/j.caeai.2024.100221

New Scientist. (2025). *New Scientist essential guide: The AI revolution*. New Scientist Ltd.

Organization for Economic Co-operation and Development. (2021). *State of implementation of the OECD AI principles: Insights from national AI policies*. OECD Publishing., DOI: 10.1787/1cd40c44-

Selwyn, N. (2019). *Should robots replace teachers? AI and the future of education*. Polity Press.

Selwyn, N. (2021). *Education and technology: Key issues and debates* (3rd ed.). Bloomsbury Academic.

UNESCO. (2023). *Guidance for generative AI in education and research*. United Nations Educational, Scientific and Cultural Organization., DOI: 10.54675/EWZM9535

Zafar, S., Shaheen, F., & Rehan, J. (2024). Use of ChatGPT and generative AI in higher education: Opportunities, obstacles, and impact on student performance. *iRASD. The Journal of Educational Research*, *5*(1), 01–12. Advance online publication. DOI: 10.52131/jer.2024.v5i1.2463

Zhao, C. (2025). AI-assisted assessment in higher education: A systematic review. *Journal of Educational Technology and Innovation*. DOI: 10.61414/jeti.v6i4.209

Zylinska, J. (2020). *AI art: Machine visions and warped dreams*. Open Humanities Press. https://openhumanitiespress.org/books/titles/ai-art/

ADDITIONAL READING

Andrejevic, M. (2020). *Automated media*. Routledge.

Bates, A. W. (2023). *Teaching in a digital age: Guidelines for designing teaching and learning* (3rd ed.). BCcampus. https://pressbooks.bccampus.ca/teachinginadigitalagev3m/

Brand, A. (2024). The ChatGPT effect: Rethinking architectural pedagogy in the AI age. *Proceedings of the Association of Collegiate Schools of Architecture (ACSA) Annual Meeting*, 112, 55–64. DOI: 10.35483/ACSA.AM.112.55

Collins, A., & Halverson, R. (2018). *Rethinking education in the age of technology: The digital revolution and schooling in America* (2nd ed.). Teachers College Press.

Du Boulay, B., Mitrovic, A., & Yacef, K. (Eds.). (2023). *Handbook of artificial intelligence in education*. Edward Elgar Publishing., https://www.e-elgar.com/shop/gbp/handbook-of-artificial-intelligence-in-education-9781800375406.html DOI: 10.4337/9781800375413

Luckin, R. (2018). *Machine learning and human intelligence: The future of education for the 21st century*. UCL Institute of Education Press.

Williamson, B., & Eynon, R. (2020). Historical threads, missing links, and future directions in AI in education. *Learning, Media and Technology*, *45*(3), 223–235. DOI: 10.1080/17439884.2020.1798995

Williamson, B., Komljenovic, J., & Gulson, K. (Eds.). (2024). *World Yearbook of Education 2024: Digitalization of education in the era of algorithms, automation and artificial intelligence*. Routledge., https://www.routledge.com/World-Yearbook-of-Education-2024-Digitalisation-of-Education-in-the-Era-of-Algorithms-Automation-and-Artificial-Intelligence/Williamson-Komljenovic-Gulson/p/book/9781032417912

Zawacki-Richter, O., & Jung, I. (Eds.). (2023). *Handbook of open, distance, and digital education*. Springer., DOI: 10.1007/978-981-19-2080-6

Zawacki-Richter, O., Kerres, M., Bedenlier, S., Bond, M., & Buntins, K. (Eds.). (2023). *Systematic review of research on artificial intelligence applications in higher education*. Springer., DOI: 10.1007/978-3-658-27602-7

KEY TERMS AND DEFINITIONS

Algorithmic Bias: The systematic distortion of outcomes produced by AI systems due to biased training data, design choices, or embedded human assumptions within algorithmic models.

Artificial Intelligence (AI): A field of computer science concerned with the development of systems capable of performing tasks that typically require human intelligence, including learning, reasoning, pattern recognition, and decision-making.

Consent and Provenance: Ethical principles ensuring that data and creative materials used by AI systems are collected, attributed, and shared transparently, with explicit acknowledgment of origin, authorship, and participation.

Creative Pedagogy: An approach to teaching that emphasizes experimentation, critical reflection, and innovation to support creative learning processes and ethical engagement with technology.

Data Privacy: The ethical and legal practice of protecting personal and sensitive information collected, processed, or analyzed by digital and AI-driven systems in educational or creative contexts.

Digital Literacy: The ability to use, understand, and critically evaluate digital technologies, including awareness of their social, cultural, and ethical implications.

Ethical AI: The development and deployment of artificial intelligence systems guided by principles of fairness, accountability, transparency, and respect for human rights and cultural diversity.

Media Education: The field and practice of teaching media production, analysis, and communication, with an emphasis on critical engagement with audiovisual technologies and algorithmic systems.

Pedagogical Innovation: The design and implementation of new teaching strategies, methods, or tools—such as AI-assisted learning—intended to enhance educational outcomes while maintaining ethical and cultural responsibility.

Responsible AI Integration: The deliberate and transparent incorporation of AI technologies into educational or creative practices in ways that respect privacy, uphold academic integrity, and promote equitable participation.

Chapter 7
Beyond the Red Pen:
Unveiling AI's Role in Writing Assessment Accuracy and Feedback Effectiveness

Fatema Ahmed Wali
http://orcid.org/0000-0003-4600-8238
Bahrain Polytechnic, Bahrain

Ranya Alesh
http://orcid.org/0009-0009-9764-5430
Bahrain Polytechnic, Bahrain

Sini Rahuman
http://orcid.org/0000-0002-8612-4068
Bahrain Polytechnic, Bahrain

Khalil E. Mohamed
Bahrain Polytechnic, Bahrain

Mona Abdulla
Bahrain Polytechnic, Bahrain

ABSTRACT

Artificial intelligence (AI) has appeared as a promising tool to support and develop assessments with efficiency, consistency, and scalability in grading (Hooda et al., 2022). Nevertheless, AI tools have been increasingly used in tertiary education, specifically in assessments, which necessitates an evaluation of their reliability and alignment with teacher evaluative standards (Vittorini, Menini & Tonelli, 2021). CoGrader is an AI-based grading platform that facilitates using rubrics to provide

DOI: 10.4018/979-8-2600-1840-8.ch007

fast and accurate grading. However, the complexity of dealing with languages in terms of contexts, genres and writing objectives may present some challenges when using CoGrader. 128 student submissions were compared through a mixed-methods approach by three faculty members and CoGrader. The study aims to provide empirical insights into how effective CoGrader is as a trustworthy alternative to teacher grading and show how practical, accurate and validated it is in Foundation and Degree-level English courses to contribute to the ongoing discourse on AI in language learning and teaching.

1. INTRODUCTION

Recent studies position Artificial intelligence (AI) as a promising valuable tool for developing assessment efficiency (Hooda et al., 2022). Higher education English as a Foreign Language written assessments have primarily depended on traditional "red-pen" teacher-marking which is valued for its contextual sensitivity yet criticised for its time-consuming nature. Nevertheless, AI tools' reliability in real grading scenarios remains contested (Vittorini, Menini & Tonelli, 2021). CoGrader is an AI-based grading platform that facilitates using rubrics to provide fast and accurate grading. However, the complexity of dealing with languages in terms of contexts, genres and writing objectives may present some challenges when using CoGrader.

128 student submissions were compared through a mixed-methods approach by three faculty members and CoGrader. The study aims to provide empirical insights into how effective CoGrader is as a trustworthy alternative to teacher grading and show how practical, accurate and validated it is in Foundation and Degree-level English courses to contribute to the ongoing discourse on AI in language learning and teaching.

Findings indicate that CoGrader applied stricter grading and revealed inconsistency with human grading, especially at the Foundation level. These results highlight the necessity of calibrating CoGrader's grading standards to be consistent with tutors' grading. The study advocates the use of CoGradaer as a supportive tool alongside human grading and not as a primary tool.

This case study investigates whether CoGrader, as an AI-driven rubric, is reliable and practical in marking written assessments within Foundation and Degree-level English as a Foreign Language courses. The study particularly aims to identify the effectiveness of CoGrader in mirroring teacher grading accuracy, how it could develop the quality of given feedback, and its influence on the efficiency of assessments. The study also investigates possible limitations and challenges related to AI-based assessment tools in higher education. Although AI adoption in higher education is on the rise, there is a lack of empirical research evaluating its effectiveness across different student proficiency levels, which underscores the significance of this study. While AI-assisted evaluation tools are widely integrated in tertiary education, the conceptual understanding of these tools mirror or differ from human evaluative marking remains limited. Many studies focus on the AI-enabled tools' surface-level accuracy aspects as well as their efficiency. However, research integrating how scoring is carried out taking into consideration the context and teacher-based evaluation is not sufficient. In response to this gap, a comparative analysis is carried out in this study to explore the aspects CoGrader matches human marking and where the discrepancies are.

The study is guided by the following hypotheses:

Hypothesis 1: CoGrader's AI-based rubric grading will show a high level of alignment with human grading standards in both Foundation and Degree-level English courses.

Hypothesis 2: CoGrader will develop grading efficiency, reducing the time spent on marking writing assessments without compromising accuracy.

Hypothesis 3: CoGrader feedback will be as constructive and actionable for students as traditional teacher feedback.

Hypothesis 4: CoGrader has specific marking gaps or inconsistencies that suggest areas for improvement in AI assessment tools.

2. BACKGROUND

2.1 Educational Assessment AI Tools

Writing tests measure a range of critical skills in both higher education and students' professional endeavours. This includes evaluating critical thinking, phrase choice, communication skills, cohesive argumentation, structured idea(s) flow in presentation. In ESL/EFL contexts, writing is traditionally assessed by instructors or external examiners, a process that is time-consuming and cognitively demanding, and potentially vulnerable to subjectivity and inconsistency. Taken together, these studies indicate that while human marking ensures contextual sensitivity, it is constrained by scalability and reliability concerns. The emergence of generative AI (GenAI) tools such as ChatGPT, Claude, and Google Gemini has introduced significant transformations in educational assessment. Their ability to generate responses, texts in various styles for both generalized, specific purposes highlight unprecedented opportunities for students and tutors through endless exploration and engagement. These machines leverage the power of Natural Language Processing (NLP), rely on a web-based corpora & knowledge bank to produce the most relevant, up-to-date information catering to the user(s)' questions or request (Lund & Wang, 2023). They enable direct access to resourceful data, empowering both students and teachers to interact in open-ended conversations Their capacity to provide rapid feedback and standardized outputs presents opportunities to reduce bias, enhance consistency, and accelerate grading processes. However, the evidence remains inconsistent regarding whether algorithmic standardization necessarily results in pedagogical validity. By using this technology, tutors could maintain a standardised marking approach, mitigate subjectivity cases, ensure the objective application of grading protocols (Baidoo-Anu & Ansah, 2023). For EFL students, AI chatbots have been becoming promising platforms providing instant, engaging feedback through a personalized lens, tailored to each learner's needs (Kartika, 2024). Other scholars measured the efficiency of GPT, Claude when grading undergraduate medical assessments. In this regard, these findings indicate that AI tools may serve as complementary evaluative agents rather than replacements for human judgment. In spite of this, some associated challenges have been reported when using LLMs for marking. Ji et al. (2023) mentioned that AI platforms (Claude/ Gemini/ GPT) can produce faulty responses, raising questions around the accuracy and trustworthiness of the information delivered. This could be due to the inequalities of data which those platforms have been trained on, leading to obvious failures to comprehend or accommodate the users' command(s). Köbis and Mehner (2021) stressed on the ethical concerns of AI substituting tutors, posing threats on the essential role tutors play in mentoring, fostering curiosity, monitoring students' discipline, and encouraging creativity. In detail, Schillings et al. (2023) pointed out that the course of teaching academic writing goes beyond vocabulary acquisition, grammar, and syntax; it entails the facilitation of complex details such as idea linking, argumentation, synthesizing, performing critical analysis. While AI tools may explain these aspects through written dialogues, no guidance can ensure learners' comprehension of such skills. Furthermore, Khademi (2023), who employed intraclass correlation to contrast GPT and Bard's marking against humans demonstrated lower reliability in AI grading compared to human markers. Overall, these studies suggest that while AI may efficiently detect micro-level linguistic errors, its capacity to evaluate higher-order writing competencies remains limited. Face-to-face or written feedback provided by tutors is most likely backed up by appropriate sources as opposed to LLMs that produce responses based on a sum of data collected from the internet.

Conversely, other notable AI-grading platforms have been trending in the modern. A noteworthy example trusted by plentiful schools is Gradescope. This website, powered by Turnitin, leverages Optical Character Recognition (OCR) technology to streamline, automate grading of numerous tests for both handwritten submissions and digital ones. Cao and Zhong (2023) who explored Gradescope for comparative analysis found that although the automated route demanded additional technical literacy and work for tutors; it eventually became efficient and fun to work on, especially with the utilization of high resolution and speed scanners. Nevertheless, it may also be essential to recognize the limitations of this software. Liow et al. (2024) outlined several shortcomings of this technology, for instance, the absence of batch data processing (CSV files extracted from Moodle), complexity in usability, difficulty of rubric configuration. While the AWS reflects promising features such as the employment of OCR, the focus on grading individual tests rather than providing an overall test mark (accumulation) remains predominant. Hansel et al. (2024) contends that without a clear comparison of students' progress throughout the course, the extent to which the intended learning outcomes are being met is immeasurable.

Thus, it can be inferred that the online grading platform is extensively used by internationally recognized schools. Then again, the existing literature echoes the voices of those who particularly specialize in STEM-based majors, portraying it as an effective tool for grading assessments of chemistry, mathematics, physics, biology, engineering. When observing through a linguistic panel, specifically in higher education, no available studies reflect its efficiency in marking ESL/ EFL writing assessments.

2.2 Strengths and Limitations of AI Feedback on Student Writing

Feedback is widely recognized as essential to writing development and academic achievement (Ryan et al., 2021). Still, as a result of limited pedagogical resources and time pressure, the provision of excellent feedback for large batches or cohorts remains a challenging dilemma. For this reason, referring to Automated Writing Evaluation (AWE) systems might be a potential solution, saving both tutors' and students' time.

Huawei and Aryadoust (2023) state that despite prior studies showcasing the effectiveness of AI feedback, the contextual and rhetorical elements are overlooked which makes AI unreliable for summative assessment grading. Web-driven feedback systems such as Grammarly and others have made a noticeable difference in the field of academia, assisting both educators and learners with detecting grammatical, syntactic errors, resulting in corrected feedback. Evidence suggests that AI performs strongly at surface-level correction but less consistently in discourse-level evaluation. With the emergence of more intelligence-driven (Generative AI) machines such as GPT, Bard, Deep Seek and more, the significance of NLP-based error detectors seems to have lost its power.

The integration of GAI in Higher Education pedagogy entails countless benefits. This includes question generation for assessment development, effort and time reduction for grading, smart academic performance monitoring through AI-based learning analytics, and crafting detailed, personalised and streamlined feedback for students (Crompton & Burke, 2023). Escalante et al. (2023) examined students' preferred form of writing feedback and the reasons behind their answers. One half preferred face-to-face feedback, the other half preferred AI-generated feedback. Those who preferred having a session with their tutor reported that they not only learn from their writing errors but are also provided with the chance to practice listening, speaking, understand the nature of the task as well as the exact requirements. In contrast, those who benefited more from AI feedback underscored the specificity and clarity of how language should be applied in writing contexts. Nonetheless, Evenddy (2024), who investigating feedback provision through NLP and Machine Learning (ML) pointed out that constructive, algorithm-based responses involve some limitations such as the necessity for extensive data sets, inconsistent feedback accuracy, and institutional resistance. Such challenges require time, teamwork and staff adaptation, further research on prompting to obtain more accurate responses. Still, Dai et al. (2023) employed ChatGPT as a main tool for undergraduate writing feedback provision. Most students found that the feedback generated was more comprehensible and detailed, easier to understand due sometimes due to being handwritten or unclear to grasp, and could be saved on their devices. The researchers also stressed the importance of AI prompting, which can, in turn, lead to significantly different outputs. In Wan & Chen's (2024) study, 70% of responses generated by ChatGPT either required minor or no alterations to the feedback delivered when uploading writing assessment answers. This was achieved as a result of successful AI (GPT) prompting, using keywords and linguistic techniques, uploading a few feedback style examples: written or visual (how teachers do it). By following this method, teachers can attain maximum benefits from the used learning machine while minimizing the risks of receiving faulty feedback or inconsistent responses.

Even so, Huawei and Aryadoust's (2023) literature review of AWE implies that several studies reported the negative scoring processes as well as their prompt complexity compared to the ones initiated by teachers. A handful of research report that with appropriate and skilful AI commanding skills, educators can attain satisfying feedback results; yet this remains and is essentially subject to the tutor's familiarity with GAI as well as their personal level of technical literacy. GAI's disruptive, algorithmic nature puzzles scholars to produce comprehensive prompts, guidelines, teaching and marking strategies (Moorhouse et al., 2023).

A few studies have systematically compared AI feedback reliability against established grading conventions in EFL writing contexts. In the event of marking a non-native English writer's essay or report, the AWE evaluates each criterion through a systematic lens rather than a pragmatic one. To elaborate, when teachers evaluate a specific student's submission, the scale goes beyond what is included in that paper, considering the student's build-up performance from scratch, their inclined progression, and the "marking culture" shared amongst team members within the department. Despite its strong ability to dictate microscopic mistakes such as wrong words, issues with spelling, logic leaps and run-on sentences, it does not take into account all the elements, nor does it possess the "human touch" or reflect any kind of teacher-generosity or compassion when grading a particular writing piece. Therefore, it can be inferred that these automated, algorithmic systems may offer service value; nonetheless, reliance on them could result in having grading inaccuracies or unhelpful feedback.

2.3 AI Feedback vs. Teacher Feedback

Pishtari et al. (2024) examined the impact that the AI-driven feedback had on the quality of designs and assessed pre- and post-training shifts in teachers' perceptions of the technology. The results showed that AI-driven feedback assists teachers in effectively achieving their design objectives.

Similarly, Wang (2024) showed the impact of corrective feedback on language learners' writing anxiety, fluency and accuracy and compared the effectiveness of feedback from human teachers and an AI-driven application. Additionally, learners in the AI-generated responses group experienced a more significant reduction in writing anxiety than their peers. The study proves beneficial insights of integrating AI applications into language learning contexts, in addition to promoting a supportive environment for students to develop their cognitive and writing skills. Prior research broadly shows that AI may foster confidence and fluency in language learning environments. Set against this, Liu (2024) contends that AWE graded content may in some instances be vague or confusing to interpret, and that responses often correct words and sentences while content problems persist. Weidlich et al. (2025) affirm this, illustrating that most students report favorable perceptions of AI for grammatical and spelling corrections "polishing"; but preferred tutors' guidance, that which sheds light on task fulfillment, quality, progression, relevance and strength of argumentation. For this reason, preference for teacher input with contextualized grounding remains dominant, with AWEs being in supplementary use.

Contrariwise, Guo and Wang (2023) studied the possible role of ChatGPT in facilitating the teaching and learning of writing English as a Foreign Language (EFL), particularly to support EFL teachers' feedback on students' writing. In this study, ChatGPT- and teacher-generated feedback were compared in terms of amount and type. The results showed that ChatGPT produced a significantly larger amount of feedback than teachers, mainly focusing on content-related and language-related issues. The results also showcased that ChatGPT, and teachers displayed tendencies towards using different feedback types when evaluating different aspects of students' writing.

In a similar context, Cao and Zhong's (2023) findings revealed that in terms of linguistic features. However, the evidence remains inconsistent regarding which modality leads to sustained long-term writing development, especially in enhancing lexical capability and referential cohesion. While teacher feedback (TF) and self-feedback (SF) showed more effectiveness in developing syntax-related skills, i.e. correct versus incorrect usage of parts of speech and grammatical forms. More critically, in a study done by Banihashem et al., (2024), the authors reported that peer reviewed feedback focused heavily on error identification as opposed to learning machine (ChatGPT) feedback, which involved a more descriptive and an "overall" analysis of what the students had written. This confirms that learning machines can provide valuable remarks at a macro scale, focusing on both strengths and points for improvement; yet, from a mechanical standpoint, tutors' formative commentary might excel, especially if the highlighted parts are the most crucial to adjust, change or fix. Additionally, Nazaretsky et al. (2023) presents more justified scores when performing automated analysis of teachers' interaction using Natural Language Processing techniques, especially when formative feedback is involved.

Nawaz et al. (2022) outlines significant inclination in students' satisfaction rates, demonstrating the effectiveness of teaching interventions and machine learning methods where student feedback can be seamlessly tracked, influencing institutional policies. Interestingly, Nawaz et al. (2022) emphasised that human analysis requires 10 times the hours to handle 10 times the amount of data; however, in text mining, while more labelled samples lead to better performance, the effect of increasing the training data becomes less apparent when the samples are large enough. While it may be challenging estimate how many samples are required to achieve an optimal performance in auto-analysing students' open responses, it is not difficult to predict that, to analyse a million student responses, there is no need to manually label 20% of the data (0.2 million).

The above was also confirmed, where AI has been widely applied to various educational technology platforms such as Virtual Mentor, Voice Assistant, Smart Content, Presentation Translator, and Global Courses, for example, MOOCs, Udemy, Google AI, Alison, Khan Academy, edX, Udacity, Coursera, etc. (6), Automatic Assessment, Personalised Learning, Educational Games, and Intelligent Tutoring System (ITS) or Intelligent Computer-Aided Instruction (ICAI) (Fitria, 2021).

Artificial Intelligence (AI) is the process of modelling human thinking and designing a smart, interactive machine, enabling it to perform human tasks or objectives. In this regard, teachers can save more energy and time on other tasks. In the same token, Open Automated Feedback (AF) allows instant responses processing speed, precision, and a scale that exceeds that of humans; still, the risk with technology is making it possible to implement poor feedback design and practices. To use AF tools effectively, teachers are required to demonstrate a wide range of competencies, such as understanding feedback, scaling up feedback to meet the needs of larger cohorts, using available resources well, and creating authentic, rich.

The literature suggests increasing growth of the effectiveness of AI-based feedback for students' written productions; nevertheless, there is not enough evidence on how consistent it is to EFL teacher-based evaluations. Robust empirical comparisons between AI-generated grades and EFL teacher evaluations remain scarce. This highlights the necessity of examining grading alignment, validity, and pedagogical reliability in hybrid assessment models.

2.4 Students' Perceptions of AI Feedback

Mixed interpretations regarding the impact of Artificial Intelligence (AI) on EFL/ESL students' learning exist. For instance, Maeng (2025) claims that learners hold attitudinal concerns of AWES due to the lengthiness of generated response content, fear of potential over-reliance, questionable work ethicality, loss of independent-thinking, and sometimes disengagement because of the "overly mechanical" responses (Jiang, 2022). Likewise, as declared by Darwin et al. (2023), outputs delivered by AI are occasionally abstract or context-insensitive, leaving room for misalignment with the author's intent. Accessibility may also work in users' favour distinctively, subject to internet availability and premium subscription privileges (Kamalov et al., 2023).

However, Sumakul et al. (2022) notes positive indications reported by learners when using a particular online site: Plot Generator. The website functions by collecting users' ideas to plot narrative stories, assists with overcoming writer's block, and can be optimized by students as well as tutors for brainstorming support. Considering the visual representations shown in Plot Generator and the data required to build those plots, learners expressed creativity enhancement, widening of imagination, and felt a sense of "engagement boost". In the same context, interviews with students have shown insights into the influence of AI assessments on motivation and engagement. The study's results showcased that AI feedback could lead to more autonomy and competence in terms of students' motivation. However, for engagement, AI assessments may reduce student attendance but increase cognitive efforts in studies. Moreover, the study reported that summative feedback can positively and negatively affect student motivation and engagement.

Students could become demotivated and disengaged if the feedback is perceived as personal and associated with a sense of failure. In contrast, if feedback is constructive and proposes improvement, students feel supported, increasing their self-esteem and confidence (Yasin, 2024). For example, Khojasteh et al. (2025), who investigated three feedback approaches when assessing intermediate-level students' writing, echoed qualitative insights of learners, and underlined the importance of adopting a dual philosophy when grading writing tasks. 88 students were assigned to one of three feedback categories: AI reviewed (group A), tutor reviewed (group B), hybrid approach (group C). While group B demonstrated obvious enhancement in lexical resources, group C showed noticeable development in their overall writing, especially in the following elements: grammar, cohesion and coherence, task achievement. From this perspective, one may state that appropriate integration of both feedback types: teachers' formative input (non-discouraging) along with AI's pedagogical evaluation for EFL/ ESFL writing students could potentially entail motivating and promising results.

2.5 Teachers' Perceptions of AI Feedback

Lin et al. (2022) conceptualized AI integration within three design frames: process-based, knowledge-based, and contextual frameworks. They identified five developmental milestones, including overcoming participation barriers, engaging in interactive design thinking, integrating experiential knowledge into AI pedagogy, promoting socially responsible AI use, and fostering holistic professional development. Collectively, these findings suggest that effective AI integration requires not only technical competence but also pedagogical and ethical awareness. In another study, two research questions were addressed: the potential of AI to enhance teaching practice and experience and the difficulties faced when utilising Artificial Intelligence education tools (AIED). Alwaqdani (2024) found that teachers acknowledged the efficiency of AI in saving time, supporting lesson design, and personalizing learning experiences. However, they also expressed concerns regarding insufficient training, potential job displacement, reduced creativity, unintended consequences, and over-reliance on AI's perceived accuracy. Nevertheless, few studies have examined how these concerns directly influence grading practices in higher education contexts. Similarly, Sheeba (2022) reported that AI applications enhance instructional efficiency and support innovative pedagogical practices. Taken together, these studies portray AI as a supportive instructional tool rather than a replacement for teacher expertise. Another study highlighted positive perceptions and attitudes towards human grading and automated processes. Nazaretsky et al. (2022) identified three primary concerns: reliability and accuracy of automated assessment, technical and workload-related challenges, and emotional factors such as trust and willingness to adopt AI in pedagogy. However, the evidence remains inconsistent regarding whether these concerns diminish over time with increased exposure and training.

Based on the current findings, this study frames AI-assisted grading as a hybrid assessment process where human grading interacts with that of AI by which a grading alignment or misalignment might emerge. This perspective allows a deeper understanding of AI grading effectiveness among different levels and grading contexts.

3 METHODOLOGY

3.1 Context and Subjects

Bahrain Polytechnic has been established by the Bahrain Government to address the need for a skilled Bahraini labour force to support economic growth and diversification. The vision of Bahrain Polytechnic is to be a world-class provider of applied higher education. This goes hand in hand with Bahrain Polytechnic's mission in producing professional and enterprising graduates with 21st-century skills necessary for the needs of the community locally, regionally, and internationally. (*About Bahrain Polytechnic*, n.d.)

To envisage the above-mentioned mission, programmes, qualifications and courses are developed in consultation with businesses, industries, professions, international education and training institutions. In the same token, EL6006 English Communication Skills A, an English course offered to degree students is aligned with Bahrain Polytechnic's strategic goals in preparing students further for the demands of English-medium undergraduate study in their chosen disciplines. In completion of EL6006, the student will be able to process and respond clearly and coherently in a well-structured manner to complex written, oral and aural information at the CEFR high B2 level encountered in defined and some undefined academic study and workplace situations. The 62 students in this study learned through principles of project-and problem-based learning, which were supported by other student-centred methodologies. Based on the principles of student-centred learning and using a variety of learning and teaching strategies, the content, assessment, instruction and materials for the course have been designed to give students the opportunity to further develop learning and demonstrate linguistic competence at the CEFR B2 level. The sample size was deemed adequate for reliability analysis based on similar AI-assisted writing assessments' studies.

The use of AI was encouraged in both courses as part of the learning process. Any such use should be acknowledged and referenced. Learning outputs generated by AI could aim at:

(1) Comparison and contrast based on specific premises and standards
(2) Critical evaluation based on given criteria such as rightness, accuracy, relevance, effectiveness, credibility, and others
(3) Annotated enhancement
(4) Ranking with justification

3.2 Human Marking and Feedback

Taking into account the objective of this study: comparing AI-marking -generated feedback versus tutor marking and overview, mixed methods were employed. Two writing rubrics were exploited in the name of evaluating students' writing performance. Rubric one was from AP5201, a foundation-level course that introduces and emphasises the fundamentals of academic writing. Rubric Two, taken from English Communication Skills A (EL6006), focuses on assessing students' analytical skills as well as their inference-drawing capabilities. (Here write the question prompts for both courses, preceded by uploading the attuned rubric on Excel; the one on Cograder might be better to keep down in 3.2). A total of 128 writing assessment submissions, 64 submissions from AP5201 and 64 submissions from EL6006, were purposefully collected and marked to ensure representation across proficiency levels and to facilitate a substantive comparison of human and AI grading. The grading process was done by three English Faculty of Professional Studies members.

3.3 AI Marking and Feedback

Amongst the numerous online platforms that support feedback provision, the primary chosen website for this study was Cograder. This web-based marking machine combines teachers' educational expertise with advanced AI technology and acts as a descriptive, personalised supporter when grading students' writing assessments. It allows teachers to provide instant and specific feedback, aiming to enhance students' writing performance. Furthermore, it could save a significant amount of time and effort when grading essays or reports, resulting in less mental fatigue as well as allowing more effort to be dedicated to teaching and research. The evaluation process can be done using multiple languages, leaving room for English and non-English language teachers, learners to leverage this platform and maximise feedback provision efficiency. Tutors can either attach each submission individually or upload all drafts in one bulk. The website automatically scans the document(s), transcribes both the wording and phrasing, preceded by grading the writing submission(s) based on the chosen rubric.

3.4 Marking Criteria

Rubric-wise, Cograder provides a series of globally recognised marking schemes that are commonly shared, used by various reputable institutions. Some examples of these standardised rubrics are California Smarter Balanced Assessment, Texas STAAR, New York Regents, Common Core State Standards and more. Additionally, provided that the AI platform is intuitive and user-friendly, it enables users to upload their own rubrics and customise each criterion as necessitated or preferred. This way, teachers can maintain full control over feedback delivery and grading decisions.

3.5 Payment Plans

Three subscription plans are available. The "Starter Route" involves no applicable fees, supports rubric crafting features and technical assistance, but is restricted to 100 submissions per month. Plan two is a more sophisticated option designed for individual tutors. It includes the abovementioned options, extends up to 350 submissions per month, includes handwritten essay guidance, Google Classroom embedding, class-performance sheet availability, grammar monitoring, as well as 48 hours of live chat and email assistance. The price for this selection is 19 US Dollars per month when billed monthly, and 15 US Dollars per month if billed annually. The institutional & district subscription plan includes all the aforementioned, along with unlimited submissions, integration with Schoology and Canvas, free access to a broader collection of international rubric libraries, AI plagiarism detection (percentage is visible too), unlimited access to reported analytics, and a 24-hour priority response support. No standard price is shown for this option; it is tailored based on the school's request.

3.6 Ethics and Plagiarism Detection

When considering Cograder's AI and plagiarism detection feature, it is important to note that no digital tool can guarantee an accurate detection percentage. The AI machine relies on pattern detection in the name of alerting the tutor to what may potentially be academically dishonest or copied, resulting in getting flagged. While the website uses advanced algorithms to ensure consistency and reliability, it is not designed to replace the tutor but rather to assist with marking and evaluation. The final call or judgement rests with the teacher, who has full control by reviewing, attuning both feedback and scores before finalising or reporting them to the students. The aim is to equip tutors with AI efficiency supported by their professional human experience and expertise.

4 FINDINGS

4.1 Foundation- Level Findings

This preliminary study explored the alignment between the scoring of teachers and the AI scoring of students' written assessments. Both the agreement between the raters and the relationship between their respective scoring patterns were assessed through several statistical methods. The results indicate different insights into grading tendencies.

To indicate the main tendencies and variability between the Teacher and CoGrader's scores, descriptive statistics were conducted. The Teachers' ratings mean score was 24.03, showing a higher average score than that of the CoGrader's mean 12.43. This significant variation in means implies that the AI likely grades students lower than the teacher. In addition, the standard deviation of Teachers' scores presented larger variability (3.55) in comparison to the CoGrader's standard deviation of 2.93, with the teachers' grading more spread out, indicating a bigger range in the awarded grades. In terms of distribution, the Teachers' scores exhibited a negative skew of -1.42, which suggests that most scores were clustered toward the higher end of the scale, with fewer students receiving low marks. On the other hand, the CoGrader's scores had a positive skew of 1.72, indicating that the AI tended to award lower scores, but with a smaller proportion of students receiving the lowest scores. These patterns underscore a clear distinction in the grading tendencies of Teachers and CoGrader.

Table 1. Foundation level descriptive statistics

Teachers' Marking		CoGrader's Marking	
Mean	24.03174603	Mean	12.42857143
Standard Error	0.446851793	Standard Error	0.368855557
Median	25	Median	12
Mode	25	Mode	12
Standard Deviation	3.546776155	Standard Deviation	2.927700219
Sample Variance	12.5796211	Sample Variance	8.571428571
Kurtosis	2.89078701	Kurtosis	5.370402961
Skewness	-1.422573675	Skewness	1.71976455
Range	17	Range	18
Minimum	12	Minimum	6
Maximum	29	Maximum	24
Sum	1514	Sum	783
Count	63	Count	63

The agreement between the Teachers' and CoGrader's ratings was calculated to measure an Intraclass Correlation Coefficient (ICC), which was -0.63656, whose negative ICC value shows poor agreement between the two raters, signifying that the scoring of teachers and CoGrader are methodically inconsistent. This negative agreement may reflect CoGrader's inability to entirely grasp human grading nuances, which proposes that the AI scoring needs advanced standardisation and alignment with the teachers' grading to guarantee more consistent marks.

Figure 1 illustrates the level of agreement between the teachers' and CoGrader's scores through the Bland-Altman plot, showing a mean bias of 11.60, implying that the teachers gave scores higher than CoGrader. The agreement's limits were found to be 5.35 and 17.86, establishing a 12.5-point difference range between the two raters' scores, which indicates that despite the consistency in grades between the teachers and CoGrader's, there is significant variability in the variations. This wide range suggests that CoGrader's scores are not aligned with the teachers. This discrepancy indicates a possible challenge in depending entirely on CoGrader for grading, as the differences could lead to flawed and biased evaluations.

The finding of minimal agreement between teachers' and CoGraders' ratings was also reinforced by the Weighted Cohen's Kappa value of 0.069 (Table 1). This value shows that even with a few partial agreements, teachers' and CoGraders' gradings continue to differ substantially. In effect, the low Kappa value indicates that CoGrader lacks consistent representation of the teachers' evaluation method, which ultimately highlights the importance of improving CoGrader's scoring criteria or algorithm.

Figure 1. Bland-Altman plot for teacher and AI scores- foundation level

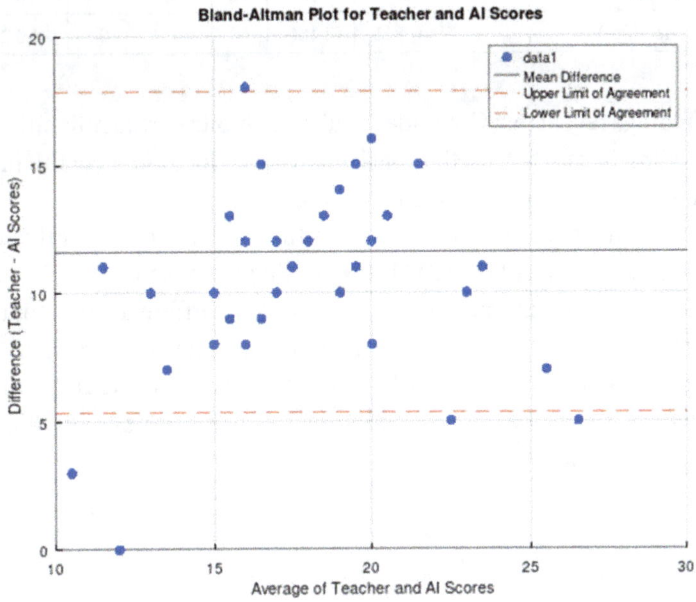

4.2 Degree-Level Findings

This study examined the consistency and alignment between Expert Tutors' grading and CoGrader's AI-based rubric scoring for Degree-level English writing assessments. The analysis focused on inter-rater reliability, descriptive statistics, and inferential measures to test whether CoGrader's marking outcomes align with human grading standards. The findings highlight both areas of overlap and notable discrepancies in the grading practices of human and AI raters.

Intraclass Correlation Coefficient (ICC) was used to evaluate the reliability of alignment between Tutor Grading and CoGrader. Table 1 illustrates the ICC (Single Measures) value 0.372 with a 95% Confidence Interval of 0.130–0.570, demonstrating reasonable agreement. Despite the statistical significance ($p < 0.001$), the consistency level is below the strong reliability threshold. The ICC increased to 0.542 when average measures were calculated, signifying stronger consistency with aggregated scores across raters, indicating that CoGrader's AI-based scoring deviates noticeably from tutors' grading.

Table 2. Intraclass correlation coefficients for teacher and AI scores

Measure	ICC	F	df1	df2	Sig	95% CI
ICC (Single Measures)	0.372	2.186	60	60	0.000	0.130–0.570
ICC (Average Measures)	0.542	2.186	60	60	0.000	0.240–0.730

These findings reveal that CoGrader's rubric exhibits partial reliability compared to tutors' grading; nevertheless, the consistency level does not meet full interchangeability and necessitates additional calibration.

Descriptive statistical analysis offered further understanding of the teacher and CoGrader scores patterns (Table 2). Tutor grading mean score was 81 compared to CoGrader's mean of 62.23, reflecting a considerable difference of about 19 points. Moreover, the dispersion of tutor grades demonstrated less dispersion ($SD = 11.91$) compared to CoGrader's grading ($SD = 12.76$). Analysis revealed mild negative skewness, suggesting higher scores predominated in both types of grading, but were less evident in CoGrader's grading.

Table 3. Degree level descriptive statistics

Descriptive statistics (Teacher Marking)			**Descriptive statistics (CoGrader's AI Marking)**	
Mean	**81**		**Mean**	**62.2295082**
Standard Error	1.524481458		Standard Error	1.633895316
Median	84		Median	65
Mode	94		Mode	67
Standard Deviation	11.90658081		Standard Deviation	12.76113036
Sample Variance	141.7666667		Sample Variance	162.8464481
Kurtosis	-0.078423955		Kurtosis	0.320297489
Skewness	-0.742735523		Skewness	-0.859417103
Range	48		Range	57
Minimum	50		Minimum	26
Maximum	98		Maximum	83
Sum	4941		Sum	3796
Count	61		Count	61

The findings of inferential tests verified that the gap between tutor scores and CoGrader scores showed a highly significant difference in the t-test ($t = 10.60$, $p < 0.001$), which was corroborated with the Wilcoxon Signed-Rank test ($W = 50.0$, $p < 0.001$). The effect size (Cohen's $d = 1.52$) showed a very big practical difference, indicating that the inconsistency between CoGrader's scores and tutors' grades is educationally valuable and statistically significant.

Weak positive correlations between tutor scores and CoGrader's scores were revealed through Pearson's correlation ($r = 0.37$), whereas Spearman's rank correlation was $r = 0.38$. The two correlations showed that the relationship between the two scores was relatively weak despite the tendency of higher scores to align. These findings indicate that CoGrader's scores do not consistently replicate the same judgments as human evaluators.

Figure 2. Bland-Altman plot for teacher and ai scores- foundation level

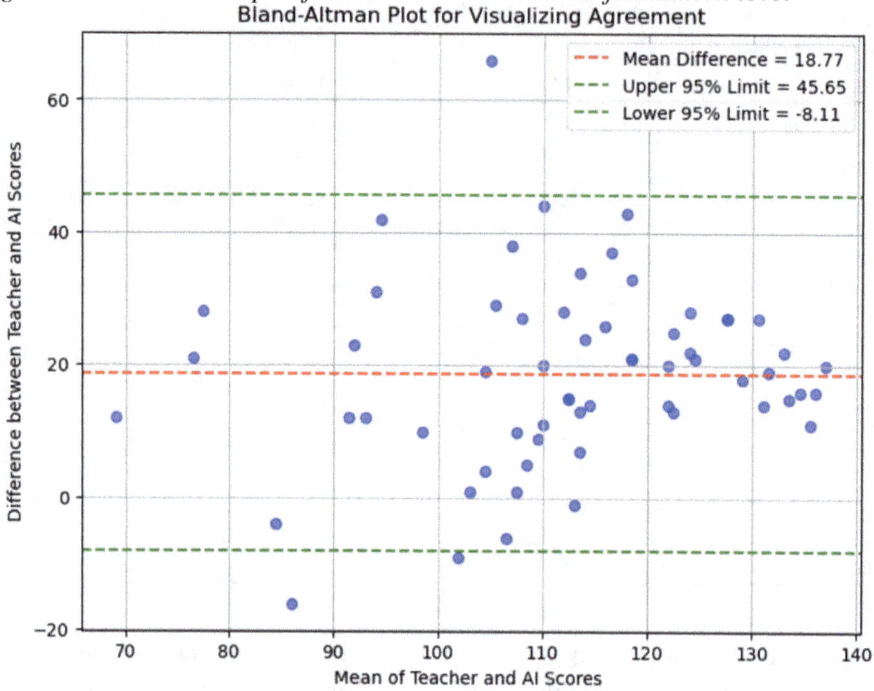

Misalignments were revealed by Bland–Altman analysis with the mean difference of 18.77 between tutors' grades and CoGrader's scores, and the limits of agreement varying from -8.11 to 45.65. Considerable variability is apparent between the two scores, with many scorers exceeding the limits, confirming that CoGrader's grading and tutors' ratings are not equivalent.

The largest discrepancies found between CoGrader's scores, and the tutors' scores were run through error analysis. For example, the extreme cases when tutors graded the writings more than 40 to 60 scores higher than CoGrader (e.g., Tutor = 92 vs CoGrader = 26) indicate that CoGrader consistently undervalued student performance, which could be attributed to strict criteria or overlooking qualitative features recognised by tutors. In most instances, CoGrader's scores were consistently lower, suggesting that it was strict or lack of contextual sensitivity.

Overall, the analysis reveals that CoGrader's scores differ substantially from tutors' grades in grading Degree-level writing despite exhibiting moderate reliability. CoGrader's current scoring model may undervalue student performance, unlike tutors who consistently assign higher grades. These findings emphasise the need to further improve CoGrader's scoring algorithms before adopting them in educational contexts.

5. DISCUSSION

Artificial intelligence (AI) continues to reshape educational assessment approaches, especially in terms of writing assessments. With the continuous growth of AI tool such as CoGrader, Turnitin Revision Assistant, Grammarly and Write & Improve, educational organisations are reviewing how significant technology is in grading, proving feedback, teaching and learning strategies and academic ethics. As AI is evolving swiftly, debates surrounding accountability, ethical principles, consistency and pedagogical roles particularly in English language settings in which writing development is intricate and contextual. This section explores prospective developments in AI-assisted writing assessments.

Recent scholarly work persistently exhibits that AI systems are challenged by reasoning within context, culturally informed interpretation and rhetorical discernment despite their linguistics accuracy and analysis (Petricini, 2025; Alshalan, 2025). Therefore, academic establishments are progressively implementing hybrid approaches in which AI executes preliminary grading or linguistic scrutiny along with human tutors corroborating or revising the scores. Fagbohun et al. (2024) and Trajkovski and Hayes (2025) indicate that educators are suggested to continue to occupy a key role in assessments and refrain from fully depending on AI-automated grading.

The dominance of hybrid assessment approaches is anticipated in the future since they maintain resource optimization with pedagogical judgement. In these approaches, error identification, superficial accuracy scoring, adherence to rubric criteria, and proposed revisions are managed by AI, whereas teachers facilitate critical thinking, creativity, reviewing argument effectiveness and following genre which ultimately (Akhter & Zaman, 2024). This approach streamlines workload without impairing equitable standards. AI-assisted moderation is a tool which facilitates AI marking audit by teachers through which they would evaluate student writing and automated feedback.

Traditional teacher grading systems furnish feedback to all learners using a consistent format irrespective of their language proficiency level or learning progression. Conversely, AI supports individualised and adaptive feedback by which feedback can sequentially change guided by students former writing practices, recurrent errors, and learning requirements. EFL research reveals that individualised AI feedback can enhance student motivation and written development (Tajik, 2025). Future writing platforms are expected to include CEFR-based learning trajectories, writing progress monitoring, learner skills mapping as well as personalized support and scaffolding where AI feedback supports students learn the reason behind the errors they commit and how not overcome them methodically.

With the continuous growth of AI in education, some challenges will prevail particularly in educational establishments with limited technological resources or expertise (Khan et al., 2024). These comprise teacher-grading and AI-grading rubric standardisation variations as well as the reluctance of educators to utilise AI-grading and considering it a threat to professional expertise (Mariano et al., 2025). There is an immediate need for effective training to use generative AI to its fullest potential understanding of its ethics, policies and the strategies to use AI-feedback pedagogically (Lindsay et al., 2025). Institutions are also urged to evaluate potential generative AI and monitor its use to promote trust and strengthen teacher confidence when using it.

Results reveal the difficulties in maintaining consistent AI-generated and human grading. The identified discrepancies between CoGrader and human graders are due to contextual aspects. It is apparent that CoGrader shows rubric application consistency while human grading seems to consider coherence, contextual appropriateness and process-based writing development which imply that that the current AI grading tools may be biased towards surface-level language aspects rather that overall writing quality, thereby reflecting the recurrent grading discrepancies. The significant discrepancies and low score concordances between the Teacher and CoGrader's scores imply that AI grading can grade with some consistency; however, AI grading remains misaligned with teacher judgments. These findings highlight significant implications for AI grading, especially where the stakes are high in learning contexts.

Theoretically, these results question the effectiveness of rubric-based AI models in complex language assessments and support a hybrid approach in which human and AI grading are utilised which is being advocated for in recent tertiary education discourse.

In sum, this research study demonstrates that notable bias and variability are exhibited in AI grading systems when compared with human grading. Despite AI grading's potential, the observed discrepancies indicate that more calibration and refinement are required for AI grading to be worth depending on educational evaluations. By resolving these shortcomings, AI models might be developed to more accurately align with human grading, which may result in more reliable and accurate evaluation methods for students' performances.

6. FUTURE RESEARCH DIRECTIONS

This study analytically evaluated the feedback quality, practicality and reliability of an AI-based rubric, CoGrader, in evaluating Degree and Foundation-level English writing. Results reveal that despite the fact that CoGrader shows moderate consistency with traditional human grading or "red-pen", pronounced disparities between both gradings are evident. CoGrader showed the tendency to grade more strictly in both courses, with marginal correlation and considerable sizes indicating potential challenges in its use as a sole grader for summative writing assessments. This study's empirical evidence represented in the authentic EFL higher education context and sample adds to the literature in this field. The findings of this study provide a theoretical understanding of AI's role in writing assessments revealing the strengths and areas that require development.

To develop AI grading effectiveness, this recommends a number of actions to be taken. Despite the moderate consistency CoGrader demonstrates with tutors, the substantial grade inconsistencies—predominantly the pronounced effect size alongside weak correlations indicate potential limitations about its effectiveness as a standalone grading tool. The tendency of CoGrader to grade more harshly than tutors could threaten fairness in grading if used alone. Several measures can be taken to develop the performance of CoGrader. Initially, CoGrader's scoring rubric and algorithm must be reviewed comprehensively in order to identify discrepancies from the Teachers' grading criteria and reduce biases found. The AI model should be calibrated with human grading behaviour to lessen the biases noted. Moreover, there is an urgent need to create a more advanced AI model to enhance alignment and coherence with human grading. Furthermore, further research should investigate the specific inconsistencies between CoGrader's and teachers' scores to clarify the logic behind CoGrader's grading compared to that of human evaluation. A number of measures are recommended to develop its reliability, including revising its rubrics to align with human assessment tendencies. Also, supplementary databases that align with tutor grading should be set up to mitigate scores' systematic underestimation. Using CoGrader as a complementary tool rather than replacing tutor grading would be recommended, as it could provide initial feedback that is then reviewed by tutors. Furthermore, extreme scoring differences can be examined to refine CoGrader's contextual, rhetorical, or stylistic features.

REFERENCES

About Bahrain Polytechnic. (n.d.). *Bahrain Polytechnic.* https://www.polytechnic.bh/about-us/

Akhter, E., & Zaman, M. A. U. (2024). Automated essay scoring and feedback systems for ESL learners: A meta-review of pedagogical impact. *American Journal of Interdisciplinary Studies*, *5*(1), 31–65. DOI: 10.63125/brzv3333

Alshalan, A. (2025). Bridging the divide: Saussurean structure and Derridean complexity in ChatGPT's meaning-making. *Arab World English Journal (AWEJ). Special Issue on Artificial Intelligence*, *5*(1), 81–95. DOI: 10.24093/awej/AI.5

Alwaqdani, M. (2024). Investigating teachers' perceptions of artificial intelligence tools in education: Potential and difficulties. *Education and Information Technologies.* Advance online publication. DOI: 10.1007/s10639-024-12903-9

Baidoo-Anu, D., & Ansah, L. O. (2023). Education in the era of generative artificial intelligence (AI): Understanding the potential benefits of ChatGPT in promoting teaching and learning. *Journal of AI*, *7*(1), 52–62. DOI: 10.61969/jai.1337500

Banihashem, S. K. B., Kerman, N. T., Noroozi, O., Moon, J., & Drachsler, H. (2024). Feedback sources in essay writing: Peer-generated or AI-generated feedback? *International Journal of Educational Technology in Higher Education*, *21*(1), 23. Advance online publication. DOI: 10.1186/s41239-024-00455-4

Cao, S., & Zhong, L. (2023). Exploring the effectiveness of ChatGPT-based feedback compared with teacher feedback and self-feedback: Evidence from Chinese to English translation. *arXiv*. https://arxiv.org/abs/2309.01645

Crompton, H., & Burke, D. (2023). Artificial intelligence in higher education: The state of the field. *International Journal of Educational Technology in Higher Education*, *20*(1), 1–22. DOI: 10.1186/s41239-023-00392-8

Dai, W., Lin, J., Jin, H., Li, T., Tsai, Y. S., Gašević, D., & Chen, G. (2023). Can large language models provide feedback to students? A case study on ChatGPT. In Chen, N.-S. (Eds.), *Proceedings of the 2023 IEEE International Conference on Advanced Learning Technologies (ICALT)* (pp. 323–325). IEEE. DOI: 10.1109/ICALT58122.2023.00100

Darwin, D. R., Mukminatien, N., Suryati, N., & Laksmi, E. D. (2023). Critical thinking in the AI era: An exploration of EFL students' perceptions, benefits, and limitations. *Cogent Education*, *11*(1), 11–18. DOI: 10.1080/2331186X.2023.2290342

Escalante, J., Pack, A., & Barrett, A. (2023). AI-generated feedback on writing: Insights into efficacy and ENL student preference. *International Journal of Educational Technology in Higher Education, 20*(1), 1–20. DOI: 10.1186/s41239-023-00425-2

Evenddy, S. S. (2024). Investigating AI's automated feedback in English language learning. *Foreign Language Instruction Probe, 3*(1), 76–87. DOI: 10.54213/flip.v3i1.401

Fagbohun, O., Iduwe, N. P., Abdullahi, M., Ifaturoti, A., & Nwanna, O. M. (2024). Beyond traditional assessment: Exploring the impact of large language models on grading practices. *Journal of Artificial Intelligence. Machine Learning and Data Science, 2*(1), 1–8.

Fitria, T. N. (2021). Artificial intelligence (AI) in education: Using AI tools for the teaching and learning process. In *Proceedings of the National Seminar on Educational Technology (PROSENAS)*. STIE AAS Press. https://prosiding.stie-aas.ac.id/index.php/prosenas/article/view/106

Guo, K., & Wang, D. (2023). To resist it or to embrace it? Examining ChatGPT's potential to support teacher feedback in EFL writing. *Education and Information Technologies*. Advance online publication. DOI: 10.1007/s10639-023-12146-0

Hansel, C. A., Ottenbreit-Leftwich, A., Quick, J. D., Greene, A. H., & Ricci, M. (2024). Gradescope in Large Lecture Classrooms: A Case Study at Indiana University: How an online grading platform enhanced student learning and instructor feedback in large-scale courses. *Journal of Teaching and Learning with Technology, 13*(1). Advance online publication. DOI: 10.14434/jotlt.v13i1.38519

Hooda, M., Rana, C., Dahiya, O., Rizwan, A., & Hossain, M. S. (2022). Artificial intelligence for assessment and feedback to enhance student success in higher education. *Mathematical Problems in Engineering, 2022*, 5215722. Advance online publication. DOI: 10.1155/2022/5215722

Huawei, S., & Aryadoust, V. (2023). A systematic review of automated writing evaluation systems. *Education and Information Technologies, 28*(1), 771–795. DOI: 10.1007/s10639-022-11200-7

Jiang, R. (2022). How does artificial intelligence empower EFL teaching and learning nowadays? A review on artificial intelligence in the EFL context. *Frontiers in Psychology, 13*, 1664–1078. DOI: 10.3389/fpsyg.2022.1049401 PMID: 36467167

Kamalov, F., Santandreu Calonge, D., & Gurrib, I. (2023). New Era of Artificial Intelligence in Education: Towards a Sustainable Multifaceted Revolution. *Sustainability (Basel), 15*(16), 12451. DOI: 10.3390/su151612451

Kartika, A. (2024). Unveiling the Merdeka Curriculum in Indonesia: Insights from Educators and Policymakers on Its Effectiveness and Implications. [INJURITY]. *Interdiciplinary Journal and Hummanity*, *3*(11), 802–819. DOI: 10.58631/injurity.v3i11.1378

Khademi, A. (2023). Can ChatGPT and Bard generate aligned assessment items?: A reliability analysis against human performance. *Journal of Applied Learning & Teaching*, *6*(1), 75–80.

Khan, M. S., Umer, H., & Faruqe, F. (2024). Artificial intelligence for low-income countries. *Humanities & Social Sciences Communications*, *11*(1), 1–13. DOI: 10.1057/s41599-024-03947-w

Khojasteh, L., Soori, A., & Javed, F. (2025). Comparing teacher E-feedback, AI feedback, and hybrid feedback in enhancing EFL writing skills. *Technology in Language Teaching & Learning*, *7*(3), 102626. DOI: 10.29140/tltl.v7n3.102626

Köbis, L., & Mehner, C. (2021). Ethical questions raised by AI-supported mentoring in higher education. *Frontiers in Artificial Intelligence*, *4*, 624050. DOI: 10.3389/frai.2021.624050 PMID: 33997774

Lin, X., Chen, L., Chan, K. K., Peng, S., Chen, X., Xie, S., Liu, J., & Hu, Q. (2022). Teachers' perceptions of teaching sustainable artificial intelligence: A design frame perspective. *Sustainability (Basel)*, *14*(13), 7811. Advance online publication. DOI: 10.3390/su14137811

Lindsay, E. D., Zhang, M., Johri, A., & Bjerva, J. (2025). The responsible development of automated student feedback with generative AI. In *2025 IEEE Global Engineering Education Conference (EDUCON)* (pp. 1–10). IEEE. DOI: 10.1109/EDUCON62633.2025.11016572

Liow, H. J. K., Yau, P. C., Tang, L., Seow, C., & Cao, Q. (2024, October). Peer-assessed (evaluated) automated grading system: a comprehensive exploration with emphasis on batch processing data visualization and rigorous peer evaluation. In *Proceedings of the 2024 international conference on artificial intelligence and teacher education* (pp. 91-96). DOI: 10.1145/3702386.3702404

Liu, W. (2024). A Systematic Review of Automated Writing Evaluation Feedback: Validity, Effects and Students' Engagement. Language Teaching Research Quarterly, 45(2667-6753), 86–105. DOI: 10.32038/ltrq.2024.45.05

Lund, B. D., & Wang, T. (2023). Chatting about ChatGPT: How may AI and GPT impact academia and libraries? *Library Hi Tech News*, *40*(3), 26–29. DOI: 10.1108/LHTN-01-2023-0009

Maeng, U. (2025). Blending AI and Instructor Feedback in EFL Writing: Learners' Motivation, Attitude, and Self-efficacy. *English Teaching*, *80*(5), 11–39. DOI: 10.15858/engtea.80.5.202512.11

Mariano, M. J., Taborete, J. J., Gampal, A., Dawisan, A., Maraganas, M. G., & Garcia, R. (2025). Analysis of AI and teacher feedback in grading students' activities. *International Journal on Studies in Education*, *7*(4), 1028–1047. DOI: 10.46328/ijonse.5148

Moorhouse, B. L., Yeo, M. A., & Wan, Y. (2023). Generative AI tools and assessment: Guidelines of the world's top-ranking universities. *Computers and Education Open*, *5*, 100151. DOI: 10.1016/j.caeo.2023.100151

Nawaz, R., Sun, Q., Shardlow, M., Kontonatsios, G., Aljohani, N. R., Visvizi, A., & Hassan, S. (2022). Leveraging AI and machine learning for the National Student Survey: Actionable insights from textual feedback to enhance quality of teaching and learning in UK higher education. *Applied Sciences (Basel, Switzerland)*, *12*(1), 514. Advance online publication. DOI: 10.3390/app12010514

Nazaretsky, T., Ariely, M., Cukurova, M., & Alexandron, G. (2022). Teachers' trust in AI-powered educational technology and a professional development program to improve it. *British Journal of Educational Technology*, *53*(4), 914–931. DOI: 10.1111/bjet.13232

Nazaretsky, T., Mikeska, J. N., & Klebanov, B. B. (2023). *Empowering teacher learning with AI: Automated evaluation of teacher attention to student ideas during argumentation-focused discussion*. ACM Digital Library., DOI: 10.1145/3576050.3576067

Petricini, T. (2025). The power of language: Framing AI as an assistant, collaborator, or transformative force in cultural discourse. *AI & Society*. Advance online publication. DOI: 10.1007/s00146-025-02586-2

Pishtari, G., Sarmiento-Márquez, E., Rodríguez-Triana, M. J., Wagner, M., & Ley, T. (2024). *Mirror mirror on the wall, what is missing in my pedagogical goals? The impact of an AI-driven feedback system on the quality of teacher-created learning designs*. ACM Digital Library., DOI: 10.1145/3636555.3636862

Ryan, T., Henderson, M., Ryan, K., & Kennedy, G. (2021). Identifying the components of effective learner-centred feedback information. *Teaching in Higher Education*. Advance online publication. DOI: 10.1080/13562517.2021.1913723

Schillings, M., Roebertsen, H., Savelberg, H., & Dolmans, D. (2023). A review of educational dialogue strategies to improve academic writing skills. *Active Learning in Higher Education, 24*(2), 95–108. DOI: 10.1177/1469787418810663

Sheeba, M. F. L. (2022). A study on perception of teachers towards AI applications in education. *XIBA Business Review, 5*(2), 23.

Sumakul, D. T. Y. G., Hamied, F. A., & Sukyadi, D. (2022). Students' perceptions of the use of AI in a writing class. *Advances in Social Science, Education and Humanities Research*. Advance online publication. DOI: 10.2991/assehr.k.220201.009

Tajik, A. (2025). Exploring the role of AI-driven dynamic writing platforms in improving EFL learners' writing skills and fostering their motivation. *Research Square*. DOI: 10.21203/rs.3.rs-5788599/v1

Trajkovski, G., & Hayes, H. (2025). AI in high-stakes and standardized testing. In *AI-assisted assessment in education: Transforming assessment and measuring learning* (pp. 313–346). Springer Nature Switzerland. DOI: 10.1007/978-3-031-88252-4_8

Vittorini, P., Menini, S., & Tonelli, S. (2021). An AI-based system for formative and summative assessment in data science courses. *International Journal of Artificial Intelligence in Education, 31*(2), 159–185. DOI: 10.1007/s40593-020-00230-2

Wan, T., & Chen, Z. (2024). Exploring generative AI assisted feedback writing for students' written responses to a physics conceptual question with prompt engineering and few-shot learning. *Physical Review. Physics Education Research, 20*(1), 010152. Advance online publication. DOI: 10.1103/PhysRevPhysEducRes.20.010152

Wang, D. (2024). Teacher- versus AI-generated (Poe application) corrective feedback and language learners' writing anxiety, complexity, fluency, and accuracy. *International Review of Research in Open and Distance Learning, 25*(3), 37–56. DOI: 10.19173/irrodl.v25i3.7646

Weidlich, J., Gotsch, F., Schudel, K., Marusic-Würscher, C., Mazzarella, J., Bolten, H., Bütler, D., Luger, S., Wohlfender, B., & Merki, K. M. (2025). Teacher, peer, or AI? Comparing effects of feedback sources in higher education. *Computers and Education Open, 9*, 100300. DOI: 10.1016/j.caeo.2025.100300

Chapter 8

Social Science Lecturers' Perspective on the Impact of AI on Students' Performance on Formative and Summative Assessment in Higher Education

Dineo Felicia Mosina
http://orcid.org/0009-0001-0687-1427
University of KwaZulu-Natal, South Africa

Dintle Masondo
University of KwaZulu-Natal, South Africa

Christina Maserole Masondo
University of South Africa, South Africa

ABSTRACT

The rapid integration of artificial intelligence (AI) into higher education has fundamentally reshaped teaching, learning, and assessment practices, raising critical questions about its viability in supporting meaningful learning outcomes. This study examines how AI is being utilised in assessment within higher education, with particular attention to its pedagogical implications and ethical challenges. Guided by the Technological Pedagogical Content Knowledge (TPACK) framework, the study

DOI: 10.4018/979-8-2600-1840-8.ch008

analyses the perspectives of three Social Sciences lecturers on students' engagement with AI across disciplinary, pedagogical, and technological domains. Drawing on qualitative participant accounts, the findings reveal that while AI can enhance writing quality, increase efficiency, and support student engagement, its uncritical and unsupervised use often undermines deep learning, disciplinary reasoning, and academic integrity.

INTRODUCTION

One of the most visible changes associated with the 4IR is the digitisation of teaching and learning practices. Digital platforms, learning management systems, online collaboration tools, and AI-driven applications have revolutionised the way knowledge is delivered, accessed, and assessed. Teaching has increasingly shifted from transmission-based models towards blended and online pedagogies that emphasise flexibility, self-paced learning, and learner autonomy. From this perspective, the 4IR has expanded the temporal and spatial boundaries of education, enabling learning beyond traditional classrooms. Artificial Intelligence (AI) has significantly transformed the teaching and learning landscape within the education system. In the wake of the Fourth Industrial Revolution, traditional methods of monitoring students' progress and capabilities have evolved to incorporate intelligent technologies. AI's impact on students' academic performance is evident in how it facilitates access to information, supports learning efficiency, and aligns educational practices with technological advancements (Mallillin & Carag et al., 2020, as cited in Mallillin, 2024). However, while AI contributes to personalised learning and efficiency, it also raises critical concerns regarding authenticity and the depth of students' engagement with learning outcomes. For instance, assessments such as assignments are now more easily generated through AI tools, prompting questions about whether students genuinely acquire the intended skills and knowledge within their modules or specialisations.

Although several studies have explored the opportunities and challenges of AI integration in education, a notable gap remains in critically analysing its *direct influence* on students' academic performance (Adewale, Azeta, Abayomi-Alli, & Sambo-Magaji, 2024). Another gap this study aims to fill is that most studies focus on students' use of AI, and few examine lecturers' perspectives in the social sciences (Sanders & Mukhari, 2024). AI technologies have introduced intelligent tutoring systems, predictive analytics, and personalised feedback tools that revolutionise the educational experience. These systems can identify students' strengths and weaknesses, recommend tailored resources, and even predict academic risks (Adewale, Azeta, Abayomi-Alli, & Sambo-Magaji, 2024). According to Mallillin (2022), AI's impact on students' academic performance lies in its ability to identify struggling learners and provide targeted interventions that enhance performance. Through such adaptive learning mechanisms, AI supports data-driven decision-making, allowing teachers to implement more effective pedagogical interventions. Social Science lecturers can offer disciplinary insights into whether AI-assisted outputs demonstrate genuine learning or superficial mimicry. Their perspectives help institutions design assessment policies that safeguard fairness, while also acknowledging AI as a legitimate learning aid rather than a threat. Understanding these perceptions is also vital for developing ethical and context-sensitive assessment frameworks (Holmes et al., 2022).

However, while AI has demonstrated positive effects on academic outcomes, its implementation raises critical pedagogical and ethical concerns. Studies such as those by Holmes et al. (2022) and Selwyn (2019) caution that AI can foster dependency, erode learner autonomy, and hinder critical thinking if students rely excessively on machine-generated content. Furthermore, AI tools can perpetuate inequalities where access to digital infrastructure and literacy remains uneven. Thus, while AI complements digital pedagogy by extending access and efficiency, it must be critically mediated by pedagogical frameworks that prioritise learner agency and inclusivity. As higher education enrolments continue to expand, a central pedagogical question arises: do students genuinely achieve disciplinary understanding or merely progress toward graduation? In the context of teacher education, for instance, future history educators must not only master content but also internalise the epistemological foundations of their discipline, critical inquiry, evidence evaluation, and interpretive reasoning. These competencies are essential for fostering critical thinking in learners, a skill long associated with emancipatory education (Freire, 1970; Giroux, 2011). However, the integration of Artificial Intelligence (AI) into higher education challenges how these outcomes are achieved and assessed.

Similarly, Giroux (2014) warns against technological determinism in education, noting that digital tools often serve neoliberal agendas of standardisation rather than fostering democratic and reflective learning. AI's algorithmic tendencies to homogenise knowledge outputs can therefore undermine the pluralism and contestation central to critical thinking, particularly in disciplines such as history that value multiple interpretations of evidence. Exploring lecturers' perspectives on AI in assessment supports institutional innovation and capacity building. Understanding their challenges, readiness levels, and ethical concerns can inform targeted professional development initiatives and policy formulation. While AI supports formative learning through personalised feedback and improved engagement, it also raises concerns about authenticity, plagiarism, and reduced critical thinking in summative contexts. Lecturers' feedback can guide the responsible adoption of AI tools that balance efficiency with equity, ensuring that formative and summative assessments remain pedagogically sound and contextually just. Thus, while AI can assist in diagnosing struggling learners and supporting academic performance (Mallillin, 2024; Adewale et al., 2024), it cannot independently produce critical thinkers. The cultivation of criticality depends on pedagogical intentionality, how educators design digital learning experiences that prioritise inquiry, reflection, and epistemic diversity. As Freire (1970) reminds us, authentic education is not the transfer of information but "the practice of freedom," where learners actively interrogate and reconstruct knowledge. Within a digital pedagogy framework, this requires positioning AI as a tool for empowerment rather than substitution, guided by educators who can mediate technology's power with ethical and critical awareness. In doing so, digital pedagogy serves as a theoretical framework for this approach.

Social Science lecturers' views are therefore crucial to ensure that AI supports formative assessment as a dialogic and developmental process rather than a mechanical evaluation (Black & Wiliam, 2009). In formative contexts, AI can provide immediate feedback and personalised scaffolding, yet only lecturers can contextualise this data within learners' socio-cultural and disciplinary frameworks (Luckin, 2018). This study examines the perspectives of social science lecturers on how AI affects students' performance in formative and summative assessments in higher education. With the rise of AI tools such as ChatGPT and automated grading systems, educators have expressed mixed views regarding their benefits and challenges. The study examines the importance of institutions striking a balance between innovation and academic integrity by developing clear AI-use policies and providing training for both lecturers and students.

LITERATURE REVIEW

The integration of AI into social science research raises critical epistemological, ethical, and methodological questions, particularly regarding bias, interpretability, and the potential reduction of nuanced qualitative insights (Kitchin, 2017). Academic performance is commonly understood as the extent to which students achieve prescribed learning outcomes within formal educational settings, often measured through grades, test scores, progression rates, and qualification attainment (York, Gibson, & Rankin, 2015). From a conventional perspective, academic performance functions as a proxy for individual ability, effort, and mastery of curriculum content, providing institutions with quantifiable indicators of educational effectiveness (Richardson et al., 2012). As Bourdieu (1986) argues, academic performance is intensely mediated by forms of cultural, social, and economic capital that advantage certain groups while systematically marginalising others. Consequently, performance outcomes frequently reflect broader patterns of inequality rather than intrinsic academic potential. However, critical scholarship problematises such narrow conceptualisations, arguing that academic performance is neither a neutral nor purely individual construct. Academic performance is widely regarded as a key indicator of the effectiveness and equity of educational systems globally. However, persistent and often stark disparities in student academic outcomes continue to challenge assumptions about uniform access to learning opportunities and merit-based success. These variations foreground a fundamental and unresolved question in educational research: "Which factors most significantly shape students' academic performance, and how do they interact across social, institutional, and individual contexts? Framed in this way, academic performance emerges not merely as an outcome of individual effort but as a complex product of structural conditions, pedagogical practices, and socio-economic influences" (Mallillin, 2024, p. 16).

Addressing this question constitutes a pressing educational concern, as it necessitates the systematic identification and critical examination of the underlying determinants of academic success in order to inform more responsive, inclusive, and effective educational interventions" (Suleiman et al., 2024, p. 2). The emergence of generative AI tools has further complicated the relationship between AI and academic performance. On one hand, such tools can function as cognitive scaffolds, assisting students with idea generation, drafting, and conceptual clarification, thereby reducing cognitive load and supporting higher-order learning (Kasneci et al., 2023). On the other hand, concerns have been raised regarding over-reliance on AI, surface learning, and the erosion of critical thinking skills. Empirical evidence suggests that when students use AI as a shortcut rather than as a learning aid, academic performance, particularly in assessments requiring conceptual understanding, may decline (Baidoo-Anu & Ansah, 2023). One of the most significant concerns is the potential for AI-facilitated academic misconduct. Tools that generate essays or answer questions automatically can encourage students to bypass critical thinking, undermining the learning objectives of assessments (Selwyn, 2019). This raises questions about whether the use of AI enhances learning or merely facilitates the reproduction of pre-existing knowledge.

From an instrumental perspective, AI has been shown to positively influence academic performance through personalised learning, adaptive feedback, and early identification of learning difficulties. Intelligent tutoring systems and learning analytics platforms tailor instructional content to individual learner profiles, enabling students to progress at their own pace and receive immediate feedback (Luckin et al., 2016). Empirical studies indicate that such personalised support can lead to measurable improvements in test scores, engagement, and course completion rates, particularly in large or resource-constrained educational settings (Zawacki-Richter et al., 2019). In this sense, AI appears to mitigate some structural limitations of traditional teaching by offering scalable academic support. However, critical scholars caution against interpreting these gains as universally transformative. Selwyn (2019) argues that AI does not operate in a social vacuum; instead, its impact on academic performance is mediated by existing inequalities related to access, digital literacy, and institutional capacity. Students from well-resourced backgrounds are more likely to benefit from AI-enhanced learning environments, while those from marginalised contexts may experience limited or superficial engagement with such technologies. Moreover, the growing reliance on AI has destabilised traditional assessment practices, complicating how academic performance is measured and interpreted. As institutions struggle to distinguish between student-generated and AI-assisted work, performance metrics may increasingly reflect technological proficiency rather than mastery of learning (Bearman et al., 2022). This raises fundamental questions about validity, academic integrity, and the meaning of "achievement" in AI-mediated educational environments, producing and potentially intensifying educational disparities rather than resolving them.

AI's influence on academic performance must also be understood within broader epistemic and pedagogical frameworks. From a critical and decolonial perspective, scholars warn that many AI systems are underpinned by Western epistemologies and data regimes that marginalise alternative ways of knowing (Williamson & Eynon, 2020). As such, AI-driven definitions of "successful performance" may privilege particular forms of knowledge production while rendering others invisible, thereby narrowing rather than expanding educational possibilities.

The absence of a coherent and integrative framework for conceptualising the multifaceted nature of academic achievement continues to constrain the design of effective educational interventions and policy responses (Suleiman et al., 2024, p. 2). This limitation is further intensified within the context of the Fourth Industrial Revolution, where rapid technological change, digitalised learning environments, and data-driven pedagogies have significantly reconfigured how academic performance is produced, measured, and interpreted (Williamson, 2017). As educators, policymakers, and higher education institutions grapple with increasingly complex learning ecosystems shaped by artificial intelligence, automation, and online modalities, the absence of a well-defined conceptual roadmap makes it challenging to align assessment practices, pedagogical strategies, and student support mechanisms with evolving educational demands. Consequently, attempts to enhance student outcomes risk remaining fragmented and reactive rather than strategically grounded in a holistic understanding of academic achievement in 4IR contexts.

UNDERSTANDING SUMMATIVE AND FORMATIVE ASSESSMENTS IN THE 4TH INDUSTRIAL REVOLUTION

Assessment is a central pedagogical practice in higher education, shaping not only how student learning is evaluated but also how learning itself is structured, experienced, and valued. Formative assessment is commonly defined as assessment for learning rather than assessment of learning. It involves ongoing feedback processes aimed at supporting students' understanding, guiding improvement, and informing teaching practices (Black & Wiliam, 1998). In higher education, formative assessment typically includes feedback on drafts, peer assessment, low-stakes tasks, and reflective activities that enable students to identify areas for improvement in their learning. Nicol and Macfarlane-Dick (2006) argue that practical formative assessment supports self-regulated learning by helping students develop the capacity to monitor, evaluate, and direct their own learning processes. From a critical perspective, formative assessment has the potential to democratise learning by shifting power away from high-stakes judgement towards dialogue and developmental feedback. Studies suggest that well-designed formative assessment enhances deep learning, conceptual understanding, and student confidence (Carless, 2015). However, scholars caution that formative assessment is often undermined in practice by institutional constraints, such as large class sizes, time pressures, and performative accountability cultures (Boud & Molloy, 2013). When feedback is delayed, unclear, or unengaged with by students, formative assessment risks becoming a procedural exercise rather than a transformative learning practice. Formative assessment in the 4IR challenges the epistemological foundations of traditional testing by privileging process over product. Digital portfolios, reflective journals, peer assessment, and collaborative problem-solving tasks assess students' capacity to engage in critical thinking, creativity, and self-regulation competencies, which are increasingly valued in 4IR economies (World Economic Forum, 2020).

Scholars argue that such practices undermine the legitimacy of rote memorisation and decontextualised knowledge recall that underpin conventional examinations (Biesta, 2010). However, critical voices caution that without careful design, digitally mediated formative assessment risks becoming surveillant and instrumental, reducing learning to data points rather than meaningful engagement (Williamson, 2017). In 4IR learning environments, formative assessment is increasingly mediated through digital platforms, learning analytics, and AI-driven feedback systems that provide real-time insights into student learning trajectories. This stands in sharp contrast to traditional tests, which often offer delayed, summative feedback that arrives too late to have a meaningful influence on learning. From a critical standpoint, formative assessment disrupts the assumption that learning can be validly captured through single-event testing, instead foregrounding learning as iterative, contextual, and socially constructed.

Whereas summative assessment plays a crucial role in maintaining academic standards and institutional credibility within higher education systems. However, critical scholars argue that summative assessment often prioritises measurement, comparability, and ranking over meaningful learning (Biesta, 2010). The impact of summative assessment on students is deeply ambivalent. On one hand, it provides clarity about expectations and motivates effort. On the other hand, heavy reliance on high-stakes summative assessment has been shown to encourage surface learning, strategic compliance, and performance anxiety (Gibbs, 2010). Furthermore, summative assessment practices may reproduce social inequalities by privileging students who are already familiar with dominant academic literacies and assessment conventions (Bourdieu & Passeron, 1990; Shay, 2008). As such, academic success, as measured through summative outcomes, may reflect cultural capital rather than learning alone. Scholars argue that this has forced higher education institutions to confront the limitations of assessments that prioritise product over learning process and originality over meaning-making (Bearman et al., 2022). As a result, summative assessment is increasingly being redesigned to incorporate reflective components, oral defences, and iterative feedback loops, thereby blurring the boundary between formative and summative assessment (Boud & Falchikov, 2007).

Nevertheless, these shifts are not without tension. While formative and redesigned summative assessments challenge traditional testing, they also operate within neoliberal accountability regimes that demand comparability, efficiency, and standardisation (Giroux, 2014; Selwyn, 2019). As such, innovative assessment practices may be co-opted into performative systems that reproduce existing power relations rather than transforming them. Furthermore, inequities in access to digital tools and assessment literacies risk disadvantaging students from historically marginalised backgrounds, raising critical questions about fairness and inclusion in 4IR assessment practices. Critically, the distinction between formative and summative assessment is increasingly blurred in contemporary higher education, particularly within outcomes-based and digitally mediated learning environments. Scholars argue that assessment should be understood as a continuum rather than a binary, with summative tasks incorporating formative elements through feedback, reflection, and iterative design (Boud, 2000). This integrative approach recognises that students learn through assessment, not merely for the purpose of assessment.

Nevertheless, power relations remain central to how assessment impacts students. From a critical pedagogical perspective, assessment functions as a regulatory mechanism that shapes student subjectivities and notions of worth (Giroux, 2014). Formative assessment can foster agency and learner autonomy, while summative assessment can discipline, rank, and exclude. The challenge for higher education, therefore, lies not in choosing between formative and summative assessment, but in critically redesigning assessment practices to foreground learning, equity, and epistemic justice.

THE VIABILITY OF ARTIFICIAL INTELLIGENCE (AI) IN ACHIEVING LEARNING OUTCOMES IN HIGHER EDUCATION

Overreliance on AI in assessments may compromise students' ability to evaluate social theories or interpret qualitative data independently and critically. Social science knowledge often requires nuanced, interpretive reasoning, which cannot be fully replicated by AI algorithms (Kitchin, 2017). The integration of AI into student assessments challenges traditional pedagogical practices. Educators must reconsider the design of assessments, academic policies, and ethical guidance to ensure that AI is used to enhance learning rather than compromise it (Floridi & Cowls, 2019).

AI has shifted from a peripheral educational technology to a core component in higher education, promising personalised learning, scalable assessment, and data-informed pedagogy. Scholarship converges on three claims: AI can individualise instruction, optimise formative feedback loops, and identify learning risks early; however, its viability depends on pedagogical alignment, ethical governance, and institutional capacity. This review synthesises the literature on how AI affects learning outcomes, organising evidence around learning theories, instructional design, assessment practices, and equity considerations, while identifying gaps and future directions.

From a pedagogical perspective, artificial intelligence (AI) supports the achievement of learning outcomes through personalised and adaptive learning. AI-driven learning management systems, intelligent tutoring systems, and analytics tools can tailor content to individual student needs, learning speeds, and prior knowledge. This responsiveness enhances student engagement, supports mastery learning, and improves conceptual understanding, particularly for outcomes related to knowledge acquisition, application, and problem-solving (Khoza & van der Walt, 2025). AI also facilitates formative assessment by providing immediate feedback, enabling students to reflect on their learning and address gaps in real-time (Nguyen, 2025).

In terms of teaching and learning innovation, AI enables educators to shift from content transmission to higher-order learning activities. When routine tasks such as grading quizzes, tracking attendance, or generating practice exercises are automated, lecturers can focus on facilitating critical thinking, discussion, collaboration, and research-based learning. This supports learning outcomes aligned with Bloom's higher cognitive domains, including analysis, evaluation, and creation (Adamakis & Rachiotis, 2025). Such innovation resonates with constructivist and connectivist learning theories, which emphasise learner-centred approaches and knowledge co-construction.

At the institutional level, AI contributes to improved learning outcomes through data-informed decision-making. Learning analytics can identify at-risk students early, enabling timely academic interventions and student support. AI-powered systems also enhance access and inclusivity by supporting students with disabilities through speech-to-text tools, language translation, and personalised learning pathways, thereby promoting equity in learning achievement (Khoza & van der Walt, 2025). These affordances align with broader goals of widening participation and addressing systemic inequalities in higher education.

However, the viability of AI is contingent upon responsible and critical implementation. Over-reliance on AI may undermine learning outcomes related to independent thinking, academic writing, and intellectual integrity if not carefully regulated. Concerns around academic dishonesty, algorithmic bias, data privacy, and unequal access to technology pose significant challenges, particularly in resource-constrained higher education contexts (Nguyen, 2025). These issues necessitate robust institutional policies, digital literacy training, and ethical guidelines for both students and staff (Adamakis & Rachiotis, 2025). AI is viable and potentially transformative in achieving learning outcomes in higher education when used as an augmentative rather than a substitutive tool. Its effectiveness depends on pedagogical alignment, educator competence, ethical governance, and contextual sensitivity. When strategically integrated, AI can enhance teaching quality, student engagement, and learning achievement while preserving the core educational values of critical inquiry and academic integrity.

DIGITAL PEDAGOGY AS A THEORETICAL FRAMEWORK

Digital pedagogy refers to the method and practice of teaching that integrates digital technologies to enhance learning, engagement, and assessment in higher education. (Morris & Stommel, 2018). Digital pedagogy extends beyond the mere use of technology in teaching; it represents a paradigm shift in how learning is designed, delivered, and experienced. It involves the thoughtful integration of digital tools to promote learner-centred, interactive, and collaborative engagement. As a theoretical framework, Technological Pedagogical Content Knowledge (TPACK), developed by Koehler and Mishra (2009), offers a crucial lens for understanding digital pedagogy. TPACK conceptualises effective teaching as the intersection of technological knowledge (TK), pedagogical knowledge (PK), and content knowledge (CK). This model highlights that effective digital pedagogy relies on a teacher's ability to integrate these domains coherently to enhance learning outcomes. According to Bayne (2015), digital pedagogy transforms traditional classroom practices by fostering critical and creative engagement with technology. Within this framework, tools such as artificial intelligence (AI), learning management systems, and digital assessment platforms are used to support both formative and summative evaluation. As higher education increasingly adopts digital transformation, digital pedagogy provides a foundation for responsible and innovative assessment design, enabling lecturers to strike a balance between technological efficiency and academic integrity, while promoting deep learning outcomes (Luckin, 2018).

Research suggests that digital pedagogy, framed through TPACK, redefines the teacher's role from content deliverer to learning facilitator (Koehler & Mishra, 2009; Trust, 2017). In AI-supported learning environments, this shift becomes even more critical. Teachers must develop not only digital competence but also critical awareness of how AI systems personalise learning, automate assessment, and influence student motivation. Digital pedagogy, therefore, offers a critical framework for analysing how educators mediate between human instruction and algorithmic intelligence.

METHODOLOGY

This study employs a qualitative self-study technique to investigate our experiences as lecturers in using AI for formative and summative assessments in higher education. The goal of the self-study is to obtain a critical understanding of our professional practice and its influence on student learning. A self-study approach enables the researcher to thoroughly analyse their own teaching practice, experiences, and thoughts. This method is based on interpretivism, stressing subjective meaning-making and reflexivity (Berry, 2007). It enables the researcher to connect personal experiences to broader educational theory and practice (Hamilton & Pinnegar, 2015). Self-study is a reflective and systematic form of inquiry in which individuals critically examine their own practices, experiences, and positionalities to generate knowledge and enhance professional understanding (Loughran, 2004). Originating within teacher education research, self-study challenges traditional distinctions between researcher and subject by positioning the self as both the site and source of knowledge production (Hamilton & Pinnegar, 1998). Rather than being an introspective or autobiographical exercise alone, self-study is grounded in rigorous methodological principles, including reflexivity, transparency, and scholarly dialogue. The self-study reflects on 3 Social Sciences lecturers on the impact of AI on students' performance on formative and summative assessments in their respective modules/ courses.

LECTURER'S REFLECTIONS ON THE IMPACT OF AI ON STUDENTS' PERFORMANCE ON FORMATIVE AND SUMMATIVE ASSESSMENT IN HIGHER EDUCATION

Dinny: As a lecturer at a university in KwaZulu-Natal, I have observed the impact of AI on students' assessments, particularly within my selected modules, where essay writing and exams are compulsory components. My modules are grounded in History, and students must develop and acquire the necessary learning outcomes for each module. Each module has different learning outcomes, but the common learning outcome is critical thinking. This learning outcome is imperative, as students are required to engage actively with the content or knowledge provided, and more so, with new ideologies. The impact that AI has had, especially in my modules, is that students' capabilities to actively share and discuss their views and perspectives on various phenomena that occur in History have been enhanced. I have observed that students have not learnt or know how to actively and ethically engage with AI. Instead, AI is being used to generate essays that adhere to the outline of the assessment criteria, rather than being used to develop students' personal thoughts or voices.

When engaging in lecture discussions, students often struggle to actively participate in different schools of thought that are essential to the course or module. However, more so, linking those schools of thought to everyday challenges within social norms. Through formative and summative assessment marks, I have noticed disparities in students' in-class assessment marks and their exam marks after the COVID-19 pandemic. For example, a student may have a high mark going into the exam but a low mark on the written exam. Thus, the question arises whether students are passive consumers of knowledge and rely heavily on AI tools to generate assignments, thereby not fully engaging with the subject matter, or if the use of AI is a means to an end. As my module is a method module that requires students to understand different theories, but more so display the application of those theories, this is where students struggle in the application, especially under exam assessments. The use of AI tools is beneficial in providing diverse knowledge and increasing information accessibility; however, a gap exists between what students have written and their actual understanding of the material. At times, when I ask a student to elaborate on their argument within an essay, they struggle to articulate or clarify what they meant. At times, students struggle to connect the arguments they construct in essays to the assessment criteria or the question being asked. Therefore, the feedback I provide to the student will consistently emphasise the need for them to engage with the literature, rather than providing a generalisation of the essay, or module or course-specific knowledge.

Within the History module, there are linguistic terms associated with the course that students often fail to use or link in their essays and papers. Thus, I prompt myself to continuously engage with students by reminding them that arguments or constructed sentences cannot be a generalisation of an argument but must link to History, to display the specialisation they are in.

Dintle: AI has a profound and wide-ranging effect on essay-based assessments, affecting learning results, academic integrity, pedagogy, and assessment design. Both the advantages and disadvantages of AI must be considered for a fair assessment. As a lecturer, I have observed the impact of AI on students' assessments, particularly in the context of essay writing in the Field of Tourism.

Within Tourism, AI is fundamentally transforming essay-based assessments and exams by challenging existing assessment approaches and providing new options for learning enhancement. Its influence is primarily determined by how it is implemented in educational settings. When managed wisely, AI may assist deeper learning and more genuine assessment; when left unmanaged, it risks jeopardising academic integrity and test validity. As a result, higher education institutions must implement adaptive, ethically informed evaluation methodologies that acknowledge AI as a long-term component of the academic environment.

When evaluating Tourism student performance in assessments, a clear distinction exists between formative and summative assessment practices. Formative assessment, which is continuous and developmental, tends to foster incremental improvement by providing students with timely feedback that supports reflection and adjustment throughout the learning process. As a result, students often demonstrate greater consistency and confidence in formative tasks, since these are low-stakes and encourage experimentation. Summative assessment, by contrast, is high-stakes and evaluative, conducted at the end of a semester to measure knowledge of the learning objectives. While it certifies achievement, summative assessment frequently reveals disparities in performance, as stronger students consolidate their skills while weaker students may struggle without ongoing scaffolding. In fields such as tourism and heritage studies, formative assessments, including reflective essays or case study discussions, capture students' ability to connect theory with practice. In contrast, summative assessments, such as final essays, demonstrate their capacity to synthesise diverse knowledge into coherent arguments. Together, these assessment modes provide complementary insights: formative assessment highlights the learning journey, while summative assessment validates the outcomes of that journey.

AI's effectiveness in student evaluations stems from its ability to enhance writing quality, provide rapid feedback, and support diverse learners. However, some of its drawbacks, including over-reliance, integrity problems, and superficial involvement, might jeopardise the attainment of genuine educational objectives. The issue for tourism and heritage education is to rethink assessments such that AI becomes a supporting tool in formative learning, while summative tasks protect uniqueness and critical reflection. AI in exams may reveal both strengths, such as digital literacy, flexibility, and clarity, as well as flaws, including a lack of inventiveness and superficial involvement. As a Tourism lecturer, it is vital to monitor AI usage through assessment design and give constructive feedback that pushes students beyond polished text to actual, critical, and practical learning. In tourism and heritage studies, this entails combining AI-supported writing with experiential, reflective, and oral components to ensure that students meet the genuine learning objectives of the module or course.

Learning outcomes are achieved most effectively when assessments are interconnected, scaffolded, and realistic with a mix of formative and summative assignments. Constructive criticism, practical learning, and monitoring ensure that students not only produce polished work but also effectively achieve the underlying objectives of the module or course. However, to guarantee that learning goals are met, instructors must provide realistic, integrated, and reflective projects that challenge students to move beyond AI outputs. The objective is to utilise AI as a supporting tool in formative learning, while summative evaluations ensure creativity, critical reflection, and the application of knowledge.

Kgari: As a lecturer at a South African University, I have witnessed numerous changes and impacts that AI has had on teaching and learning within the social sciences. AI assists students in enhancing the quality of their essays in terms of language and content. Students can obtain more recent references that enhance the information required for excellent content. Students perform better in formative assessments than in summative assessments because AI helps them organise and edit their work in language. Drawbacks are in copying and pasting in essays. Students plagiarise, and they do not edit the answers AI gives. However, it is effective in helping students respond to assessments and meet the objectives set for them. In many instances, it is challenging to identify students' abilities and weaknesses because they do not utilise them appropriately. They just cut and paste information. As a lecturer, I must teach students how to utilise AI in their assessments. The assignments I set must be AI-aligned and help them avoid plagiarism, while encouraging creativity. Therefore, it is necessary to question whether students have achieved the learning outcomes for the selected module, especially if the modules are continuous assessment modules with no written exams. The increase in student admissions in each module places pressure on ensuring that students understand and also meet the learning outcomes outlined for the module.

LECTURERS IN DISCUSSION ON THE USE OF AI

Participants Dinny and Kgari emphasise that this learning outcome is imperative because it requires students to engage actively with disciplinary knowledge and to interrogate new ideologies, rather than passively reproducing content. From her perspective, the introduction of AI in History modules has had a mixed impact. On the one hand, she observes that AI has enhanced students' capacity to share and discuss their views and perspectives on historical phenomena, suggesting that AI may function as an entry point for participation and dialogic engagement. This finding aligns with research suggesting that AI tools can enhance access to information and facilitate surface-level engagement and discussion in the social sciences (Baidoo-Anu & Ansah, 2023).

On the other hand, Dinny's account reveals a critical gap between participation and authentic learning. She notes that students "have not learnt or know how to actively and ethically engage with AI". Kgari shares the same sentiment, "in many instances, it is challenging to identify students' abilities and weaknesses because they do not utilise them appropriately. They simply cut and paste information", instead of using generative AI to produce essays that closely conform to assessment criteria without developing their own historical voice or interpretive stance. Holmes et al. (2022) and Selwyn (2019) caution that AI can foster dependency, erode learner autonomy, and hinder critical thinking if students rely excessively on machine-generated content. This reflects broader scholarly concerns that AI use in higher education often prioritises performance and compliance over epistemic development, resulting in outputs that meet formal requirements while undermining critical thinking, originality, and disciplinary reasoning (Williamson, 2017). In this sense, AI risks reshaping assessment practices in ways that privilege technical alignment with rubrics rather than the cultivation of independent historical analysis and ethical scholarship.

Dinny's observations, therefore, highlight a tension central to contemporary debates on AI and learning outcomes: while AI may enhance efficiency, access, and participation, its uncritical use can erode the very learning outcomes that History education seeks to achieve, particularly the development of personal voice, critical interpretation, and ethical engagement with knowledge. As Solak (2025) argues, the growing authority of algorithmic tools in knowledge production raises epistemological concerns for the social sciences, where meaning-making, context, and reflexivity are foundational to the field. Without explicit pedagogical guidance on the ethical use of AI and critical engagement, AI can become a substitute for thinking rather than a scaffold for learning, thereby widening the gap between apparent academic success and the genuine attainment of higher-order learning outcomes.

Participant Dintle highlights the dual nature of AI in student evaluations, noting that its effectiveness lies in its capacity to enhance writing quality, deliver rapid feedback, and support diverse learners. This perspective aligns with scholarly research suggesting that AI-enabled tools can improve clarity, coherence, and linguistic accuracy in student writing, while also offering timely feedback that supports iterative learning and inclusivity, particularly for students from diverse linguistic and educational backgrounds this viewpoint, AI appears to function as a pedagogical support mechanism that can facilitate access to assessment expectations and potentially reduce barriers to participation. On the other hand, extensive reliance on high-stakes summative assessment has been widely critiqued for encouraging surface learning, strategic compliance, and heightened performance anxiety, rather than sustained conceptual understanding (Gibbs, 2010). Moreover, summative assessment practices have been shown to reproduce existing social inequalities by privileging students who possess prior familiarity with dominant academic literacies and assessment conventions, thereby reinforcing the role of cultural capital in academic success (Bourdieu & Passeron, 1990; Shay, 2008). In this context, achievement as measured through summative outcomes may reflect students' capacity to navigate assessment norms rather than the depth of their learning.

These longstanding critiques have gained renewed urgency in the context of AI-mediated assessment practices. Scholars argue that the increasing emphasis on polished outputs and measurable performance has exposed the limitations of assessment regimes that prioritise product over process and originality over meaning-making (Bearman et al., 2022). Dintle's account foregrounds this tension, illustrating how AI can enhance the technical quality of student work and increase efficiency in evaluation, while simultaneously risking the erosion of the epistemic purposes of assessment if its use remains unregulated and pedagogically under-scaffolded. In the absence of explicit guidance on the ethical use of AI and critical engagement,

Empirical evidence indicates that when students use AI as a shortcut rather than as a cognitive scaffold, academic performance, particularly in assessments that require conceptual understanding, synthesis, and critical reasoning, may decline (Baidoo-Anu & Ansah, 2023). Participant Kgari's reflections strongly corroborate this concern, foregrounding the growing risk of AI-facilitated academic misconduct in higher education. Kgari identifies copying and pasting AI-generated responses into essays without editing or critical engagement as a prevalent practice, noting that such behaviour obscures students' authentic abilities, learning gaps, and conceptual weaknesses. This observation reinforces scholarly arguments that unregulated AI use can decouple assessment performance from genuine learning, rendering assessment outputs unreliable indicators of student competence.

At the same time, Kgari acknowledges the pedagogical potential of AI, particularly its effectiveness in supporting students in responding to assessments and aligning their work with stated learning objectives. This duality reflects a central tension in contemporary assessment debates: AI can enhance efficiency, access, and structural alignment with assessment criteria, yet simultaneously undermine epistemic integrity when it replaces rather than supports student thinking (Williamson, 2017; Bearman et al., 2022). From a TPACK perspective, this indicates a disruption of content knowledge, as AI-generated outputs risk flattening disciplinary complexity and marginalising students' reasoning, voice, and interpretive agency. Rather than deepening engagement with content, AI becomes a surrogate for disciplinary thinking. Across participants' narratives, there is a shared recognition that pedagogical strategies have not yet fully adapted to the realities of AI-mediated learning. Dintle acknowledges AI's effectiveness in enhancing writing quality, supporting diverse learners, and providing rapid feedback elements that align with inclusive and formative pedagogical principles. Importantly, TPACK conceptualises technological knowledge not as technical proficiency alone, but as an understanding of how technologies shape knowledge production and learning practices. The participants' experiences suggest that students often have functional access to AI tools but lack a critical awareness of their epistemic implications, ethical boundaries, and limitations.

Nevertheless, the participants also point toward a constructive path forward. Kgari's assertion that lecturers must teach students how to use AI signals a shift toward pedagogical responsibility and intentional design. This aligns with TPACK's emphasis on educators as designers of learning experiences who mediate the relationship between content, pedagogy, and technology. When lecturers actively scaffold AI use, positioning it as a tool for idea generation, feedback, and critical engagement rather than content substitution, AI has the potential to support deeper learning and more authentic achievement of learning outcomes. Participant Dinny's observations foreground a growing disjunction between formative and summative assessment outcomes in the post-COVID-19 higher education context. Through both formative and summative assessment marks, Dinny notes a recurring pattern in which students achieve relatively high marks in continuous assessment tasks, yet perform poorly in high-stakes written examinations. This supports scholarly concerns that AI-mediated assessment can inflate formative marks without a corresponding increase in conceptual understanding, thereby weakening the predictive validity of formative assessment for summative performance (Gibbs, 2010; Bearman et al., 2022). From an assessment perspective, formative assessment is intended to support learning through feedback, reflection, and the development of conceptual understanding. In contrast, summative assessment evaluates the extent to which learning outcomes have been achieved (Black & Wiliam, 2009). However, Dinny's account suggests that this alignment may be increasingly compromised. To address this, scholars argue for assessment designs that integrate formative and summative purposes more coherently, emphasising reflective engagement, process-based evaluation, and opportunities for students to articulate their reasoning (Shay, 2008; Black & Wiliam, 2009).

In the absence of such redesign, AI risks exacerbating existing tensions between assessment for learning and assessment of learning, ultimately undermining the achievement of authentic learning outcomes. Participant Dintle reinforces this perspective, noting that while AI can support students in responding to formative tasks by enhancing writing quality and providing rapid feedback, it may also foster superficial engagement when students over-rely on AI-generated outputs rather than developing their own ideas. By contrast, summative assessments are high-stakes, evaluative tasks conducted at the end of a module or semester to certify achievement and measure attainment of the intended learning outcomes (Gibbs, 2010). Dintle's account highlights that summative assessments frequently reveal disparities in performance. This disparity echoes concerns in the literature that uncritical reliance on AI can artificially inflate formative performance, masking genuine learning gaps and creating a disconnect between formative confidence and summative achievement (Bearman et al., 2022). Consequently, integrating AI into assessment requires careful pedagogical planning that aligns formative and summative tasks, emphasises ethical and reflective use of AI, and ensures that learning outcomes are authentically assessed.

CONCLUSION

Analysed through the TPACK framework, the participants' accounts illustrate that the challenges associated with AI in higher education do not stem from technology itself, but from insufficient integration across technological, pedagogical, and content domains. Without deliberate alignment, AI risks reinforcing surface learning, academic misconduct, and performative assessment practices. However, when embedded within a coherent TPACK-informed pedagogical strategy, AI can become a powerful enabler of disciplinary engagement, ethical learning, and meaningful achievement of learning outcomes in higher education. Consequently, the observed gap between formative and summative performance signals a broader assessment challenge in higher education: the need to realign assessment practices with learning outcomes in the context of digital and AI-mediated learning. To address this, scholars argue for assessment designs that integrate formative and summative purposes more coherently, emphasising reflective engagement, process-based evaluation, and opportunities for students to articulate their reasoning (Shay, 2008; Black & Wiliam, 2009). In the absence of such redesign, AI risks exacerbating existing tensions between assessment for learning and assessment of learning, ultimately undermining the achievement of authentic learning outcomes.

REFERENCES

Adamakis, M., & Rachiotis, T. (2025). *Artificial Intelligence in Higher Education: A State-of-the-Art Overview of Pedagogical Integrity*. Artificial Intelligence Literacy, and Policy Integration., DOI: 10.3390/encyclopedia5040180

Adewale, M. D., Azeta, A., Abayomi-Alli, A., & Sambo-Magaji, A. (2024). Impact of artificial intelligence adoption on students' academic performance in open and distance learning: A systematic literature review. *Heliyon, 10*(22), e40025. Advance online publication. DOI: 10.1016/j.heliyon.2024.e40025 PMID: 39605813

Baidoo-Anu, D., & Ansah, L. O. (2023). Education in the era of generative artificial intelligence (AI): Understanding the potential benefits of ChatGPT in promoting teaching and learning. *Journal of AI, 7*(1), 52–62. DOI: 10.61969/jai.1337500

Bayne, S. (2015). What is the matter with 'technology-enhanced learning'? *Learning, Media and Technology, 40*(1), 5–20. DOI: 10.1080/17439884.2014.915851

Bearman, M., Dawson, P., Ajjawi, R., Tai, J., & Boud, D. (2022). Reconsidering assessment for learning in a digital age. *Assessment & Evaluation in Higher Education, 47*(1), 1–14.

Berry, A. (2007). *Tensions in teaching about teaching: Understanding practice as a teacher educator* (Vol. 5). Springer Science & Business Media.

Biesta, G. (2010). *Good education in an age of measurement*. Paradigm.

Black, P., & Wiliam, D. (1998). Assessment and classroom learning. *Assessment in Education: Principles, Policy & Practice, 5*(1), 7–74. DOI: 10.1080/0969595980050102

Black, P., & Wiliam, D. (2009). Developing the theory of formative assessment. *Educational Assessment, Evaluation and Accountability, 21*(1), 5–31. DOI: 10.1007/s11092-008-9068-5

Boud, D., & Falchikov, N. (2007). *Rethinking assessment in higher education. Routledge. Boud, D., & Falchikov, N. (2007). Rethinking assessment in higher education*. Routledge.

Boud, D., & Molloy, E. (2013). Rethinking models of feedback for learning. *Assessment & Evaluation in Higher Education, 38*(6), 698–712. DOI: 10.1080/02602938.2012.691462

Bourdieu, P. (1986). The forms of capital. In J. Richardson (Ed.), *Handbook of theory and research for the sociology of education* (pp. 241–258). Greenwood.

Bourdieu, P., & Passeron, J. C. (1990). *Reproduction in education, society and culture* (Vol. 4). Sage.

Carless, D. (2015). *Excellence in university assessment.* Routledge. DOI: 10.4324/9781315740621

Floridi, L., & Cowls, J. (2019). A unified framework of five principles for AI in society. *Harvard Data Science Review, 1*(1).

Freire, P. (1970). *Pedagogy of the oppressed.* Herder and Herder.

Gibbs, G. (2010). *Using assessment to support student learning*. Leeds Met Press.

Giroux, H. A. (2011). *On critical pedagogy.* Bloomsbury Academic.

Giroux, H. A. (2014). *Neoliberalism's war on higher education.* Haymarket Books.

Hamilton, M. L., & Pinnegar, S. (1998). Conclusion: The value and the promise of self-study. In Hamilton, M. L. (Ed.), *Reconceptualising teaching practice: Self-study in teacher education* (pp. 235–246). Falmer Press.

Hamilton, M. L., & Pinnegar, S. (2015). *Self-study of practice as a genre of qualitative research: Theory, methodology, and practice.* Springer.

Holmes, W., Bialik, M., & Fadel, C. (2022). *Artificial intelligence in education: Promises and implications for teaching and learning.* Center for Curriculum Redesign.

Kasneci, E., Sessler, K., Küchemann, S., Bannert, M., Dementieva, D., Fischer, F., Gasser, U., Groh, G., Günnemann, S., Hüllermeier, E., Krusche, S., Kutyniok, G., Michaeli, T., Nerdel, C., Pfeffer, J., Poquet, O., Sailer, M., Schmidt, A., Seidel, T., & Kasneci, G. (2023). ChatGPT for good? On opportunities and challenges of large language models for education. *Learning and Individual Differences, 103*, 102274. DOI: 10.1016/j.lindif.2023.102274

Khoza, N. G., & van der Walt, F. (2025). A systematic review on AI-enhanced pedagogies in higher education in the Global South. *Frontiers in Education, 10*, 1667884. Advance online publication. DOI: 10.3389/feduc.2025.1667884

Kitchin, R. (2017). Thinking critically about and researching algorithms. *Information Communication and Society, 20*(1), 14–29. DOI: 10.1080/1369118X.2016.1154087

Koehler, M. J., & Mishra, P. (2009). What is technological pedagogical content knowledge (TPACK)? *Contemporary Issues in Technology & Teacher Education, 9*(1), 60–70.

Loughran, J. (2004). A history and context of self-study of teaching and teacher education practices. In Loughran, J. J. (Eds.), *International handbook of self-study of teaching and teacher education practices* (pp. 7–39). Springer. DOI: 10.1007/978-1-4020-6545-3_1

Luckin, R. (2018). *Machine learning and human intelligence: The future of education for the 21st century*. UCL Press.

Luckin, R., Holmes, W., Griffiths, M., & Forcier, L. B. (2016). *Intelligence unleashed: An argument for AI in education*. Pearson.

Mallillin, L. L. D. (2024). Artificial intelligence (AI) towards students' academic performance. *Innovare Journal of Education, 12*(4), 16–21. DOI: 10.22159/ijoe.2024v12i4.51665

Morris, S., & Stommel, J. (2018). *An urgency of teachers: The work of critical digital pedagogy*. Hybrid Pedagogy.

Nguyen, T. T. (2025). Artificial Intelligence in Higher Education: A *Systematic Review of Impacts, Barriers, and Emerging Trends. IOSR Journal of Research & Method in Education*, 15(3), 53–61. Available at: www.iosrjournals.org

Nicol, D. J., & Macfarlane-Dick, D. (2006). Formative assessment and self-regulated learning: A model and seven principles of good feedback practice. *Studies in Higher Education, 31*(2), 199–218. DOI: 10.1080/03075070600572090

Richardson, M., Abraham, C., & Bond, R. (2012). Psychological correlates of university students' academic performance. *Psychological Bulletin, 138*(2), 353–387. DOI: 10.1037/a0026838 PMID: 22352812

Sanders, D. A., & Mukhari, S. S. (2024). Lecturers' perceptions of the influence of AI on a blended learning approach in a South African higher education institution. *Discover Education, 3*(1), 135. DOI: 10.1007/s44217-024-00235-2

Selwyn, N. (2019). *Should robots replace teachers? AI and the future of education*. Polity Press.

Shay, S. (2008). Beyond social constructivist perspectives on assessment. *Teaching in Higher Education, 13*(5), 595–605. DOI: 10.1080/13562510802334970

Suleiman, I. B., Okunade, O. A., Dada, E. G., & Ezeanya, U. C. (2024). Key factors influencing students' academic performance. *Journal of Electrical Systems and Information Technology, 11*(1), 41. DOI: 10.1186/s43067-024-00166-w

Trust, T. (2017). Using the TPACK framework to examine teachers' knowledge of educational technology integration. *Journal of Digital Learning in Teacher Education, 33*(1), 21–27.

Williamson, B. (2017). Big data in education. *Sage (Atlanta, Ga.).*

Williamson, B., & Eynon, R. (2020). Historical threads, missing links, and future directions in AI in education. *Learning, Media and Technology, 45*(3), 223–235. DOI: 10.1080/17439884.2020.1798995

World Economic Forum. (2020). Schools of the future: Defining new models of education for the Fourth Industrial Revolution.

York, T. T., Gibson, C., & Rankin, S. (2015). Defining and measuring academic success. *Practical Assessment, Research & Evaluation, 20*(5), 1–20.

Zawacki-Richter, O., Marín, V. I., Bond, M., & Gouverneur, F. (2019). Systematic review of research on artificial intelligence applications in higher education. *International Journal of Educational Technology in Higher Education, 16*(39), 39. DOI: 10.1186/s41239-019-0171-0

Zhou, Q., Suraworachet, W., Pozdniakov, S., Martinez-Maldonado, R., Bartindale, T., Chen, P., Richardson, D., & Cukurova, M. (2021). Investigating students' experiences with collaboration analytics for remote group meetings. *Lecture Notes in Computer Science, 12748*, 472–485. DOI: 10.1007/978-3-030-78292-4_38

Chapter 9
AI-Driven Learning Environments and Adaptive Learning Technologies

Nikhil Kumar Goyal
http://orcid.org/0009-0007-4532-8033
Noida International University, Greater Noida, India

Ayesha Farooqi
http://orcid.org/0009-0000-4556-4211
Poornima University, Jaipur, India

Vasileios Paliktzoglou
http://orcid.org/0009-0001-0326-1156
Bahrain Polytechnic, Bahrain

Udit Mamodiya
http://orcid.org/0000-0002-8022-4252
Poornima University, Jaipur, India

ABSTRACT

Learning technologies and AI-powered learning environments are radically changing the way education is provided in modern times through providing individualized, data intensive, and highly adaptive learning experiences. The systems utilize the techniques of artificial intelligence, including machine learning, natural language processing, learning analytics, and so on, in order to analyze learner behaviors, performance trends, cognitive and emotional reactions on a continuous basis. According to such insights, AI programs dynamically adjust content difficulty,

DOI: 10.4018/979-8-2600-1840-8.ch009

learning patterns, feedback rate and assessment styles to the needs of individual learners. The chapter covers the theoretical aspects of the AI-enhanced learning environment such as its architecture, mechanics, personalization policies, and implementation in different learning settings. It also studied intelligent tutoring system (ITS), real-time adaptive feedback loop, emotion smart personalisation and learning success predictive analytics.

1. INTRODUCTION

1.1 Evolution of Technology-Enhanced Learning

The history of introducing technology in the field of education is connected with the first computer-assisted instructional methods up to the modern advanced learning scenarios based on AI. At the beginning, digital learning tools were not dynamic, as they provided learners with the same information irrespective of the background and learning rate. These earlier systems enhanced the availability of information but were not able to be customized and adapted to differences in student abilities. Educational platforms were slowly transformed into adaptive functionality as data availability was growing and computing capability was becoming more powerful. These systems might divide the learners according to the performance trends and suggest slightly different learning directions, although personalisation was minimised and predetermined by rules (Anderson & Dron, 2011).

Figure 1. Technology-enhanced learning

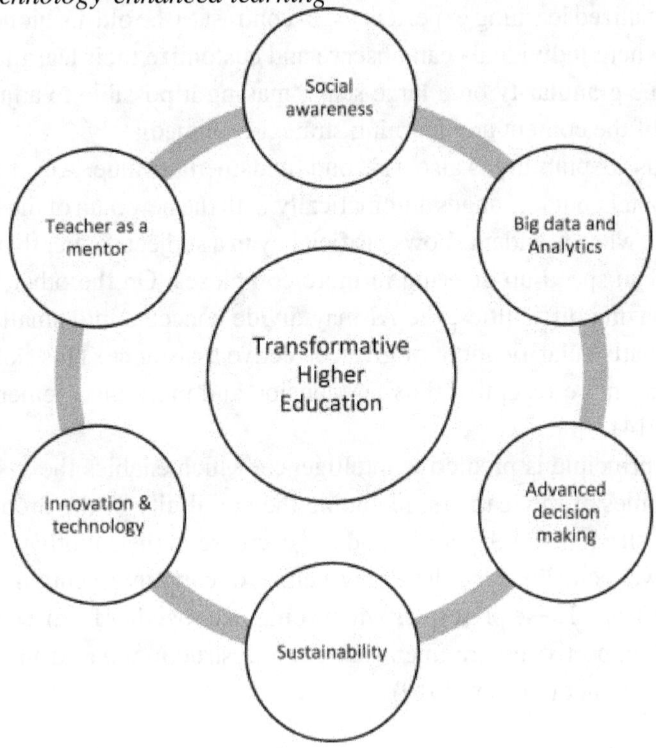

The AI transforms this to be based on dynamic, data-driven decision-making capabilities. Current AI-based learning systems use machine learning algorithms that can process large volumes of learner interaction and determine patterns that were not easily observable by human teachers. This development allowed the systems to personalize instruction by responding immediately to the progress of learners, their preferences and their expected requirements. This has evolved over the years including complex adaptive quizzes to virtual tutors, cognitive modelling systems, emotion responsive systems and AIs driven immersive learning experiences over time. Such redesign is an indication of pushing content delivery tools towards smart environments that can facilitate the learning process of learners in an active way.

1.2 Main Postulates of AI-driven learning

The AI-based learning systems have a number of underlying principles that determine their difference to the typical digital learning systems. The initial principle is the personalization that is data-driven and will enable AI systems to constantly gather and examine the interactions of learners i.e., how quickly they react, how many of their attempts are erroneous, navigation patterns, and even emotions to develop individualized learning experiences. In contrast to the old-fashioned approach to teaching, where individuals can observe and customize their learning, AI offers insights of fine granularity on a large scale, making it possible to adjust the level of difficulty of the content and learning strategies immediately.

Continuous adaptability is also a second fundamental value. AI is not just a differentiated content but it changes automatically with the new data of the learners. As an illustration, when a student shows proficiency in a subject sooner than requested, the program can speed up or bring in more complexes. On the other hand, when a student is having difficulties, the AI may divide concepts into smaller subparts, move to alternative clarification, or give corrective assistance. This flexibility also makes learning more receptive thus less tension and more involvement (Baker & Inventado, 2014).

The third principle is predictive intelligence, which enables the system to predict the outcomes of the learners, including the possibility of the dropouts, future performance, shortfalls in the skills, and the decrease in their motivation. This anticipatory power contributes to the strengthening of early interventions by teachers or the system itself. These principles when combined together form a personalized, proactive and supportive environment, and frame instructions based on the changing needs of each learner (Bower, 2019).

1.3 AI-based Learning Environments Architecture

The AI-based learning systems are based on the multilayered structures, which combine the components of data gathering, analytic operations, and the delivery of personalized content. The first layer is the data acquisition that comprises of capturing interactions of the learners with the learning management systems (LMS), online tests, online learning modules, and sensor-based devices. The types of data streams can be behavioral measures, keystrokes, quiz performance or even facial expressions or other biometric measures like eye tracking in more sophisticated systems. This stream of data is fundamental to the AI-based personalization.

The second level is that of data processing and analytical modeling in which machine learning codes study data collected and deduce consequential patterns. Decision trees, neural networks, reinforcement learning agent, and natural language processing model are some algorithms which underlie different capabilities, including predicting learning challenges in a learner to offering personalized feedback. This analytical engine is in charge of transforming raw data into actionable insights so that the system could know what is going on with the learner, cognitively and emotionally (Dillenbourg et al., 1996).

The last layer is adaptive content delivery whereby the suggestions, customized activities, feedback, and learning orientation are accorded to the learner. This layer guarantees a smooth level of interaction between the system and the student and may be made via dashboards, virtual dispensers, or some sort of interactive learning module. Its architecture is scalable, and thousands of learners simultaneously can be provided with individual experiences without impairing the working of systems. In totality, all these architectural elements provide a coherent environment that will be able to sustain intelligent, autonomous, and responsive learning.

1.4 AI Application in Learning Environment

The application of AI in education systems integrates different applications, and each of them has its own advantages, helping to facilitate various elements of the educational process. Intelligent tutoring systems (ITS) are one of the applications through which human tutors are imitated and can assist the learner step-by-step, respond to questions, identify misconception and modify instruction depending on the behavior of students. ITS apply cognitive models to the thinking process of the learners to know where they are probably performing poorly and therefore they can provide targeted intervention.

Learning analytics and prediction is another significant use since systems process massive amounts of data in order to determine trends and predict student performance. Such tools are used to trace progress of students, identify the possibility of drop out and optimize curriculum strategies by the institutions. The algorithms of machine learning used in this category allow making strategic decisions and long-term planning with the purpose of enhancing student achievement.

The third use is dedicated to adaptive assessments, which adjust the level of difficulty of the questions in real-time, depending on the answers of students. This will enable measuring student knowledge more accurately in the case of not having to conduct long and grueling examinations. Moreover, the learning process can be improved by the use of natural language processing (NLP) in the form of chatbots, automated feedback systems, and writing assistance with AI support. These systems assist students with respect to clarity and formative feedback, which are given as soon as it is required (Education and Employers, 2018).

Collectively, these applications represent the wide range of possibilities of AI-driven learning environments to revolutionize the process of instruction, assessment, and support, and the overall interaction of the learner.

2. ADAPTIVE LEARNING TECHNOLOGIES AND THEIR CORE FUNCTIONALITIES

2.1 Understanding Adaptive Learning Systems

Adaptive learning technologies are a significant break as compared to traditional digital education technologies in that, they provide a unique ways of learning which constantly realigns to meet the progress, behavioral, and cognitive requirements of the learner. In contrast to the inflexible order of use presented by the statical e-learning modules, the adaptive learning system decodes student-permitted information and adjusts instruction dynamically through the application of the algorithmic intelligence. This kind of individual customization is particularly applicable in differentiated classrooms where the students come with prior knowledge that may have different speeds of learning and even understanding of the knowledge covered. Adaptive systems can also help a person master the underlying concepts of a subject before progressing on because they recognize the proficiency gaps in advance so that each student gets the instruction they need to acquire the basic concepts first.

Figure 2. Structure of the adaptive learning system

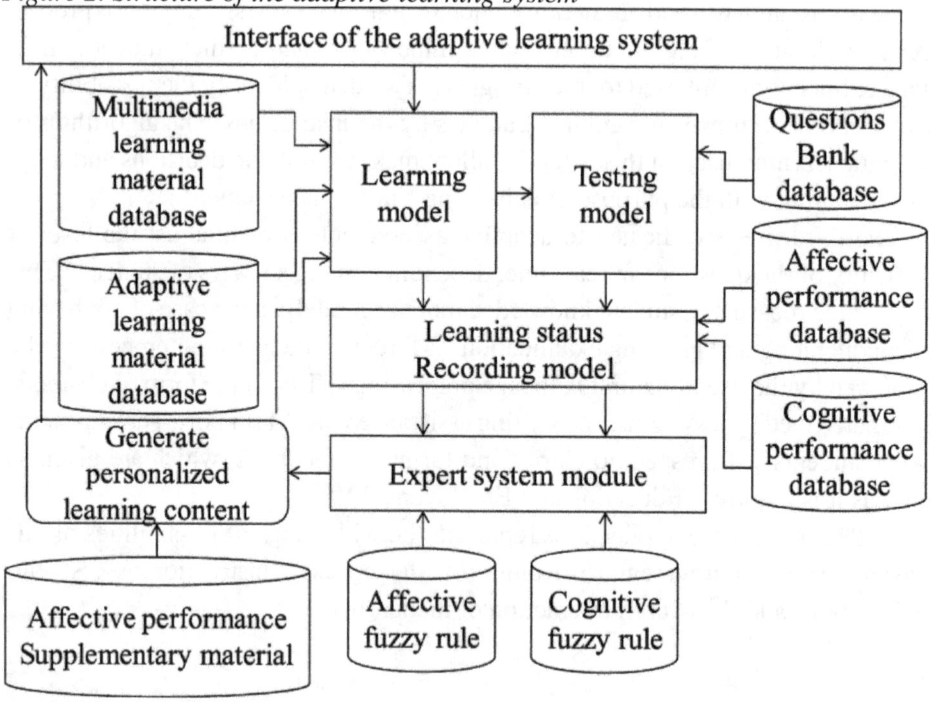

The systems are largely dependent on the machine learning, predictive analytics, and cognitive modelling. Machine learning helps the system see the trends in performance of students e.g., constant mistakes, frequent breaks or fast learning, meaning different levels of understanding. Predictive models assert the chance of a learner experiencing difficulty in the future subject to be learned, and cognitive models are that which mimic the cognitive activities involved in learning, such as how false beliefs are created or how much of what is learned is remembered. Collectively, these elements allow adaptive learning system to provide dynamic learning environments that are student-centred and instantly responsive to variations in performance, behavior, and motivation (Eom et al., 2006).

The adaptive learning systems are very effective due to the fact that they blend the automation and pedagogical intelligence. Though AI controls the customizations, based on educational theories of mastery learning, spaced repetition, and formative assessment these systems are designed. This will see the adaptive technology being applied towards the cognitive and emotional aspects of learning. Consequently, learners feel less frustrated, more confident, and have more valuable interaction to make which plays a major role in enhancing learning results and retention.

2.2 Mechanisms of real-time personalization

The anticipation of transformations in adaptive learning technologies is real-time, i.e., personalization. These systems continuously keep track of activities of learners including response patterns, frequency of interactions, time spent at tasks, and type of errors and modify learning environment. This information is used by the AI engine to decide when the learners should seek further clarification, when they can move on to higher stimuli and when they should be provided with corrective information. This incessant tracking can allow a fluid learning process in which the difficulty in content and instructional plans can change in response to moment-to-moment performance of the learner.

One important personalization process in the real-time is the dynamically adaptive content difficulty. The system becomes more complex when the student answers easier questions several times correct and provides attention and challenge to the student. On the other hand, frequent mistakes will result in simplified descriptions, illustrations, or other means of instruction offered by the system. This will make sure that the learners are kept in the optimum zone of proximal development that is not too difficult and at the same time too easy, which entails deeper meaning and better confidence (Gikas & Grant, 2013).

The adaptive feedback is also another mechanism. AI systems provide specific, practical advice, which is based on individual mistakes, instead of generic words such as correct or incorrect. As an illustration, when a particular student continues to have misunderstandings concerning a mathematical concept, the system can point out the particular step where the misunderstanding arises and give specific examples or hints. It can also be in the form of motivational nudges in systems which can be used to remind progress or trigger encouragement to a learner when they experience indicators of fatigue or loss of interest. These interventions in personal formats imitate the human tutoring and the learning process becomes more adorable and accommodative.

2.3 Smart Content Sequencing and Pathway Optimisation

Adaptive learning systems do not just go through the material, they are capable of sequencing instructional modules in an intelligent manner, depending on the profile of a specific learner. This is achieved by studying the past history of performance and the present levels of mastery and applying them to identify the most effective learning route. The system determines what is needed as a pre requirements of knowledge and makes sure that the learner pays back on what has been taught before moving ahead with the learning process. This prevents the cases when the students move to difficult subjects without learning the previous ones and this may frustrate and bankrupt in the conventional learning environment.

In sequencing, algorithm takes into account various variables; the relevance of every idea in the course, the proficiency pattern of the learner, the relationship among various ideas and the expected performance results. To illustrate, when a learner has been shown to have mastered algebraic manipulation well but is facing problem with word problems, the system may rearrange modules so that the learner can understand the comprehension techniques and come back to applications. This makes teaching to match the needs in the cognitive ability of the individuals instead of the standardized timing schedules.

Streamlined routes are especially useful in large educational institutions, i.e. university or MOOC, where the teacher cannot individually track the progress of all students. AI makes sure that every learner works along the most productive path, with no redundant repetitions taking place and core abilities being strengthened. With simplified learning travel, adaptive systems step down on the amount of time that can be spent in educating as well as the amount of the cognitive load, making the general learning results better. Such personalization is something that could not be achieved manually, which outlines the disruptive role of AI in the contemporary education (Hodges et al., 2020).

2.4 Feedback Loops and Assessment based Adaptation

The assessment becomes the core of the adaptive learning technologies that facilitate personalization and the ability to make constant advancements. These are systems that integrate a blend of formative, diagnostic, and micro-assessment to learners to measure their level of understanding at fine levels. Adaptive assessments are continuous and do not interrupt learning unlike other tests, which are static and episodic. The system can include questions in the activities, track the behavioral indicators, or assess the responses based on the natural language processing, provided by the students. This continual evaluation enables the AI engine to refresh the profile of the students as they proceed.

Feedback loops are essential in the adaptation process where outcome of assessment would guide the next stage of instruction. In instances of the learner suffering, the system would automatically give the specific content, explanations, or remedial materials. In case of mastery, then the learner moves on in more complicated areas. Such feedback feedback loops develop a continuous improvement cycle, which allows the learners to develop at their own pace, with timely guidance provided (Järvelä et al., 2015).

Notably, the assessment-based adjustment can benefit students and educators alike. Students get continuous feedback which improves reflection and self-management. Teachers can access specific performance dashboards based on identifying trends in a class and specific learning areas. This allows teachers to state more specific interventions, mentoring at individual scale, and to develop more efficient instructional plans. Finally, adaptation-based on assessment increases the levels of transparency, decreases the learning gaps and promotes more justifiable educational results (Johnson et al., 2015).

3. INTELLIGENT TUTORING SYSTEMS AND AUTOMATED INSTRUCTIONAL SUPPORT

3.1 The Architecture of Intelligent Tutoring Systems

One of the most successful applications of AI in education is intelligent Tutoring Systems (ITS) which is created to simulate the processes of decision making and pedagogy of highly qualified human tutors. The four main interrelated components of an ITS include student model, domain model, pedagogical model and interface. This student model is constantly updating a comprehensive profile of the learner, relying on the information about performance, the misconceptions, time which is spent to complete the tasks and the indications of the behavior. The changing profile allows the system to estimate how a tutor can detect the preparedness, frustration, or confidence of a learner. The domain model is the repository of knowledge, which is the expertise and stores the structured concepts of learning, problem type and pathways of solution. It guarantees accuracy of content on presentation, relevance, and pedagogical validity.

The pedagogical model serves as an instructional brain of the system and decides when to go through with new material, how to give feedback, and the teaching methods to be applied. As an example, it can determine whether the learner needs to be scaffolded, provided with worked examples, conceptual explanations, or imitation assignments or not, depending on performance observations. This model has the advantage of maintaining an instruction within the cognitive load principles as well as learning theories. Lastly, interface bridges the gap between the learners and the system either by the way of a conversation, visual explanations, simulation, or interactive activity. Quality of interface is directly related to engaging the learners, usability and emotional comfortability (Kizilcec et al., 2016).

The combination of these elements helps ITS to provide subtle, reactive and contextual learning goods. In contrast to traditional e-learning tools which consist mainly of content delivery platforms, ITS proactively makes reason about both our needs as learners and produces customized instruction. This dynamism in analysis, adaptation, and response makes them very potent accomplices of considering various learning styles, using learners with disabilities, and helping students in learning complex areas like mathematics, programming, engineering, and language learning.

3.2 Natural Language Understanding and Conversational Support

Present-day ITS greatly depend on the use of natural language understanding (NLU) and conversational AI to aid more human interaction processes between machines and learners. They do not simply require the learner to select answers given in a particular format or in multiple choices, but instead can be able to understand open-ended text, voice recognition and even disjointed ways an individual is explaining themselves. This enables the learners to articulate themselves in natural language thereby rendering the digital learning space more natural and less limiting. The NLU-driven systems would be able to detect conceptual mistakes, unclear rationale, and analyze the completeness of the explanations, which will provide the level of understanding that is similar to that of the human tutor.

ITS with conversational agents can be used to support intelligent and interactive conversations that go beyond error-correction. These agents may pose probing questions, they may encourage the learner to explain their reasoning, or they may take learners through step-by-step instructions when solving a complicated problem. This form of interaction, based on questions, fosters metacognition which enables learners to reflect on the way they think and identify any wrong beliefs. Moreover, conversational support is also more accessible to learners who cannot easily employ conventional methods of learning, including learners with dyslexia or writing difficulty.

These relationships have an emotional-support role. Conversational agents can deanxiety, maintain attention, and instill confidence in learners by modulating the tones and selective language, using empathy, and prompts that encourage the learning process. They are able to see signs of disengagement, like brief and hasty reactions or extended inactivity, and provide motivation or relaxation. Conversational ITS can thus not only aid in cognitive but also affective growth which makes them a whole person learning experience to the learner that caters to both affective and academic needs (Koedinger & Corbett, 2006).

3.3 The Automated Feedback, Scaffolding and Diagnosis of error

Their capacity to offer automatically, real time, and personalized feedbacks is one of the strongest functions of ITS. In traditional learning conditions, the correction of the errors is usually less effective because of the delays in the feedback, provided by grading periods or the absence of an instructor. Conversely, ITS approaches raise learner responses in real-time, and compare them to anticipated reasoning schemes, establishing the specific point at which an error happens. This granularity allows the system to provide feedback that cylinders on the root cause instead of providing answers that have been labelled as right and wrong.

Another significant characteristic of automatic instructional support is scaffolding. ITS is able to provide graduated help, where hints or remnants of the solution are given, followed by partial and then full demonstration of a solution given as necessary. This is much of what expert strategies in tutoring are like and makes sure that learners are well challenged. The system is provided to reduce scaffolding as the learners advance to achieve mastery and independence. The active kind of support enhances the conceptual learning and eliminates the formation of long-standing misunderstanding.

In ITS, error diagnosis does not just stop at getting the wrong answers but detecting patterns that can help one establish that there are conceptual problems. To give an example, when a student continually commits mistakes of negative signs in algebra, it is observed that there is a conceptual error, and the system will identify it that each error will not be individual. ITS has the capability of providing remedial modules, specific exercises, or other explanations depending on the needs of the learner by anticipating the probable causes of errors. Such a forecasting and remedial attribute helps boost learning performance and memory the most (Koper, 2001).

3.4 Customization by Modelling Learner and Tracking Knowledge

The ITS has learning capabilities that focus on learner modeling. The system keeps dynamic record of the knowledge states in learners, language cognitive capabilities, and behavioral predispositions due to its ability in gathering continuous data concerning the learner and their status about what they know, what they do not know, and how they would do in the next task. Bayesian Knowledge Tracing and Deep Knowledge Tracing are knowledge tracing algorithms that can approximate the likelihood that a learner has mastered every concept. These are the probabilities that can be used to choose the learning activities and set pace of instruction.

ITS through learner modeling detect when the repetition is no longer effective to learners and they are ready to move on. The system on the other hand identifies when learners risk forgetting previously learnt content and issues review exercises based on the spaced repetition principles. Such a method will make learning efficient, personal and cognitively adjusted to the personal development.

Additionally, sophisticated ITS are integrated with affective and behavioral modeling with indicators like hesitation, rapid and opportunity guessing, or an emotion found on a face or a text being examined by using facial recognition or text sentiment analysis. It enables the system to modify instructional strategies not only based on the cognitive performance but at the same time on the emotional states like frustration, or boredom. The use of multimodal personalization can enhance the interests of learners, lower the number of dropouts, and provide a learning environment that is more conducive and understanding (Means et al., 2010).

4. LEARNING ANALYTICS AND DATA-DRIVEN PERSONALIZATION

4.1 Foundations of Learning Analytics in AI-Driven Education

Learning analytics is the foundation of adaptive learning experiences as it helps the educational data and converts it into useful information. At the most basic level, learning analytics refers to the process of gathering, processing, and exploring data that are the result of interactions among learners, which can include clicks, task duration, and attempting quizzes, navigation, and even emotional cues that multimodal sensors can record. This is a rich data that allows educators and systems to see the behavior of learners in a way that could have not been reached by usual classroom observation. AI emphatically enhances the strength of learning analytics by exposing invisible patterns of how learners think, learn and struggle.

Learning analytics is based on a number of computational methods. Machine learning models find out the connection between learner behaviors and performance outcomes, including finding predictors of early disengagement. Clustering algorithms divide learners into groups according to their similar learning traits, so as it is possible to customize them at group level. Predictive analytics focuses on the anticipated future performance trends and skill development trends. Also, the network analysis is useful to plot and trace peer interactions within collaborative learning environments, exposing social aspects that can determine the effectiveness of learning. These methods allow seeing the picture of the learner experience in an AI-driven setting holistically.

The insights of learning analytics are not confined to student support, and are also used in curriculum design and institutional decisions. Teachers will be able to define the topics that contribute to misunderstanding over and over again and modify the teaching methods. Institutions are able to monitor program level measures of success, manage resources efficiently, and measure effectiveness of teaching interventions. The introduction of learning analytics into the education process would mean that the AI-based settings would generate a self-perpetuating cycle of refinement that leads to the improvement of the quality of teaching and the results that learners achieve (Moore, 1989).

4.2 Behavioral, Cognitive and Affective Insights

Learning analytics is integrated onto AI to capture aspects of learner behavior more than scholarly performance alone. Such patterns as task completion, time on task, and engagement frequency are examined using behavioral analytics. These measures demonstrate that learners do not just read some superficial material, but they engage in the learning process. As an example, longer response times can indicate confusion by seeing very fast completion times that could be, conversely, disengaged or guessing. These insights assist systems and instructors to intervene at the opportune time in order to maintain engagement and eliminate dropout.

Cognitive analytics is a glimpse into the manner in which the learners internalize information. On the basis of such models as Bayesian Knowledge Tracing and Deep Knowledge Tracing, AI systems learn the degree of mastery, recognize misunderstandings and estimate the learning curves. This enables the platform to customize learning in line with the cognitive preparedness. There are other aspects that can be determined using cognitive analytics: specific variation in learning strategies (i.e., whether a student likes repetitive drilling or abstract explanations) which can be used to ensure that the learning system is adjusted to cognitive peculiarities of a given individual and not standardized learning instruction (Nambiar, 2018).

Affective analytics will be another dimension that will identify the emotions of frustration, boredom, confusion, and motivation. AI systems identify emotional reactions, which affect the effectiveness of learning through textual sensual analysis, voice tone, and facial expressions. As an example, continuous frustration can be an indicator that the scaffold should be as well as more basic guidance, as boredom can be an indicator that the content is not challenging enough. Through the incorporation of affective understanding within the adaptive processes, systems do have the capacity to develop emotionally supportive learning conditions that can keep the learners highly motivated, confident, and cognitively at the learning priming level.

4.3 Predictive Modeling of Customized Applications

Predictive modelling allows AI systems to anticipate future learning results, according to the existing behavioural and performance trends. These models make approximate predictions based on past data and live explanations on whether a learner will get through a course, absorb a concept, or fail to do so in the coming content. As an illustration, indications of weakness on basic subjects can be forecasted to cause problems in further subjects, and the system can prescribe specific remedial courses. This ability to predict enables learning not to be reactive but proactive and thus the interventions are made earlier to prevent the performance deterioration to a greater extent.

Individualized paths are made by comparing the supposed results and tracing the optimal learning paths. In case a student feels that he will have trouble with a concept, a preparatory module or interactive simulation might be offered concerning the learning style of the student. On the other hand the high pace learners can be provided with accelerated track, enrichment or more difficult projects. This dynamic methodology is such that each learner gets the appropriate teaching at appropriate time and the most is learnt (Picciano, 2017).

The predictive analytics also aids the instructors by identifying the learners who are at risk. The trends that are viewed in dashboards include dwindling engagement, stagnant mastery, or a forecasted performance decrease. The teachers can then focus on the interventions to avoid academic failure by focusing on personalized tutoring, mentoring, or motivational guidance. Predictive modeling enhances the whole learning environment by readying machine intelligence with human knowledge (Reeves & Lin, 2011).

4.4 Institutional and Pedagogical Decision Support

Learning analytics is essential in the critical decision support and not only at the learner level but also at institutional level and in the pedagogy. Trends in course aggregated performance and feedback data help education leaders evaluate the success of the course. An example of this is where when large percentages of students are faced with difficulties in any segment of the curriculum the institutions can change the course materials, retrain the teachers or redesign the test. These revelations develop powerful quality assurance systems that see to it that instructional design is improved continuously.

To instructors, learning analytics dashboards are effective teaching aids. They provide graphic views of the performance distributions by the classes, mastery rates on the concept levels, and patterns of engagement by learners. These perspectives enable instructors to modify the instructional practices, invest more resources into instructional support, and individualize the teaching in accordance with the learning profiles. The evidence based pedagogy boosts pedagogical clarity, minimizes the pedagogical gap, and promotes a more fair learning context (Mikropoulos & Natsis, 2011).

On a larger level, learning analytics can help the institution to discover systemic patterns in retention, completion, and student satisfaction. Such insights are used in making strategic choices, like updating the curriculum, investing in technology, and policies to make sure that the learning systems are forward looking. By incorporating it, learning analytics is in a position to enable institutions to make decisions based on intuition, but grounded on rigorous and evidence-based education planning.

5. EMOTION-AWARE AND CONTEXT-AWARE ADAPTIVE LEARNING

5.1 The Role of Emotion in Learning

Affective emotions have a strong influence on cognitive skills, including attention, memory and problem resolution, and become the fundamental aspects of adaptive learning. The conventional digital learning systems in most cases overlook the emotional aspects and view the learners as rational beings that process information in the same manner. Conversely, AI-driven environments appreciate emotional states, frustration, anxiety, or enthusiasm as being influencing the interaction of learners with the content. Learning technologies that are emotion aware are trying to analyze such states to make sure that the interventions match not only cognitive requirements but also emotional preparation.

Multimodal input sensors to AI systems, including facial expression, voice tone, writing styles, physiologic cues and interaction behaviour, are used to detect emotions. These indicators expose changes in engagement, confidence and motivation. As an example, when a learner takes long before replying, the system might conclude that he/she is unsure or nervous. Here the sensitivity of AI detection enables the empathetic response of the AI in terms of encouragement or cut of workload to mitigate stress. Adaptive learning is more humanized and friendly by incorporation of emotional intelligence (Slater & Wilbur, 1997).

Systems that are sensitive to emotions are especially useful with students who have at least anxiety, low self-efficacy, or poor academic confidence. These systems ensure that a good learning environment is maintained by means of understanding emotional distress early and provide the appropriate support. They set the stage of emotionally intelligent AI tutors that positively affect the student well-being and academic achievements. This renders emotion-awareness a significant component of next generation adaptive learning ecology.

5.2 Multimodal Emotion Detection Technology

The idea of multimodal emotion detection will be used to integrate various data streams in order to obtain a comprehensive picture of the emotional condition of the learner. Facial recognition systems use micro-expressions (e.g., movement of eyebrows or tension of mouth) to determine the emotion, e.g. being confused or frustrated. Voice analysis measures pitch, tone and speech rhythm in order to diagnose stress or exhaustion. Text sentiment analysis works out the emotional tone of the written answers and discloses certain signs of confidence, discouragement, or curiosity. Physiological sensors search the variables such as heart rate or skin specific conduction and use it to determine the intensity of emotion.

Combining streams of emotions, AI systems become more accurate and reliable as opposed to using a single input stream. This performs a multimodal fusion, which allows the system to be aware of the discrepancies such as when the facial expression of a student indicates he is confused but their explanations in writing look confident. In this instance, the system may give clarifying questions to find out what the real state of emotion or thought is. This cross-verifying capability increases the strength of detection of emotions.

Emotion detection that relies on multiple methods enables learning platforms to have a dynamic approach to learning. In the instance where the system detects an increasing frustration, it could present easier tasks, give hints or switch the style of presentation of an alternative explanation. When boredom sets in, it can add the gamification factor or raise the complexity of the work. In general, AI-powered systems can provide a more dynamic, interactive, and human-centered learning experience because of the response to emotions on a real-time basis (Merchant et al., 2014).

5.3 Context-Sensitive Personalization and Environment Intelligence

Context-based adaptive learning goes beyond looking at the inner aspects of the learner and includes the area and environment parameters. Such systems learn the context of the user like location, time of day, type of device, internet availability, and noise levels among others to use this information to maximize the learning process. An example would be where should the system realise that the learner is working in a noisy environment using a mobile phone, it could change the content formatting by substituting the videos with the text information to alleviate cognitive pressure. Such sensitivity will make learning effective, whatever is the external situation.

Context-sensitive intelligence also focuses upon daily habits and routines. The software can recognize when productivity is at its highest and recalculate study schedules based on the usage data. Students who tend to study better in the evenings can be given tasks which are more complex than the rest within the evenings but the students with problems with concentrating in the mornings can be given lighter work before the day. This individualized timeframe maintains long-term learning and perspectives of enhanced engagement (Wen et al., 2023).

Moreover, the systems that are context-aware can support disabled or special-need learners through adjusting the complexity of the interface, content modality, and pacing. In the case of the visually impaired learners, the system can put more emphasis on audio explanations. In the case of learners who are motor impaired, it can make navigation controls easier. Adaptive systems can provide greater levels of inclusiveness by mediating environmental and personal context to facilitate an equal opportunity and develop more inclusive learning environments.

5.4 Increasing the Engagement With the Help of Emotion and Context Synergy

Emotion-conscious and context-conscious personalisation together will produce a highly empathetic learning atmosphere that is similar to the carefulness of human educators. Whenever emotional and contextual analytics are combined, the system can tune interventions in a more specific way. An example is when a learner exhibits indicators of exhaustion and a system notices that he or she is studying late at night, it may prescribe such a break or suggest that the learner reviews the materials later.

This synergy helps avoid overloading the brain with cognition and retention in the long term due to the conformity of learning to physiological and psychological cycles.

Motivation is also promoted by emotion, as well as context synergy. The cognitive processing is enhanced when the learners are subjected to the positive emotional states in the environment favorable to the learning processes. The AI systems support these conditions by providing individual encouragement, modifying the form of the content, or adding new interesting and interactive features at the right moment. This assists to sustain flow- a psychological state of feeling in which learners experience a state of being in a complete state of immersion and attention resulting in more meaningful learning informations (Dunleavy & Dede, 2014).

The combination strategy also helps in persisting and long-term academic success of students. Understanding the environmental issues, emotional agony, or any loss of interest, when AI systems regularly detect them, the systems elicit prompt responses and keep the learner focused. This responsiveness as a whole makes digital learning a favorable ecosystem in which students are able to feel respected, heard, and empowered. Cognitive needs are met through the contextual needs by connecting the former to the latter and the latter to cognitive needs, making AI personalized, humane, and emotionally intelligent.

6. CHALLENGES IN AI-DRIVEN LEARNING ENVIRONMENTS

6.1 Data Privacy, Security, and Consent Management

The artificial intelligence-based learning environments use continuous data monitoring, both the academic achievements, the behavioral trends, the engagement rate, the click-stream data, and even the emotional signals registered using the advanced sensory systems. Although such information is needed to create individual learning trajectories, it also creates a major issue of privacy and informed consent. Not every student can comprehend the extent of data gathering and the means by which data is analyzed and stored as well as shared with the services of third parties, particularly in relation to minors. Adopters of AI-based learning platforms must consequently assure transparency of the data collection process, communicate and renew consent, and impose meaningful control over personal information to the students (Ibáñez & Delgado-Kloos, 2018).

Security is another very essential parameter of this challenge. When AI systems are collecting groups of data based on diverse educational sources, there is a higher risk of at least one data breach. Attacks on educational facilities are on the increase, as the personal information of students is also frequently the most insecure due to the averted institutional cybersecurity. Data integrity compromises may affect the students in the long term (identity theft or profiling). Therefore, there should be strict cybersecurity policies such as encryption, differential privacy, secure authentication, and constant monitoring. Also, it is very important to comply with regulatory schemes like GDPR, FERPA, and laws on data protection in the regions to ensure the preservation of credibility and trust. After all, the advantages of AI-based personalized learning may be lost to the dangers that compromise the well-being of the students, unless there is a solid privacy and security baseline.

6.2 Algorithmic Bias, Fairness, and Equity

The intelligence of AI algorithms in adaptive learning systems can only be as just as the information that it is trained on. Numerous educational datasets are inherently biased in socioeconomic, linguistic, gender-based and cultural ways, which can unintentionally be used to affect the results of algorithmic modelings. To illustrate, when an adaptive learning system is mostly trained on data of students in urban and well-resourced schools, it might yield incorrect outputs or other inappropriate learning trajectories when applied to students in rural or disadvantaged populations and communities. That bias may also generate self-reinforcing trends, in which disadvantaged learners are already disadvantaged and may end up with less enrichment time and challenging content to quell inequities instead of alleviating the inequities (Ivanashko et al., 2024).

Educational AI will need fairness measures of auditing the training data to detect skewed trends, implementing bias-reduction methods, and making the outputs of the models frequently reviewed by people. Furthermore, the institutions should put in mind inclusive algorithm design to present various learning styles, language heritage, and cognitive diversity. In the absence of conscious regulation, AI-based environments will be able to recreate systematic inequalities found in traditional learning environments. Implementation therefore requires a continuous process to control that the credo of personalization may not be executed by striving to the detriment of equity or even equality.

6.3 Excessive Dependence on Automation and the Declining Role of the Human Educators

Learning environments based on AI offer never-before-seen automation, be it grading and delivery of instruction, tracking of student engagement, or prediction of performance. The uncontrollable use of AI, however, can pose several dangers to the people aspect of teaching. Teachers provide emotional assistance, guidance, and delicate insight into situational circumstances of a student- all these features that AI technology cannot fully duplicate. Provided that institutions start perceiving AI as a substitute, instead of a complement to the work of the educator, they will be in danger of undermining the fabric of relationships that the acquisition of knowledge engages with.

More so, students can get too dependent on adaptive systems that lead them through all stages of learning process. Personalization can only enhance the results, but excessive dependence on automatic feedback has the potential to suppress the development of self-regulatory skills critical to achievement (setting goals, reflection, persistence and also independent problem-solving). Enhancing AI on repetitive, data-driven tasks but teaching it on high-impact areas, such as socio-emotional support, facilitating creative learning, and contextualizing AI-generated insights is hence needed. This balance can be used to make sure that technology complements humans, as opposed to crowdsourcing out human agency in learning.

6.4 Transparency, Explainability and Student Trust

Artificial intelligence-based adaptive learning systems can be viewed as complicated black boxes; it is challenging when an educator and a learner predict how such outputs as difficulty adjustments, content suggestions, or performance projections are created. Such unclear nature may undermine trust and cause resistance among students in cases where AI-generated judgment is perceived to be unjust or fallacy. Such a level of explainability will be more vital in high stakes academic work where making an algorithmic decision might affect academic advancement or even post-academic education.

As a way to earn trust, educational AI systems should include explainable AI (XAI) techniques which explicitly explain why and why a recommendation was made. The students and teachers must be in a position to question the system: Why was this content recommended? Why was my level of difficulty changed? What were some of the factors used to predict this performance? Intuitive descriptions not only enhance acceptability but also facilitate self-consciousness in students as well as metacognition development. Furthermore, open dialogue on the possibilities of AI, drawbacks, and inadmissible human control will mean that learners will regard the technology as a beneficial tool, but not as a mysterious force (Bond et al., 2024).

6.5 Learning Analytics and Responsible Innovation

The high rate of adoption of AI across learning systems poses more ethical concerns on surveillance, agency, and the intent of learning analytics. As an example, other systems monitor such micro-behaviors as patterns of the keyboards, eye movement, or time per screen. Although these pieces of data may make the differentiation of an individual personalized, they may also produce the impression of surveillance which hurts intrinsic motivation. Institutions should establish strict limits such as the use of data and ensure that the learning analytics does not violate student autonomy and psychological health (Azzam & Charles, 2024).

Educational AI responsible innovation demands a governance framework which is both inclusive of educators, technological practitioners, policymakers, and learners. Ethical standards need to discuss the right level of monitoring, retention periods of data, partnerships with vendors that are responsible, and accountability measures in case of an AI system failure or due to adverse effects of the products. In the long run, the aim would be to develop learning practices in which AI would be utilized in a responsible way to empower students instead of limit them so that the technological advancement will not be accomplishing at the expense of greater educational values like autonomy, dignity, and lifelong learning.

7. FUTURE DIRECTIONS AND EMERGING INNOVATIONS IN AI-DRIVEN LEARNING ENVIRONMENTS

7.1 Next-Generation Adaptive Learning Models and Hyper-Personalization

The adaptive learning will evolve into an ever-evolving, more sophisticated, and highly context-aware, with the novel adaptive learning environments shifting past the traditional rule-based personalization, as the AI technologies will progress. The concept of hyper-personalization will combine various data, such as academic achievements and real-time emotional indicators, cognitive loads, and behavioral standards, to form a dynamically updated learner profile. It will not only suggest the right learning contents, but also identify the cases of frustration, fatigue, or disengagement of the learner and automatically direct the learning path. As the use of affective computing increases, AI will support individually learning cognitive and emotional needs by offering feedback in their own desired style, pacing, and level of support (Okoye et al., 2024).

Real-time adaptation is also further expanded by the existence of the large language models [LLM] and the foundation models. These models have the ability to produce customized explanations, orchestrate complex ideas, build individual practice tasks, and provide the human tutoring simulation of dialogue. Future versions can introduce the ability to make reasoning about the beliefs of students with certain misconceptions, modulate explanations, and predict possible problems in the learning process in future. Hyper-personalized systems will broadly start to act as intelligent learning companions and not be simply a recommendation engine but have a wider role in the personalized learning process and will alter the concept of individualized instruction as well as the type of interaction between a student and an AI in the digital learning environment.

7.2 Intensive Learning Experiences With Extended Reality (XR), Metaverse Classrooms, and Intelligent Simulations

Immersive technologies are going to form a fundamental part of the future of AI-driven learning, and they include virtual reality (VR), augmented reality (AR) and mixed reality (MR). These AR devices will incorporate AI in them to cause adaptive learning simulations to device actual student performance in real time. As an example, the AR-based science laboratories can change the difficulty of the experiment based on the students level of achievement and VR provided the opportunity to simulate the high-risk situation like to manage an emergency, to conduct a surgery, or to run an engineering task in a safe, controlled digital environment. It is with this, together with AI, that environments become immersive and intelligent, providing context-sensitive information and automated feedback, as well as real-time behavioral control.

Another giant in the immersive learning is the advent of the educational metaverse. The avatars, intelligent tutoring agents, and collaborative working environment, as well as interactive simulations can be conducted in AI-enabled metaverse classrooms. In such settings, adaptive learning will be able to study the interactions of individuals and groups to make collaborative learning optimal, allocate equal roles and roles, and create equal participation. The natural language understanding enables the virtual agents to take part in group discussion, conflict management, or persuading the quieter students to speak out. With the XR hardware becoming increasingly more affordable, smart immersive studies will have a role to play in revolutionizing experiential learning.

7.3 Multimodal Learning Analytics and Cognition-Aware AI Systems

Multimodal learning analytics will be the next stage in the AI in the field of education, combining the inputs of texts, recipes, facial expressions, gesture patterns, physiological signals, and device interactions. Such analytics will facilitate cognitive-conscious AI systems that deduce mental conditions of confusion, intrinsic motivation, cognitive overload, and being able to master concepts. This understanding can be used to act pro-actively in the learning systems, e.g. making material simpler when there is a peak in cognitive load or more difficult when there is an indication of mastery.

Multimodal analytics will also enable flawless cross- Environmental and device-to-environment learning in the future. Regardless of whether a student is interacting via a smartphone, VR headset, smart classroom panel, or wearable device, AI systems will form a coherent union of the data to keep the learner profiles in line with one another. It is an ongoing tracking that leads the way to the personal learning trajectories that can be developed beyond the classroom setting and modified according to the schedule of the learning individual, and assist the learner in self-regulated learning behaviors. Further, the development of edge computing will allow more computing to be done locally on the devices thereby enhancing data protection and eliminating the need to use the cloud server to store sensitive data.

7.4 Federated Artificial Intelligence, Privacy-Sensitive Personalization, and Ethical Intelligence

Privacy-preserving models like federated learning, differential privacy, and encrypted computation will grow to be more accepted in future AI-based learning settings as the ethical concerns begin to gain prominence. Federated AI allows the models to be trained using distributed data, e.g. student devices or institution servers, without transferring sensitive information to a single point. The solution reduces the risk of privacy and at the same time encourages the construction of powerful predictive models. Differential privacy also ensures the identity of students by adding mathematical noise to datasets, without affecting the analytical worth.

Next-generation learning technologies will make ethical intelligence one of their focal requirements. The AI systems will require auditing fairness, transparency, and detection of bias techniques to be built in. Institutions can also use special-purpose gadgets, known as AI ethics dashboards, which display the performance of algorithms, identify suspicious cases, and record automated actions to be examined by humans. The innovations will be accountable and promote responsible learning analytics use. The future of AI-driven learning will not only be more technologically advanced but also moral, and it will position innovation and the human qualities of autonomy, dignity, and fair access (Demartini et al., 2024).

7.5 Collaborative AI, Human-AI Co Teaching, and Augmented Educator Roles

As new technologies become more common in the teaching field, teachers are sure to collaborate with AI systems under co-teaching models. The principle of AI will be used to deal with personalized tutoring, data-based insights, and adaptable content delivery whereby educators work on critical thinking development, emotional support, and mentorship. Joint AI systems will enable instructors to co-create the learning paths, discover high-risk learners at the very beginning to support them, and coordinate classroom operations in a smoother manner. Quite on the contrary, AI will transform the role of teachers enabling them to make practical decisions, lessen the work of the administration and increase the scope of their pedagogical activity (Bower & Vlachopoulos, 2018).

Also, real-time classroom analytics, i.e. student engagement trends, group dynamics, or concept mastery metrics, will be provided by the advanced teacher-support systems to effect on-the-fly changes in the teaching approaches. The use of AI in professional development will also involve providing recommendation of specific training depending on classroom observations and teacher performance data. This transformation of human-AI partnership will transform the teaching profession into a more tactical, expressive and intellectually intellectual.

CONCLUSION

Among other things, AI based learning, and adaptive learning technology are transforming the world of education by bringing with them a degree of personalization, intensity, and interactivity never witnessed before. These technologies are applicable by means of advanced analytics, cognitive computing and dynamic content delivery systems; they allow the learning journeys that are highly adaptive to the needs, talents, and ambitions of an individual. They enable institutions to leave standardized teaching to differentiated and learner-oriented teaching that changes constantly as students move forward. Consequently, learning turns out to be meaningful, efficacious, and more accessible to fill gaps in the achievement and guarantee diverse learners the support they need to succeed.

Simultaneously, AI progress in the education field requires considerations such as ethics, governance, and critical human aspects of learning. Even though intelligent systems may supply real-time information, suggest individualized resources, and mediate simulated experiences, the emotional, social, and motivational learning components have yet to be replaced with human interaction. Teachers play a significant role in the process of helping students reason, develop creativity and fostering resiliency, and these tasks cannot be performed by AI. Therefore, AI holds the key to the future in the field of education through balanced cooperation when technology will complement human abilities, and it will not substitute them. This collaboration enables educators to work on mostly productive pedagogical tasks when artificial intelligence does simple computing and data analysis.

In the future, adaptive learning ecosystems will be even more improved through the application of emerging technologies, including extended reality, multimodal analytics, federated AI, and hyper-personalization. The innovations offer dense, contextual, affectively intelligent and globally aware learning environments. Nevertheless, to make it possible, the institutions should not only invest in technological infrastructure but ethical frameworks, training of educators, and inclusive design principles. Reconciling between innovation and responsibility, AI-powered learning platforms have the potential to produce a paradigm shift in the way individuals acquire knowledge, in addition to enhancing academic equity and preparing civilizations to a future where both human and artificial intelligence combine and collaborate to enhance knowledge and access.

REFERENCES

Anderson, T., & Dron, J. (2011). Three generations of distance education pedagogy. *International Review of Research in Open and Distance Learning*, *12*(3), 80–97. DOI: 10.19173/irrodl.v12i3.890

Azzam, A., & Charles, T. (2024). A review of artificial intelligence in K-12 education. *Open Journal of Applied Sciences*, *14*(8), 2088–2100. DOI: 10.4236/ojapps.2024.148137

Baker, R. S., & Inventado, P. S. (2014). Educational data mining and learning analytics. In *Handbook of Educational Psychology* (pp. 600–620). Routledge.

Bond, M., Zawacki-Richter, O., & Perez-Sanagustin, M. (2024). A meta systematic review of AI in higher education. *International Journal of Educational Technology in Higher Education*, *21*(1), 20. DOI: 10.1186/s41239-023-00436-z

Bower, M. (2019). Can virtual reality experiences support learning? *Research in Learning Technology*, *27*(1), 21545.

Bower, M., & Vlachopoulos, P. (2018). A critical analysis of technology-enhanced learning design frameworks. *British Journal of Educational Technology*, *49*(6), 981–997. DOI: 10.1111/bjet.12668

Demartini, C. G., Sciascia, L., Bosso, A., & Manuri, F. (2024). Artificial intelligence bringing improvements to adaptive learning in education: A case study. *Sustainability (Basel)*, *16*(3), 1347. DOI: 10.3390/su16031347

Dillenbourg, P., Baker, M., Blaye, A., & O'Malley, C. (1996). The evolution of research on collaborative learning. In *Learning in Humans and Machines* (pp. 189–211). Pergamon.

Dunleavy, M., & Dede, C. (2014). Augmented reality teaching and learning. Handbook of Research on Educational Communications and Technology. DOI: 10.1007/978-1-4614-3185-5_59

. Education and Employers. (2018). *How AI is transforming higher education.*

Eom, Y., Wen, H., & Ashill, N. (2006). Determinants of students' perceived learning outcomes in online education. *Decision Sciences Journal of Innovative Education*, *4*(2), 215–235. DOI: 10.1111/j.1540-4609.2006.00114.x

Gikas, J., & Grant, M. M. (2013). Mobile computing devices in higher education. *The Internet and Higher Education*, *19*, 18–26. DOI: 10.1016/j.iheduc.2013.06.002

Hodges, C., Moore, S., Lockee, B., Trust, T., & Bond, A. (2020). The difference between emergency remote teaching and online learning. *EDUCAUSE Review*.

Ibáñez, M. B., & Delgado-Kloos, C. (2018). AR for STEM learning: A systematic review. *Computers & Education*, *123*, 109–123. DOI: 10.1016/j.compedu.2018.05.002

Ivanashko, O., Kozak, A., Knysh, T., & Honchar, K. (2024). The role of artificial intelligence in shaping the future of education: Opportunities and challenges. *Futurity Education*, *4*(1), 126–146.

Järvelä, S., Kirschner, P. A., Panadero, E., Malmberg, J., Phielix, C., Jaspers, J., Koivuniemi, M., & Järvenoja, H. (2015). Enhancing socially shared regulation in collaborative learning groups: Designing for CSCL regulation tools. *Educational Technology Research and Development*, *63*(1), 125–142. DOI: 10.1007/s11423-014-9358-1

. Johnson, L., Adams Becker, S., Estrada, V., & Freeman, A. (2015). *NMC Horizon Report: 2015 Higher Education Edition.*

Kizilcec, R. F., Pérez-Sanagustín, M., & Maldonado, J. J. (2016). Self-regulated learning strategies predict learner behavior in MOOCs. *Computers & Education*, *104*, 18–33. DOI: 10.1016/j.compedu.2016.10.001

Koedinger, K. R., & Corbett, A. T. (2006). *Cognitive tutors: Technology bringing learning science to the classroom*. Cambridge Handbook of the Learning Sciences.

Koper, R. (2001). *Modeling units of study from a pedagogical perspective*. Open University of the Netherlands.

Means, B., Toyama, Y., Murphy, R., Bakia, M., & Jones, K. (2010). *Evaluation of evidence-based practices in online learning*. US Department of Education.

Merchant, Z.. (2014). Effectiveness of VR-based instruction. *Computers & Education*, *70*, 29–40. DOI: 10.1016/j.compedu.2013.07.033

Mikropoulos, T. A., & Natsis, A. (2011). Educational virtual environments: A ten-year review. *Computers & Education*, *56*(3), 769–780. DOI: 10.1016/j.compedu.2010.10.020

Moore, M. G. (1989). Three types of interaction. *American Journal of Distance Education*, *3*(2), 1–7. DOI: 10.1080/08923648909526659

Nambiar, R. M. K. K. (2018). Artificial intelligence: A new path to democratizing higher education? *Studies in Higher Education*, *43*(11), 2044–2056.

Okoye, K., Daruich, S. D. N., Castaño, R., Escamilla, J., & Hosseini, S. (2024). Analyzing the impact of digitized-education toward the future of education: A comparative study based on students' evaluation of teaching data. *Studies in Educational Evaluation*, *82*, 101359. DOI: 10.1016/j.stueduc.2024.101359

Picciano, A. G. (2017). Theories and frameworks for online education. *Online Learning : the Official Journal of the Online Learning Consortium*, *21*(3), 166–190. DOI: 10.24059/olj.v21i3.1225

Reeves, T. C., & Lin, L. (2011). The research we have is not the research we need. *Educational Technology*, *51*(4), 1–21.

Slater, M., & Wilbur, S. (1997). A framework for immersive virtual environments. *Presence (Cambridge, Mass.)*, *6*(6), 603–616. DOI: 10.1162/pres.1997.6.6.603

Wen, Y., Wu, L., He, S., Ng, N. H. E., Teo, B. C., Looi, C. K., & Cai, Y. (2023). Integrating augmented reality into inquiry-based learning approach in primary science classrooms. *Educational Technology Research and Development*, *71*(4), 1631–1651. DOI: 10.1007/s11423-023-10235-y PMID: 37359487

Chapter 10
From Personalization to Responsibility: AI-Driven Adaptive Learning Environments

Shikha Khullar
http://orcid.org/0009-0000-5598-3145
Poornima University, Jaipur, India

Abdus Sobhan
http://orcid.org/0009-0009-5139-1172
Varendra University, Rajshahi, Bangladesh

Nitu Tank
http://orcid.org/0009-0001-9782-4764
Poornima University, Jaipur, India

Priya Swami
http://orcid.org/0009-0004-6366-8152
Poornima University, Jaipur, India

ABSTRACT

The concept of artificial intelligence (AI) is transforming the educational process due to the opportunities offered by artificial intelligence to create adaptive learning experiences that scale personalized instruction. The chapter explores the theoretical underpinning, architecture, and adaption of AI-based learning systems, such as learner modeling, content adaptation, and continuous assessment. Although these technologies offer better learning results and instructional performance, their data-driven and algorithmic character serve as a major source of ethical concerns. The chapter critically examines the problems of bias, fairness, privacy and surveil-

DOI: 10.4018/979-8-2600-1840-8.ch010

lance throughout the lifecycle of adaptive learning systems. It also talks about the importance of explainable AI in promoting transparency, trust, and responsible human-AI cooperation in education. Using both empirical and practical examples, the chapter suggests a combined ethical risk-reduction framework that balances technical innovation and ethical governance.

1. INTRODUCTION

The Full adoption of the use of artificial intelligence (AI) in the education sector represents a revolutionary shift that may change the process of teaching and learning as a whole. This transition is already in motion as the search of educational experiences that are scalable, efficient, and tailored to the specific needs of the student is made. The article by Luckin, Holmes, Griffiths, and Forcier (2016) is not the only one that outlines the opportunity that AIEd has to it the instruction problem that the standard ones have been placing the students in since it will be making the support provided adaptive and responsive. Conversely, the algorithms and high level of data of these systems also brings about a lot of ethical concerns which are quite grave and should be put to serious and careful examination. The critical analysis of bias, privacy, and ethics as the primary concerns of the responsible development and implementation of AI-based learning environments and adaptive learning technologies is among the key contributions of this chapter.

AI's entry into the education sector could be correctly attributed to the impossibility of solving pedagogical issues that were present for a long time. Conventional classroom models usually find it hard to deal with the variations present in students' prior knowledge, cognitive powers, and rates of learning. AI does this by replacing human diagnostic and personalization. In fact, one of the forms of AI, cognitive tutoring systems, is an example of this, showing that it is possible to apply the principles of the learning sciences and thus giving the students personalized and mastery-based instruction (Koedinger & Corbett, 2006). The very target of this whole operation is to utilize the computational force in a manner that empowering the teachers, that is, providing different levels of support in a manner that will promote both improving results and making it easier for students everywhere to get through to quality instruction (Baker, 2016).

The transition from traditional e-learning to AI-based learning environments has been a huge technological and pedagogical breakthrough. The first e-learning platforms and Learning Management Systems were mainly digital storages of unchangeable content, providing very little interactivity or customization. The arrival of AIEd denotes the transition from content delivery systems to systems that smartly control the entire learning process. Today's AI-powered environments function through an uninterrupted loop of data gathering, model-based reasoning, and adaptive reaction, which encourages a very lively interaction between the student and the system (du Boulay, 2016).

It is necessary to provide a precise explanation of adaptive learning technologies. These are specialized, one-of-a-kind AIEd systems that personalize teaching dynamically. Interactive systems that use computational models of the student, the subject, and teaching methods are described as being able to automatically adjust educational content, order, duration, and response (Shute & Zapata-Rivera, 2012). Their application varies from simple adaptive navigation based on rules to complex intelligent tutoring systems that apply machine learning for cognitive modelling, with the primary aim of maximizing the learning path to suit the individual cognitive, emotional, and metacognitive requirements.

The ethical, bias, and privacy issues being the most important in this regard are primarily due to the powerful capabilities of these systems. The use of adaptive technologies entails the constant gathering and algorithmic analysis of fine-grained student data, which thus increases the likelihood of student privacy issues, surveillance, and data security concerns (Zeide, 2019). Besides, the algorithms that control adaptation have the potential to foster or even worsen existing societal biases. Baker and Hawn (2021) explain how the bias in algorithms in educational systems can result in giving disadvantageous treatment to students from underprivileged backgrounds if the training data or model goals mirror the inequities of the past. So, the goal of technological personalization has to always be together with the promise of fairness, transparency, and ethical governance, and vice versa.

This necessity led to the objectives and contributions of this chapter. The chapter's main goal is to build the conceptual and technical foundations of AI-supported learning environments, scrutinize the different models and methods which support adaptation, examine the causes and strategies for bias mitigation, and give a detailed account of the privacy risks as well as the regulatory frameworks. Moreover, it will look into the role of explainability in trust building and will have a discussion of the empirical evidence from the actual implementations. It will also develop a synthesized, critical framework as a primary contribution that links technical innovation with ethical responsibility. The proposal is that this framework will be useful for researchers, developers, educators, and policymakers to work through this intricate AI in the education landscape, ensuring that the movement towards personalized learning is done in a thoughtful way that takes into account the rights of individuals and also the movement towards fairer educational practice.

2. CONCEPTUAL FOUNDATIONS OF AI-DRIVEN LEARNING ENVIRONMENTS

It is necessary to become acquainted with three major conceptual grounds to construct and to roll out the AI-based education environments that are both effective and moral: the past and present technical evolution of Artificial Intelligence in Education (AIEd) history; the acknowledged learning theories that underpin and direct adaptive features; and the technical frameworks that implement these principles into operational systems. The main interrelated foundations are recognized in this section and at the same time, are prepared for the forthcoming analysis of adaptive models, methods and their moral implications.

2.1 Artificial Intelligence in Education (AIEd)

Artificial Intelligence in Education is a subject that crosses many boundaries and is primarily focused on using AI techniques to solve major education problems while also making scientific learning more knowledgeable. Its past evolution is a mere reflection of AI's journey, transitioning from difficult, symbolic systems to relaxed, data-driven methods. You could trace back the roots of AIEd to the 1950s and 60s when the first computer-assisted instruction (CAI) systems offered only basic drill-and-practice exercises. The biggest leap forward came with the introduction of Intelligent Tutoring Systems (ITS) in the 1970s and 1980s such as SCHOLAR and SOPHIE that combined knowledge representation and model-based reasoning to pretend a more subtle tutorial conversation (Woolf, 2009). A major change in educational technology occurred with the principle of using computational models to direct instruction established in this period. The development of cognitive tutors, which relied on psychological theories like ACT-R, further sophisticated this method by simulating the human thinking process and giving support where and when needed (Koedinger & Corbett, 2006). The current time is characterized by the rapid growth of data-heavy adaptive learning systems and the use of learning analytics, all thanks to the progress in AI and the availability of huge educational datasets (Baker & Inventado, 2014).

Various advanced methods make up the technical arsenal of current AIEd systems. The main techniques that support Machine Learning (ML) and Deep Learning (DL) are used in many applications, such as forecasting of student performance, learning patterns clustering, and handling of complex multimodal data. Natural Language Processing (NLP) is the technology that gives the systems the power to understand the language, generate it and evaluate it, thus enabling interactions that are very similar to human ones, conducting automatic writing assessments, and performing collaborative discourse analysis (Graesser et al., 2018). Reinforcement Learning

(RL) is the method applied to enhance the quality of educational decisions, where, through repeated interaction, systems learn the best sequence of instructional actions to maximize the development of long-term learning benefits (Mandel et al., 2014). Knowledge Representation and Reasoning (KRR) methods form the backbone of the technology development and are still very useful in classifying domain knowledge, maintaining current models of the learner, and defining the teaching rules that result in system adaptability (Aleven et al., 2016).

2.2 Learning Theories Supporting Adaptive Systems

Learning environments powered by AI technology are not just software tools but rather pedagogical innovations whose layout is to be directed by strong learning theories. They adaptivity has its educational value in doing so as it fits with the way that humans gain, process, and build knowledge. Different foundational learning theories i.e. behaviorism, cognitivism and constructivism all contribute to the formulation of different design principles. Behaviorism's strength lies in its understanding of stimulus, response, and reinforcement and is mirrored in systems which give instant feedback and break down complex skills into reinforced sub-tasks (Skinner, 1958). Cognitivism's concern with monitoring mental processes leads to the development of cognitive tutors that are capable of simulating a learner's knowledge state as well as misconceptions to provide just-in-time instructional support (Anderson et al., 1995). Constructivism sees learning as an application of creating knowledge and thus the design is informed by AI acting as a scaffold or facilitator in explorative learning environments and collaborative tools rather than as a direct instructor (Suthers, 2006).

The theories eventually meet each other in their mutual support of the personalized and mastery-based learning paradigms. Adaptive technologies are the main means of personalization and are intended to adjust the teaching to the individual student's characteristics. This is quite similar to the mastery learning theory which claims that pupils have to reach a certain level of competence in one unit before moving on to the next one (Bloom, 1968). AI systems implement this by constantly measuring mastery using such methods as Bayesian Knowledge Tracing and regulating the order of content delivery accordingly. Moreover, today's AIEd viewpoints are aiming at promoting self-regulation learning (SRL) to an increasing degree alongside the regular teaching process, by letting students select their goals, giving them access to the monitoring of their progress through dashboards, and encouraging them to do the reflecting on their methods, thus empowering them with skills for lifelong learning beyond that particular context (Roll & Winne, 2015).

2.3 Architecture of AI-Driven Learning Environments

AIEd's conceptual and theoretical principles are implemented via an integrated architectural framework, often referred to as a three-layer model consisting of data, intelligence, and application. The data layer is the basic support of the architecture and contains all the information that the system has processed. It not only contains detailed data on learners' performances like metrics, logs of interactions, and time spent on the task but also the structured data of content like learning objects, their metadata, and prerequisite relationships, and the supply of any setting-related data such as the environment, time, and device, which also belong to the context. The ethical handling, security, and trustworthiness of this data layer are the major requirements for any responsible system. As shown in Figure 1, the three-layer architecture of AI-driven learning environments, highlighting the interaction between data collection, intelligent modeling, and application-level personalization under overarching ethical considerations.

Figure 1. An architectural overview of AI-driven learning environments

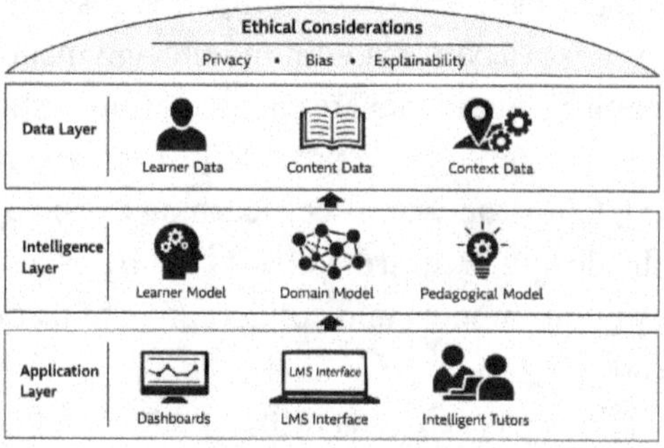

The intelligence layer serves as the main engine for processing, where raw data is turned into insights that can be acted upon. In this layer, the very important computational models are: the domain model that represents the subject matter, the learner model that indicates the inferred state of the student, and the pedagogical model that specifies the strategies for intervention. This layer is where the algorithms for knowledge tracing, recommendation, and classification take place, and where learning analytics are done to create insights. The design and functioning of this layer are the ones that mainly bring up issues of algorithmic bias and fairness. The application layer, on the other hand, is the one that is user-facing interface. This layer includes instructor and administrator dashboards that show analytics for decision support visually, the learner's main interaction environment which might be integrated within a Learning Management System (LMS) or be a separate platform, and specific implementations such as intelligent tutors that run structured tutorial dialogues. This is the point where the system's intelligence is finally revealed at the application layer, and the end-user can most tangibly experience transparency, explainability, and trust.

3. ADAPTIVE LEARNING TECHNOLOGIES: MODELS AND METHODS

The most significant transformation that can come from AI-based education systems is the result of the use of specific adaptive learning technologies. These technologies are the core of the process through which data, architecture, and theory are converted into custom educational experiences. This section presents the fundamental models and techniques that enable this flexibility focusing on three intertwined aspects: the development of the dynamic learner models, the algorithms that manage content adaptation and recommendation, and the systems for automatic assessment and feedback.

3.1 Learner Modelling

The adaptive system's main computational model of the student is the learner model, which is a representation of the student's changing cognitive, emotional, and behavioral aspects. It serves as a dynamic hypothesis that informs and directs all the personalization choices made by the system. The updating of cognitive knowledge is mainly done through Knowledge Tracing, which is traditionally executed using Bayesian Knowledge Tracing to infer the skill level from the history of responses (Corbett & Anderson, 1995). On the other hand, modern techniques apply deep learning frameworks such as Deep Knowledge Tracing to model intricate knowledge structures and time dependencies (Piech et al., 2015).

Learner profiling results in a multidimensional model that incorporates various aspects of the student's profile such as cognitive modeling (information processing), affective modeling (e.g., measuring engagement through interaction or expression analysis) (Baker et al., 2010), and behavioral modeling (e.g., help-seeking patterns). The main objective of this integration is to predict the best learning paths and support needs.One of the main issues is the cold-start problem, where new user modeling is hindered by a lack of initial data, and data sparsity, which imposes limits in drawing reliable conclusions based on the data collected. Some of the strategies used to overcome these challenges include making use of population priors, initial self-assessments, and transfer learning.

3.2 Content Adaptation and Recommendation

A learner model that is well-formed delivers the possibility of personalized instruction through content adaptation and recommendation algorithms. Adaptive sequencing designates the best pedagogical order for presenting the concepts, problems, or activities. Mastery-based sequencing, supported by knowledge tracing, makes sure the prerequisite skills are acquired before the transition to the next level. In addition, other algorithms control the cognitive load, and the scheduling of reviews is done to fight forgetting based on principles like spaced repetition (Pavlik & Anderson, 2008).

The algorithms for content recommendation choose particular learning objects (like texts, videos, exercises) for every single learner. They take their roots from the research conducted on recommender systems, using collaborative filtering (taking into account the likes of similar learners), content-based filtering (aligning item characteristics to previous success), or even more advanced hybrid and knowledge-based techniques. The latter one uses domain ontologies to guarantee the pedagogical coherence and conceptual soundness (Manouselis et al., 2011). One of the main considerations in the designing process is to find the right point between exploration (providing new content) and exploitation (making use of already effective material).

An essential necessity is to make sure that adaptation is multi-mode and inclusive. Different formats (text, audio, video, simulation) should be used to present the content in such a way that various learner requirements are met by the systems. In addition, inclusive design means that the algorithms will have to take the disadvantage scenario and fight against it. This will entail bias checking and on purpose shaping of proposals so that counteracting the bad effect would not only be directed towards the learner's disability, linguistic background, or learning path but would also provide equal access to the best resources. The main aim is to release and increase the educational process.

3.3 Assessment and Feedback Mechanisms

The effectiveness of a learning environment is, in the first place, directly related to its power of accurate assessment and meaningful feedback. In AI-powered systems, these functions change from being sporadic events to being constant, automatic, and adapting processes that are at the core of learning (Ifenthaler & Yau, 2020). As a result, the personalization loop is closed whereby learner states can be diagnosed in real time and teaching methods changed accordingly.

Adaptive technologies impose a stronger need for formative assessment to be more heavily focused upon than summative assessment. Integrated formative assessment is able to produce and provide continuous data on progress and misconceptions, thereby assisting the system in making changes (Shute & Rahimi, 2017). The summative evaluation of the final outcomes is still relevant, but in adaptive systems, the aggregated formative data can often provide strong summative insights without the need for separate high-stakes testing, which in turn offers a more comprehensive picture of the competency development process (Pelánek, 2017). Learner interaction analysis through algorithms makes "stealth assessment" possible, where the evaluation is made a part of the learning activities without any interruption (Shute & Ventura, 2013).

Automated grading and feedback generation are the corner stones of scalable personalization. Moreover, although such reliability is only applicable to highly structured areas, the prowess of Natural Language Processing has already opened up the way that semi-structured and even unstructured responses could be graded automatically (Shermis & Burstein, 2013). In general, automated feedback is categorized as falling into one of three: knowledge of response (correctness), knowledge of correct response (the answer), and elaborated feedback (explanations or hints). The most developed adaptive systems give priority to elaborated feedback in order to facilitate the learner's conceptual understanding. To illustrate, an intelligent tutor can identify a particular area of misunderstanding in physics, and then provide a complementary remedial example (VanLehn, 2011), using cognitive models and error libraries to tackle the root causes.

The feedback's pedagogical power hinges on its elucidation. Unclear feedback entails distrust and diminishes applicability. Thus, the principles of Explainable AI (XAI) are vital. By making the feedback explainable, the system's evaluation gets revealed to both the student and teacher in a way that is easy to understand. For the students, it not only tells them what is incorrect but also why and how to get better, hence promoting metacognitive skills (Roll & Winne, 2015). For the teachers, the explainable analytics dashboards not only show the total scores but also the system's reasoning regarding the learning patterns of the whole class, thus, allowing them to make pedagogical interventions that are based on facts (Holstein et al., 2019). Figure 2 illustrates the adaptive learning process model, highlighting the continuous feedback loop between learner interaction, modeling, content adaptation, and assessment.

Figure 2. An adaptive learning process model

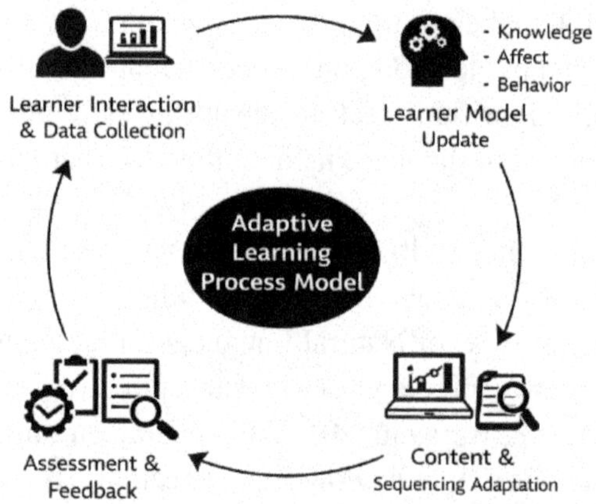

4. DATA, BIAS, AND FAIRNESS IN ADAPTIVE LEARNING SYSTEMS

Adaptive learning system workings are by their nature, totally dependent on periodic data collection and analysis performed on a huge scale. The personalization process through this data-oriented method is the heart of the matter, yet it gives rise to challenges that are huge and connected with the algorithm bias and systemic unfairness. The incorporation of bias in the datasets that are utilized for the training of these systems is mainly due to the influence of current and past social conditions, and the technologies that are developed through them will not just mirror the bias but also escalate it. This section discusses critically the educational data architecture, identifies various sources of bias that are typical for AI-assisted learning, and finally mentions rules and techniques that are necessary for building fairness-aware adaptive systems.

4.1 Educational Data Ecosystem

Adaptive learning systems operate within a complex data ecosystem consisting not only of academic performance metrics but also of logs of behavioral interactions and biometric or affective data. The latter, which can be collected through various means including sensors or inferred from patterns like eye-tracking or keystroke dynamics, aims to uncover learner states such as engagement and cognitive load (Slade & Prinsloo, 2013).

To get the raw data to the point of being insightful and doable there must be preprocessing pipelines with a structured approach. The first stage of data accumulation is going on through the learning platform where the application logging mechanisms are placed. The raw data stream consists of various parts, and it is first cleaned by removing outliers and treating missing values, then transformed into structured formats, and finally integrated from different sources to make a single learner record. Feature engineering is the main step in which raw interaction logs are changed into pedagogically significant indicators. Some of them can be measuring "persistence" through multiple attempts on one problem or determining "response latency" to conclude whether there is confidence or hesitation. The pipeline design is a very important and not so neutral process. The choices about which data will be collected, the manner in which it will be grouped, and the features that will be formed will not only have direct but also indirect influence over the models that follow and may even implant the existing social biases into the core of the system unconsciously (Sweeney, 2013).

4.2 Sources of Bias in AI Driven Learning

Bias in adaptive learning systems can occur at various stages of the data algorithm pipeline, resulting in unfair or discriminatory effects on certain groups of learners. Algorithmic bias denotes the occurrence of systematic and reproducible errors that lead to inequitable results. This might arise from the formal definition of the algorithm's objective function. To illustrate, an algorithm aimed solely at maximizing average test scores of all students might evolve methods that are beneficial to the larger demographic and, at the same time, unfavorable to the smaller ones whose learning styles and previous readiness differ (Baker & Hawn, 2021).

The main reason behind algorithmic bias is dataset bias which is the situation where the training data used for model building is not representative of the population of the target learners. These datasets often reflect the historical discrimination in the fields of education (access, resource allocation, and achievement). As a result, the models may not work well for people from minority groups, low-income families or certain areas. A famous case is found in the field of natural language processing: suppose the model is trained mainly using text from one dialect of a language; in that case, it may misunderstand the answers or give less helpful feedback to students who speak different dialects or use non-standard grammar (Hobert & Meyer von Wolff, 2021).

The socio-cultural, gender, and language biases to a lesser degree or more pronouncedly represent the problem. The society's stereotypes can be reflected in the instructional content and historical interaction data that lead to biased recommendations. For instance, the system based on past patterns might purport to female student's content related to STEM or to male students the humanities. Linguistic bias poses a greater threat to non-native speakers and students from diverse linguistic backgrounds; their writing may get less accurate automated evaluation and poorer feedback. A major risk is the bias getting exaggerated through adaptive feedback loops. The system may suggest easier material if it has falsely assessed a student's ability, through biased data, at the beginning. The student receives less challenging work and this limited opportunity can bring about a slower pace of learning, and eventually, the new data will still support the low estimation of the system, thereby forming a self-reinforcing cycle of reduced outcomes (O'Neil, 2016).

4.3 Fairness Aware Adaptive Learning

Tackling the issue of bias will mean that there is going to be a commitment to fairness aware adaptive learning. Fairness metrics need to be defined, bias detection and mitigation need to be done, and inclusive design principles need to be adopted. Fairness in educational AI is determined by the context in which it is applied and is frequently quantified with statistical metrics like demographic parity, equality of opportunity, or predictive parity (Verma & Rubin, 2018). The choice of a metric brings with it ethical trade-offs that can be justified in terms of the educational objectives.

The technical replies are constituted, among other things, by model auditing which identifies and reports disproportionate performance in different subgroups and by the application of mitigation techniques that are categorised into the following three stages: pre-processing (where data is debiased), in-processing (where fairness constraints are added to the algorithms), and post-processing (where outputs are adjusted) (Mehrabi et al., 2021). This, in the case of adaptive systems, might translate into the recommended actions being automatically and continuously adjusted according to the fairness audits.

The technical procedures, however, should be rooted in inclusive, value sensitive design. The participation of the stakeholders, that is the educators, students, and communities, is necessary to spot the harms as well as the needs. It is necessary to be open about the logic and the limitations of the system. At last, fairness can be counted as a basic and a non-negotiable design requirement, which will not be a retrospective fix; equity will be rooted in the whole system lifecycle (Friedman & Hendry, 2019).

5. PRIVACY, SECURITY, AND ETHICAL CHALLENGES

Adaptive learning systems, being heavily reliant on vast data collection and sophisticated algorithms, introduce a lot of issues regarding students' privacy, data protection, and ethical responsibility. The installation of such systems leads to a difficult situation in which, on one hand, surveillance, data misuse, and less freedom for students are counted as the main disadvantages, while, on the other hand, personalization of teaching is considered as the main advantage. This part of the paper discusses the main privacy concerns raised by AI-based education, evaluates the existing legal and regulatory measures, and suggests basic moral principles for constructing dependable systems.

5.1 Privacy Risks in AI Driven Learning Environments

The primary function of adaptive learning is based on constant, detailed monitoring of student activity, referred to as student surveillance, and it involves much more than just the ordinary academic assessment. In addition to this, systems keep track of each student's detailed interactions, such as clicks, keyboard presses, and movement on the screen, thus developing very comprehensive cognitive and behavioral profiles. This widespread collection of data has raised the question of whether there is an excessive collection of data where the information collected is more than what is required for teaching purposes. On the one hand, such data may improve algorithms, but on the other hand, it increases the risk of function creep being the usage of data for unapproved purposes which are usually intrusive, such as behavioral profiling, making predictions in non-academic areas, or even commercial exploitation (Zeide, 2019). Recent studies have explored blockchain-integrated AI systems with ensemble learning for secure and tamper-resistant environments, demonstrating improved anomaly detection and system integrity (Khullar et al., 2025).

In the realm of technical privacy risks, two issues stand out especially clearly - re-identification and inference. Even if a dataset has been thoroughly anonymized by getting rid of direct identifiers such as student names or IDs, the abundance and distinctiveness of the data coming from behaviors can still make it possible to identify individuals through connections with other datasets. Additionally, using machine learning and advanced analytics can lead to making very sensitive inferences about a student that were not even communicated in any way. A system might predict signs of a learning disability, mental health issues, low-income background, or troubled family relations based on a student's performance, classroom presence and writing style (Rubel & Jones, 2016). The traits learned in this way could result in people getting labeled, the school adopting a certain view of the student's abilities, or even unauthorized sharing of health-related data that is harmful to the student's privacy and might hurt the student physically or emotionally.

5.2 Data Protection and Regulatory Frameworks

The regulations that include the protection of data and compliance are both complicated, and despite that, they are the main issues within the sphere of education. Compliance remains one of the most common issues in the international arena of data protection and, regulation-wise, educational data. The European Union (GDPR) is a strict regulation known as the General Data Protection Regulation that is similar to a global standard and the Western countries must accept the same. An example is that of the United States, which has a law named Family Educational Rights and Privacy Act (FERPA) ensuring that student education records are not accessed by unauthorized individuals. Nevertheless, it remains highly unclear to what extent it is encompassed by how vast sums of behavioural data were generated by adaptive learning platforms (Regan & Jesse, 2019). International learning technologies have an even more complex regulatory situation due to the introduction of education-specific data privacy laws by different regions. These frameworks are founded on the three major concepts of informed consent, transparency and data ownership. It is very difficult to ensure that those students and parents at schools will give informed consent in a genuine manner, as the power imbalance will lead to it being perceived as a way to avoid the incredibly data-intensive platform, which seems to imply that the person, in turn, is resigning to the highly valuable educational tools. Transparency requires the communications between the universities and the vendors to express all the data collecting, using, access and retention. The issue of ownership of data remains controversial, it is typically discussed between learning institutions, the vendors of platforms, and learners themselves. The ethical practice requires that the learners, as the data subjects, should have considerable control over their online footprints, as well as the rights to access, correct and delete their data and to be aware of the important algorithmic conclusions about themselves (Hoel and Chen, 2019).

5.3 Ethical Design Principles

The change in compliance with the law to an ethical design must be followed by the application of active principles of ethical design. These principles revolve around accountability and responsibility. The accountability of the consequences of the AI-based systems, including the errors of the algorithms or biased outcomes, should be distributed between vendors, academic institutions, and administrators. The principle of human in the loop is a crucial one, as it ensures that the teachers possess a great degree of control and the final decision-making power. The idea is that AI should assist teachers, not take over their role, and the systems should be designed to offer useful insights to teachers rather than making fully independent, high stakes decisions about students (Holstein et al., 2019).

Value sensitive design, on the other hand, does not only justify but also enforces the integration of ethical considerations into the technical design process through a methodological framework. This process requires the explicit identification of stakeholder values - autonomy, fairness, trust, and human dignity, among others - and the transformation of those values into requirements and features that are architectural (Friedman & Hendry, 2019). As an example, it could be necessary to provide for the audit of the system, to allow external scrutiny of the algorithms, or to develop user interfaces that offer explanations of the decisions made for teachers. Lastly, designers should be very frank about the ethical trade-offs involved in personalization. The search for the best learning patterns might be in conflict with the freedom of students as hyper-personalization could restrict the participation and exploration of the learner. There is a trade-off, on the one hand, between the personalization's data usefulness and privacy's data minimization. There are also these trade-offs that need to be recognized and balanced through stakeholder discussions that include everyone. This is vital for the growth of adaptive learning technologies that are not just effective but also socially responsible and morally defensible. Figure 3 summarizes the key ethical risks in AI-driven adaptive learning systems and the corresponding mitigation strategies across the system lifecycle.

Figure 3. An ethical risk-mitigation framework

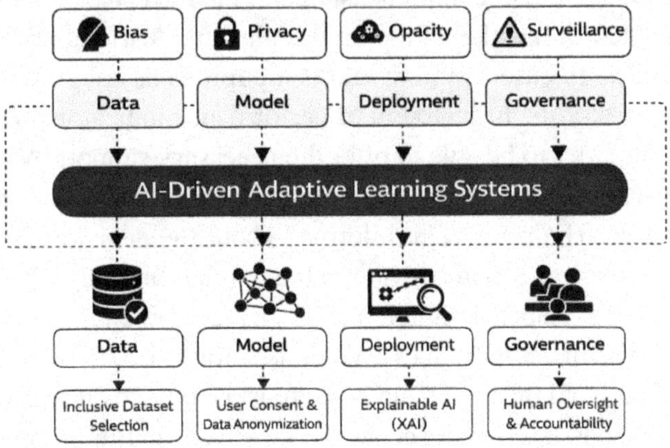

6. EXPLAINABILITY AND TRUST IN ADAPTIVE LEARNING TECHNOLOGIES

The development of AI-powered adaptive learning systems has reached a level of sophistication that has created a significant paradox: their efficacy is increasing, but their internal decision-making is becoming more and more opaque to teachers and students. Opaqueness or lack of transparency may cause the erosion of trust that is the very basis of the educational relationship. For this reason, Explainable AI (XAI) has come to be regarded as an indispensable research area within the educational technology landscape. This section delineates the teaching and moral imperative of explainability, assesses the techniques of rendering models comprehensible to various customer segments, and debates the basic linkage of transparency, trust, and end-user acceptance.

6.1 Need for Explainable AI (XAI) in Education

The demand for the transparency of educational AI is not just a general preference for transparent systems but rather a very specific need for pedagogical, ethical and practical reasons. From a teaching point of view, learning that is effective often requires knowing the "why" behind the feedback, corrections, and recommended pathways. An unexplainable recommendation from a system works as a black box instruction, which can prevent a learner from developing a proper understanding of the subject and acquiring metacognitive skills (Holmes et al., 2022). For a teacher, the lack of clarity is just as challenging. If a teacher does not know the grounds for the AI's judgment of student comprehension and the next steps it suggests, he/she cannot properly incorporate the AI tool in teaching and learning or intervene in an appropriate manner. In case a system marks a pupil as at-risk, the teacher would want to be informed of the behavioural or performance indicators that contributed to that marking in order to be able to offer the necessary support (Miller, 2019).

Explainability, from an ethical standpoint, is the basic principle behind accountability and fairness. The right to be informed about the decision-making process is more and more seen as a primary rule in the regulation of algorithms. When an adaptive system, for example, assigns a final grade, recommends a remedial track, or diagnoses a learning difficulty, makes a major decision that determines the course of a student's education, all the parties involved must be able to question and comprehend the reason behind it (Gunning et al., 2019). This is of utmost importance since it is the only way of recognizing and challenging biases, as mentioned in Section 4. If there is no explainability, it will not be possible to carry out significant audits or to make sure that the systems are functioning as planned and are free of discrimination. Recent research has emphasized the role of explainable intelligence and trust modeling in building ethical, human-centric AI systems (Khullar et al., 2026).

6.2 Model Interpretability for Educators and Learners

The successful explainability process is that the interpretative insights should be provided on the basis of the different users' roles and their expertise. In the case of teachers, it is necessary to transform the outputs of the algorithm into a pedagogical guide that is practical for the teachers. An example of this is the dashboard analytics, which should work not only by identifying a student as at risk but also by giving the reason through the connection of system inferences to specific, observable events, such as engagement time drop and occurred failures on a certain concept that is less than that of the peers (Holstein et al., 2019). This way educators get to make their judgments that are informed and contextually based.

There is a significant difference in ways of explanation. Some of the systems use clearly comprehensible models like decision trees, but may lose some predictive power. In the more complex black box models such as deep neural networks, post hoc methods of explanation are used. Some of these include feature importance techniques like LIME or SHAP that identify the inputs with the largest contribution to a prediction, and counterfactual explanations that demonstrate what a different input would have caused in terms of the outcome. The learners anticipate that the explainability in the system must be in the form of easy feedback and revelation of the system operations. One of them could include visual knowledge maps that will show the progress of the learners or even short messages that are clarifying the adaptive choices (ex: Your performance is why the next unit will have more practice in decimals). This transparency facilitates learner agency, fosters growth mentality, and results in trust in the system recommendations.

6.3 Trust, Transparency, and User Acceptance

Explainability's ultimate aim is to build trust, which is the single most significant factor influencing user acceptance and the continuous, efficient use of adaptive learning technologies. Trust here is not a simple concept; it includes sects such as trust in the system being right (performance trust), trust that it is treating everyone fairly and that it has good intentions (purpose trust), and trust that its operations are open and comprehensible (process trust) (Kizilcec, 2016). A shortage of openness immediately undermines process trust that may later lead to a general lack of confidence in the system's performance and purpose.

In the field of technology acceptance, one of the most important factors is trust which always mediates the impact of perceived usefulness and perceived ease of use. The teachers' skepticism towards the system's suggestions will lead to a lack of their usage in teaching, no matter how effective the system has been in trials. Likewise, students may lose their interest or feel anxious if they consider the system as an unyielding examiner rather than a patient teacher. Thus, proactive transparency through carefully designed explainability should be regarded not only as an extra feature but as a basic requirement in the design for adoption of the technology. It grants the users the possibility to set their trust at the right level, knowing both the strengths and weaknesses of the system.

To create reliable systems, one must constantly commit to open conversations. This entails being upfront about the system's capabilities and limitations, admitting to mistakes honestly, providing user-friendly means for users to challenge outputs, and creating user interfaces that make explanations visible instead of concealing them behind intricate menus. When the emphasis is on making things clear for users, the creators of adaptive learning technologies can transition from developing systems that users are forced to use, to developing systems that teachers and students willingly use because they comprehend, trust, and appreciate their part in the educational process.

7. CASE STUDIES AND PRACTICAL IMPLEMENTATIONS

The various theoretical frameworks, models, and ethical discussions that are associated with AI-assisted learning environments are - at the end of the day - based on and tested by real-world applications. This part of the study looks at specific examples of AI-assisted learning systems and combines the empirical results of their use. Examining both the technological application and the outcomings provides the most important proof for the effectiveness, difficulties, and everyday realities of adaptive learning technologies, thus linking the research and practice.

7.1 AI-Driven Learning Platforms

Out of all the AI-driven platforms that have popped up, diverse ones have surfaced taking the principles of adaptivity literally but in different ways. Intelligent Tutoring Systems (ITS) are one of the categories that have developed to the fullest extent and have done intensive research on. These systems are mimicking human tutors one-on-one by giving step-by-step support, context-sensitive feedback and personalized problem sequencing. MATHia of Carnegie Learning is a typical example of an ITS for math grounded on cognitive science principles. It is known as a cognitive model mimicking how students learn certain math concepts giving rise to diagnosing misconceptions with utmost precision and hence, providing personalized hints and feedback instantly (Koedinger & Corbett, 2006). The other well-known ITS is Auto Tutor which provides students help in learning physics, computer literacy, and critical thinking by using a natural language dialogue and having conversational interactions that scaffold deeper explanations (Graesser et al., 2018). These systems are showing the advantages of deep domain modeling and interactive, guided problem-solving.

Together with pure ITS, adaptive capability has been added to larger-scale systems such as MOOCs (Massive Open Online Courses) and LMS (Learning Management Systems) as an integrated feature. Leading platforms like Coursera and edX are gradually taking up the adaptive features of personalized course suggestions and learning pathways that are aware of prerequisites. More advanced adaptive LMS platforms like Knewton (which is now part of Pearson) or Smart Sparrow offer authoring tools that educators and instructional designers can use to create adaptive learning experiences by setting rules, conceptual maps, and feedback logic. The majority of these systems concentrate on adaptive content sequencing and assessment that rely on learners' interactions data to alter the material flow in real-time. For example, the system may send a student who does not pass a quiz on an essential concept to a remedial lesson automatically while the student who passed could either move on or opt for enrichment material. The said practices show the adaptability of the logic that enables it to transfer from extensive cognitive tutoring to personalization of wider curriculum.

7.2 Empirical Findings from Real-World Deployments

The use of these platforms has resulted in an increasing amount of empirical research focusing on their influence on learning outcomes, student participation, and the ethical aspects of their applications. Throughout the different meta-analyses carried out on the effectiveness of Intelligent Tutoring Systems (ITS), they have always established that there are positive and at times, variable effects on learning when compared to traditional classroom instruction or non-adaptive computer-based instruction. In a comprehensive review of more than 50 controlled studies, Kulik and Fletcher (2016) concluded that learners getting support from ITS invariably excelled on tests, and the average effect size was thus worthwhile for educational purposes. The instant feedback, the enforcement of mastery learning, and the careful matching of the difficulty of the problems with the students' abilities are usually cited as the reasons behind such effectiveness.

In addition to final scores, research examines students' engagement and behavior as outcomes. According to the studies, a significant benefit of using adaptive systems is that they can enhance students' persistence and time spent on-task by moderate frustration (with the help of suitable challenges) and boredom (by not exposing learners to unnecessary repetition) (Baker et al., 2010). Nevertheless, these advantages do not come automatically. On the one hand, poorly calibrated systems, while, on the other hand, students' lack of understanding of the system can result in students' confusion, manipulation of the system, and disengagement. The empirical evidence reinforces the notion that pedagogical design and usability are just as important as the sophistication of the underlying algorithm.

At the same time, real-world usages have uncovered ethical and privacy problems which are very clear. Different situations point out that giving informed consent is difficult, as students and their parents have to deal with long and hard-to-understand privacy policies that they cannot comprehend. During the period in which various educational tech companies suffered serious security issues, students' very private info was leaked, thus pointing out the lack of proper security measures (Regan & Jesse, 2019). Besides that, empirical checks have reported the presence of bias in algorithms used in the systems. Say, for instance, the very analysis of a widely adopted adaptive learning system that would show its recommendation engine is systematically directing less difficult material to students of a specific demographic group, even after accounting for their initial performance, thus continuing the opportunity gap (Baker & Hawn, 2021). These implications observed are in line with the theoretical concerns mentioned in Sections 4 and 5, that is, the ethical risks are already felt in practice and thus, besides having to be actively governed, they need to be monitored continuously and to be subject to prompt design modifications.

The combination of case studies and empirical evidence sheds light on a complicated matter. Teachers can make AI-supported learning systems their allies in improving the results and the number of students taking part in the learning process, provided the systems have quality pedagogy and excellent algorithms as their backbone. Nevertheless, their introduction is not a matter of technology alone; it is a social and technical issue that presents difficult choices among the personalization and the privacy, the efficiency and the equity, and the automation and the human supervision. The experiences derived from these applications in practice will help to ensure the responsible development and deployment of adaptive learning technologies in the future.

8. CHALLENGES, LIMITATIONS, AND OPEN RESEARCH ISSUES

AI-driven adaptive learning systems go through a complex process of development and deployment which is still not very effective due to the challenges such systems have to face. These barriers consist of technical, ethical and methodological areas that need to be addressed through a well-defined research agenda for the future.

In this section, we will explain these problems, emphasizing the most important technical challenges, the issues of social and ethical aspects that are still around, and the shortcomings of present research paradigms that are most noticeable.

The initial group of obstacles is made up of basic technical issues relating to scalability and robustness. Even though adaptive systems are quite good in limited research environments, their scaling to the point of serving large and varied populations would entail the problems of data infrastructure, computation cost, and model generalization. The cold start issue, which means that a model is unable to learn by a system due to the lack of data, continues to be one of the main barriers for effective personalization for new users (Scheffel et al., 2021). Besides, guaranteeing the robustness of a system is a tricky affair. Performance of the models goes down with concept drift, where performance is affected by changes to the content or the student behavior over time. Besides, they are also at risk of learners employing adversarial tactics, like guessing answers systematically to earn hints, which promotes getting through without real learning and goes against the pedagogical goal (Baker et al., 2010).

Apart from the technical side, there are still serious ethical and socio technical limitations. One of the main worries is that human agency might be weakened. The use of algorithms in personalization could easily lead to the reduction of learner's autonomy, accidental discovery, and the acquiring of self-regulated learning skills. When teachers overly rely on the system-generated recommendations, they may lose their professional expertise and discretion, thus their role might be reduced to that of a system monitor rather than an instructional leader (Selwyn, 2019). In addition, the issues of algorithmic bias and data privacy that were discussed earlier are not solved problems but rather persistent socio technical conflicts. Some technical debiasing approaches can be only partially effective and can also result in new trade-offs, while privacy preserving measures usually result in a reduction of utility. It is also true that in educational settings, the accountability for algorithmic decisions is very vague and this gives rise to the question of who is responsible when errors or harms take place.

Today's research and evaluation techniques reveal significant shortcomings. The current body of literature primarily relies on short quantitative measures like post-test scores, at the same time it is neglecting the long-term effects that are more important such as retention of knowledge, transfer of skills, and learner motivation. Furthermore, the research often lacks ecological validity, thus it does not accurately depict the integration of these systems into the real classroom environment, the teacher's practices, and the curriculum (Luckin et al., 2016). A major hindrance is the absence of common standards and methods for the evaluation of ethical conduct that are coherent and consistent. Fairness, transparency, and accountability metrics and rigorous assessments are not yet generally applied in conjunction with the measures of learning gain, resulting in a large gap in the holistic understanding of the impact of these technologies.

9. FUTURE DIRECTIONS AND CONCLUSION

The progression of AI in education demands a transition from merely adaptive systems to those that are ethically grounded, trustworthy, and equitable. This last part delineates major future directions and proposes the chapter's main conclusions while stressing that responsible development hinges on the union of technical ability with robust ethical protection. The convergence of AI inference, IoT, and big data is expected to drive next-generation intelligent and scalable learning ecosystems (Khullar & Tank, 2026).

The future decision-making hangs on three interconnected priorities. Firstly, the responsible AI must become the operational aspect of the company which would involve creating detailed design standards, exhaustive auditing, and multi-faceted evaluation. The systems have to be built in such a way that there would be transparency and accountability in them which would be an ongoing process and trust can be built through users getting to understand (Holmes et al., 2022). The aim is to develop gadgets that will automatically empower the educator's skills and the learner's control (Jobin, Ienca, & Vayena, 2019). Secondly, the conflict that exists between personalization and privacy has to be removed with the help of technical innovation. In fact, there is no doubt that the modern-day paradigms such as federated learning, which allows for model training over decentralized data without the need for any central collection, are of utmost importance in lessening the risks related to data (McMahan et al., 2017). Also, the organization of different privacy measures like differential privacy will be the basis for a whole set of privacy protection mechanisms. Thirdly, to ensure that the new technologies are used properly, each company has to have good policy rules and interdisciplinary cooperation. The educational authorities should make it a point that there are always algorithmic impact assessments and fairness audits going on while the governance should keep inviting various groups to take part in its oversight (Reich & Ito, 2017). The solving of the socio-technical difficulties will need continuous collaboration of computer science, learning science, ethics, and policy. This chapter has successfully dissected the technical underpinnings of adaptive learning, the ethical risks being one of them. These risks are algorithmic bias, privacy erosion, and opaque decision-making among others. The presented evidence has proved these to be practical obstacles that are in direct line with the world's trust and outcomes. Hence, the researchers are required to couple the longitudinal studies with the establishment of uniformly accepted standards for moral performance education alongside learning gains

(Holmes et al., 2022). The faculty should be given professional development that would help them to assess the AI tools critically as well as integrate them, and the goal is to keep them as the main teaching experts (Selwyn, 2019). The government and the institution heads are supposed to come up with governance systems where surety of algorithmic accountability exists and the stakeholders are the ones who talk (Reich & Ito, 2017).

REFERENCES

Aleven, V., McLaughlin, E. A., Glenn, R. A., & Koedinger, K. R. (2016). Instruction based on adaptive learning technologies. In Mayer, R. E., & Alexander, P. A. (Eds.), *Handbook of research on learning and instruction* (2nd ed., pp. 522–560). Routledge.

Anderson, J. R., Corbett, A. T., Koedinger, K. R., & Pelletier, R. (1995). Cognitive tutors: Lessons learned. *Journal of the Learning Sciences*, *4*(2), 167–207. DOI: 10.1207/s15327809jls0402_2

Baker, R. S. (2016). Stupid tutoring systems, intelligent humans. *International Journal of Artificial Intelligence in Education*, *26*(2), 600–614. DOI: 10.1007/s40593-016-0105-0

Baker, R. S., D'Mello, S. K., Rodrigo, M. M. T., & Graesser, A. C. (2010). Better to be frustrated than bored: The incidence, persistence, and impact of learners' cognitive-affective states during interactions with three different computer-based learning environments. *International Journal of Human-Computer Studies*, *68*(4), 223–241. DOI: 10.1016/j.ijhcs.2009.12.003

Baker, R. S., & Hawn, A. (2021). Algorithmic bias in education. *International Journal of Artificial Intelligence in Education*, *32*(4), 1052–1092. DOI: 10.1007/s40593-021-00285-9

Baker, R. S., & Inventado, P. S. (2014). Educational data mining and learning analytics. In Larusson, J. A., & White, B. (Eds.), *Learning analytics: From research to practice* (pp. 61–75). Springer., DOI: 10.1007/978-1-4614-3305-7_4

Bloom, B. S. (1968). Learning for mastery. *Evaluation Comment*, *1*(2), 1–12.

Corbett, A. T., & Anderson, J. R. (1995). Knowledge tracing: Modeling the acquisition of procedural knowledge. *User Modeling and User-Adapted Interaction*, *4*(4), 253–278. DOI: 10.1007/BF01099821

du Boulay, B. (2016). Artificial intelligence as an effective classroom assistant. *IEEE Intelligent Systems*, *31*(6), 76–81. DOI: 10.1109/MIS.2016.93

Friedman, B., & Hendry, D. G. (2019). *Value sensitive design: Shaping technology with moral imagination*. The MIT Press. DOI: 10.7551/mitpress/7585.001.0001

Graesser, A. C., Hu, X., & Sottilare, R. (2018). Intelligent tutoring systems. In Fischer, F., Hmelo-Silver, C. E., Goldman, S. R., & Reimann, P. (Eds.), *International handbook of the learning sciences* (pp. 246–255). Routledge. DOI: 10.4324/9781315617572-24

Gunning, D., Stefik, M., Choi, J., Miller, T., Stumpf, S., & Yang, G. Z. (2019). XAI: Explainable artificial intelligence. *Science Robotics*, *4*(37), eaay7120. Advance online publication. DOI: 10.1126/scirobotics.aay7120 PMID: 33137719

Hobert, S., & Meyer von Wolff, R. (2021). Say hello to your new automated tutor: A structured literature review on pedagogical conversational agents. *Proceedings of the 54th Hawaii International Conference on System Sciences*, 1105–1114. https://doi.org/DOI: 10.24251/HICSS.2021.135

Hoel, T., & Chen, W. (2019). Privacy and data protection in learning analytics should be motivated by an educational maxim: Towards a proposal. *Research and Practice in Technology Enhanced Learning*, *14*(1), 1–13. DOI: 10.1186/s41039-019-0115-2 PMID: 30595748

Holmes, W., Porayska-Pomsta, K., Holstein, K., Sutherland, E., Baker, T., Shum, S. B., Santos, O. C., Rodrigo, M. T., Cukurova, M., Bittencourt, I. I., & Koedinger, K. R. (2022). Ethics of AI in education: Towards a community-wide framework. *International Journal of Artificial Intelligence in Education*, *32*(3), 504–526. DOI: 10.1007/s40593-021-00239-1

Holstein, K., McLaren, B. M., & Aleven, V. (2019). Co-designing a real-time classroom orchestration tool to support teacher-AI complementarity. *Journal of Learning Analytics*, *6*(2), 27–52. DOI: 10.18608/jla.2019.62.3

Ifenthaler, D., & Yau, J. Y.-K. (2020). Utilising learning analytics to support study success in higher education: A systematic review. *Educational Technology Research and Development*, *68*(4), 1961–1990. DOI: 10.1007/s11423-020-09788-z

Jobin, A., Ienca, M., & Vayena, E. (2019). The global landscape of AI ethics guidelines. *Nature Machine Intelligence*, *1*(9), 389–399. DOI: 10.1038/s42256-019-0088-2

Khullar, S., Mounika, G. R., Chauhan, S. S., Garg, G., Priyanka, T. P., & Kaliappan, S. (2025). Advanced hybrid ensemble learning for blockchain-enabled secure voting: Leveraging random forest, XGBoost, and neural networks for robust anomaly detection and integrity assurance. *Proceedings of the 1st International Conference on Advancement in Futuristic Technologies (ICAFT)*, 1–7. https://doi.org/10.1109/ICAFT66710.2025.11452780

Kizilcec, R. F. (2016). How much information? Effects of transparency on trust in an algorithmic interface. *Proceedings of the 2016 CHI Conference on Human Factors in Computing Systems*, 2390–2395. https://doi.org/DOI: 10.1145/2858036.2858402

Koedinger, K. R., & Corbett, A. T. (2006). Cognitive tutors: Technology bringing learning sciences to the classroom. In Sawyer, R. K. (Ed.), *The Cambridge handbook of the learning sciences* (pp. 61–77). Cambridge University Press.

Kulik, J. A., & Fletcher, J. D. (2016). Effectiveness of intelligent tutoring systems: A meta-analytic review. *Review of Educational Research, 86*(1), 42–78. DOI: 10.3102/0034654315581420

Luckin, R., Holmes, W., Griffiths, M., & Forcier, L. B. (2016). *Intelligence unleashed: An argument for AI in education.* Pearson.

Mandel, T., Liu, Y. E., Levine, S., Brunskill, E., & Popovic, Z. (2014). Offline policy evaluation across representations with applications to educational games. *Proceedings of the 13th International Conference on Autonomous Agents and Multiagent Systems (AAMAS 2014)*, 1077–1084. DOI: 10.65109/TNVS8310

Manouselis, N., Drachsler, H., Vuorikari, R., Hummel, H., & Koper, R. (2011). Recommender systems in technology enhanced learning. In Ricci, F., Rokach, L., Shapira, B., & Kantor, P. B. (Eds.), *Recommender systems handbook* (pp. 387–415). Springer., DOI: 10.1007/978-0-387-85820-3_12

McMahan, H. B., Moore, E., Ramage, D., Hampson, S., & Arcas, B. A. (2017). Communication-efficient learning of deep networks from decentralized data. *Proceedings of the 20th International Conference on Artificial Intelligence and Statistics (AISTATS)*, 1273–1282.

Mehrabi, N., Morstatter, F., Saxena, N., Lerman, K., & Galstyan, A. (2021). A survey on bias and fairness in machine learning. *ACM Computing Surveys, 54*(6), 1–35. DOI: 10.1145/3457607

Miller, T. (2019). Explanation in artificial intelligence: Insights from the social sciences. *Artificial Intelligence, 267*, 1–38. DOI: 10.1016/j.artint.2018.07.007

O'Neil, C. (2016). *Weapons of math destruction: How big data increases inequality and threatens democracy.* Crown Publishing Group.

Pavlik, P. I., & Anderson, J. R. (2008). Using a model to compute the optimal schedule of practice. *Journal of Experimental Psychology. Applied, 14*(2), 101–117. DOI: 10.1037/1076-898X.14.2.101 PMID: 18590367

Pelánek, R. (2017). Bayesian knowledge tracing, logistic models, and beyond: An overview of learner modeling techniques. *User Modeling and User-Adapted Interaction, 27*(3-5), 313–350. DOI: 10.1007/s11257-017-9193-2

Piech, C., Bassen, J., Huang, J., Ganguli, S., Sahami, M., Guibas, L. J., & Sohl-Dickstein, J. (2015). Deep knowledge tracing. *Advances in Neural Information Processing Systems*, *28*, 505–513.

Regan, P. M., & Jesse, J. (2019). Ethical challenges of edtech, big data and personalized learning: Twenty first century student sorting and tracking. *Ethics and Information Technology*, *21*(3), 167–179. DOI: 10.1007/s10676-018-9492-2

Reich, J., & Ito, M. (2017). *From good intentions to real outcomes: Equity by design in learning technologies*. Digital Media and Learning Research Hub.

Roll, I., & Winne, P. H. (2015). Understanding, evaluating, and supporting self-regulated learning using learning analytics. *Journal of Learning Analytics*, *2*(1), 7–12. DOI: 10.18608/jla.2015.21.2

Rubel, A., & Jones, K. M. L. (2016). Student privacy in learning analytics: An information ethics perspective. *The Information Society*, *32*(2), 143–159. DOI: 10.1080/01972243.2016.1130502

Scheffel, M., Drachsler, H., & Specht, M. (2021). The five facets of learning analytics: A framework for building trust and transparency. *Computers and Education: Artificial Intelligence*, *2*, 100037. DOI: 10.1016/j.caeai.2021.100037

Selwyn, N. (2019). *Should robots replace teachers? AI and the future of education*. Polity Press.

Shermis, M. D., & Burstein, J. (Eds.). (2013). *Handbook of automated essay evaluation: Current applications and new directions*. Routledge. DOI: 10.4324/9780203122761

Shute, V. J., & Rahimi, S. (2017). Review of computer-based assessment for learning in elementary and secondary education. *Journal of Computer Assisted Learning*, *33*(1), 1–19. DOI: 10.1111/jcal.12172

Shute, V. J., & Ventura, M. (2013). *Measuring and supporting learning in games: Stealth assessment*. The MIT Press. DOI: 10.7551/mitpress/9589.001.0001

Shute, V. J., & Zapata-Rivera, D. (2012). Adaptive educational systems. In Durlach, P. J., & Lesgold, A. M. (Eds.), *Adaptive technologies for training and education* (pp. 7–27). Cambridge University Press. DOI: 10.1017/CBO9781139049580.004

Skinner, B. F. (1958). Teaching machines. *Science*, *128*(3330), 969–977. DOI: 10.1126/science.128.3330.969 PMID: 13592277

Slade, S., & Prinsloo, P. (2013). Learning analytics: Ethical issues and dilemmas. *The American Behavioral Scientist*, *57*(10), 1510–1529. DOI: 10.1177/0002764213479366

Suthers, D. D. (2006). Technology affordances for intersubjective meaning making: A research agenda for CSCL. *International Journal of Computer-Supported Collaborative Learning*, *1*(3), 315–337. DOI: 10.1007/s11412-006-9660-y

Sweeney, L. (2013). Discrimination in online ad delivery. *Communications of the ACM*, *56*(5), 44–54. DOI: 10.1145/2447976.2447990

VanLehn, K. (2011). The relative effectiveness of human tutoring, intelligent tutoring systems, and other tutoring systems. *Educational Psychologist*, *46*(4), 197–221. DOI: 10.1080/00461520.2011.611369

Verma, S., & Rubin, J. (2018). Fairness definitions explained. *Proceedings of the International Workshop on Software Fairness (FairWare '18)*, 1–7. https://doi.org/ DOI: 10.1145/3194770.3194776

Woolf, B. P. (2009). *Building intelligent interactive tutors: Student-centered strategies for revolutionizing e-learning*. Morgan Kaufmann.

Zeide, E. (2019). Artificial intelligence in higher education: Applications, promise and perils, and ethical questions. *EDUCAUSE Review*, *54*(3). https://er.educause.edu/articles/2019/8/artificial-intelligence-in-higher-education-applications-promise-and-perils-and-ethical-questions

Chapter 11
Future of AI in Education

Uzma Mumtaz
National Small Industries Corporation, India

Anand Bharathi
http://orcid.org/0000-0002-7367-8264
Vellore Institute of Technology, India

Vinoth Kumar S.
http://orcid.org/0009-0001-9523-6651
Patrician College of Arts and Science, India

Anjali Shukla
http://orcid.org/0009-0003-3064-9775
Jain University, India

Bharath Raj N.
http://orcid.org/0009-0006-8250-3120
Jain University, India

Abdullah Malik
http://orcid.org/0000-0002-0149-5549
Jain University, India

J. Jenefer
Vallal P.T. Lee Chengalvaraya Naicker Arts and Science College, India

S. Nilavarasan
Alagappa University, India

ABSTRACT

The rapid evolution of Artificial Intelligence (AI) in pedagogical and andragogical frameworks demands shifts in teaching, learning, and assessment practices. This chapter explores the future of AI in education using conceptual and bibliometric approaches, examining historical, current, and emerging trends. A bibliometric analysis (1970–2025) maps publication growth, thematic structures, leading researchers, and collaboration patterns. The findings show a shift from rule-based AI used mainly for administrative support to generative, human-centered, and adaptive systems that enhance personalized learning, intelligent assessment, and educator AI collaboration. The chapter also addresses ethical concerns, governance, and policy requirements to ensure accountable and transparent AI use. By integrating

DOI: 10.4018/979-8-2600-1840-8.ch011

theory with empirical evidence, it outlines implications and future directions for researchers, educators, policymakers, and institutions, emphasizing sustainable, inclusive, and meaningful educational innovation.

INTRODUCTION AND CONCEPTUAL BACKGROUND OF THE STUDY

AI technology is rapidly changing the way the world conducts business, manages governments, and interacts with society (Dunleavy & Margetts, 2025; Elamin, 2024). In the educational realm, the impact of AI is perhaps more profound than any other emerging technology because AI forces a substantial restructuring of the entire system of knowledge creation, delivery, evaluation, and the experience of learning (Cope et al., 2021; Chen et al., 2020; George & Wooden, 2023). Education AI technology has developed in alignment with the rest of society. From the early-introduced computer-assisted instructional systems, now technologies in the form of generative AI systems that possess high-level reasoning and dialogue capabilities advanced education technology rapidly (Lang et al., 2025; Pratschke, 2024; Yadav, 2025). To devise a better understanding of the overall future of this technology in education, an interdisciplinary approach that is multifaceted on the historical context and the conceptual, and anticipatory analytic for the future is recommended.

AI can be defined as the ability of computer systems to execute operations that typically demand human intellect such as reasoning, learning, perception, language and comprehension, and decision making (Korteling et al., 2021). In the field of education, AI includes a wide range of technologies and methods that aim to support and improve teaching, learning, assessment, and management of education systems (Chen et al., 2020; Luckin & Cukurova, 2019). Such systems have the ability to modify and adapt to the needs of the learner, the goals of the instructor, and the objectives of the educational institution through the use of data, models, algorithms, and feedback mechanisms.

The roots of AI's development are in the symbolic systems and rule-based systems of the mid 20th century, where the goal was to mimic human thinking using logic and decision-making frameworks (Confalonieri et al., 2021; Calegari et al., 2020). Although the early systems were rigid and not easily scalable, they provided the pioneering ideas for the future systems. Machine learning was one of the major breakthroughs whereby systems are able to learn from and adapt to data, as well as understand patterns in learner behavior and performance to make predictions without explicit instructions (Jordan & Mitchell, 2015; Strielkowski et al., 2023). The most recent advancements in AI are the modern deep learning systems that include multiple layers of neural networks and allow for the processing of complex data in the form of text, speech, and images to provide more contextually sensitive solutions that are educationally focused (Chen et al., 2024; Mundlamuri et al., 2025).

AI usage in education has changed since the start of its implementation. It was previously seen as using AI for administrative task, but now is moving towards pedagogical AI (Dai et al., 2025). Initial practice deployments with AI were to aid with grading, scheduling, and other operational functions (Aldriye et al., 2019). AI is now being integrated with Intelligent Tutoring Systems, Predictive Analytics, and Adaptive Learning to assist with self-directed learning, teaching informed by data, and personalized learning (Strielkowski et al., 2025). Learning Analytics is one of the most important developments of the revised AI paradigm in education and uses AI to process educational data for insights with actionable suggestions for teachers and administrators.

With the emergence of AI, LLMs, ChatGPT, and other conversational agents, educational AI has been transformed (Ramos & Casas, 2025). Unlike previous, more narrow, AI tools, LLMs have wide-ranging language comprehension and production capabilities and can take on the role of tutor, content creator, and reflective learning partner (Chen et al., 2024). Their dialogue, explanation, and feedback responsiveness have the potential to significantly transform teaching and learning... as well as the issues of authorship, academic dishonesty, epistemic authority, and assessment practices (Bansal et al., 2024; Bidry et al., 2025).

There is both a growth of potential and urgent concern in the education sector with the increasing use of AI. With the possibility of personalizing learning for students, increasing the ease of accessibility, providing assistance to educators and improving learning outcomes, AI can revolutionize educational practices and outcomes in multiple contexts (Singh et al., 2025). In contrast to this, the increased use of AI in education can pose ethical, inequitable, and opaque concerns, particularly in how the educational community preserves the ability to make choices, the governance of educational data, and the role of educators (Slimi & Carballido, 2023). In light of the aforementioned discourse, the most urgent and ethical articulation of AI in education centers on the importance of 'augmented' human capacity. This means educationally focused AI tools designed to extend the professionalism of educators. In the teaching and learning process, Synergy and educational practices out of autonomous support for learners, advocates, educators, and students (Ryan, 2025; Schmager et al. 2025). It has been universally accepted, to varying degrees, that the development of AI in education must be guided by principles of fairness, accountability, transparency, and inclusivity and ethical (Hosseini Tabaghdehi & Ayaz, 2025).

This chapter aims to integrate conceptual building blocks and prospect illuminating insights to provide clarity to the likely future of AI in education. Based on the authors' extensive bibliometric and thematic analyses, the chapter attempts to situate the development of AI in educational ecosystems, identify the major driver(s), both in technology and concept, of AI in education, and assess the impact on educators, institutions, policymakers, and researchers, to elaborate on major issues and research deficiencies that need attention.

METHODOLOGY

Table 1. Inclusion and exclusion criteria

Criteria Applied	Inclusion / Exclusion Description	Records Remaining (n)
Time period	Studies published between 1932 and 2025	65,518
Document type	**Included:** Articles only	26,063
Publication stage	**Included:** Final stage publications	24,581
Subject relevance	**Included:** AI and Education keywords	14,492
Language	**Included:** Language specific studies	**13,664**

Source: Developed by Authors

Table 1 summarizes the stepwise screening and selection processes applied in the study to identify the pertinent literature. The first step involved an exhaustive search within a specified time frame (1932-2025) which returned 65,518 records. After records were filtered to include only academic articles to retain academic rigor, the records were reduced to 26,063. A final stage publication only filter reduced the records to 24,581. Keyword based filtering to retain thematic relevance and present the publications within the scope of "Artificial Intelligence" and "Education" limited the records to 14,492. A narrowing language filter reduced the records to 13,664. The systematic filtering applied to the records ensured the studies were pertinent to the literature and sufficient in having undergone peer-review to facilitate qualitative and bibliometric analysis.

RESULTS

Descriptive Bibliometric Overview

Table 2. Summary statistics

Metric	Value
Timespan	1970 – 2025
Sources	3,893
Documents	13,644
Annual Growth Rate	16.83%
Authors	53,555
Authors of Single Author Documents	1,854
International Co Authors	24.13%
Co Authors per Document	4.55
Author's Keywords (DE)	23,995
Document Average Age	4.43 years
Average Citations per Document	23.45

Source: Developed by Authors

The bibliometric profile of the dataset shows sustained growth and increasing scholarly activity over the 55-year period of 1970-2025. This suggests long-term and lasting scholarly interest. Spanning 3,893 unique sources (including journals and books) the 13,644 documents published indicates the broad and well-established research area. With an annual growth rate of 16.83%, the area of research demonstrates significant growth especially over the recent past, further highlighting its increasing relevance to the scholarly community. The average age document of 4.43 years illustrates a highly recent body of literature. The average of 23.45 citations per document indicates moderately strong impact and influence of the research area to the scholarly community.

Data shows evidence of thorough theme formation, indicated by 23,995 author keywords which reveal advanced conceptual progress. This shows great diversity, indicating that the research field has developed considerably both in idea formulation, methodology, and subtopics. The pattern of authorship clearly indicates the scale and collaborative nature of the field with 53,555 authors. Of note, 1,854 authors had works that were solely their own, which further indicates that the field leans collaborative in nature. This observation of collaboration is strengthened by the fact that the publication count is significantly greater than the number of single authors, which is 1,973. Average of 4.55 authors on a single document shows that the research is generally team-based, and 24.13% of authorship of the research being international indicates that great cross border collaboration exists in the research. This suggests that collaborative effort is well utilized in the research undertaken, which raises its worth and improves the quality of the work. The fact that the only document types in the dataset are research articles, 13,644 in total shows that the researchers are grounding their work on strong evidence, and that evidence has undergone the scrutiny of the peer-review, which indicates high academic rigor and increases reliability of the dataset. All in all, bibliometric data shows a highly collaborative research field that is growing very quickly, and is connected to many other research fields through collaboration. The fact that there are many multi-authored publications shows that there are many interdisciplinary collaborations in the research. The diverse set of keywords suggests that the data is indicating multiple evolving research areas.

GROWTH AND SCOPE OF AI IN EDUCATION RESEARCH

Figure 1. Annual scientific production

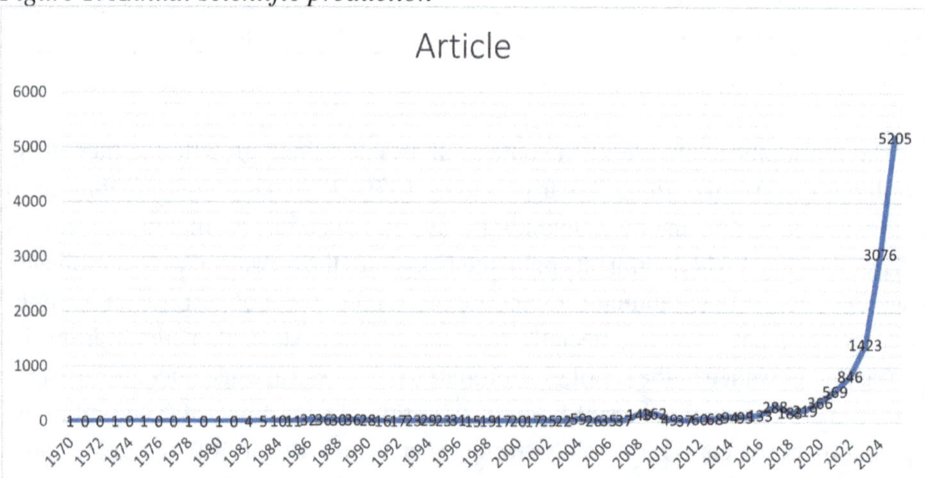

Source: Developed by Authors

The research conducted from 1970 to 2025 shows a clear evolution in the research field annually. The first few years of research (1970 - 1981) had the lowest scholarly productivity, and isolated publications started to appear. This demonstrates that the field was in its formative years with little to no interest from the academic community. From the early 1980's to mid 1995's, research publications started to grow additionally. This slow and steady growth demonstrated the development of foundational ideas, along with the early stages of empirical work. The growth of the publications continued moderately between 1996 and 2007 and had a stable pace, which suggests that the field was settling down. From 2008 and beyond, a notable change occurred and there was a substantial increase in publications. This period was the first notable increase of publications due to an increase in interest for research from multiple disciplines. The most notable increase in publications occurred from 2017 onwards, where there was a sharp increase with 2025 being the highest in recorded history. This increase is extremely notable and signifies the relevant importance the field holds for AI in Education and the technology and policies of residents globally. The field has reached a level of development indicative of a significant and rapid growth of the field and its areas of applications in the last several years.

Table 3. Most influential and highly cited research works

TC	Document Title	Author	TC / Year	DOI
10843	Dermatologist level classification of skin cancer with deep neural networks	Esteva (2017)	1,084.30	10.1038/nature21056
4298	The movie lens datasets: History and context	Harper (2015)	358.17	10.1145/2827872
3120	Artificial Intelligence (AI): Multidisciplinary perspectives on emerging challenges, opportunities, and agenda for research, practice and policy	Dwivedi (2021)	520	10.1016/j.ijinfomgt.2019.08.002
2296	Artificial Intelligence in Education: A Review	Chen (2020)	328	10.1109/ACCESS.2020.2988510
1495	Make3D: Learning 3D scene structure from a single still image	Saxena (2009)	83.06	10.1109/TPAMI.2008.132

continued on following page

Table 3. Continued

TC	Document Title	Author	TC / Year	DOI
1492	A Survey on Explainable Artificial Intelligence (XAI): Toward Medical XAI	Tjoa (2021)	248.67	10.1109/TNNLS.2020.3027314
1431	How Does ChatGPT Perform on the United States Medical Licensing Examination? The Implications of Large Language Models for Medical Education and Knowledge Assessment	Gilson (2023)	357.75	10.2196/45312
1360	Introduction to radiomics	Mayerhoefer (2020)	194.29	10.2967/JNUMED.118.222893
1341	Tensor Decomposition for Signal Processing and Machine Learning	Sidiropoulos (2017)	134.1	10.1109/TSP.2017.2690524
1260	Machine learning in manufacturing: Advantages, challenges, and applications	Wuest (2016)	114.55	10.1080/21693277.2016.1192517

Source: Developed by Authors

Table 3 shows the top influential and cited research studies in the field of artificial intelligence and its use in the educational sector, illustrating the extent to which these works have contributed to the evolution of phenomena as well as scholarly and practical use.

Esteva et al. (2017) won the award for the most influential of the group with her study on skin cancer classification at the level of a dermatologist using deep neural networks. With 10,800 total citations and 1,000 a year, the level of interest demonstrates the impact that AI research has made in the field of medical diagnostics. It has also influenced the field of engineering and clinical decision making.

Harper and Konstan's (2015) publication regarding the Movie Lens datasets and how it revolutionized the field of recommender systems is also of great impact. The high number of citations illustrates the effect shared datasets have in what is being described as a cross-economical standard of research. This phenomenon also applies to the work of Dwivedi et al. (2021). The authors have a cross-sectional view of the field of AI in relation to the various opportunities, challenges, and policy proposed frameworks. The growing annual citations of the publication indicate growing interest in the governance, ethics, and implementation of AI strategically.

Review based studies also feature prominently. The synthesis and clarity infused in the rapidly changing field as demonstrated by the works of Chen (2020) and Tjoa (2021) who have reviewed Artificial Intelligence in Education and surveyed Explainable AI (XAI) in medicine respectively is what the academic community expresses largely and advocates. The citation streak is a strong indicator of practice reliance for the purpose of trend, gap and future direction identification.

The continued steady citation count of works like Saxena et al.'s Make3D (2009) illustrates the piece's longer lasting relevance for computer vision and 3D scene understanding. On the other hand, the machine learning applied studies in manufacturing (Wuest et al., 2016) and the use of tensor decomposition for signal processing (Sidiropoulos et al., 2017) demonstrate that AI techniques are present in the work of the industry and engineering fields.

The 2023 publication of Gilson et al. examining the medical exam performance of ChatGPT is among the more recent works to have been published. It has gained a great number of citations per year, demonstrating the immediate and strong interest of the academia in the large language models and the effect on the teaching-traditional evaluation of profession processes.

Table 4. Highly influential authors

TC	%	Author	TD
2050	12.38446	Chiu, Thomas k.f.	13
1989	12.01595	Chai, Ching Sing	16
1841	11.12185	Haleem, Abid	5
1841	11.12185	Javaid, Mohd	5
1785	10.78354	Bozkurt, Aras	10
1263	7.630037	Tlili, Ahmed	10
1227	7.412554	Hwang, Gwojen	14
1221	7.376306	Adarkwah, Michael Agyemang	5
1171	7.074246	Crompton, Helen	5
1141	6.89301	Cukurova, Mutlu	6
1024	6.18619	Dai, Yun	11

Source: Developed by Authors

Table 4 shows a number of authors who have made an impact in the field and have received a significant number of citations. It is clear that Thomas K. F, Chiu is the most influential, because he has the greatest number of citations (2050) among 13 documents and is evident that his work has been regularly utilized by other researchers.

Ching Sing Chai is next with 1989 citations from 16 documents. Chai is slightly less cited than Chiu but has more publications. This suggests that Chai has consistently contributed to the active research community.

With 5 documents each, Abid Haleem and Mohd Javaid have 1841 citations each. Their low document count but high citations indicate that their work is highly influential and of strong quality.

Table 5. Top influential journal

tc	journal	tp	publisher
12494	Nature	14	Nature Research
9261	Sustainability (Switzerland)	237	Multidisciplinary Digital Publishing Institute (MDPI)
8171	Ieee access	188	Institute of Electrical and Electronics Engineers Inc.
5903	International journal of artificial intelligence in education	98	Springer
5626	Computers and education: artificial intelligence	114	Elsevier B.V.
4951	Education and information technologies	120	Springer
4471	Jmir medical education	101	JMIR Publications Inc.
4110	International journal of information management	5	Elsevier B.V.
3825	Ieee transactions on pattern analysis and machine intelligence	27	IEEE Computer Society
3807	International journal of educational technology in higher education	29	Springer Science and Business Media Deutschland GmbH

Source: Developed by Authors

Nature has the highest influence on research with 12,494 citations from 14 publications. This means that even with few publications, the impact is very high. Next is Sustainability (Switzerland), with 9,261 citations and a very high volume of 237 publications. This shows both high productivity and high research visibility. IEEE Access also has a strong influence with 8,171 citations from 188 publications. Computers and Education: Artificial Intelligence (5,626 citations, 114 publications) and Education and Information Technologies (4,951 citations, 120 publications) have influence and indicate a strong research interest on AI in education.

Table 6. Top country

Citations	Country	Documents
119897	United states	3734
41311	China	1988
37967	United Kingdom	1031
22047	Australia	585
18880	Germany	615
18032	Canada	558
17300	India	607
11950	Spain	606
10291	Saudi Arabia	502
9282	Netherlands	212
9008	Hong Kong	223

Source: Developed by Authors

Table 6 illustrates the data by country, where the US holds the most dominant position, as evidenced by 119,897 citations from 3,734 documents, clearly signaling not only his copious productivity, but also his considerable impact on the world stage of research. In second place is China, with 41,311 citations from 1,988 documents, underscoring its fast development in research. The United Kingdom is also noted to have 37,967 citations from 1,031 publications, signaling a strong impact, while both Australia and Germany are rather even with regard to citations and documents. India, with 607 documents, garnered 17,300 citations, signaling a good, strong, and developing pertinence. The data clearly illustrates that a higher volume of publications, in conjunction with the quality of research, significantly enhances a country's citation impact.

Table 7. Top organisation

Citations	Organization	Documents
14495	Stanford engineering, Stanford, ca, united states	26
12024	Stanford university school of medicine, Stanford, ca, united states	39
5748	College of science and engineering, Minneapolis, mn, united states	5
2136	School of computer science, Pittsburgh, pa, united states	15
1979	Harvard medical school, Boston, ma, united states	69
1915	University of Toronto faculty of medicine, Toronto, on, Canada	61
1913	Department of curriculum and instruction, Chinese university of Hong Kong, Hong Kong, Hong Kong	24
1841	Department of mechanical engineering, Jamia Millia Islamia, new Delhi, India	5

continued on following page

Table 7. Continued

Citations	Organization	Documents
1832	Yale school of medicine, New haven, ct, united states	24
1777	Beijing normal university, Beijing, China	27

Source: Developed by Authors

As seen from the organizational analysis from the table 7, the most influential contributor is Stanford University with Stanford Engineering having the highest impact per paper with 14,495 citations stemming from 26 documents, and Stanford University School of Medicine having 12,024 citations with 39 papers. This is also the case with the College of Science and Engineering, Minneapolis, and Jamia Millia Islamia, who have demonstrated an impressive number of citations stemming from only five documents. Also, the established medical and academic institutions represented by Harvard Medical School, Yale School of Medicine, and University of Toronto Faculty of Medicine have shown remarkable productivity and solid citations. The findings reinforce the fact that quality of research is to be prioritized over quantity.

Table 8. Keyword

Occurrences	%	Keyword
12688	33.0133	Artificial intelligence
5356	13.93594	Human
4334	11.27677	Article
4235	11.01918	Education
3967	10.32186	Humans
2071	5.388598	ChatGPT
2070	5.385996	Female
1938	5.042542	Male
1774	4.615825	Medical education
1724	4.485728	Adult

Source: Developed by Authors

Table 8 indicates that Artificial Intelligence has been mentioned 12,688 times, dominating the focus. Terms like Human (5,356) and Humans (3,967) show a strong people-centric perspective. Article (4,334) signifies a scholarly focus, while Education (4,235) and medical education (1,774) demonstrate AI's relevance to learning and training in the health profession. Interest in particular AI applications is shown through ChatGPT (2,071). AI is often discussed alongside demographics with the terms Female (2,070), Male (1,938), and Adult (1,724) indicating a focus on gender and age. AI is predominantly discussed in relation to humans and education.

Figure 2. Word cloud

Source: *Developed by Authors*

Figure 3. Co authorship network

Source: *Developed by Authors*

The VOSviewer co authorship network presented as figure 3 shows the co authorship network of 15 authors divided in 3 clusters who have established 27 co authorship links with a total link strength of 44, which reflects a moderate level of research collaboration. The largest cluster, (red) has a greater number of connections than the others in the co authorship network, signifying the majority of authors in this cluster have a more significant role than the authors in the other clusters. This is especially true for Wayne Holmes, who is positioned as the most dominant collaborator in this cluster, which suggests that Holmes has contributed significantly to the co authorship of the research most related to artificial intelligence in education, learning analytics, and innovative pedagogy. Other authors in this cluster, Koedinger, Santos, Boticarío, Kukurova, Riienties, Järvelä, and Gašević, have very strong and substantial links to one another. The second cluster (green) is the first cluster that illustrates the bridging role within the core and periphery of this network. From this perspective, Ahmed Tlili and Aras Bozkurt are the most significant authors in this cluster. In many cases, this cluster is characterized by interdisciplinary, and cross-regional collaboration, especially related to open education, digital education, and education policy. The third cluster (blue) is more specialized and smaller than the other two, comprising Guerrero Roldán, Rodríguez González, and Bañeres, which illustrates the strongest ties to one another in this cluster, but weaker ties to others, which reflects a more concentrated area of research in educational technology. The network demonstrates a mature and evolving field with a strong direction, thematic leadership, and significant knowledge flows in cross-cluster exchange.

Figure 4. Thematic analysis

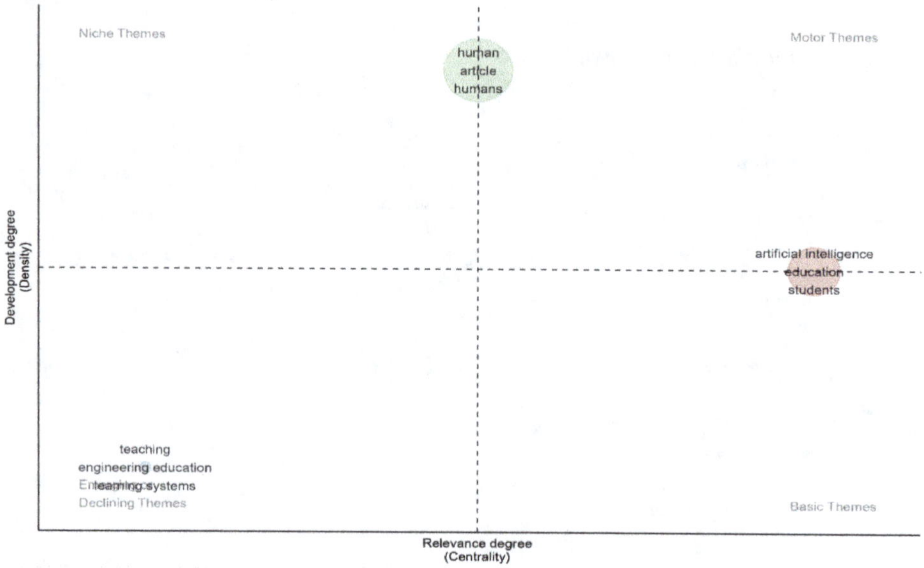

Figure 5. Cluster analysis

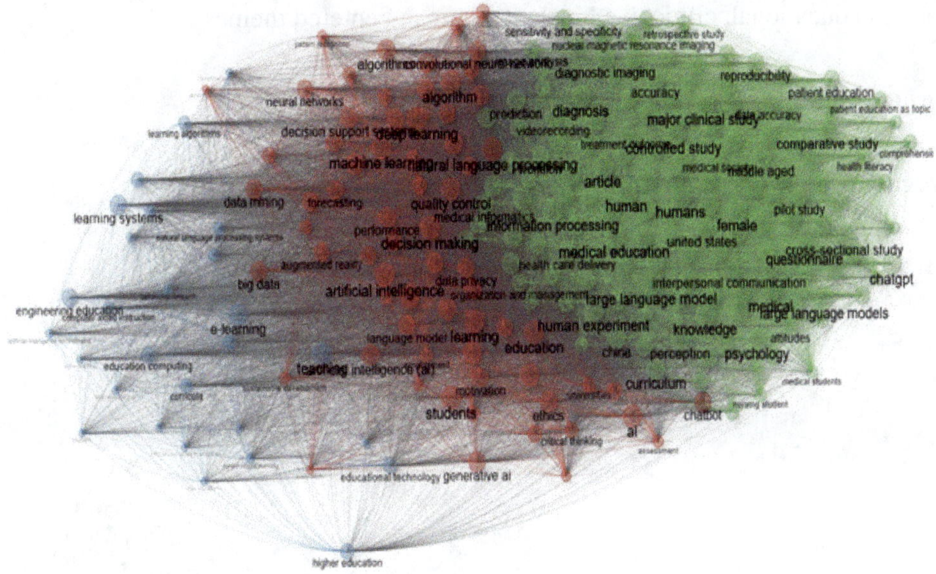

Source: *Developed by Authors*

Figures 4 and 5 present the results of thematic and cluster analyses, respectively, the results of which provide an overall well-structured and clear landscape of AI research that can be differentiated by strategic themes by quadrant, and dissected by centrality (relevance) and density (development). The motor theme quadrant is primarily made up of artificial intelligence, education, and students, which means that these topics are especially central and well developed, driving the core research agenda and serving as the primary engines of scholarly output. To this end, the large green thematic cluster which encompasses humans, medical education, large language models, ChatGPT, diagnostic accuracy, questionnaires, clinical studies, etc. conveys an impressive array of rapidly growing and methodologically sophisticated empirical and applied work at the intersection of AI, healthcare, and education. The basic themes quadrant comprises the more foundational high-human, high-article, high-human, high-education-, and education- concepts, which are highly central but less dense, suggesting that these trends are undersubscribed relative to their importance. By a margin of contrast, the so-called declining or emerging themes quadrant demonstrates the extent to which teaching, engineering education, learning systems, and e learning are concerned over an apparent relative decline in research attention focused on them, or a transition toward integration with newer AI paradigms (e.g., generative AI and decision support systems). The restricted number of niche themes indicates less fragmented research strands and greater thematic cohesion. The thematic structure shows a transition from conventional educational technologies to more sophisticated AI applications. There is a notable convergence across educational, clinical, ethical, and human-centered themes.

AUTHOR CO CITATION NETWORKS

Figure 6. Co citation networks

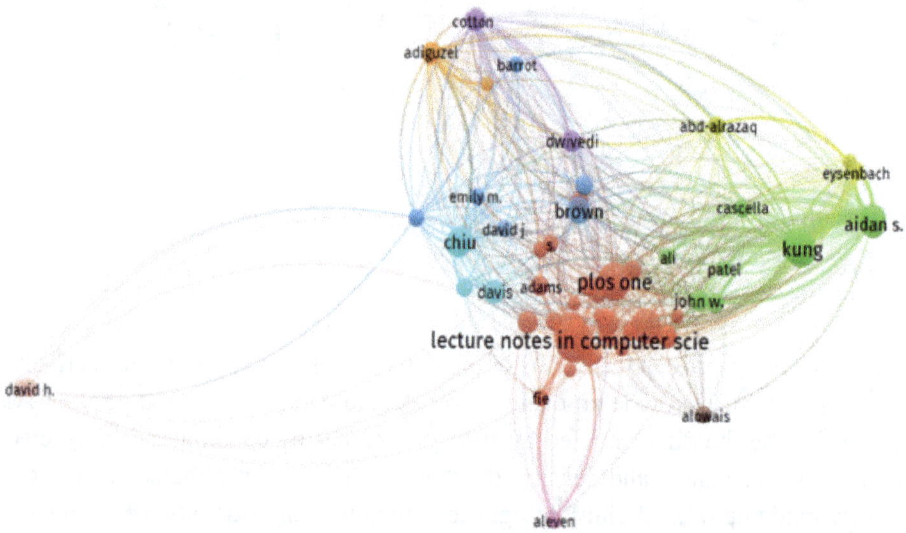

Source: *Developed by Authors*

Figure 6 illustrates a VOSviewer citation network visualization where the author level data set with the 50 citation minimum hit the 75 highly cited items threshold from 29,685 authors. The visualization shows a highly complex, dense, and scholarly structure described by 10 clusters, 1,031 links, and a very high total link strength of 5,664 which suggests an influential and highly connected structure of knowledge. The visualization indicates the presence of a number of central publications above the individual author level, with significant central and unique publication sources being Lecture Notes in Computer Science and PLOS ONE. The visualization shows the significant and central role of these venues as publishers of interdisciplinary research in AI and educational research in computer science. The strong link clusters around the central hubs show key authors and venues as Kung, Aidan S, Cascella,

Eysenbach, Brown, Dwivedi, Chiu, and David J. and demonstrate high citation and co-citation counts in their research. The green and yellow clusters, led by Kung and Eysenbach, demonstrate strong connections in the domains of health informatics, digital technologies, and widespread applied AI, while the red cluster led by Lecture Notes in Computer Science shows a significant foundational and conference scholarship. Some of the smaller peripheral nodes, like David H. and Aleven, show fewer but significant connections, suggesting specialized roles.

FINDINGS

The findings illustrate that impact in the field is largely determined by thematically central and well-developed areas instead of volume. At the document level, studies set in motor themes, and in particular the ones related to AI in education, students, medical education, LLMs, and ChatGPT, receive the most scholarly attention. These themes tend to be both highly relevant and methodologically mature, which means that studies that tackle real-world problems in education and healthcare with empirical evidence and an interdisciplinary approach receive the most attention and have the highest citation impact. The focus on human, clinical, and educational applications further indicates the movement away from technical AI research to studies that are socially relevant and focused on applications.

At the level of authors, the findings show that a relatively small number of leading scholars have an outsized influence on the field's intellectual landscape. Thomas K. F. Chiu and Ching Sing Chai, for instance, are prominent features of key thematic clusters, which indicates substantial scholarly impact and persistence. The analysis reveals that high impact in citations is not always caused by high productivity; in fact, several authors have significantly impactful citations from less publications, provided these publications are clearly articulated and central to the theme.

At the source, country, and institutional levels, the results reaffirm that quality, reputation, and collaboration are more important than quantity of publications. High impact journals e.g. Nature, demonstrate high citation rates despite low publication rates, and journals such as Sustainability and IEEE Access exhibit high citation rates and high publication rates. The United States is by far the leader in both citations and documents, followed by China and the United Kingdom. Stanford University and Harvard Medical School lead in citation impact, illustrating the importance of the quality of research and the quality of the institution in determining the influence of research.

9. FUTURE DIRECTIONS OF AI IN EDUCATION

The future of Artificial Intelligence in education relies on technology, pedagogy, and ethics coming together. The educational approaches of AI technology including generative and adaptive AI, will enhance educational teaching and learning by integrating individualized learning to allow personal, competency based education. Concomitantly innovative frameworks of Human and AI cooperation will view AI as an educator's design, evaluate, and integrate assistant, and not as a replacer of human decisions. Furthermore, AI will reshape evaluation through ongoing constructive feedback and genuine assessment methods. The implications surrounding bias, transparency, and accountability will continue to be an important concern. The future of AI in education will rely on policies and ethical principles on AI that protect privacy, fairness and transparency and explainable AI. To get the right AI in education system to protect the right of a society, and to improve the quality of education, a multi stakeholder system will be essential.

Table 9. Future research directions of AI in education

Theme	Key Focus Areas	Implications for Education
Generative & Adaptive AI	Generative AI for content creation, lesson planning, feedback; adaptive systems using real time learner data; personalized and competency based models	Enables individualized learning paths, flexible pacing, and mastery based progression; requires strong governance to ensure quality, equity, and standardization
Augmented Intelligence	Teacher–AI partnerships; AI as instructional and administrative support; focus on mentorship and socio emotional learning	Reduces administrative workload; enhances instructional quality; reinforces human agency by prioritizing augmentation over automation
Intelligent Assessment Systems	Continuous and formative assessment; process based evaluation; simulations and project based learning	Improves feedback quality and authenticity of assessment; raises concerns about bias, transparency, fairness, and accountability
Governance & Ethics	Bias mitigation, explainability, data privacy, regulatory frameworks, multi stakeholder involvement	Ensures ethical, transparent, and socially aligned AI adoption; safeguards learner data and institutional trust

Source: Developed by Authors

IMPLICATIONS

The implications of artificial intelligence involve educators, institutions, policy makers, and researchers, showing the need for unified and responsible implementation. For some educators, AI means the opportunity to redesign a curriculum and a set of teaching practices to advance, individualize, and support inquiry and collaboration. However, this also means teaching staff will need to develop a set of new skills known as AI Literacy, that will allow for a critical analysis of AI, and will foster the ethical and responsible use of AI for teaching practice. To that end, professor training (both induction and continual) will need to include training to develop innovative teaching practices, including instruction and the pedagogy of the content, as well as practice ethics. At the institutional and policy levels, innovation and ethics will need to be supported by investment in distributed digital infrastructure, system development, and the regulation of data privacy. The application of AI to research on the education system will create significant research opportunities across disciplines, including cultural, educational, and human–AI collaborations. The growth of this field will be the result of intergovernmental collaboration across educational disciplines, computer science, ethics, and the social sciences to generate systematic and evidence-based research.

CONCLUSION

This chapter has analyzed the prospects of AI within the educational sector by using a conceptual and future driven approach to complement a large scale bibliometric study. From the findings, the author states that the true nature of AI's transformative potential lies not within automation but rather within the possibility of AI supporting human centered, ethical and inclusive educational approaches. AI has the potential to advance the future of education by joining the technological innovation and pedagogy and governance framework. Ultimately, the future of AI in education hinges on the collective decisions of teachers, educational institutions, policymakers, and researchers. The thoughtful design, responsible use, and ongoing research/adquisition will establish a capacity to ensure that AI is a means of tackling new issues rather than a means of reinforcing existing issues. Ideas in this chapter are meant to guide the former and to support a more thoughtful and responsible use of AI in education.

LIMITATIONS OF THE CHAPTER

Although the findings of this chapter are impressive, there are still certain limitations regarding the presentation of the findings of this chapter that warrant recognition. The bibliometric analysis assesses solely studies in the Scopus database, leaving out possible studies in other major citation databases like the Web of Science (WoS), and in addition, there is a lack of integrations or merges, leading to possible omissions of pertinent studies in other databases. Besides, there is the absence of any quality stratification of the journals or citation ranking and journal ranking based filters such as the Q1 quartile, the A* or A rank, the FT50 lists, and other similar journal elitist indicators. In contrast, all of the eligible peer reviewed articles that satisfied the inclusion criteria were treated equally. While this type of inclusion positively reduces selection bias and captures the broadest possible intellectual landscape, it also greatly reduces the ability to differentiate the findings based on the level of prestige of the journal or the quality tier. Citation-based measures also tend to favor older publications, leading to an underestimation of the impact of more recent publications, especially in rapidly changing domains such as generative AI and large language models. The chapter also takes a conceptual and bibliometric synthesis of the data, and does not include any primary empirical data, leaving a possibility of conducting future research in the area by utilizing other data bases and mixed method research designs.

REFERENCES

Aldriye, H., Alkhalaf, A., & Alkhalaf, M. (2019). Automated grading systems for programming assignments: A literature review. *International Journal of Advanced Computer Science and Applications, 10*(3). Advance online publication. DOI: 10.14569/IJACSA.2019.0100328

Bansal, G., Chamola, V., Hussain, A., Guizani, M., & Niyato, D. (2024). Transforming conversations with AI—A comprehensive study of ChatGPT. *Cognitive Computation, 16*(5), 2487–2510. DOI: 10.1007/s12559-023-10236-2

Bidry, M., Hanine, M., Ouaguid, A., & Obidallah, W. J. (2025). Transforming Education With Generative AI: A Comprehensive Review of Advancements, Challenges, and Future Opportunities. *IEEE Access : Practical Innovations, Open Solutions, 13*, 202938–202955. DOI: 10.1109/ACCESS.2025.3636891

Calegari, R., Ciatto, G., Denti, E., & Omicini, A. (2020). Logic-based technologies for intelligent systems: State of the art and perspectives. *Information (Basel), 11*(3), 167. DOI: 10.3390/info11030167

Chen, J., Liu, Z., Huang, X., Wu, C., Liu, Q., Jiang, G., Pu, Y., Lei, Y., Chen, X., Wang, X., Zheng, K., Lian, D., & Chen, E. (2024). When large language models meet personalization: Perspectives of challenges and opportunities. *World Wide Web (Bussum), 27*(4), 42. DOI: 10.1007/s11280-024-01276-1

Chen, L., Chen, P., & Lin, Z. (2020). Artificial intelligence in education: A review. *IEEE Access : Practical Innovations, Open Solutions, 8*, 75264–75278. DOI: 10.1109/ACCESS.2020.2988510

Confalonieri, R., Coba, L., Wagner, B., & Besold, T. R. (2021). A historical perspective of explainable artificial intelligence. *Wiley Interdisciplinary Reviews. Data Mining and Knowledge Discovery, 11*(1), e1391. DOI: 10.1002/widm.1391

Cope, B., Kalantzis, M., & Searsmith, D. (2021). Artificial intelligence for education: Knowledge and its assessment in AI-enabled learning ecologies. *Educational Philosophy and Theory, 53*(12), 1229–1245. DOI: 10.1080/00131857.2020.1728732

Dai, R., Thomas, M. K. E., & Rawolle, S. (2025). The roles of AI and educational leaders in AI-assisted administrative decision-making: A proposed framework for symbiotic collaboration. *Australian Educational Researcher, 52*(2), 1471–1487. DOI: 10.1007/s13384-024-00771-8

Dunleavy, P., & Margetts, H. (2025). Data science, artificial intelligence and the third wave of digital era governance. *Public Policy and Administration*, *40*(2), 185–214. DOI: 10.1177/09520767231198737

Elamin, M. O. I. (2024). AI through the ages: Unlocking key opportunities and navigating challenges in the history and future of artificial intelligence. *International Journal of Religion*, *5*(12), 1152–1166. DOI: 10.61707/tarzcj89

George, B., & Wooden, O. (2023). Managing the strategic transformation of higher education through artificial intelligence. *Administrative Sciences*, *13*(9), 196. DOI: 10.3390/admsci13090196

Hosseini Tabaghdehi, S. A., & Ayaz, Ö. (2025). AI ethics in action: A circular model for transparency, accountability and inclusivity. *Journal of Managerial Psychology*. Advance online publication. DOI: 10.1108/JMP-03-2024-0177

Jordan, M. I., & Mitchell, T. M. (2015). Machine learning: Trends, perspectives, and prospects. *Science*, *349*(6245), 255–260. DOI: 10.1126/science.aaa8415 PMID: 26185243

Korteling, J. E., van de Boer-Visschedijk, G. C., Blankendaal, R. A., Boonekamp, R. C., & Eikelboom, A. R. (2021). Human-versus artificial intelligence. *Frontiers in Artificial Intelligence*, *4*, 622364. DOI: 10.3389/frai.2021.622364 PMID: 33981990

Lang, Q., Wang, M., Yin, M., Liang, S., & Song, W. (2025). Transforming education with generative AI (GAI): Key insights and future prospects. *IEEE Transactions on Learning Technologies*, *18*, 230–242. DOI: 10.1109/TLT.2025.3537618

Luckin, R., & Cukurova, M. (2019). Designing educational technologies in the age of AI: A learning sciences-driven approach. *British Journal of Educational Technology*, *50*(6), 2824–2838. DOI: 10.1111/bjet.12861

Mundlamuri, R., Gunnam, G. R., Mysari, N. K., & Pujuri, J. (2025). The Evolution of AI: From Classical Machine Learning to Modern Large Language Models. *IEEE Access : Practical Innovations, Open Solutions*, *13*, 178302–178341. DOI: 10.1109/ACCESS.2025.3621344

Pratschke, B. M. (2024). *Generative AI and education: Digital pedagogies, teaching innovation and learning design*. Springer Nature. DOI: 10.1007/978-3-031-67991-9

Ramos, L. T., & Casas, E. (2025). Applications, trends, and perspectives of large language models in education: A literature review. *Authorea Preprints*. DOI: 10.36227/techrxiv.176413429.91587404/v1

Ryan, M. (2025). We're only human after all: A critique of human-centred AI. *AI & Society*, *40*(3), 1303–1319. DOI: 10.1007/s00146-024-01976-2 PMID: 40225308

Schmager, S., Pappas, I. O., & Vassilakopoulou, P. (2025). Understanding Human-Centred AI: A review of its defining elements and a research agenda. *Behaviour & Information Technology*, *44*(15), 1–40. DOI: 10.1080/0144929X.2024.2448719

Singh, T. M., Reddy, C. K. K., Murthy, B. R., Nag, A., & Doss, S. (2025). Ai and education: Bridging the gap to personalized, efficient, and accessible learning. In *Internet of behavior-based computational intelligence for smart education systems* (pp. 131–160). IGI Global.

Slimi, Z., & Carballido, B. V. (2023). Navigating the Ethical Challenges of Artificial Intelligence in Higher Education: An Analysis of Seven Global AI Ethics Policies. *TEM journal, 12*(2).

Strielkowski, W., Grebennikova, V., Lisovskiy, A., Rakhimova, G., & Vasileva, T. (2025). AI-driven adaptive learning for sustainable educational transformation. *Sustainable Development (Bradford)*, *33*(2), 1921–1947. DOI: 10.1002/sd.3221

Strielkowski, W., Vlasov, A., Selivanov, K., Muraviev, K., & Shakhnov, V. (2023). Prospects and challenges of the machine learning and data-driven methods for the predictive analysis of power systems: A review. *Energies*, *16*(10), 4025. DOI: 10.3390/en16104025

Yadav, S. (2025). Reimagining education with advanced technologies: transformative pedagogical shifts driven by artificial intelligence. In *Impacts of Generative AI on the Future of Research and Education* (pp. 1–26). IGI Global.

Compilation of References

Abdelkader, A. A. M., Hassan, H., & Abdelkader, M. (2024). The role of artificial intelligence in designing higher education courses: Benefits and challenges. In Lytras, M. D., Alkhaldi, A., Malik, S., Serban, A. C., & Aldosemani, T. (Eds.), *The evolution of artificial intelligence in higher education* (pp. 83–97). Emerald Publishing Limited., DOI: 10.1108/978-1-83549-486-820241005

About Bahrain Polytechnic. (n.d.). *Bahrain Polytechnic*. https://www.polytechnic.bh/about-us/

Abulibdeh, A., Zaidan, E., & Abulibdeh, R. (2024). Navigating the confluence of artificial intelligence and education for sustainable development in the era of industry 4.0: Challenges, opportunities, and ethical dimensions. *Journal of Cleaner Production, 437*, 140527. DOI: 10.1016/j.jclepro.2023.140527

Adamakis, M., & Rachiotis, T. (2025). *Artificial Intelligence in Higher Education: A State-of-the-Art Overview of Pedagogical Integrity*. Artificial Intelligence Literacy, and Policy Integration., DOI: 10.3390/encyclopedia5040180

Adetayo, A. J. (2023). Artificial intelligence chatbots in academic libraries: The rise of ChatGPT. *Library Hi Tech News, 40*(3), 18–21. DOI: 10.1108/LHTN-01-2023-0007

Adewale, M. D., Azeta, A., Abayomi-Alli, A., & Sambo-Magaji, A. (2024). Impact of artificial intelligence adoption on students' academic performance in open and distance learning: A systematic literature review. *Heliyon, 10*(22), e40025. Advance online publication. DOI: 10.1016/j.heliyon.2024.e40025 PMID: 39605813

Agrawal, G. (2024). Accountability, trust, and transparency in AI systems from the perspective of public policy: Elevating ethical standards. In *AI healthcare applications and security, ethical, and legal considerations* (pp. 148–162). IGI Global. DOI: 10.4018/979-8-3693-7452-8.ch009

Akbar, M. A., Khan, A. A., Mahmood, S., Rafi, S., & Demi, S. (2024). Trustworthy artificial intelligence: A decision-making taxonomy of potential challenges. *Software, Practice & Experience*, *54*(9), 1621–1650. DOI: 10.1002/spe.3216

Akgun, S., & Greenhow, C. (2022). Artificial intelligence in education: Addressing ethical challenges in K-12 settings. *AI and Ethics*, *2*(3), 431–440. DOI: 10.1007/s43681-021-00096-7 PMID: 34790956

Akhtar, M. A. K., Kumar, M., & Nayyar, A. (2024). Transparency and accountability in explainable AI: Best practices. In *Towards ethical and socially responsible explainable ai: Challenges and opportunities* (pp. 127–164). Springer Nature Switzerland. DOI: 10.1007/978-3-031-66489-2_5

Akhter, E., & Zaman, M. A. U. (2024). Automated essay scoring and feedback systems for ESL learners: A meta-review of pedagogical impact. *American Journal of Interdisciplinary Studies*, *5*(1), 31–65. DOI: 10.63125/brzv3333

Akinrinola, O., Okoye, C. C., Ofodile, O. C., & Ugochukwu, C. E. (2024). Navigating and reviewing ethical dilemmas in AI development: Strategies for transparency, fairness, and accountability. *GSC Advanced Research and Reviews*, 18(3), 050-058. DOI: 10.30574/gscarr.2024.18.3.0088

Al Fraidan, A. (2025). Procedural Transparency and Legal Accountability to Sustain AI-Mediated Language Assessment in Saudi Arabia. *SAGE Open*, *15*(4), 21582440251396113. DOI: 10.1177/21582440251396113

Alam, A. (2023). Developing a curriculum for ethical and responsible AI: A university course on safety, fairness, privacy, and ethics to prepare next generation of AI professionals. In *Intelligent communication technologies and virtual mobile networks* (pp. 879–894). Springer Nature Singapore. DOI: 10.1007/978-981-99-1767-9_64

Aldriye, H., Alkhalaf, A., & Alkhalaf, M. (2019). Automated grading systems for programming assignments: A literature review. *International Journal of Advanced Computer Science and Applications*, *10*(3). Advance online publication. DOI: 10.14569/IJACSA.2019.0100328

Aler Tubella, A., Mora-Cantallops, M., & Nieves, J. C. (2024). How to teach responsible AI in Higher Education: Challenges and opportunities. *Ethics and Information Technology*, *26*(1), 3. DOI: 10.1007/s10676-023-09733-7

Aleven, V., McLaughlin, E. A., Glenn, R. A., & Koedinger, K. R. (2016). Instruction based on adaptive learning technologies. In Mayer, R. E., & Alexander, P. A. (Eds.), *Handbook of research on learning and instruction* (2nd ed., pp. 522–560). Routledge.

Ali, S. I., Albadoo, S. F., & Al Mubarak, M. (2025). Ethical Ramifications and Remedial Approaches on Bias in Artificial Intelligence. In *Sustainable Digital Technology and Ethics in an Ever-Changing Environment* (Vol. 2, pp. 95–108). Springer Nature Switzerland. DOI: 10.1007/978-3-031-86708-8_8

Alonso-Rodríguez, A. M. (2024). Towards an ethical framework for artificial intelligence in education. *Teoría de la Educación. Revista Interuniversitaria, 36*(1), 31821. Advance online publication. DOI: 10.14201/teri.31821

Alshalan, A. (2025). Bridging the divide: Saussurean structure and Derridean complexity in ChatGPT's meaning-making. *Arab World English Journal (AWEJ). Special Issue on Artificial Intelligence*, *5*(1), 81–95. DOI: 10.24093/awej/AI.5

Alvarez, J. M., Colmenarejo, A. B., Elobaid, A., Fabbrizzi, S., Fahimi, M., Ferrara, A., Ghodsi, S., Mougan, C., Papageorgiou, I., Reyero, P., Russo, M., Scott, K. M., State, L., Zhao, X., & Ruggieri, S. (2024). Policy advice and best practices on bias and fairness in AI. *Ethics and Information Technology*, *26*(2), 31. DOI: 10.1007/s10676-024-09746-w

Alwaqdani, M. (2024). Investigating teachers' perceptions of artificial intelligence tools in education: Potential and difficulties. *Education and Information Technologies*. Advance online publication. DOI: 10.1007/s10639-024-12903-9

Al-Zahrani, A. M., & Alasmari, T. M. (2024). Exploring the impact of artificial intelligence on higher education: The dynamics of ethical, social, and educational implications. *Humanities & Social Sciences Communications*, *11*(1), 912. DOI: 10.1057/s41599-024-03432-4

Anderson, J. R., Corbett, A. T., Koedinger, K. R., & Pelletier, R. (1995). Cognitive tutors: Lessons learned. *Journal of the Learning Sciences*, *4*(2), 167–207. DOI: 10.1207/s15327809jls0402_2

Anderson, T., & Dron, J. (2011). Three generations of distance education pedagogy. *International Review of Research in Open and Distance Learning*, *12*(3), 80–97. DOI: 10.19173/irrodl.v12i3.890

Anwar, N., Rahaman, R., Widodo, A. M., Sekti, B. A., Erzed, N., Santiago Tangkudung, R. R., . . . Budhisantosa, N. (2025). Sustainable cybersecurity in the AI era: Innovations in green computing and security. In *Sustainable Information Security in the Age of AI and Green Computing* (pp. 603–620). DOI: 10.4018/979-8-3693-8034-5.ch030

Association of Southeast Asian Nations. (2024). *ASEAN guide on AI governance and ethics*. ASEAN Secretariat.

Association of Southeast Asian Nations. (2025). *Expanded ASEAN guide on generative AI governance and ethics*. ASEAN Secretariat.

Awashreh, R. (2025a). Leadership strategies for managing change and fostering innovation over private higher education: Academic institutions in Oman. In R. Awashreh, *Evolving strategies for organizational management and performance evaluation* (pp. 399–422). IGI Global. DOI: 10.4018/979-8-3373-0149-5.ch018

Awashreh, R. (2025b). Managing business continuity and resilience in higher education institutions without compromising the quality of education. In R. Awashreh, *Enhancing resilience in business continuity management* (pp. 295–326). IGI Global. DOI: 10.4018/979-8-3693-8809-9.ch010

Awashreh, R. (2026). Advancing innovative entrepreneurship in higher education: Suggested framework. In R. Awashreh, *Sustainable innovation in the Middle East and North Africa (MENA) region* (pp. 121–154). IGI Global. DOI: 10.4018/979-8-3373-0908-8.ch005

Awashreh, R., & Almi, H. (2026). Do universities need rankings?: Rethinking biases, transparency, and alternative models. In R. Awashreh & H. Almi, *Influence of university rankings on institutions: Ethics, controversies, and competition* (pp. 1–32). IGI Global. DOI: 10.4018/979-8-3373-7518-2.ch001

Awashreh, R., & Hassiba, A. (2025b). Democratizing personalized learning through mentorship reform in private higher education. In R. Awashreh, *Democratizing education with AI and the future of personalized learning* (pp. 207–236). IGI Global. DOI: 10.4018/979-8-3373-2302-2.ch007

Awashreh, R. (2024a). Omani private universities: Debates between progress in human development but weak education quality. *The International Journal of Educational Organization and Leadership*, *32*(1), 1–15. DOI: 10.18848/2329-1656/CGP/v32i01/1-15

Awashreh, R. (2024b). Be aware: Navigating challenges in AI-driven higher education. *The International Journal of Interdisciplinary Educational Studies*, *20*(1), 203–218. DOI: 10.18848/2327-011X/CGP/v20i01/203-218

Awashreh, R. (2025c). Navigating leadership dynamics: Insights and strategies across domains. In *Optimizing leadership and governance in higher education* (pp. 203–232). IGI Global., DOI: 10.4018/979-8-3693-3534-5.ch010

Awashreh, R., & Al Ghunaimi, H. (2025). Rethinking the PhD: Aligning higher education with market needs and practical skills. *Forum for Linguistic Studies*, *7*(2), 254–264. DOI: 10.30564/fls.v7i2.7942

Awashreh, R., & Hassiba, A. (2025a). Revolutionizing education with AI: Personalized learning, predictive analytics, and gamification. In *Insights into digital business, human resource management, and competitiveness* (pp. 149–170). IGI Global., DOI: 10.4018/979-8-3693-9440-3.ch006

Awashreh, R., & Mohamed, Y. (2024). Comparative study of leadership perceptions in government and education sectors: Insights from the UAE and Oman. *The International Journal of Organizational Diversity*, *24*(2), 109–123. DOI: 10.18848/2328-6261/CGP/v24i02/109-123

Azzam, A., & Charles, T. (2024). A review of artificial intelligence in K-12 education. *Open Journal of Applied Sciences*, *14*(8), 2088–2100. DOI: 10.4236/ojapps.2024.148137

Baidoo-Anu, D., & Ansah, L. O. (2023). Education in the era of generative artificial intelligence (AI): Understanding the potential benefits of ChatGPT in promoting teaching and learning. *Journal of AI*, *7*(1), 52–62. DOI: 10.61969/jai.1337500

Baker, R. S. (2016). Stupid tutoring systems, intelligent humans. *International Journal of Artificial Intelligence in Education*, *26*(2), 600–614. DOI: 10.1007/s40593-016-0105-0

Baker, R. S., D'Mello, S. K., Rodrigo, M. M. T., & Graesser, A. C. (2010). Better to be frustrated than bored: The incidence, persistence, and impact of learners' cognitive-affective states during interactions with three different computer-based learning environments. *International Journal of Human-Computer Studies*, *68*(4), 223–241. DOI: 10.1016/j.ijhcs.2009.12.003

Baker, R. S., & Hawn, A. (2021). Algorithmic bias in education. *International Journal of Artificial Intelligence in Education*, *31*(4), 1052–1092. DOI: 10.1007/s40593-021-00285-9

Baker, R. S., & Inventado, P. S. (2014). Educational data mining and learning analytics. In *Handbook of Educational Psychology* (pp. 600–620). Routledge.

Baker, R. S., & Inventado, P. S. (2014). Educational data mining and learning analytics. In Larusson, J. A., & White, B. (Eds.), *Learning analytics: From research to practice* (pp. 61–75). Springer., DOI: 10.1007/978-1-4614-3305-7_4

Banihashem, S. K. B., Kerman, N. T., Noroozi, O., Moon, J., & Drachsler, H. (2024). Feedback sources in essay writing: Peer-generated or AI-generated feedback? *International Journal of Educational Technology in Higher Education*, *21*(1), 23. Advance online publication. DOI: 10.1186/s41239-024-00455-4

Bansal, G., Chamola, V., Hussain, A., Guizani, M., & Niyato, D. (2024). Transforming conversations with AI—A comprehensive study of ChatGPT. *Cognitive Computation, 16*(5), 2487–2510. DOI: 10.1007/s12559-023-10236-2

Barocas, S., & Selbst, A. D. (2016). Big data's disparate impact. *California Law Review, 104*(3), 671–732.

Bayne, S. (2015). What is the matter with 'technology-enhanced learning'? *Learning, Media and Technology, 40*(1), 5–20. DOI: 10.1080/17439884.2014.915851

Bearman, M., Dawson, P., Ajjawi, R., Tai, J., & Boud, D. (2022). Reconsidering assessment for learning in a digital age. *Assessment & Evaluation in Higher Education, 47*(1), 1–14.

Beetham, H., & Sharpe, R. (Eds.). (2019). *Rethinking pedagogy for a digital age: Principles and practices of design* (3rd ed.). Routledge., DOI: 10.4324/9781351252805

Berry, A. (2007). *Tensions in teaching about teaching: Understanding practice as a teacher educator* (Vol. 5). Springer Science & Business Media.

Bidry, M., Hanine, M., Ouaguid, A., & Obidallah, W. J. (2025). Transforming Education With Generative AI: A Comprehensive Review of Advancements, Challenges, and Future Opportunities. *IEEE Access : Practical Innovations, Open Solutions, 13*, 202938–202955. DOI: 10.1109/ACCESS.2025.3636891

Biesta, G. (2010). *Good education in an age of measurement.* Paradigm.

Bilki, Z., Satar, M., & Sak, M. (2023). Critical digital literacy in virtual exchange for ELT teacher education: An interpretivist methodology. *ReCALL, 35*(1), 58–73. DOI: 10.1017/S095834402200009X

Black, P., & Wiliam, D. (1998). Assessment and classroom learning. *Assessment in Education: Principles, Policy & Practice, 5*(1), 7–74. DOI: 10.1080/0969595980050102

Black, P., & Wiliam, D. (2009). Developing the theory of formative assessment. *Educational Assessment, Evaluation and Accountability, 21*(1), 5–31. DOI: 10.1007/s11092-008-9068-5

Bloom, B. S. (1968). Learning for mastery. *Evaluation Comment, 1*(2), 1–12.

Bogina, V., Hartman, A., Kuflik, T., & Shulner-Tal, A. (2022). Educating software and AI stakeholders about algorithmic fairness, accountability, transparency and ethics. *International Journal of Artificial Intelligence in Education, 32*(3), 808–833. DOI: 10.1007/s40593-021-00248-0

Bond, M., Zawacki-Richter, O., & Perez-Sanagustin, M. (2024). A meta systematic review of AI in higher education. *International Journal of Educational Technology in Higher Education, 21*(1), 20. DOI: 10.1186/s41239-023-00436-z

Boud, D., & Falchikov, N. (2007). *Rethinking assessment in higher education. Routledge. Boud, D., & Falchikov, N. (2007). Rethinking assessment in higher education*. Routledge.

Boud, D., & Molloy, E. (2013). Rethinking models of feedback for learning. *Assessment & Evaluation in Higher Education, 38*(6), 698–712. DOI: 10.1080/02602938.2012.691462

Bourdieu, P. (1986). The forms of capital. In J. Richardson (Ed.), *Handbook of theory and research for the sociology of education* (pp. 241–258). Greenwood.

Bourdieu, P., & Passeron, J. C. (1990). *Reproduction in education, society and culture* (Vol. 4). Sage.

Bower, M. (2019). Can virtual reality experiences support learning? *Research in Learning Technology, 27*(1), 21545.

Bower, M., & Vlachopoulos, P. (2018). A critical analysis of technology-enhanced learning design frameworks. *British Journal of Educational Technology, 49*(6), 981–997. DOI: 10.1111/bjet.12668

Brandão, A., Pedro, L., & Zagalo, N. (2024). Teacher Professional Development for a Future with Generative Artificial Intelligence—An Integrative Literature Review. *Digital Education Review, 45*(45), 151–157. DOI: 10.1344/der.2024.45.151-157

Bucholc, M., Komornik, Ł., & Piasna, A. (2022). The world algorithmic order: Data, platforms, and the global condition. *Big Data & Society, 9*(1), 1–12. DOI: 10.1177/20539517221078981

Bùi, T. T. D., & Tong, T. V. A. (2025). The impact of AI writing tools on academic integrity: Unveiling English-majored students' perceptions and practical solutions. *AsiaCALL Online Journal, 16*(1), 83–110. Advance online publication. DOI: 10.54855/acoj.251615

Calderwood, S. J. (2025). Surveillance Digitisation, Performativity, and Teacher-Student Relationships in a Blended Learning Setting. *Postdigital Science and Education*, 1–25.

Calegari, R., Ciatto, G., Denti, E., & Omicini, A. (2020). Logic-based technologies for intelligent systems: State of the art and perspectives. *Information (Basel), 11*(3), 167. DOI: 10.3390/info11030167

Camilleri, M. A. (2023). Artificial intelligence governance: Ethical considerations and implications for social responsibility. *Expert Systems: International Journal of Knowledge Engineering and Neural Networks.* Advance online publication. DOI: 10.1111/exsy.13406

Cancela-Outeda, C. (2024). The EU's AI act: A framework for collaborative governance. *Internet of Things : Engineering Cyber Physical Human Systems, 27,* 101291. DOI: 10.1016/j.iot.2024.101291

Cao, G., Liang, M., & Li, X. (2018). How to make the library smart? The conceptualization of the smart library. *The Electronic Library, 36*(5), 811–825. DOI: 10.1108/EL-11-2017-0248

Cao, S., & Zhong, L. (2023). Exploring the effectiveness of ChatGPT-based feedback compared with teacher feedback and self-feedback: Evidence from Chinese to English translation. *arXiv*. https://arxiv.org/abs/2309.01645

Carless, D. (2015). *Excellence in university assessment.* Routledge. DOI: 10.4324/9781315740621

Chan, C., & Hu, W. (2023). *Students' voices on generative AI: Perceptions, benefits, and challenges in higher education.* arXiv. https://doi.org//arxiv.2305.00290DOI: 10.48550

Chan, C. K. Y. (2023). A comprehensive AI policy education framework for university teaching and learning. *International Journal of Educational Technology in Higher Education, 20*(1), 38. DOI: 10.1186/s41239-023-00408-3

Charles, K., Yousuf, A., Chow Chua, H., Matthews, S., Harnett, J., & Hinton, T. (2025). AI in action: Changes to student perceptions when using generative artificial intelligence for the creation of a multimedia project-based assessment. *European Journal of Pharmacology, 998,* 177508. Advance online publication. DOI: 10.1016/j.ejphar.2025.177508 PMID: 40086582

Chen, H. (2024). The ethical challenges of educational artificial intelligence and coping measures: A discussion in the context of the 2024 World Digital Education Conference. Science Insights Education Frontiers, 20(2), 3263-3281.

Chen, J., Liu, Z., Huang, X., Wu, C., Liu, Q., Jiang, G., Pu, Y., Lei, Y., Chen, X., Wang, X., Zheng, K., Lian, D., & Chen, E. (2024). When large language models meet personalization: Perspectives of challenges and opportunities. *World Wide Web (Bussum), 27*(4), 42. DOI: 10.1007/s11280-024-01276-1

Chen, L., Chen, P., & Lin, Z. (2020). Artificial intelligence in education: A review. *IEEE Access : Practical Innovations, Open Solutions, 8*, 75264–75278. DOI: 10.1109/ACCESS.2020.2988510

Cheong, B. C. (2024). Transparency and accountability in AI systems: Safeguarding wellbeing in the age of algorithmic decision-making. *Frontiers in Human Dynamics, 6*, 1421273. DOI: 10.3389/fhumd.2024.1421273

Cheong, H.-I., Lyons, A., Houghton, R. W., & Majumdar, A. (2023). Secondary qualitative research methodology using online data within the context of social sciences. *International Journal of Qualitative Methods, 22*(2), 16094069231180160. DOI: 10.1177/16094069231180160

Cobo, C., & Rivera-Vargas, P. (2023). What is 'algorithmic education' and why do education institutions need to consolidate new capacities? In *The new digital education policy landscape* (pp. 210–225). Routledge. DOI: 10.4324/9781003373018-14

Coglianese, C. (2024). Procurement and artificial intelligence. In *Handbook on Public Policy and Artificial Intelligence* (pp. 235–248). Edward Elgar Publishing. DOI: 10.4337/9781803922171.00026

Confalonieri, R., Coba, L., Wagner, B., & Besold, T. R. (2021). A historical perspective of explainable artificial intelligence. *Wiley Interdisciplinary Reviews. Data Mining and Knowledge Discovery, 11*(1), e1391. DOI: 10.1002/widm.1391

Cope, B., Kalantzis, M., & Searsmith, D. (2021). Artificial intelligence for education: Knowledge and its assessment in AI-enabled learning ecologies. *Educational Philosophy and Theory, 53*(12), 1229–1245. DOI: 10.1080/00131857.2020.1728732

Corbett, A. T., & Anderson, J. R. (1995). Knowledge tracing: Modeling the acquisition of procedural knowledge. *User Modeling and User-Adapted Interaction, 4*(4), 253–278. DOI: 10.1007/BF01099821

Cox, A. (2022). How artificial intelligence might change academic library work: Applying the competencies literature and the theory of the professions. *Journal of the Association for Information Science and Technology, 74*(3), 367–380. DOI: 10.1002/asi.24635

Crompton, H., & Burke, D. (2023). Artificial intelligence in higher education: The state of the field. *International Journal of Educational Technology in Higher Education, 20*(1), 1–22. DOI: 10.1186/s41239-023-00392-8

Cummings, M. L. (2017). Automation bias in intelligent time critical decision support systems. In *AIAA Infotech at Aerospace Conference*. DOI: 10.4324/9781315095080-17

Daher, R. (2025). Integrating AI literacy into teacher education: A critical perspective paper. *Discover Artificial Intelligence*, *5*(1), 217. Advance online publication. DOI: 10.1007/s44163-025-00475-7

Dai, R., Thomas, M. K. E., & Rawolle, S. (2025). The roles of AI and educational leaders in AI-assisted administrative decision-making: A proposed framework for symbiotic collaboration. *Australian Educational Researcher*, *52*(2), 1471–1487. DOI: 10.1007/s13384-024-00771-8

Dai, W., Lin, J., Jin, H., Li, T., Tsai, Y. S., Gašević, D., & Chen, G. (2023). Can large language models provide feedback to students? A case study on ChatGPT. In Chen, N.-S. (Eds.), *Proceedings of the 2023 IEEE International Conference on Advanced Learning Technologies (ICALT)* (pp. 323–325). IEEE. DOI: 10.1109/ICALT58122.2023.00100

Darwin, D. R., Mukminatien, N., Suryati, N., & Laksmi, E. D. (2023). Critical thinking in the AI era: An exploration of EFL students' perceptions, benefits, and limitations. *Cogent Education*, *11*(1), 11–18. DOI: 10.1080/2331186X.2023.2290342

David, A., Yigitcanlar, T., Desouza, K., Li, R. Y. M., Cheong, P. H., Mehmood, R., & Corchado, J. (2024). Understanding local government responsible AI strategy: An international municipal policy document analysis. *Cities (London, England)*, *155*, 105502. DOI: 10.1016/j.cities.2024.105502

de Putter-Smits, L. G. A., Pols, C. F. J., Dekkers, P. J. J. M., Runhaar, P. R., Timmer, M., & Van der Veen, J. T. (2025). Exploring the role of generative AI in science teacher education programs: A qualitative study. *International Journal of Educational Research Open*, *9*, 100492. Advance online publication. DOI: 10.1016/j.ijedro.2025.100492

Demartini, C. G., Sciascia, L., Bosso, A., & Manuri, F. (2024). Artificial intelligence bringing improvements to adaptive learning in education: A case study. *Sustainability (Basel)*, *16*(3), 1347. DOI: 10.3390/su16031347

Dieterle, E., Dede, C., & Walker, M. (2024). The cyclical ethical effects of using artificial intelligence in education. *AI & Society*, *39*(2), 633–643. DOI: 10.1007/s00146-022-01497-w PMID: 36185064

Dignum, V. (2019). *Responsible artificial intelligence: How to develop and use AI in a responsible way*. Springer. DOI: 10.1007/978-3-030-30371-6

Dillenbourg, P., Baker, M., Blaye, A., & O'Malley, C. (1996). The evolution of research on collaborative learning. In *Learning in Humans and Machines* (pp. 189–211). Pergamon.

Ding, A. C. E., Shi, L., Yang, H., & Choi, I. (2024). Enhancing teacher AI literacy and integration through different types of cases in teacher professional development. *Computers and Education Open*, *6*, 100178. DOI: 10.1016/j.caeo.2024.100178

Domínguez Figaredo, D., & Stoyanovich, J. (2023). Responsible AI literacy: A stakeholder-first approach. *Big Data & Society*, *10*(2), 20539517231219958. DOI: 10.1177/20539517231219958

Drachsler, H., & Greller, W. (2016). Privacy and analytics: It's a delicate issue a checklist for trusted learning analytics. *Journal of Educational Technology & Society*, *19*(1), 89–99.

du Boulay, B. (2016). Artificial intelligence as an effective classroom assistant. *IEEE Intelligent Systems*, *31*(6), 76–81. DOI: 10.1109/MIS.2016.93

Dunleavy, M., & Dede, C. (2014). Augmented reality teaching and learning. Handbook of Research on Educational Communications and Technology. DOI: 10.1007/978-1-4614-3185-5_59

Dunleavy, P., & Margetts, H. (2025). Data science, artificial intelligence and the third wave of digital era governance. *Public Policy and Administration*, *40*(2), 185–214. DOI: 10.1177/09520767231198737

Dwivedi, Y. K., Kshetri, N., Hughes, L., Slade, E. L., Jeyaraj, A., Kar, A. K., Baabdullah, A. M., Koohang, A., Raghavan, V., Ahuja, M., Albanna, H., Albashrawi, M. A., Al-Busaidi, A. S., Balakrishnan, J., Barlette, Y., Basu, S., Bose, I., Brooks, L., Buhalis, D., & Wright, R. (2023). Opinion paper: "So what if ChatGPT wrote it?" Multidisciplinary perspectives on opportunities, challenges and implications of generative conversational AI for research, practice and policy. *International Journal of Information Management*, *71*, 102642. DOI: 10.1016/j.ijinfomgt.2023.102642

Elamin, M. O. I. (2024). AI through the ages: Unlocking key opportunities and navigating challenges in the history and future of artificial intelligence. *International Journal of Religion*, *5*(12), 1152–1166. DOI: 10.61707/tarzcj89

Eom, Y., Wen, H., & Ashill, N. (2006). Determinants of students' perceived learning outcomes in online education. *Decision Sciences Journal of Innovative Education*, *4*(2), 215–235. DOI: 10.1111/j.1540-4609.2006.00114.x

Escalante, J., Pack, A., & Barrett, A. (2023). AI-generated feedback on writing: Insights into efficacy and ENL student preference. *International Journal of Educational Technology in Higher Education*, *20*(1), 1–20. DOI: 10.1186/s41239-023-00425-2

Eubanks, V. (2018). *Automating inequality: How high-tech tools profile, police, and punish the poor*. St. Martin's Press.

Evenddy, S. S. (2024). Investigating AI's automated feedback in English language learning. *Foreign Language Instruction Probe, 3*(1), 76–87. DOI: 10.54213/flip.v3i1.401

Fagbohun, O., Iduwe, N. P., Abdullahi, M., Ifaturoti, A., & Nwanna, O. M. (2024). Beyond traditional assessment: Exploring the impact of large language models on grading practices. *Journal of Artificial Intelligence. Machine Learning and Data Science, 2*(1), 1–8.

Farahani, M. Sh. (2024). *Artificial intelligence and inequality: Challenges and opportunities*. Qeios., DOI: 10.32388/7HWUZ2

Fassbender, W. J. (2024). "I can almost recognize its voice": AI and its impact on ethical teacher-centaur labor. *English Teaching, 23*(1), 104–117. DOI: 10.1108/ETPC-08-2023-0101

Ferguson, R. (2019). Ethical challenges for learning analytics. *Journal of Learning Analytics, 6*(3), 25–30. DOI: 10.18608/jla.2019.63.5

Filgueiras, F. (2024). Artificial intelligence and education governance. *Education, Citizenship and Social Justice, 19*(3), 349–361. DOI: 10.1177/17461979231160674

Fitria, T. N. (2021). Artificial intelligence (AI) in education: Using AI tools for the teaching and learning process. In *Proceedings of the National Seminar on Educational Technology (PROSENAS)*. STIE AAS Press. https://prosiding.stie-aas.ac.id/index.php/prosenas/article/view/106

Floridi, L., & Cowls, J. (2019). A unified framework of five principles for AI in society. *Harvard Data Science Review, 1*(1).

Floridi, L., Cowls, J., Beltrametti, M., Chatila, R., Chazerand, P., Dignum, V., Luetge, C., Madelin, R., Pagallo, U., Rossi, F., Schafer, B., Valcke, P., & Vayena, E. (2018). AI4People—An ethical framework for a good AI society. *Minds and Machines, 28*(4), 689–707. DOI: 10.1007/s11023-018-9482-5 PMID: 30930541

Freire, P. (1970). *Pedagogy of the oppressed*. Herder and Herder.

Friedman, B., & Hendry, D. G. (2019). *Value sensitive design: Shaping technology with moral imagination*. The MIT Press. DOI: 10.7551/mitpress/7585.001.0001

Fu, Y., & Weng, Z. (2024). Navigating the ethical terrain of AI in education: A systematic review on framing responsible human-centered AI practices. *Computers and Education: Artificial Intelligence, 7*, 100306. DOI: 10.1016/j.caeai.2024.100306

Gaskins, N. (2023). Interrogating algorithmic bias: From speculative fiction to liberatory design. *TechTrends*, *67*(3), 417–425. DOI: 10.1007/s11528-022-00783-0 PMID: 36160677

George, B., & Wooden, O. (2023). Managing the strategic transformation of higher education through artificial intelligence. *Administrative Sciences*, *13*(9), 196. DOI: 10.3390/admsci13090196

Gibbs, G. (2010). *Using assessment to support student learning*. Leeds Met Press.

Gikas, J., & Grant, M. M. (2013). Mobile computing devices in higher education. *The Internet and Higher Education*, *19*, 18–26. DOI: 10.1016/j.iheduc.2013.06.002

Giroux, H. A. (2011). *On critical pedagogy*. Bloomsbury Academic.

Giroux, H. A. (2014). *Neoliberalism's war on higher education*. Haymarket Books.

Goosen, W., & Mugumo, V. P. (2024). A framework for the application of AI in higher education in association with APPETD and Swiss Institute for Management and Innovation. In *Proceedings of the International Conference on Medical Imaging, Electronic Imaging, Information Technologies, and Sensors (MIEITS 2024)*. SPIE. DOI: 10.1117/12.3030740

Gouseti, A., Lakkala, M., Raffaghelli, J., Ranieri, M., Roffi, A., & Ilomäki, L. (2024). Exploring teachers' perceptions of critical digital literacies and how these are manifested in their teaching practices. *Educational Review*, *76*(7), 1751–1785. DOI: 10.1080/00131911.2022.2159933

Graesser, A. C., Hu, X., & Sottilare, R. (2018). Intelligent tutoring systems. In Fischer, F., Hmelo-Silver, C. E., Goldman, S. R., & Reimann, P. (Eds.), *International handbook of the learning sciences* (pp. 246–255). Routledge. DOI: 10.4324/9781315617572-24

Gunning, D., Stefik, M., Choi, J., Miller, T., Stumpf, S., & Yang, G. Z. (2019). XAI: Explainable artificial intelligence. *Science Robotics*, *4*(37), eaay7120. Advance online publication. DOI: 10.1126/scirobotics.aay7120 PMID: 33137719

Guo, K., & Wang, D. (2023). To resist it or to embrace it? Examining ChatGPT's potential to support teacher feedback in EFL writing. *Education and Information Technologies*. Advance online publication. DOI: 10.1007/s10639-023-12146-0

Hamilton, M. L., & Pinnegar, S. (1998). Conclusion: The value and the promise of self-study. In Hamilton, M. L. (Ed.), *Reconceptualising teaching practice: Self-study in teacher education* (pp. 235–246). Falmer Press.

Hamilton, M. L., & Pinnegar, S. (2015). *Self-study of practice as a genre of qualitative research: Theory, methodology, and practice*. Springer.

Hansel, C. A., Ottenbreit-Leftwich, A., Quick, J. D., Greene, A. H., & Ricci, M. (2024). Gradescope in Large Lecture Classrooms: A Case Study at Indiana University: How an online grading platform enhanced student learning and instructor feedback in large-scale courses. *Journal of Teaching and Learning with Technology, 13*(1). Advance online publication. DOI: 10.14434/jotlt.v13i1.38519

Hanshaw, G., & Sullivan, C. (2025). Exploring barriers to AI course assistant adoption: A mixed-methods study on student non-utilization. *Discover Artificial Intelligence, 5*(1), 178. Advance online publication. DOI: 10.1007/s44163-025-00312-x

Henadirage, A., & Gunarathne, N. (2025). Barriers to and opportunities for the adoption of generative artificial intelligence in higher education in the global south: Insights from Sri Lanka. *International Journal of Artificial Intelligence in Education, 35*(1), 245–281. DOI: 10.1007/s40593-024-00439-5

Herane, M. (2024, January 16). AI in education, balancing innovation with ethics. *Higher Education Digest.* Retrieved from https://www.highereducationdigest.com/ai-in-education-balancing-innovation-with-ethics/

Hobert, S., & Meyer von Wolff, R. (2021). Say hello to your new automated tutor: A structured literature review on pedagogical conversational agents. *Proceedings of the 54th Hawaii International Conference on System Sciences*, 1105–1114. https://doi.org/DOI: 10.24251/HICSS.2021.135

Hodges, C., Moore, S., Lockee, B., Trust, T., & Bond, A. (2020). The difference between emergency remote teaching and online learning. *EDUCAUSE Review.*

Hoel, T., & Chen, W. (2019). Privacy and data protection in learning analytics should be motivated by an educational maxim: Towards a proposal. *Research and Practice in Technology Enhanced Learning, 14*(1), 1–13. DOI: 10.1186/s41039-019-0115-2 PMID: 30595748

Holmes, W., Bialik, M., & Fadel, C. (2019). *Artificial intelligence in education: Promises and implications for teaching and learning*. Center for Curriculum Redesign.

Holmes, W., Porayska-Pomsta, K., Holstein, K., Sutherland, E., Baker, T., Shum, S. B., Santos, O. C., Rodrigo, M. T., Cukurova, M., Bittencourt, I. I., & Koedinger, K. R. (2022). Ethics of AI in education: Towards a community-wide framework. *International Journal of Artificial Intelligence in Education, 32*(3), 504–526. DOI: 10.1007/s40593-021-00239-1

Holstein, K., McLaren, B. M., & Aleven, V. (2019). Co-designing a real-time classroom orchestration tool to support teacher-AI complementarity. *Journal of Learning Analytics, 6*(2), 27–52. DOI: 10.18608/jla.2019.62.3

Hooda, M., Rana, C., Dahiya, O., Rizwan, A., & Hossain, M. S. (2022). Artificial intelligence for assessment and feedback to enhance student success in higher education. *Mathematical Problems in Engineering, 2022*, 5215722. Advance online publication. DOI: 10.1155/2022/5215722

Hosseini Tabaghdehi, S. A., & Ayaz, Ö. (2025). AI ethics in action: A circular model for transparency, accountability and inclusivity. *Journal of Managerial Psychology*. Advance online publication. DOI: 10.1108/JMP-03-2024-0177

Huang, L. (2023). Ethics of artificial intelligence in education: Student privacy and data protection. *Science Insights Education Frontiers, 16*(2), 2577–2587. DOI: 10.15354/sief.23.re202

Huawei, S., & Aryadoust, V. (2023). A systematic review of automated writing evaluation systems. *Education and Information Technologies, 28*(1), 771–795. DOI: 10.1007/s10639-022-11200-7

Ibáñez, M. B., & Delgado-Kloos, C. (2018). AR for STEM learning: A systematic review. *Computers & Education, 123*, 109–123. DOI: 10.1016/j.compedu.2018.05.002

Ifenthaler, D., & Yau, J. Y.-K. (2020). Utilising learning analytics to support study success in higher education: A systematic review. *Educational Technology Research and Development, 68*(4), 1961–1990. DOI: 10.1007/s11423-020-09788-z

Igbokwe, I. C. (2023). Application of artificial intelligence (AI) in educational management. *International Journal of Scientific and Research Publications, 13*(3), 300. DOI: 10.29322/IJSRP.13.03.2023.p13536

Ilomäki, L., Lakkala, M., Kallunki, V., Mundy, D., Romero, M., Romeu, T., & Gouseti, A. (2023). Critical digital literacies at school level: A systematic review. *Review of Education, 11*(3), e3425. DOI: 10.1002/rev3.3425

Isiaku, L., Muhammad, A. S., Kefas, H. I., & Ukaegbu, F. C. (2024). Enhancing technological sustainability in academia: Leveraging ChatGPT for teaching, learning, and evaluation. *Quality Education for All, 1*(1), 385–416. DOI: 10.1108/QEA-07-2024-0055

Ivanashko, O., Kozak, A., Knysh, T., & Honchar, K. (2024). The role of artificial intelligence in shaping the future of education: Opportunities and challenges. *Futurity Education, 4*(1), 126–146.

Järvelä, S., Kirschner, P. A., Panadero, E., Malmberg, J., Phielix, C., Jaspers, J., Koivuniemi, M., & Järvenoja, H. (2015). Enhancing socially shared regulation in collaborative learning groups: Designing for CSCL regulation tools. *Educational Technology Research and Development*, *63*(1), 125–142. DOI: 10.1007/s11423-014-9358-1

Jeyaraman, M., Ramasubramanian, S., Balaji, S., Jeyaraman, N., Nallakumarasamy, A., & Sharma, S. (2023). ChatGPT in action: Harnessing artificial intelligence potential and addressing ethical challenges in medicine, education, and scientific research. *World Journal of Methodology*, *13*(4), 170–178. DOI: 10.5662/wjm.v13.i4.170 PMID: 37771867

Jiang, R. (2022). How does artificial intelligence empower EFL teaching and learning nowadays? A review on artificial intelligence in the EFL context. *Frontiers in Psychology*, *13*, 1664–1078. DOI: 10.3389/fpsyg.2022.1049401 PMID: 36467167

Jindal, M., Chaiyachati, K. H., Fung, V., Manson, S. M., & Mortensen, K. (2023). Eliminating health care inequities through strengthening access to care. *Health Services Research*, *58*(S3, Suppl 3), 300–310. DOI: 10.1111/1475-6773.14202 PMID: 38015865

Jin, Y., Yan, L., Echeverria, V., Gašević, D., & Martinez-Maldonado, R. (2025). Generative AI in higher education: A global perspective of institutional adoption policies and guidelines. *Computers and Education: Artificial Intelligence*, *8*, 100348. DOI: 10.1016/j.caeai.2024.100348

Jobin, A., Ienca, M., & Vayena, E. (2019). The global landscape of AI ethics guidelines. *Nature Machine Intelligence*, *1*(9), 389–399. DOI: 10.1038/s42256-019-0088-2

Johnston, H., Wells, R. F., Shanks, E. M., Boey, T., & Parsons, B. N. (2024). Student perspectives on the use of generative artificial intelligence technologies in higher education. *International Journal for Educational Integrity*, *20*(1), 2. Advance online publication. DOI: 10.1007/s40979-024-00149-4

Jordan, M. I., & Mitchell, T. M. (2015). Machine learning: Trends, perspectives, and prospects. *Science*, *349*(6245), 255–260. DOI: 10.1126/science.aaa8415 PMID: 26185243

Kamalov, F., Santandreu Calonge, D., & Gurrib, I. (2023). New era of artificial intelligence in education: Towards a sustainable multifaceted revolution. *Sustainability (Basel)*, *15*(16), 12451. DOI: 10.3390/su151612451

Kartika, A. (2024). Unveiling the Merdeka Curriculum in Indonesia: Insights from Educators and Policymakers on Its Effectiveness and Implications. [INJURITY]. *Interdiciplinary Journal and Hummanity, 3*(11), 802–819. DOI: 10.58631/injurity.v3i11.1378

Kasneci, E., Sessler, K., Küchemann, S., Bannert, M., Dementieva, D., Fischer, F., Gasser, U., Groh, G., Günnemann, S., Hüllermeier, E., Krusche, S., Kutyniok, G., Michaeli, T., Nerdel, C., Pfeffer, J., Poquet, O., Sailer, M., Schmidt, A., Seidel, T., & Kasneci, G. (2023). ChatGPT for good? On opportunities and challenges of large language models for education. *Learning and Individual Differences, 103*, 102274. DOI: 10.1016/j.lindif.2023.102274

Khademi, A. (2023). Can ChatGPT and Bard generate aligned assessment items?: A reliability analysis against human performance. *Journal of Applied Learning & Teaching, 6*(1), 75–80.

Khan, M. S., Umer, H., & Faruqe, F. (2024). Artificial intelligence for low-income countries. *Humanities & Social Sciences Communications, 11*(1), 1–13. DOI: 10.1057/s41599-024-03947-w

Kharrufa, A., & Johnson, I. G. (2024). The potential and implications of generative AI on HCI education. DOI: 10.1145/3658619.3658627

Khojasteh, L., Soori, A., & Javed, F. (2025). Comparing teacher E-feedback, AI feedback, and hybrid feedback in enhancing EFL writing skills. *Technology in Language Teaching & Learning, 7*(3), 102626. DOI: 10.29140/tltl.v7n3.102626

Khoo, O., Sreberny, A., & Thiranagama, S. (Eds.). (2022). *Environment, media and popular culture in Southeast Asia*. Amsterdam University Press., DOI: 10.5117/9789463722642

Khoza, N. G., & van der Walt, F. (2025). A systematic review on AI-enhanced pedagogies in higher education in the Global South. *Frontiers in Education, 10*, 1667884. Advance online publication. DOI: 10.3389/feduc.2025.1667884

Khullar, S., Mounika, G. R., Chauhan, S. S., Garg, G., Priyanka, T. P., & Kaliappan, S. (2025). Advanced hybrid ensemble learning for blockchain-enabled secure voting: Leveraging random forest, XGBoost, and neural networks for robust anomaly detection and integrity assurance. *Proceedings of the 1st International Conference on Advancement in Futuristic Technologies (ICAFT)*, 1–7. https://doi.org/10.1109/ICAFT66710.2025.11452780

Kiemde, S. M. A., & Kora, A. D. (2022). Towards an ethics of AI in Africa: Rule of education. *AI and Ethics, 2*(1), 35–40. DOI: 10.1007/s43681-021-00106-8

Kim, N. W., Ko, H.-K., Myers, G., & Bach, B. (2024). ChatGPT in data visualization education: A student perspective (Preprint). /arXiv.2405.00748DOI: 10.1109/VL/HCC60511.2024.00022

Kim, B. J., Jeong, S., Cho, B. K., & Chung, J. B. (2025). AI Governance in the Context of the EU AI Act. *IEEE Access : Practical Innovations, Open Solutions, 13*, 144126–144142. DOI: 10.1109/ACCESS.2025.3598023

Kitchin, R. (2017). Thinking critically about and researching algorithms. *Information Communication and Society, 20*(1), 14–29. DOI: 10.1080/1369118X.2016.1154087

Kizilcec, R. F. (2016). How much information? Effects of transparency on trust in an algorithmic interface. *Proceedings of the 2016 CHI Conference on Human Factors in Computing Systems*, 2390–2395. https://doi.org/DOI: 10.1145/2858036.2858402

Kizilcec, R. F., & Lee, H. (2022). Algorithmic fairness in education. In *The ethics of artificial intelligence in education* (pp. 174–202). Routledge. DOI: 10.4324/9780429329067-10

Kizilcec, R. F., Pérez-Sanagustín, M., & Maldonado, J. J. (2016). Self-regulated learning strategies predict learner behavior in MOOCs. *Computers & Education, 104*, 18–33. DOI: 10.1016/j.compedu.2016.10.001

Kloker, S., Bazanya, M., & Kateete, T. (2024). I don't trust you (anymore)! The effect of students' LLM use on lecturer-student trust in higher education. DOI: 10.58653/nche.v12i1.6

Knight, J., Dooly, M., & Barberà, E. (2023). Getting smart: Towards critical digital literacy pedagogies. *Social Semiotics, 33*(2), 326–349. DOI: 10.1080/10350330.2020.1836815

Köbis, L., & Mehner, C. (2021). Ethical questions raised by AI-supported mentoring in higher education. *Frontiers in Artificial Intelligence, 4*, 624050. DOI: 10.3389/frai.2021.624050 PMID: 33997774

Koedinger, K. R., & Corbett, A. T. (2006). *Cognitive tutors: Technology bringing learning science to the classroom*. Cambridge Handbook of the Learning Sciences.

Koedinger, K. R., & Corbett, A. T. (2006). Cognitive tutors: Technology bringing learning sciences to the classroom. In Sawyer, R. K. (Ed.), *The Cambridge handbook of the learning sciences* (pp. 61–77). Cambridge University Press.

Koehler, M. J., & Mishra, P. (2009). What is technological pedagogical content knowledge (TPACK)? *Contemporary Issues in Technology & Teacher Education, 9*(1), 60–70.

Komljenovic, J. (2022). The future of value in digitalised higher education: Why data privacy should not be our biggest concern. *Higher Education*, *83*(1), 119–135. DOI: 10.1007/s10734-020-00639-7 PMID: 33230347

Kooli, C., & Chakraoui, R. (2025). AI-driven assistive technologies in inclusive education: Benefits, challenges, and policy recommendations. *Sustainable Futures : An Applied Journal of Technology, Environment and Society*, *10*, 101042. Advance online publication. DOI: 10.1016/j.sftr.2025.101042

Koper, R. (2001). *Modeling units of study from a pedagogical perspective*. Open University of the Netherlands.

Korteling, J. E., van de Boer-Visschedijk, G. C., Blankendaal, R. A., Boonekamp, R. C., & Eikelboom, A. R. (2021). Human-versus artificial intelligence. *Frontiers in Artificial Intelligence*, *4*, 622364. DOI: 10.3389/frai.2021.622364 PMID: 33981990

Krumsvik, R. J. (2020). Home schooling, remote teaching and digital Bildung in societal crisis. *Nordic Journal of Digital Literacy*, *15*(2), 71–85. DOI: 10.18261/issn.1891-943x-2020-02-01

Kulik, J. A., & Fletcher, J. D. (2016). Effectiveness of intelligent tutoring systems: A meta-analytic review. *Review of Educational Research*, *86*(1), 42–78. DOI: 10.3102/0034654315581420

Lang, Q., Wang, M., Yin, M., Liang, S., & Song, W. (2025). Transforming education with generative AI (GAI): Key insights and future prospects. *IEEE Transactions on Learning Technologies*, *18*, 230–242. DOI: 10.1109/TLT.2025.3537618

Lee, D., Arnold, M., Srivastava, A., Plastow, K., Strelan, P., Ploeckl, F., Lekkas, D., & Palmer, E. (2024). The impact of generative AI on higher education learning and teaching: A study of educators' perspectives. *Computers & Education. Artificial Intelligence*, *6*, 100221. Advance online publication. DOI: 10.1016/j.caeai.2024.100221

Leelavathi, R., & Surendhranatha, R. C. (2024). ChatGPT in the classroom: Navigating the generative AI wave in management education. *Journal of Research in Innovative Teaching & Learning*. Advance online publication. DOI: 10.1108/JRIT-01-2024-0017

Lee, S. C., Baby, T., Vongvit, R., Lee, J., Kim, Y. W., Cha, M. C., & Yoon, S. H. (2026). Development and validation of Generative AI Competence Scale (GenAIComp) among university students. *Technology in Society*, *84*, 103059. Advance online publication. DOI: 10.1016/j.techsoc.2025.103059

Li, N. (2023). Ethical considerations in artificial intelligence: A comprehensive discussion from the perspective of computer vision. *SHS Web of Conferences*, 179(1), 04024. DOI: 10.1051/shsconf/202317904024

Lim, T., Gottipati, S., & Cheong, M. L. F. (2023). Ethical considerations for artificial intelligence in educational assessments. In *Creative AI tools and ethical implications in teaching and learning* (pp. 32–79). IGI Global., DOI: 10.4018/979-8-3693-0205-7.ch003

Lin, C. C., Huang, A. Y. Q., & Lu, O. H. T. (2023). Artificial intelligence in intelligent tutoring systems toward sustainable education: A systematic review. *Smart Learning Environments*, *10*(1), 41. DOI: 10.1186/s40561-023-00260-y

Lindsay, E. D., Zhang, M., Johri, A., & Bjerva, J. (2025). The responsible development of automated student feedback with generative AI. In *2025 IEEE Global Engineering Education Conference (EDUCON)* (pp. 1–10). IEEE. DOI: 10.1109/EDUCON62633.2025.11016572

Lin, J., Liao, Z., Dai, J., Wang, M., Yu, R., Yang, H., & Liu, C. (2025). Digital and artificial intelligence-assisted cephalometric training effectively enhanced students' landmarking accuracy in preclinical orthodontic education. *BMC Oral Health*, *25*(1), 623. Advance online publication. DOI: 10.1186/s12903-025-05978-4 PMID: 40275285

Lin, X., Chen, L., Chan, K. K., Peng, S., Chen, X., Xie, S., Liu, J., & Hu, Q. (2022). Teachers' perceptions of teaching sustainable artificial intelligence: A design frame perspective. *Sustainability (Basel)*, *14*(13), 7811. Advance online publication. DOI: 10.3390/su14137811

Liow, H. J. K., Yau, P. C., Tang, L., Seow, C., & Cao, Q. (2024, October). Peer-assessed (evaluated) automated grading system: a comprehensive exploration with emphasis on batch processing data visualization and rigorous peer evaluation. In *Proceedings of the 2024 international conference on artificial intelligence and teacher education* (pp. 91-96). DOI: 10.1145/3702386.3702404

Liu, W. (2024). A Systematic Review of Automated Writing Evaluation Feedback: Validity, Effects and Students' Engagement. Language Teaching Research Quarterly, 45(2667-6753), 86–105. DOI: 10.32038/ltrq.2024.45.05

Liu, Q., & Khalil, M. (2023). Understanding privacy and data protection issues in learning analytics using a systematic review. *British Journal of Educational Technology*, *54*(6), 1715–1747. DOI: 10.1111/bjet.13388

Loughran, J. (2004). A history and context of self-study of teaching and teacher education practices. In Loughran, J. J. (Eds.), *International handbook of self-study of teaching and teacher education practices* (pp. 7–39). Springer. DOI: 10.1007/978-1-4020-6545-3_1

Luckin, R. (2018). *Machine learning and human intelligence: The future of education for the 21st century*. UCL Press.

Luckin, R., & Cukurova, M. (2019). Designing educational technologies in the age of AI: A learning sciences-driven approach. *British Journal of Educational Technology*, *50*(6), 2824–2838. DOI: 10.1111/bjet.12861

Luckin, R., Holmes, W., Griffiths, M., & Forcier, L. (2016). *Intelligence unleashed: An argument for AI in education*. Pearson.

Lund, B. D., & Wang, T. (2023). Chatting about ChatGPT: How may AI and GPT impact academia and libraries? *Library Hi Tech News*, *40*(3), 26–29. DOI: 10.1108/LHTN-01-2023-0009

Lund, B., Omame, I., Tijani, S., & Agbaji, D. (2020). Perceptions toward Artificial Intelligence among Academic Library Employees and Alignment with the Diffusion of Innovations' Adopter Categories. *College & Research Libraries*, *865*, 865. Advance online publication. DOI: 10.5860/crl.81.5.865

Maeng, U. (2025). Blending AI and Instructor Feedback in EFL Writing: Learners' Motivation, Attitude, and Self-efficacy. *English Teaching*, *80*(5), 11–39. DOI: 10.15858/engtea.80.5.202512.11

Maimela, C., & Mbonde, P. (2025). Artificial intelligence in South African universities: Curriculum transformation and decolonisation—aid or obstacle? *Frontiers in Sociology*, *10*, 1543471. DOI: 10.3389/fsoc.2025.1543471 PMID: 40697567

Mallillin, L. L. D. (2024). Artificial intelligence (AI) towards students' academic performance. *Innovare Journal of Education*, *12*(4), 16–21. DOI: 10.22159/ijoe.2024v12i4.51665

Mandel, T., Liu, Y. E., Levine, S., Brunskill, E., & Popovic, Z. (2014). Offline policy evaluation across representations with applications to educational games. *Proceedings of the 13th International Conference on Autonomous Agents and Multiagent Systems (AAMAS 2014)*, 1077–1084. DOI: 10.65109/TNVS8310

Mannuru, N. R., Shahriar, S., Teel, Z. A., Wang, T., Lund, B. D., Tijani, S., … Vaidya, P. (2025). Artificial intelligence in developing countries: The impact of generative artificial intelligence (AI) technologies for development. *Information Development, 41*(3 Special Issue: "Artificial Intelligence initiatives"), 1036–1054. DOI: 10.1177/02666669231200628

Manouselis, N., Drachsler, H., Vuorikari, R., Hummel, H., & Koper, R. (2011). Recommender systems in technology enhanced learning. In Ricci, F., Rokach, L., Shapira, B., & Kantor, P. B. (Eds.), *Recommender systems handbook* (pp. 387–415). Springer., DOI: 10.1007/978-0-387-85820-3_12

Mariano, M. J., Taborete, J. J., Gampal, A., Dawisan, A., Maraganas, M. G., & Garcia, R. (2025). Analysis of AI and teacher feedback in grading students' activities. *International Journal on Studies in Education*, *7*(4), 1028–1047. DOI: 10.46328/ijonse.5148

Martínez, M. A. (2026). Epistemic extractivism in engaged urban and housing research: Implications and counter-measures. *International Journal of Urban and Regional Research*, 1468-2427.70055. DOI: 10.1111/1468-2427.70055

McKay, M. H. (2024, June). Realizing the Promise of AI Governance Involving Humans-in-the-Loop. In *International Conference on Human-Computer Interaction* (pp. 107–123). Cham: Springer Nature Switzerland. DOI: 10.1007/978-3-031-76827-9_7

McMahan, H. B., Moore, E., Ramage, D., Hampson, S., & Arcas, B. A. (2017). Communication-efficient learning of deep networks from decentralized data. *Proceedings of the 20th International Conference on Artificial Intelligence and Statistics (AISTATS)*, 1273–1282.

Means, B., Toyama, Y., Murphy, R., Bakia, M., & Jones, K. (2010). *Evaluation of evidence-based practices in online learning*. US Department of Education.

Mehrabi, N., Morstatter, F., Saxena, N., Lerman, K., & Galstyan, A. (2021). A survey on bias and fairness in machine learning. *ACM Computing Surveys*, *54*(6), 1–35. DOI: 10.1145/3457607

Memarian, B., & Doleck, T. (2023). Fairness, Accountability, Transparency, and Ethics (FATE) in Artificial Intelligence (AI) and higher education: A systematic review. *Computers and Education: Artificial Intelligence*, *5*, 100152. DOI: 10.1016/j.caeai.2023.100152

Merchant, Z.. (2014). Effectiveness of VR-based instruction. *Computers & Education*, *70*, 29–40. DOI: 10.1016/j.compedu.2013.07.033

Mikropoulos, T. A., & Natsis, A. (2011). Educational virtual environments: A ten-year review. *Computers & Education*, *56*(3), 769–780. DOI: 10.1016/j.compedu.2010.10.020

Miller, T. (2019). Explanation in artificial intelligence: Insights from the social sciences. *Artificial Intelligence*, *267*, 1–38. DOI: 10.1016/j.artint.2018.07.007

Mogavi, R. H., Deng, C., Kim, J. J., Zhou, P., Kwon, Y. D., Metwally, A. H. S., Tlili, A., Bassanelli, S., Bucchiarone, A., Gujar, S., Nacke, L. E., & Hui, P. (2024). ChatGPT in education: A blessing or a curse? A qualitative study exploring early adopters' utilization and perceptions. *Computers in Human Behavior: Artificial Humans*, *2*(1), 100027. DOI: 10.1016/j.chbah.2023.100027

Moore, M. G. (1989). Three types of interaction. *American Journal of Distance Education*, *3*(2), 1–7. DOI: 10.1080/08923648909526659

Moorhouse, B. L., Yeo, M. A., & Wan, Y. (2023). Generative AI tools and assessment: Guidelines of the world's top-ranking universities. *Computers and Education Open*, *5*, 100151. DOI: 10.1016/j.caeo.2023.100151

Morris, S., & Stommel, J. (2018). *An urgency of teachers: The work of critical digital pedagogy*. Hybrid Pedagogy.

Mouta, A., Torrecilla-Sánchez, E. M., & Pinto-Llorente, A. M. (2025). Comprehensive professional learning for teacher agency in addressing ethical challenges of AIED: Insights from educational design research. *Education and Information Technologies*, *30*(3), 3343–3387. DOI: 10.1007/s10639-024-12946-y

Mundlamuri, R., Gunnam, G. R., Mysari, N. K., & Pujuri, J. (2025). The Evolution of AI: From Classical Machine Learning to Modern Large Language Models. *IEEE Access : Practical Innovations, Open Solutions*, *13*, 178302–178341. DOI: 10.1109/ACCESS.2025.3621344

Mutambara, A. G. (2025). *Artificial Intelligence: A driver of inclusive development and shared prosperity for the Global South*. CRC Press. DOI: 10.1201/9781003511014

Nakai, K., & Kanehisa, M. (1992). A knowledge base for predicting protein localization sites in eukaryotic cells. *Genomics*, *14*(4), 897–911. DOI: 10.1016/S0888-7543(05)80111-9 PMID: 1478671

Nambiar, R. M. K. K. (2018). Artificial intelligence: A new path to democratizing higher education? *Studies in Higher Education*, *43*(11), 2044–2056.

Nawaz, R., Sun, Q., Shardlow, M., Kontonatsios, G., Aljohani, N. R., Visvizi, A., & Hassan, S. (2022). Leveraging AI and machine learning for the National Student Survey: Actionable insights from textual feedback to enhance quality of teaching and learning in UK higher education. *Applied Sciences (Basel, Switzerland)*, *12*(1), 514. Advance online publication. DOI: 10.3390/app12010514

Nazaretsky, T., Ariely, M., Cukurova, M., & Alexandron, G. (2022). Teachers' trust in AI-powered educational technology and a professional development program to improve it. *British Journal of Educational Technology*, *53*(4), 914–931. DOI: 10.1111/bjet.13232

Nazaretsky, T., Mikeska, J. N., & Klebanov, B. B. (2023). *Empowering teacher learning with AI: Automated evaluation of teacher attention to student ideas during argumentation-focused discussion*. ACM Digital Library., DOI: 10.1145/3576050.3576067

New Scientist. (2025). *New Scientist essential guide: The AI revolution*. New Scientist Ltd.

Nguyen, T. T. (2025). Artificial Intelligence in Higher Education: A *Systematic Review of Impacts, Barriers, and Emerging Trends. IOSR Journal of Research & Method in Education*, 15(3), 53–61. Available at: www.iosrjournals.org

Nguyen, A., Ngo, H. N., Hong, Y., Dang, B., & Nguyen, B. P. T. (2023). Ethical principles for artificial intelligence in education. *Education and Information Technologies*, *28*(4), 4221–4241. DOI: 10.1007/s10639-022-11316-w PMID: 36254344

Nicol, D. J., & Macfarlane-Dick, D. (2006). Formative assessment and self-regulated learning: A model and seven principles of good feedback practice. *Studies in Higher Education*, *31*(2), 199–218. DOI: 10.1080/03075070600572090

Novelli, C., Taddeo, M., & Floridi, L. (2024). Accountability in artificial intelligence: What it is and how it works. *AI & Society*, *39*(4), 1871–1882. DOI: 10.1007/s00146-023-01635-y

O'Neil, C. (2016). *Weapons of math destruction: How big data increases inequality and threatens democracy*. Crown Publishing Group.

Oberg, G. (2025). Moral injury in teaching: The systemic roots of ethical conflict and emotional burnout in education. *Educational Review*, •••, 1–24.

OECD. (2023). *OECD digital education outlook 2023: Towards an effective digital education ecosystem*. OECD Publishing., DOI: 10.1787/9872e201-

Ofosu-Ampong, K. (2024). Artificial intelligence research: A review on dominant themes, methods, frameworks, and future research directions. *Telematics and Informatics Reports, 14*, 100127. DOI: 10.1016/j.teler.2024.100127

Okoye, K., Daruich, S. D. N., Castaño, R., Escamilla, J., & Hosseini, S. (2024). Analyzing the impact of digitized-education toward the future of education: A comparative study based on students' evaluation of teaching data. *Studies in Educational Evaluation, 82*, 101359. DOI: 10.1016/j.stueduc.2024.101359

Omidvar, S., & Meihami, H. (2025). Exploring the "what" and "how" of opportunities and challenges of AI in EFL teacher education. *Computers and Education: Artificial Intelligence, 9*, 100443. Advance online publication. DOI: 10.1016/j.caeai.2025.100443

Organization for Economic Co-operation and Development. (2021). *State of implementation of the OECD AI principles: Insights from national AI policies.* OECD Publishing., DOI: 10.1787/1cd40c44-

Ou, S. (2024). Transforming education: The evolving role of artificial intelligence in students' academic performance. *International Journal of Education and Humanities, 13*(2), 163–173. DOI: 10.54097/cc1x7r95

Pammer-Schindler, V., & Rosé, C. (2022). Data-related ethics issues in technologies for informal professional learning. *International Journal of Artificial Intelligence in Education, 32*(3), 609–635. DOI: 10.1007/s40593-021-00259-x

Pant, A., Hoda, R., Tantithamthavorn, C., & Turhan, B. (2024). Ethics in AI through the practitioner's view: A grounded theory literature review. *Empirical Software Engineering, 29*(67), 67. Advance online publication. DOI: 10.1007/s10664-024-10465-5

Papagiannidis, E., Mikalef, P., & Conboy, K. (2025). Responsible artificial intelligence governance: A review and research framework. *The Journal of Strategic Information Systems, 34*(2), 101885. DOI: 10.1016/j.jsis.2024.101885

Patias, I., Miteva, D., & Peltekova, E. (2026). Using Old Lessons for New AI – A Trainer for Project Risk Management. In *Lecture Notes in Computer Science* (Vol. 16119 LNAI, pp. 155–167). DOI: 10.1007/978-3-032-05607-8_16

Pavlik, P. I., & Anderson, J. R. (2008). Using a model to compute the optimal schedule of practice. *Journal of Experimental Psychology. Applied, 14*(2), 101–117. DOI: 10.1037/1076-898X.14.2.101 PMID: 18590367

Pelánek, R. (2017). Bayesian knowledge tracing, logistic models, and beyond: An overview of learner modeling techniques. *User Modeling and User-Adapted Interaction, 27*(3-5), 313–350. DOI: 10.1007/s11257-017-9193-2

Petricini, T. (2025). The power of language: Framing AI as an assistant, collaborator, or transformative force in cultural discourse. *AI & Society*. Advance online publication. DOI: 10.1007/s00146-025-02586-2

Pham, S. T. H. (2025). An empirical investigation of the experience of educators and politicians with the emergence of artificial intelligence in education. *Technology in Society, 83*, 102965. Advance online publication. DOI: 10.1016/j.techsoc.2025.102965

Picciano, A. G. (2017). Theories and frameworks for online education. *Online Learning : the Official Journal of the Online Learning Consortium, 21*(3), 166–190. DOI: 10.24059/olj.v21i3.1225

Piech, C., Bassen, J., Huang, J., Ganguli, S., Sahami, M., Guibas, L. J., & Sohl-Dickstein, J. (2015). Deep knowledge tracing. *Advances in Neural Information Processing Systems, 28*, 505–513.

Pishtari, G., Sarmiento-Márquez, E., Rodríguez-Triana, M. J., Wagner, M., & Ley, T. (2024). *Mirror mirror on the wall, what is missing in my pedagogical goals? The impact of an AI-driven feedback system on the quality of teacher-created learning designs*. ACM Digital Library., DOI: 10.1145/3636555.3636862

Porayska-Pomsta, K. (2024). A manifesto for a pro-actively responsible AI in education. *International Journal of Artificial Intelligence in Education, 34*(1), 73–83. DOI: 10.1007/s40593-023-00346-1

Poyares, M. (2025). Migrant Data Extractivism: Tech and Borders at the Limit of Rights. *International Migration (Geneva, Switzerland), 63*(4), e70065. DOI: 10.1111/imig.70065

Pratschke, B. M. (2024). *Generative AI and education: Digital pedagogies, teaching innovation and learning design*. Springer Nature. DOI: 10.1007/978-3-031-67991-9

Prinsloo, P., & Kaliisa, R. (2022). Data privacy on the African continent: Opportunities, challenges and implications for learning analytics. *British Journal of Educational Technology, 53*(4), 894–913. DOI: 10.1111/bjet.13226

Prinsloo, P., & Slade, S. (2017). Ethics and learning analytics. *British Journal of Educational Technology, 48*(2), 387–392.

Prinsloo, P, Slade, S., & Khalil, M. (2022). The answer is (not only) technological: Considering student data privacy in learning analytics. *British Journal of Educational Technology, 53*(4), 876–893. DOI: 10.1111/bjet.13216

Radu, R. (2021). Steering the governance of artificial intelligence: National strategies in perspective. *Policy and Society*, *40*(2), 178–193. DOI: 10.1080/14494035.2021.1929728

Ramos, L. T., & Casas, E. (2025). Applications, trends, and perspectives of large language models in education: A literature review. *Authorea Preprints*. DOI: 10.36227/techrxiv.176413429.91587404/v1

Rashid, A. B., & Kausik, M. A. K. (2024). AI revolutionizing industries worldwide: A comprehensive overview of its diverse applications. *Hybrid Advances*, *7*, 100277. DOI: 10.1016/j.hybadv.2024.100277

Ravyse, W. S., Blignaut, A. S., Leendertz, V., & Woolner, A. (2016). Success factors for serious games to enhance learning: A systematic review. *Virtual Reality (Waltham Cross)*, *21*(1), 31–58. DOI: 10.1007/s10055-016-0298-4

Reeves, B. (2022). Assessing ethical capability: A framework for supporting teacher judgement of student proficiency. *Australian Educational Researcher*, *49*(4), 779–804. DOI: 10.1007/s13384-021-00442-y

Reeves, T. C., & Lin, L. (2011). The research we have is not the research we need. *Educational Technology*, *51*(4), 1–21.

Regan, P. M., & Jesse, J. (2019). Ethical challenges of edtech, big data and personalized learning: Twenty first century student sorting and tracking. *Ethics and Information Technology*, *21*(3), 167–179. DOI: 10.1007/s10676-018-9492-2

Reich, J., & Ito, M. (2017). *From good intentions to real outcomes: Equity by design in learning technologies*. Digital Media and Learning Research Hub.

Richardson, M., Abraham, C., & Bond, R. (2012). Psychological correlates of university students' academic performance. *Psychological Bulletin*, *138*(2), 353–387. DOI: 10.1037/a0026838 PMID: 22352812

Roll, I., & Winne, P. H. (2015). Understanding, evaluating, and supporting self-regulated learning using learning analytics. *Journal of Learning Analytics*, *2*(1), 7–12. DOI: 10.18608/jla.2015.21.2

Roshanaei, M., Olivares, H., & Lopez, R. (2023). Harnessing AI to foster equity in education: Opportunities, challenges, and emerging strategies. *Journal of Intelligent Learning Systems and Applications*, *15*(4), 123–143. DOI: 10.4236/jilsa.2023.154009

Rubel, A., & Jones, K. M. L. (2016). Student privacy in learning analytics: An information ethics perspective. *The Information Society*, *32*(2), 143–159. DOI: 10.1080/01972243.2016.1130502

Rudin, C. (2019). Stop explaining black box machine learning models for high stakes decisions and use interpretable models instead. *Nature Machine Intelligence, 1*(5), 206–215. DOI: 10.1038/s42256-019-0048-x PMID: 35603010

Ryan, M. (2025). We're only human after all: A critique of human-centred AI. *AI & Society, 40*(3), 1303–1319. DOI: 10.1007/s00146-024-01976-2 PMID: 40225308

Ryan, T., Henderson, M., Ryan, K., & Kennedy, G. (2021). Identifying the components of effective learner-centred feedback information. *Teaching in Higher Education*. Advance online publication. DOI: 10.1080/13562517.2021.1913723

Salas-Pilco, S. Z., Xiao, K., & Hu, X. (2022). Artificial intelligence and learning analytics in teacher education: A systematic review. *Education Sciences, 12*(8), 569. DOI: 10.3390/educsci12080569

Sanders, D. A., & Mukhari, S. S. (2024). Lecturers' perceptions of the influence of AI on a blended learning approach in a South African higher education institution. *Discover Education, 3*(1), 135. DOI: 10.1007/s44217-024-00235-2

Santomartino, S. M., & Yi, P. H. (2022). Systematic Review of Radiologist and Medical Student Attitudes on the Role and Impact of AI in Radiology. *Academic Radiology, 29*(11), 1748–1756. DOI: 10.1016/j.acra.2021.12.032 PMID: 35105524

Sargiotis, D. (2024). Fostering ethical and inclusive AI: A human-centric paradigm for social impact. SSRN *Electronic Journal.* DOI: 10.2139/ssrn.4879372

Scheffel, M., Drachsler, H., & Specht, M. (2021). The five facets of learning analytics: A framework for building trust and transparency. *Computers and Education: Artificial Intelligence*, 2, 100037. DOI: 10.1016/j.caeai.2021.100037

Schiff, D. (2022). Education for AI, not AI for education: The role of education and ethics in national AI policy strategies. *International Journal of Artificial Intelligence in Education, 32*(3), 527–563. DOI: 10.1007/s40593-021-00270-2

Schillings, M., Roebertsen, H., Savelberg, H., & Dolmans, D. (2023). A review of educational dialogue strategies to improve academic writing skills. *Active Learning in Higher Education, 24*(2), 95–108. DOI: 10.1177/1469787418810663

Schmager, S., Pappas, I. O., & Vassilakopoulou, P. (2025). Understanding Human-Centred AI: A review of its defining elements and a research agenda. *Behaviour & Information Technology, 44*(15), 1–40. DOI: 10.1080/0144929X.2024.2448719

Schwartz, R., Vassilev, A., Greene, K., Perine, L., Burt, A., & Hall, P. (2024). *Towards a standard for identifying and managing bias in artificial intelligence* (NIST Special Publication 1270). National Institute of Standards and Technology. https://nvlpubs.nist.gov/nistpubs/SpecialPublications/NIST.SP.1270.pdf

Sekti, B. A. (2025a). Foundations of Artificial Intelligence Ethics. In *Navigating Social Trust in the AI Era* (pp. 23–47). DOI: 10.4018/979-8-3373-7011-8.ch002

Sekti, B. A. (2025b). Machine Learning vs. AI: Key Concepts. In *Implementing Enterprise Cybersecurity With AI* (pp. 1–27). DOI: 10.4018/979-8-3373-2252-0.ch001

Selwyn, N. (2019). *Should robots replace teachers? AI and the future of education*. Polity Press.

Selwyn, N. (2021). *Education and technology: Key issues and debates* (3rd ed.). Bloomsbury Academic.

Shay, S. (2008). Beyond social constructivist perspectives on assessment. *Teaching in Higher Education, 13*(5), 595–605. DOI: 10.1080/13562510802334970

Sheeba, M. F. L. (2022). A study on perception of teachers towards AI applications in education. *XIBA Business Review, 5*(2), 23.

Shermis, M. D., & Burstein, J. (Eds.). (2013). *Handbook of automated essay evaluation: Current applications and new directions*. Routledge. DOI: 10.4324/9780203122761

Sholla, S., & Reshi, I. A. (2024). Ethical reasoning in technology: using computational approaches to integrate ethics into AI systems. Journal of Information, Communication and Ethics in Society.

Shute, V. J., & Rahimi, S. (2017). Review of computer-based assessment for learning in elementary and secondary education. *Journal of Computer Assisted Learning, 33*(1), 1–19. DOI: 10.1111/jcal.12172

Shute, V. J., & Ventura, M. (2013). *Measuring and supporting learning in games: Stealth assessment*. The MIT Press. DOI: 10.7551/mitpress/9589.001.0001

Shute, V. J., & Zapata-Rivera, D. (2012). Adaptive educational systems. In Durlach, P. J., & Lesgold, A. M. (Eds.), *Adaptive technologies for training and education* (pp. 7–27). Cambridge University Press. DOI: 10.1017/CBO9781139049580.004

Siemens, G., & Baker, R. (2012). Learning analytics and educational data mining: Towards communication and collaboration. In *Proceedings of the 2nd International Conference on Learning Analytics and Knowledge* (pp. 252–254). DOI: 10.1145/2330601.2330661

Singhal, A., Neveditsin, N., Tanveer, H., & Mago, V. (2024). Toward fairness, accountability, transparency, and ethics in AI for social media and health care: Scoping review. *JMIR Medical Informatics*, *12*, e50048. DOI: 10.2196/50048 PMID: 38568737

Singh, T. M., Reddy, C. K. K., Murthy, B. R., Nag, A., & Doss, S. (2025). Ai and education: Bridging the gap to personalized, efficient, and accessible learning. In *Internet of behavior-based computational intelligence for smart education systems* (pp. 131–160). IGI Global.

Skinner, B. F. (1958). Teaching machines. *Science*, *128*(3330), 969–977. DOI: 10.1126/science.128.3330.969 PMID: 13592277

Slade, S., & Prinsloo, P. (2013). Learning analytics: Ethical issues and dilemmas. *The American Behavioral Scientist*, *57*(10), 1510–1529. DOI: 10.1177/0002764213479366

Slater, M., & Wilbur, S. (1997). A framework for immersive virtual environments. *Presence (Cambridge, Mass.)*, *6*(6), 603–616. DOI: 10.1162/pres.1997.6.6.603

Slimi, Z., & Carballido, B. V. (2023). Navigating the Ethical Challenges of Artificial Intelligence in Higher Education: An Analysis of Seven Global AI Ethics Policies. *TEM journal*, *12*(2).

Strielkowski, W., Grebennikova, V., Lisovskiy, A., Rakhimova, G., & Vasileva, T. (2025). AI-driven adaptive learning for sustainable educational transformation. *Sustainable Development (Bradford)*, *33*(2), 1921–1947. DOI: 10.1002/sd.3221

Strielkowski, W., Vlasov, A., Selivanov, K., Muraviev, K., & Shakhnov, V. (2023). Prospects and challenges of the machine learning and data-driven methods for the predictive analysis of power systems: A review. *Energies*, *16*(10), 4025. DOI: 10.3390/en16104025

Suleiman, I. B., Okunade, O. A., Dada, E. G., & Ezeanya, U. C. (2024). Key factors influencing students' academic performance. *Journal of Electrical Systems and Information Technology*, *11*(1), 41. DOI: 10.1186/s43067-024-00166-w

Sumakul, D. T. Y. G., Hamied, F. A., & Sukyadi, D. (2022). Students' perceptions of the use of AI in a writing class. *Advances in Social Science, Education and Humanities Research*. Advance online publication. DOI: 10.2991/assehr.k.220201.009

Sun, J. C. (2023). Gaps, guesswork, and ghosts lurking in technology integration: Laws and policies applicable to student privacy. *British Journal of Educational Technology*, *54*(6), 1604–1618. DOI: 10.1111/bjet.13379

Susanto, G. W. A., Maulana, H., Putri, P. H., Purwaningrahayu, R. D., Wijaya, A. A., Sekti, B. A., & Karuniawan, A. (2023). Stability Analysis to Select the Stable and High Yielding of Black Soybean (Glycine max (L) Merril) in Indonesia. *International Journal of Agronomy*, *2023*, 1–14. Advance online publication. DOI: 10.1155/2023/7255444

Suthers, D. D. (2006). Technology affordances for intersubjective meaning making: A research agenda for CSCL. *International Journal of Computer-Supported Collaborative Learning*, *1*(3), 315–337. DOI: 10.1007/s11412-006-9660-y

Sweeney, L. (2013). Discrimination in online ad delivery. *Communications of the ACM*, *56*(5), 44–54. DOI: 10.1145/2447976.2447990

Tahir, M., Amanat, I., & Awan, S. M. (2024). Ethical considerations and challenges in the integration of artificial intelligence in education: A systematic review. *Journal of Education and Management Studies*, *3*(4), 35–50. Advance online publication. DOI: 10.69565/jems.v3i4.314

Tajik, A. (2025). Exploring the role of AI-driven dynamic writing platforms in improving EFL learners' writing skills and fostering their motivation. *Research Square*. DOI: 10.21203/rs.3.rs-5788599/v1

Tallberg, J., Erman, E., Furendal, M., Geith, J., Klamberg, M., & Lundgren, M. (2023). The global governance of artificial intelligence: Next steps for empirical and normative research. *International Studies Review*, *25*(3), viad040. Advance online publication. DOI: 10.1093/isr/viad040

Tan, S. (2023). Harnessing artificial intelligence for innovation in education. In *Learning intelligence: Innovative and digital transformative learning strategies* (pp. 335–363). Springer., DOI: 10.1007/978-981-19-9201-8_8

Tapalova, O., & Zhiyenbayeva, N. (2022). Artificial Intelligence in Education: AIEd for Personalised Learning Pathways. *Electronic Journal of e-Learning*, *20*(5), 639–653. DOI: 10.34190/ejel.20.5.2597

Trajkovski, G., & Hayes, H. (2025). AI in high-stakes and standardized testing. In *AI-assisted assessment in education: Transforming assessment and measuring learning* (pp. 313–346). Springer Nature Switzerland. DOI: 10.1007/978-3-031-88252-4_8

Trust, T. (2017). Using the TPACK framework to examine teachers' knowledge of educational technology integration. *Journal of Digital Learning in Teacher Education*, *33*(1), 21–27.

Tufail, S., Riggs, H., Tariq, M., & Sarwat, A. I. (2023). Advancements and Challenges in Machine Learning: A comprehensive review of models, libraries, applications and algorithms. *Electronics (Basel), 12*(8), 1789. DOI: 10.3390/electronics12081789

UNESCO. (2023). *Guidance for generative AI in education and research.* United Nations Educational, Scientific and Cultural Organization., DOI: 10.54675/EWZM9535

United Arab Emirates. (2024). *UAE guiding principles on AI policy.* UAE Government. Retrieved from https://ai.gov.ae/wp-content/uploads/2024/10/UAE-Guiding-on-ai-policy-EN-V3.pdf

VanLehn, K. (2011). The relative effectiveness of human tutoring, intelligent tutoring systems, and other tutoring systems. *Educational Psychologist, 46*(4), 197–221. DOI: 10.1080/00461520.2011.611369

Vartiainen, H., Kahila, J., Tedre, M., López-Pernas, S., & Pope, N. (2025). Enhancing children's understanding of algorithmic biases in and with text-to-image generative AI. *New Media & Society, 27*(9), 5342–5368. DOI: 10.1177/14614448241252820

Verma, S., & Rubin, J. (2018). Fairness definitions explained. *Proceedings of the International Workshop on Software Fairness (FairWare '18)*, 1–7. https://doi.org/ DOI: 10.1145/3194770.3194776

Vittorini, P., Menini, S., & Tonelli, S. (2021). An AI-based system for formative and summative assessment in data science courses. *International Journal of Artificial Intelligence in Education, 31*(2), 159–185. DOI: 10.1007/s40593-020-00230-2

Walter, Y. (2024). Embracing the future of Artificial Intelligence in the classroom: The relevance of AI literacy, prompt engineering, and critical thinking in modern education. *International Journal of Educational Technology in Higher Education, 21*(1), 15. Advance online publication. DOI: 10.1186/s41239-024-00448-3

Wang, S., Wang, F., Zhu, Z., Wang, J., Tran, T., & Du, Z. (2024). Artificial intelligence in education: A systematic literature review. *Expert Systems with Applications, 252*(Part A), 124167. DOI: 10.1016/j.eswa.2024.124167

Wang, D. (2024). Teacher- versus AI-generated (Poe application) corrective feedback and language learners' writing anxiety, complexity, fluency, and accuracy. *International Review of Research in Open and Distance Learning, 25*(3), 37–56. DOI: 10.19173/irrodl.v25i3.7646

Wan, T., & Chen, Z. (2024). Exploring generative AI assisted feedback writing for students' written responses to a physics conceptual question with prompt engineering and few-shot learning. *Physical Review. Physics Education Research, 20*(1), 010152. Advance online publication. DOI: 10.1103/PhysRevPhysEducRes.20.010152

Weidlich, J., Gotsch, F., Schudel, K., Marusic-Würscher, C., Mazzarella, J., Bolten, H., Bütler, D., Luger, S., Wohlfender, B., & Merki, K. M. (2025). Teacher, peer, or AI? Comparing effects of feedback sources in higher education. *Computers and Education Open*, *9*, 100300. DOI: 10.1016/j.caeo.2025.100300

Wen, Y., Wu, L., He, S., Ng, N. H. E., Teo, B. C., Looi, C. K., & Cai, Y. (2023). Integrating augmented reality into inquiry-based learning approach in primary science classrooms. *Educational Technology Research and Development*, *71*(4), 1631–1651. DOI: 10.1007/s11423-023-10235-y PMID: 37359487

Wheatley, A., & Hervieux, S. (2019). Artificial intelligence in academic libraries: An environmental scan. *Information Services & Use*, *39*(4), 347–356. DOI: 10.3233/ISU-190065

Williamson, B. (2017). Big data in education: The digital future of learning, policy and practice.

Williamson, B. (2017). Big data in education. *Sage (Atlanta, Ga.)*.

Williamson, B., & Eynon, R. (2020). Historical threads, missing links, and future directions in AI in education. *Learning, Media and Technology*, *45*(3), 223–235. DOI: 10.1080/17439884.2020.1798995

Williams, R., Cloete, R., Cobbe, J., Cottrill, C., Edwards, P., Markovic, M., Naja, I., Ryan, F., Singh, J., & Pang, W. (2022). From transparency to accountability of intelligent systems: Moving beyond aspirations. *Data & Policy*, *4*, e7. DOI: 10.1017/dap.2021.37

Woolf, B. P. (2009). *Building intelligent interactive tutors: Student-centered strategies for revolutionizing e-learning*. Morgan Kaufmann.

World Economic Forum. (2020). Schools of the future: Defining new models of education for the Fourth Industrial Revolution.

Wu, C., Zhang, H., & Carroll, J. M. (2024). AI governance in higher education: Case studies of guidance at Big Ten universities. *Future Internet*, *16*(10), 354. DOI: 10.3390/fi16100354

Xue, L., & Pang, Z. (2022). Ethical governance of artificial intelligence: An integrated analytical framework. *Journal of Digital Economy*, *1*(1), 44–52. DOI: 10.1016/j.jdec.2022.08.003

Yadav, S. (2025). Reimagining education with advanced technologies: transformative pedagogical shifts driven by artificial intelligence. In *Impacts of Generative AI on the Future of Research and Education* (pp. 1–26). IGI Global.

Yan, Y., & Liu, H. (2025). Ethical framework for AI education based on large language models. *Education and Information Technologies, 30*(8), 10891–10909. DOI: 10.1007/s10639-024-13241-6

Yassin, N. I., Omran, S., Houby, E. M. E., & Allam, H. (2017). Machine learning techniques for breast cancer computer aided diagnosis using different image modalities: A systematic review. *Computer Methods and Programs in Biomedicine, 156*, 25–45. DOI: 10.1016/j.cmpb.2017.12.012 PMID: 29428074

York, T. T., Gibson, C., & Rankin, S. (2015). Defining and measuring academic success. *Practical Assessment, Research & Evaluation, 20*(5), 1–20.

Yu, L., & Yu, Z. (2023). Qualitative and quantitative analyses of artificial intelligence ethics in education using VOSviewer and CitNetExplorer. *Frontiers in Psychology, 14*, 1061778. DOI: 10.3389/fpsyg.2023.1061778 PMID: 36968737

Zafar, S., Shaheen, F., & Rehan, J. (2024). Use of ChatGPT and generative AI in higher education: Opportunities, obstacles, and impact on student performance. *iRASD. The Journal of Educational Research, 5*(1), 01–12. Advance online publication. DOI: 10.52131/jer.2024.v5i1.2463

Zawacki-Richter, O., Marín, V. I., Bond, M., & Gouverneur, F. (2019). Systematic review of research on artificial intelligence applications in higher education – where are the educators? *International Journal of Educational Technology in Higher Education, 16*(39), 39. Advance online publication. DOI: 10.1186/s41239-019-0171-0

Zeide, E. (2019). Artificial intelligence in higher education: Applications, promise and perils, and ethical questions. *EDUCAUSE Review, 54*(3). https://er.educause.edu/articles/2019/8/artificial-intelligence-in-higher-education-applications-promise-and-perils-and-ethical-questions

Zhai, C., Wibowo, S., & Li, L. D. (2024). The effects of over-reliance on AI dialogue systems on students' cognitive abilities: A systematic review. *Smart Learning Environments, 11*(28), 28. Advance online publication. DOI: 10.1186/s40561-024-00316-7

Zhai, X., Chu, X., Chai, C. S., Jong, M. S. Y., Istenic, A., Spector, M., Liu, J. B., Yuan, J., & Li, Y. (2021). A review of artificial intelligence (AI) in education from 2010 to 2020. *Complexity, 2021*(1), 8812542. Advance online publication. DOI: 10.1155/2021/8812542

Zhao, C. (2025). AI-assisted assessment in higher education: A systematic review. *Journal of Educational Technology and Innovation*. DOI: 10.61414/jeti.v6i4.209

Zhou, Q., Suraworachet, W., Pozdniakov, S., Martinez-Maldonado, R., Bartindale, T., Chen, P., Richardson, D., & Cukurova, M. (2021). Investigating students' experiences with collaboration analytics for remote group meetings. *Lecture Notes in Computer Science, 12748*, 472–485. DOI: 10.1007/978-3-030-78292-4_38

Zylinska, J. (2020). *AI art: Machine visions and warped dreams.* Open Humanities Press. https://openhumanitiespress.org/books/titles/ai-art/

About the Contributors

Vasileios Paliktzoglou, an academic and industry professional, holds a Ph.D. in Computer Science from the University of Eastern Finland. He is an active contributor to academia, serving as a guest and associate editor for prestigious journals like the Journal of Information Systems Education (JISE) and IAFOR Journal of Education. He has been a keynote speaker at several academic and industry events, sharing his insights on social computing, collaborative learning, and emerging technologies in higher education. Dr. Paliktzoglou also actively participates in international research projects, highlighting his commitment to advancing knowledge and innovation as the Book Series Editor for the "Emerging Technologies in Education" at Vernon Press and "AI and Education" at STAR Scholars Press. His expertise continues to shape the academic and research landscape at Bahrain Polytechnic.

***

Mona Abdulla is a Maths Tutor in the School of Professional Development at Bahrain Polytechnic. A founding member of the institution since 2008, she previously served as Maths Programme Manager in the Faculty of Foundation for over six years and brings extensive experience in developing Mathematics and Engineering Physics courses. She has taught a wide range of Maths courses across foundation and degree levels, including Data Analysis, Engineering Mathematics, Mathematics for Business and ICT, and Technical Mathematics. She also served for seven years as a Maths and Science Senior Tutor at Bahrain Training Institute. Her professional interests include integrating Problem-Based Learning into Maths curricula. She has strong leadership and management experience and has actively contributed to several Quality Department projects.

Raffi Akbar Saputra is an IT professional with a strong interest in Information Technology and digital technology development. He focuses on the application of information systems and technology-based solutions to improve efficiency, productivity, and innovation across various sectors. With a strong motivation for continuous learning, Raffi actively expands his knowledge of emerging technologies, including data-driven systems and modern computing solutions. His adaptive and problem-solving-oriented mindset enables him to contribute to the development of practical and relevant technology solutions in both academic and professional settings.

Ranya Alesh is a Senior English Lecturer at Bahrain Polytechnic. She has been teaching English as a Second Language, developing curricula, and ensuring that quality standards and policies are implemented in alignment with Quality Matters standards. Her research interests include Quality Education Best Practices and Success Stories, Effectiveness of Asynchronous Activities in English Learning and Teaching, Comparative Literature, and Change Management Techniques.

Raed Atef is an Assistant Professor of Governance and Public Policy. He has served as a faculty member, researcher, and consultant with various organizations. He is actively involved in consulting, research, and training with government agencies, NGOs, and the private sector. He has worked with several universities and has published numerous research papers and studies

Khalil Ebrahim is a Lecturer and Course Coordinator in English Language and Applied Linguistics. He holds an MA in Linguistics from the United Kingdom and has professional experience in assessment design, curriculum development, and digital pedagogy in higher education. His research interests include AI-assisted writing assessment, automated feedback systems, and the pedagogical integration of artificial intelligence in language education.

Padmavati E. Gundgurti earned her B.Tech. in Information Science and Engineering from Visvesvaraya Technological University in 201,Belagavi, Karnataka, she completed her post graduation in M.Tch in 2013 from Visvesvaraya Technological University, Belagavi, Karnataka and she is pursuing her Ph.D. in Computer Science and Engineering, specializing in Artifical Intelligence from CMR University affilated to Visvesvaraya Technological University, Belagavi, Karnataka. With over 10 years of teaching experience at VTU PG Center Kalaburagi and Central University of Karnataka, Kadaganchi, Kalaburagi she has instructed both undergraduate and postgraduate students. She is currently the Lecturer of Department of Computer Science and Engineering, BVRIT HYDERABAD College of Engineering for Women. Padmavati E. Gundgurti has published two Indian patent. Published 4 papers in international journals,and 8 papers in international conference. She is an active reviewer for reputed conferences and journals. During my academic journey, I have coordinated several significant events, including guest lectures on "Trends in Software Engineering" and "Workshop on Introduction Industry 4.0 and Internet of Things, Cloud Computing", as well as hands-on sessions on "Cloud Computing" and the IBM Bootcamp & 24-hour Hackathon. I received an appreciation letter for being the feedback topper and a certificate in the NPTEL. I also participated in the Assistive Technology Lab on the International Day of People with Different Abilities, where I developed the "R.E.D" (Read out Expiry Date) app. Additionally, I conducted a workshop in collaboration with Facebook (Meta) on the Spark AR Developer Training Program and received certificates of appreciation for guiding projects on Image Deblurring and Credit Card Fraud Detection, which were presented at the 5th National Level IEEE Project Competition.Guided and mentor of various Hackathons and received sponsorship for the project.

Jenefer J is an Assistant Professor with a Ph.D. in Management from Alagappa University. She specializes in Finance. She earned her B.Com from Stella Maris College and her MBA from Pondicherry University. Her primary research interests focus on agricultural commodity futures. In addition to her core specialization, she actively explores emerging areas in finance such as sustainable finance, financial market integration, risk management strategies, behavioral finance, and fintech-driven innovations in commodity trading. She has published in Scopus-indexed and UGC CARE-listed journals, contributed book chapters, and presented her research at international conferences. Her ongoing research continues to expand into interdisciplinary domains, reflecting her commitment to exploring evolving financial markets.

Shikha Khullar is an academic and researcher specializing in artificial intelligence, adaptive learning technologies, and the ethical governance of intelligent systems. Her work focuses on the design, evaluation, and responsible deployment of AI-driven educational technologies, with particular attention to issues of bias, privacy, transparency, and explainability. She has contributed to scholarly research and edited volumes on AI applications across education and emerging digital systems, bridging technical innovation with ethical and societal considerations.

Vinoth Kumar S is a dedicated research scholar in Commerce, currently pursuing his Ph.D. at the University of Madras. He obtained his undergraduate and postgraduate degrees from the reputed University of Madras, securing distinction and being recognized as the Best Academic Performer during his master's program. He further completed his Master of Philosophy in Commerce, strengthening his academic and research expertise. His research interests centre on Sustainability, Financial Literacy, and Change Management, addressing contemporary economic and organizational challenges. Vinoth has published and presented numerous research papers at national and international conferences. Notably, he received the Best Paper Award at an international conference organized by Great Lakes Institute of Management, Gurgaon, recognizing the quality and impact of his scholarly contribution. He is currently serving as a Research Assistant in an ICSSR-funded project, contributing actively to academic research initiatives. Additionally, he has coordinated and successfully completed several projects and programs supported by Central and State Government agencies, demonstrating strong leadership and organizational capabilities.

Udit Mamodiya is an Associate Professor and Associate Dean (Research) at Poornima University in Jaipur, Rajasthan, India. With a robust academic and professional background, he has significantly contributed to the fields of renewable energy sources, reliability analysis, expert systems, and decision support systems. Dr. Mamodiya has authored over 60 research papers indexed in prestigious databases such as SCI, Scopus, and UGC Care, showcasing his commitment to advancing knowledge in his areas of expertise. Additionally, he has authored ten books published by national publishers, further enriching the academic community with valuable resources. An innovator at heart, Dr. Mamodiya holds an impressive portfolio of intellectual property, including 50 utility patents (both national and international) along with 20 design patents and copyrights. His entrepreneurial spirit is exemplified by securing 1 Crore in funding from the All India Council for Technical Education (AICTE) to establish the IDEA Lab at Poornima University, aimed at fostering innovation and research among students and faculty.

Rampelli Manojkumar received his Ph.D. in Power Engineering from the Indian Institute of Technology Guwahati in 2023. He obtained his Master of Technology in Power and Energy Systems from the National Institute of Technology Karnataka, Surathkal, India, in 2015. He is currently an Assistant Professor in the Department of Electrical and Electronics Engineering at BVRIT Hyderabad College of Engineering for Women. He is currently the Editorial Board Member of Scientific Reports, Early Career Editor for the International Journal of Ambient Energy and the Guest Editor for PLOS ONE. He has been a speaker at the IEEE Smart Grid webinar series and has contributed to multiple funded research projects on smart transformer-based microgrid systems and distributed generation management. He has published 10 Q1 journal papers, including articles in IEEE Transactions on Power Systems, IEEE Transactions on Industrial Informatics, and Sustainable Cities and Society. His research expertise spans energy management, hybrid AC/DC distribution systems, energy storage, and power electronics applications in modern distribution systems. Additionally, he is an active reviewer for around 30 SCI journals, including IEEE

Transactions on Industrial Informatics, IEEE Systems Journal, Journal of Energy Storage, Applied Energy, etc. He has also been actively involved in faculty training programs focused on teaching and learning enhancement, including instructional design, formative assessment, and teaching analytics, thereby strengthening his interdisciplinary expertise in education and technology integration.

Azalia Primadita Muchransyah, Ph.D., is a filmmaker, writer, and scholar from Indonesia. She received her doctorate in Media Study from the University at Buffalo, SUNY, in 2021. Her research and creative interests span media studies, film studies and production, documentary and hybrid forms, HIV studies, feminist studies, and media activism in Indonesia. Her dissertation explored alternative documentary production and distribution to examine the paradoxes of HIV advocacy from a media ecology perspective. A two-time Fulbright grantee, she has received awards including the UB Three Minute Dissertation Award and fellowships from the Gender Institute and the Mark Diamond Research Fund. Her recent publications address topics such as AI filmmaking, the metaverse, the comparison between professional and smartphone cameras, and alternative film screening venues. She was nominated for the Citra Award for Best Animated Short Film at Festival Film Indonesia 2022 for Nusa Antara, an animated documentary that has since screened internationally.

Sini Rahuman is an Assistant Professor of Mathematics at Bahrain Polytechnic, where she teaches a range of mathematics courses, including Mathematics for Computing, Technical Mathematics, Business Mathematics and Foundation Mathematics. She is also actively involved in course development and material preparation. Her research interests include Computational Fluid Dynamics (CFD), Applied Mathematics, Artificial Intelligence, Machine Learning, Deep Learning, and Reinforcement Learning.

Anand Bharathi S is an Assistant Professor at VIT Business School (VITBS), VIT University, Vellore, India. He holds a B.E. from Anna University, an MBA from Bharathiar University, and a Ph.D. in Management from Alagappa University. His academic and research expertise lies in digital marketing, search engine optimization (SEO), search engine marketing (SEM), social media marketing (SMM), and data-driven marketing analytics. He has published research articles in peer-reviewed and indexed journals and contributed book chapters to Scopus-indexed publications. In addition to his academic contributions, he brings significant industry experience as a digital marketing strategist, leading SEO, SEM, and analytics-driven campaigns across education and consulting sectors. His research interests include AI-driven SEO, digital search ecosystems, generative engine optimization (GEO), answer engine optimization (AEO), and emerging innovations in data-driven digital marketing.

T. Aditya Sai Srinivas is an accomplished academician currently serving as an Associate Professor in the Department of Computer Science and Engineering at Ravindra College of Engineering for Women, Kurnool. He holds a Ph.D. in Internet of Things (IoT) from the prestigious VIT University, Vellore, where he specialized in cutting-edge IoT frameworks and intelligent systems. With a strong research orientation, he has published over 50 research papers in reputed international journals. His academic contributions extend beyond research, having authored multiple textbooks in computer science and engineering. Dr. Srinivas is actively involved in mentoring students and guiding innovative projects in emerging technologies like ML, IoT, and FL. He is also a regular contributor to academic conferences and technical symposiums. His work reflects a commitment to both scholarly excellence and practical application in the evolving tech landscape.

Binastya Anggara Sekti has been a lecturer at the Faculty of Computer Science, Esa Unggul University, Jakarta, since 2016. He is actively involved in the Artificial Intelligence and Information Security Study Group. He holds a Bachelor's degree in Informatics Engineering from the Bandung Institute of Technology and a Master's degree in Information Systems Management from Trisakti University, Jakarta. Prior to entering academia, he accumulated over 25 years of professional experience as an IT practitioner in various companies across Jakarta. His work focused on developing data centers for internet service providers and delivering IT solutions for the manufacturing and oil & gas sectors. His research interests include artificial intelligence, cybersecurity, and the development of IT infrastructure.

Jogen Sharma is a Ph.D. Research Scholar in Library and Information Science at KIIT Deemed to be University, Bhubaneswar, Odisha, India and Assistant Librarian at the India International Centre (IIC), New Delhi, India. His academic and professional work centers on bibliometric research, digital transformation, and sustainable library practices. He has contributed widely through publications in reputed journals, edited volumes and conferences. His expertise includes implementing advanced technologies to modernize academic libraries and supporting institutional research needs. He is actively involved in professional associations and is committed to advancing innovation and sustainability in Library and Information Science.

Abdus Sobhan is an undergraduate student in Computer Science and Engineering (CSE) at Varendra University, Rajshahi, Bangladesh. His research interests include Quantum Computing, Artificial Intelligence (AI), Machine

Learning (ML), Deep Learning, and Blockchain. He has been actively involved in research and academic activities, with a focus on applying AI, ML, and emerging computational paradigms to real-world challenges.

Fatema Wali is an Associate Professor of English at Bahrain Polytechnic, and she has been teaching English as a Second Language, developing curricula, designing e-learning courses, and managing teams. Her research interests include On-line language learning, English as a Second Language, Computer Assisted Language Learning, Interdisciplinary Education, Entrepreneurship Education and Problem Based Learning.

Index

Symbols

A

C

D

E

F

W

www.ingramcontent.com/pod-product-compliance
Lightning Source LLC
LaVergne TN
LVHW081537300926
849161LV00006B/1471
9798260018408